Supernatural Japan

MICHIGAN MONOGRAPH SERIES IN JAPANESE STUDIES

NUMBER 107

CENTER FOR JAPANESE STUDIES
UNIVERSITY OF MICHIGAN

Supernatural Japan

Izumi Kyōka and the Global Fantastic

Pedro Thiago Ramos Bassoe

University of Michigan Press
Ann Arbor

Published in the United States of America by the
University of Michigan Press
First published March 2026

A CIP catalog record for this book is available from the British Library.

Library of Congress Control Number: 2025035490
LC record available at https://lccn.loc.gov/2025035490

ISBN 978-0-472-07799-1 (hardcover : alk. paper)
ISBN 978-0-472-05799-3 (paper : alk. paper)
ISBN 978-0-472-90575-1 (open access ebook)

DOI: https://doi.org/10.3998/mpub.14463158

The University of Michigan Press's broader open access publishing program is made possible thanks to additional funding from the University of Michigan Office of the Provost and the generous support of contributing libraries.

Cover illustration: Komura Settai, back endpaper illustration from *The Red Plum Blossom Collection* (*Kōbaishū*, 1918): living lion's head mask (*shishi no kashira*). Courtesy of Izumi Kyōka Kinenkan Museum.

The authorized representative in the EU for product safety and compliance is Easy Access System Europe, Mustamäe tee 50, 10621 Tallinn, Estonia, gpsr.requests@easproject.com

Dedicated to my grandmother, Vilma.

Contents

Digital materials related to this title can be found on the Fulcrum platform via the following citable URL: https://doi.org/10.3998/mpub.14463158

Acknowledgments

The writing of this book was made possible by professors who gave their time teaching me how to write, research, and formulate arguments. My dissertation advisor, Daniel O'Neill, introduced me to the archives of Meiji print culture, encouraged me to think more critically about my writing, and helped to develop the title of this book. Alan Tansman helped shape my ability to write academic prose and often provided crucial advice for editing and revising written materials. Beate Fricke taught me art history and introduced me to a new field of research through review and discussion of Japanese print culture and visual art at the East Asian Library at the University of California, Berkeley. Mark Unno, at the University of Oregon, taught me how to write academic essays, while also providing knowledge of Buddhism that has significantly informed my study of Japanese literature. At Keiō University in Japan, Matsumura Tomomi led me through readings of some of Kyōka's more difficult texts, including several stories that directly inspired the main themes of this book. Guohe Zheng introduced me to the language and literature of Japan, thereby inspiring this unexpected academic journey.

Throughout the writing of this book, mentors and colleagues have provided invaluable advice for revising arguments and striving to make a greater impact with my writing. In addition to those mentioned above, scholars who helped shape this project include H. Mack Horton, Jason Webb, Glynne Walley, Rebecca Copeland, and Jonathan Zwicker. I was also offered crucial support and advice by colleagues and mentors at Purdue University, including Jennifer William, Beate Allert, and Angelica Duran. In addition, I would like to thank Emma Ben Hadj for checking my translations from French. In Japan, I received assistance in making contacts and acquiring images from my colleague Tominaga Maki, a scholar of Izumi Kyōka. I also benefited from interactions with many other scholars of Kyōka, including Suzuki Aya,

Hinode Yumi, and many members of the Izumi Kyōka Kenkyūkai (Research Society). Throughout my years of study and research, I have been fortunate to benefit from conversation and connection with friends in academia, with whom I have shared interests in topics such as literature, languages, art, and music, including Matthew Mewhinney, Jon Pitt, Chelsea Ward, Lisa Hoffmann-Kuroda, and Hannah Airriess, among many others.

In Japan, I received assistance in acquiring images and surveying archives of print culture and visual materials relating to Kyōka from various curators and scholars at several museums and libraries. Foremost, I would like to thank Anakura Tamaki of the Izumi Kyōka Kinenkan Museum, who helped me to acquire many of the images that appear in this book. In addition, I would like to express my gratitude to the following individuals and organizations: Yamamoto Sagiri of Waseda University Library, Orii Takae of Kawagoe Shiritsu Bijutsukan (Kawagoe City Art Museum), Shinohara Yū of Saitama Kenritsu Bijutsukan (Museum of Modern Art, Saitama), Ichikawa Yoshika of Shiseidō Kigyō Shiryōkan (Shiseidō Corporate Museum), Shōchiku Co., Ltd., Watanabe Akiko of Kanagawa Kindai Bungakukan (Kanagawa Museum of Modern Literature), Horita Satomi of Bussi-en, Kanazawa, Takeo Satoshi of Groovy Inc., Takeuchi Miki of Keiō University Mita Media Center, Deborah Rudolph of C. V. Starr East Asian Library at the University of California, Berkeley, and Aoike Tōru of Kokuritsu Kokkai Toshokan (National Diet Library, Japan). Research at the National Diet Library, Keiō University, the Izumi Kyōka Kinenkan Museum in Kanazawa, and various libraries and museums in Tokyo was supported by the Fulbright Scholarship for Graduate Student Research, funded by the Fulbright Program. Research at art museums and archives in Saitama and Shizuoka prefectures was supported by the Northeast Asia Council Japan Grant, funded by the Association for Asian Studies. A conference on Izumi Kyōka and literature of the fantastic, in support of the writing, editing, and promotion of this book, was sponsored by the College of Liberal Arts at Purdue University.

It is with deep gratitude that I thank my wife, Aisulu, who has supported me in many ways over the years, and with whom I have shared many meaningful experiences. I also thank my children, Altyn and Emil, who are both talented, responsible, and interesting people. I thank my mother, Heloisa, and my father, Jeff, for their love and support throughout my life. Other family members whom I wish to thank include my brothers, Shannon, Sky, and Anthony, and my aunts, uncles, cousins, and grandparents. Shannon was my good friend and grew up enjoying the same Japanese cartoons and video games that I did, and so I think that he would have appreciated the publication of this book.

Illustrations

Introduction

1. Izumi Kyōka as Global Author

Izumi Kyōka (1873–1939) was one of the most popular, influential, and critically acclaimed authors of literature of the fantastic in modern Japan. He wrote some of the most famous stories of the fantastic in modern Japanese literature, including *The Holy Man of Mt. Kōya* (*Kōya hijiri*, 1900), a story that depicts a meeting between a monk and a mysterious woman who appears to have magical powers; *The Grass Labyrinth* (*Kusameikyū*, 1908), a tale of apparitions set in a haunted mansion; and *The Castle Tower* (*Tenshu monogatari*, 1917), a fantasy play set in a castle populated by goblins and fairies. Despite the clearly modern elements and global influences of Kyōka's fiction, Kyōka has often been characterized as one of the most traditional Japanese authors of the modern era, whose work carried on the forms and themes of the literature of the Edo period (1603–1868). In this book, I argue that Kyōka was a groundbreaking author of modern fiction with supernatural themes, whose work diverged in profound ways from traditional Japanese literature, and who established literature of the fantastic as a modern genre in Japan. I argue that Kyōka created a new form of modern fantasy literature by combining influences from traditional Japanese genres, such as picture books known as *kusazōshi* ("grass books") and Nō theater, with global literature that was translated into Japanese beginning in the Meiji period (1868–1912). As I will show, Kyōka's global influences included Hans Christian Andersen (1805–1875), Prosper Mérimée (1803–1870), Guy de Maupassant (1850–1893), Jules Verne (1828–1905), Gerhart Hauptmann (1862–1946), Apuleius (2nd century), and the *Arabian Nights*. Combining such influences, Kyōka created literature that was far newer and more experimental than has generally been recognized.

In scholarship, Kyōka has often been upheld as a representative of "pure" Japanese literature in the modern era, or as an author who rejected modern literary values, aesthetics, and techniques.[1] During an era when modern authors in Japan drew influence from a panoply of Western writers, including Gustave Flaubert (1821–1880), Émile Zola (1840–1902), Ivan Turgenev (1818–1883), Leo Tolstoy (1828–1910), and Henrik Ibsen (1828–1906), among many others, to create recognizably modern novels and short stories with realistic themes and settings, Kyōka is said to have based his tales of ghosts, geisha, and the supernatural almost entirely on East Asian precedents. Kyōka's influences are often traced to premodern Japanese and Chinese literature and other art forms, such as the stately and otherworldly art of Nō theater,[2] the popular ghost stories of Ueda Akinari (1734–1809),[3] the ethereal poetry of Li He (790–816),[4] and the grand martial epic of *The Water Margin* (Japanese: *Suikoden*; Chinese: *Shuihuzhuan*, Ming Dynasty).[5] Altogether, scholars have linked Kyōka's fiction to almost every notable genre of premodern Japanese literature, as does Mita Hideaki, who lists Kyōka's primary influences as *setsuwa* (Buddhist sermons or fables), *yomihon* (premodern fiction with themes of valor and morality), *ninjōbon* (books about geisha and love affairs), *sharebon* (books about fashion and the pleasure quarters), *kusazōshi*, Nō theater, kabuki theater, storytelling arts such as *yose*, and other traditional art forms.[6] Mita acknowledges that Kyōka read some European literature in translation, but concludes that these readings had no substantial influence on the author.

At times, critics have also found that Kyōka's fiction bears conspicuous signs of modernity, or shares traits with the work of writers of fantasy literature from around the world, although such evaluations have generally been sporadic or lack details of Kyōka's specific global influences and modern literary techniques. Still, such evaluations have provided a basis and important clues for the current study. In one of the first essays ever written on Kyōka, "Izumi Kyōka and Romanticism" ("Izumi Kyōka to romanchiku," 1907), by critic Saitō Nonohito (a.k.a. Saitō Shinsaku), Saitō compares Kyōka to German romantic writers, including E. T. A. Hoffmann (1776–1822), Novalis (1772–1801), and Ludwig Tieck (1773–1853), in part due to similarities in the historical contexts of their work, produced during eras of profound social transformation marked by the rise of positivism and the waning of traditional and religious worldviews. Saitō observes similarities particularly between Kyōka and Tieck, including in intimations of sublime, hidden depths in their romantic narratives, and in their frequent evocations of misty, moonlit nights, although he laments that Kyōka appears to be operating virtually alone as a writer of fantastic fiction in early-twentieth-century Japan.[7]

In another early article, from 1911, scholar Ikuta Chōkō compares Kyōka to Hoffmann and Edgar Allan Poe (1809–1849)—he refers to Kyōka specifically as a "romantiker" and describes him as an author with the visual imagination of a Pre-Raphaelite painter.[8] Writing in 1949, a decade after Kyōka's death, author Katsumoto Seiichirō provocatively argued that Kyōka "established the foundation" of his fiction on Western literature and painting and referred to Kyōka as "an Eastern disciple" of primarily French and German novelists, including Mérimée, Hoffmann, and Stendhal (1783–1842), as well as Swiss symbolist painter Arnold Böcklin (1827–1901).[9]

In later scholarship, critics have found striking similarities between Kyōka's writing and fantasy literature from Europe, and particularly from France, based on resonant interests and themes. Scholar Waki Akiko, in *Gensō no ronri: Izumi Kyōka no sekai* (*The Logic of Fantasy: The World of Izumi Kyōka*, 1974), compares Kyōka's fiction to that of foundational French writer of the fantastic Gerard de Nerval (1808–1855), due to shared themes of nostalgia, return to the hometown, and longing for an absent mother.[10] In *Gensō kūkan no tōzai: Furansu bungaku o tōshite mita Izumi Kyōka* (*Spaces of the Fantastic East and West: Izumi Kyōka as Seen through French Literature*, 1990), scholars of French literature find similarities between fiction by Kyōka and that of various French writers, including Charles Nodier (1780–1844), Gerard de Nerval, Théophile Gautier (1811–1872), Auguste Villiers de l'Isle Adam (1838–1889), Henri Bosco (1888–1976), Mérimée, and Maupassant.[11] Contributors to the volume examine similarities and divergences in these authors' approaches to topics including animism, polytheism, Buddhism, Christianity, angels, demons, depictions of "other worlds" (*takai*), and the veneration of sacred feminine figures. Despite the many insightful observations in such scholarship, however, it must be noted that there is no evidence that Kyōka was familiar with almost any of the Western writers listed above, with the exceptions of Mérimée, Maupassant, and possibly Hoffmann. Thus, the mechanisms by which Kyōka's literature acquired its globalized qualities, or the factors leading to perceptions of the modernity of his work, remain unexplained.

The global nature of Kyōka's fiction is further suggested in comments made by major Japanese authors, who have remarked that Kyōka's literature somehow feels foreign or exotic, thereby overturning the idea that his work was "purely" Japanese. Such comments reframe the context of Kyōka's writing and encourage readers to discover new horizons in his work. Novelist Mishima Yukio (1925–1970), for example, once wrote that Kyōka's stories often seem to take place in the mountains and forests of Germany, rather than in Japan, whereas novelist, scholar, and translator of French literature Shibusawa Tatsuhiko (1928–1987) expressed surprise that the fantastic worlds of Kyōka's fiction were produced by a Japanese author at all.[12] Novelist Tsushima Yūko (1947–2016), on a similar note, wrote that, while reading Kyōka in Paris, she suddenly felt as though the author was not as "Japanese" (*Nihonteki*) as he had generally been portrayed by scholars and that he was somehow a writer who could be appreciated universally, in any time or place.[13]

In this book, rather than arguing that the influence of traditional Japanese literature in Kyōka's fiction has been overstated, because such influence is undisputedly important, I seek to elucidate the networks and combinations of Japanese and global fiction that met in Kyōka's work, while also presenting this confluence as an origin point for the hybrid forms of Japanese fantasy literature that continue to be popular in Japan and around the world today. Like foundational writers of literature of the fantastic from modern Europe, Kyōka drew on the themes and structures of literature and popular storytelling from the past and set them in new contexts, while experimenting with basic elements of language and narrative to create distinctly modern works of fiction. Just as European authors looked to the folktales, myths, and epics of the past for images of supernatural creatures such as phantoms, vampires, werewolves, fairies, and elves, who they brought into modern settings, Kyōka adapted imagery of gods, buddhas, shape-shifting animals, and traditional Japanese monsters known as *yōkai* in fiction that clearly reflects the concerns and realities of the modern world. Kyōka also adapted formal elements from traditional Japanese genres, such as the rhythmic structures of Nō and *temari uta* ("nursery rhymes") and narratives centering on the revelation of miraculous powers and images, as commonly found in Nō, *kusazōshi*, and popular Buddhist tales.

In this study, among premodern genres, I focus on examining one of the most important influences on Kyōka's imagination of the fantastic—illustrated books known as *kusazōshi*, or otherwise *gōkan* ("collected volumes"), *ehon* ("picture books"), or *ezōshi* ("picture booklets"). I argue that *kusazōshi* were a major source of fantasy elements for Kyōka's fiction, due to their prominent themes of magic, monsters, and powerful heroes who set out on epic adventures, at times resembling modern genre fantasy. *Kusazōshi* have long been acknowledged as a major inspiration for Kyōka, but specific details about their influence on his stories remain scarce.

As for the global elements of Kyōka's fiction, I focus on establishing clear connections between Kyōka and his global sources of influence, while also identifying trends and developments in the broader literary environment in Japan that arose in response to the translation of Western literature. I argue that Kyōka was profoundly influenced by the work of several European authors, including Andersen, Hauptmann, and Mérimée, as well as by the Middle Eastern collection of supernatural tales, the *Arabian Nights*, also known as *One Thousand and One Nights* (*Alf layla wa-layla* in Arabic). Among such works, I emphasize the *Arabian Nights* as one of the most important influences on Kyōka's fiction throughout his life.[14] From the *Arabian Nights*, Kyōka adapted imagery of supernatural beings, eroticism, magic, and intricately detailed fantasy settings, as well as the literary technique of elaborate multipart frame narratives.[15] Another key influence on Kyōka's early development as a writer was *The Improvisatore* (*Improvisatoren*, 1835) by Andersen, a novel that combines elements of realism with scenes of fantasy and a fairytale-like atmosphere. *The Improvisatore* was translated by author Mori Ōgai (1862–1922) during the Meiji period and was a major influence on the wider development of literary romanticism in Japan. Kyōka was also deeply influenced by *The Sunken Bell* (*Die versunkene Glocke*, 1896) by Hauptmann, a fairy play (*märchendrama*) that Kyōka co-translated, or rather edited and rewrote, based on a translation by scholar of German literature Tobari Chikufū (1873–1955). Kyōka's favorite European author during the second half of his career was Mérimée, an author who wrote famous tales of living statues, phantoms, and metamorphosis. Kyōka was also impressed by the work of Maupassant, a modern writer of sensationalist tales, as demonstrated by references to the quality of Maupassant's writing in Kyōka's essays. Kyōka and Maupassant are compared in this book as literary figures who occupied similar positions in their respective cultural contexts, as foundational authors of literature of the fantastic in Japan and in France, and also as writers who wrote fiction that reflected similar concerns with the modern world, including themes of modern medicine, psychology, and the borders of superstition and belief.

The list of global works that Kyōka referenced clearly in his writing offers a strong starting point for considering the position of his literature in a comparative context. Altogether, in his fiction and essays, Kyōka references the following works of global literature: "Mademoiselle Fifi" (1882) by Guy de Maupassant, "The Etruscan Vase" ("La vase étrusque," 1828), *A Chronicle of the Reign of Charles IX* (*Chronique du règne de Charles IX*, 1829), and "Carmen" (1845) by Prosper Mérimée, *The Improvisatore* by Hans Christian Andersen, *Michael Strogoff* (*Michel Strogoff*, 1876) by Jules Verne, *The Golden Ass* by Apuleius, and the *Arabian Nights*. Muramatsu Sadataka, one of the first scholars of Kyōka's fiction, mentions that Kyōka spoke with him personally about another work by Mérimée, "The Vision of Charles XI" ("Vision de Charles

XI," 1829).[16] Kyōka co-translated a single play during his lifetime, *The Sunken Bell* by Hauptmann, and he mentions preparing the final version of a manuscript for the translation of another play, *The Miser* (*L'avare*, 1668) by Molière (1622–1673), as translated by his literary mentor Ozaki Kōyō (1867–1903). As an adult, Kyōka owned a copy of the *Arabian Nights* in Japanese translation, as well as a collection of works by Russian romantic author Mikhail Lermontov (1814–1841). Another foreign work of literature that Kyōka read early in life was *The Golden Ass* by Apuleius, a second-century text written in Latin by a writer from North Africa that is set in Thessaly, Greece. Kyōka references Zola, Turgenev, and Ibsen by name in one of his essays, although he does not mention any particular works that he read by any of these authors, and he mentions Tolstoy in a *tanka*, or a Japanese-style poem. Scholars have also speculated that Kyōka read fiction by Alexandre Dumas (1802–1870), Victor Hugo (1802–1885), and Oscar Wilde (1854–1900) based on parallel imagery and plot developments in certain works. Finally, Kyōka references two collections of foreign stories in translation in his essays, the *Foam on the Waves Collection* (*Minawashū*, 1892) by Mori Ōgai, with stories by writers including Hoffmann, G. E. Lessing (1729–1781), Heinrich von Kleist (1777–1811), Aloisia Kirschner (1854–1930), Turgenev, Tolstoy, Alphonse Daudet (1840–1897), Washington Irving (1783–1859), Bret Harte (1836–1902), and Pedro Calderón de la Barca (1600–1681), and *Collection of Masterpieces from the West* (*Taisei meichoshū*, 1907) by translator Baba Kochō (1869–1940), with stories by Maupassant, Turgenev, Honoré de Balzac (1799–1850), and Henryk Sienkiewicz (1846–1916).

In addition to such references, the modernity of Kyōka's fiction is demonstrated by his literary style. While Kyōka preserved certain themes, narrative devices, and linguistic elements from premodern Japanese literature in his work, his writing diverges too drastically from his sources to be considered as the mere continuation of a literary tradition. One has only to read a work by a premodern author who inspired Kyōka, such as Motokiyo Zeami (ca. 1363–ca. 1443), Matsuo Bashō (1644–1694), Ueda Akinari, Jippensha Ikku (1765–1831), Santō Kyōden (1761–1816), Shikitei Sanba (1776–1822), or Ryūtei Tanehiko (1783–1842), and a story by Kyōka in succession and the stark difference will be clear. Crucially, unlike the premodern writers who inspired him, Kyōka wrote most of his fiction in modern Japanese (*gendaigo*), rather than classical Japanese (*bungo*). By writing in *gendaigo*, Kyōka produced a literary idiom that was much closer to the modern, spoken language. He also experimented with grammar, such as by obfuscating and overlapping subjects or omitting sentence parts to a greater extent than the language normally allows, or by juxtaposing literary images with minimal syntactical connection. Moreover,

Kyōka's use of descriptive language was objective in ways that earlier literature rarely was—his stories feature extensive and detailed descriptions of settings (sometimes running into many pages) including mountain landscapes, seaside villages, inns, restaurants, alleyways, and even the occasional hospital or train compartment. Passages of scenic description in Edo period literature, by comparison, tend to be much shorter and more poetic or figural in expression. The overall effect of Kyōka's literary experimentation is the production of a fictional world that combines classical Japanese imagery with dense visual descriptions of modern, realistic settings, in ways that are indicative of the author's experiences with diverse literary traditions from around the world.

2. Kyōka and Literature of the Fantastic: *Gensō Bungaku*

Among modern Japanese authors, Kyōka most clearly fits the role of the founding figure of modern fantasy literature, or *gensō bungaku*, in Japan. Around the early twentieth century, Kyōka was one of very few Japanese writers who worked consistently with supernatural themes. Although other authors also wrote stories of the fantastic around the same time, including Kōda Rohan (1867–1947), Natsume Sōseki (1867–1916), Tanizaki Jun'ichirō (1886–1965), Okamoto Kanoko (1889–1939), Akutagawa Ryūnosuke (1892–1927), and Kawabata Yasunari (1899–1972), few other authors were so steadfast in writing stories about ghosts and monsters, or produced as much literature with as much supernatural content as Kyōka. Contemporary critics largely ignored Kyōka's supernatural stories, focusing instead on evaluating the realistic or naturalistic novel as the representative genre of the modern era.[17] Beginning in the late 1960s and early 1970s, however, critics began to reevaluate Kyōka's contributions to the formation of fantasy literature in Japan and to the canon of modern Japanese literature more broadly. This reevaluation was spurred by a rise of interest in "the fantastic," or *le fantastique*, as a distinctive literary genre of the modern world, along with a search to identify lineages of fantasy writing in Japan. The scholars who championed Kyōka in the 1970s were often comparativist critics who specialized in the study of European literature, such as Kawamura Jirō, a scholar and translator of German literature who also wrote groundbreaking scholarship on literature of the fantastic from Japan;[18] Tanemura Suehiro, a prominent scholar of German literature who translated fantasy and horror fiction into Japanese;[19] Shibusawa Tatsuhiko, a major scholar and translator of French literature;[20] and Waki Akiko, a scholar and translator of English-language fantasy novels for young readers.[21]

As scholar Sunaga Asahiko notes, the term *gensō bungaku* (literally meaning "literature of the illusory") was popularized as the standard translation of "*littérature fantastique*" in Japan circa the 1970s by Shibusawa, among other scholars.[22] Eventually, the term came to encompass many genres that subverted the expectations of realist or naturalist fiction, including "fairytales, fantasy, gothic literature, romantic literature, the supernatural, and horror."[23] In recent times, the term *gensō bungaku* has often been used in Japan to market genre fantasy or formula fantasy in ways that parallel the use of "fantasy literature" in the United States. In popular publications, the term is often used in a general sense to refer to any literature with supernatural themes, from premodern Japanese tales to contemporary fantasy fiction from around the world, thereby mirroring the polyvalence of terms such as "fantasy" and "the fantastic" in English.

Kyōka's central position in the foundation of modern fantasy literature in Japan is suggested by frequent references to his work throughout publications on the topic of *gensō bungaku*, including in critical studies, popular encyclopedias, and readers' introductions to the genre. Almost all books on *gensō bungaku*, from popular to academic works, include at least an entry or chapter on Kyōka and the importance of his fiction in the formation of *gensō bungaku* as a modern literary genre in Japan. One encyclopedia includes a section of top-ten favorite works by eight writers, all of whom include at least one work by Kyōka, the only author whose work is featured in all eight of the lists. Four authors list "The Holy Man of Mt. Kōya" as a favorite text, while the others list "A Tale of a Dragon of the Deep" ("Ryūtandan," 1896), *One Day in Spring* ("Shunchū" / "Shunchū gokoku," 1906), "A Quiet Obsession" ("Mayu kakushi no rei," 1924), and *The Swamp Woman* (*Numa fujin*, 1908).[24] Kawamura Jirō opens his response with the statement: "It would be nice if I could just list 'everything by Kyōka' as one of my choices . . .'"[25]

In English-language scholarship, Kyōka has been recognized for his contributions to Japanese fantasy literature in ways that emphasize the innovative qualities of his work. In the most prominent study of *gensō bungaku* in English, *The Fantastic in Modern Japanese Literature: The Subversion of Modernity* (1996), Susan J. Napier describes Kyōka as "arguably the greatest of Japanese fantasy writers, and certainly the greatest chronicler of fantastic females in Japanese literature."[26] Napier also explores affinities between Kyōka's writing and the contemporary literary genre of magical realism, particularly due to tensions that Kyōka sets up between aspects of the supernatural and the real, tradition and modernity, the old and the new Japan.[27] Scholar Cody Poulton similarly explores elements of fantasy in Kyōka's literature, in part by comparing his work to global traditions of folklore, fairytales, and mythology. Poulton describes *The Holy Man of Mt. Kōya* as possessing a "mythical, archetypal quality" that has somehow struck readers from various cultural backgrounds as deeply familiar, including readers in Western contexts, who might find similarities between Kyōka's fiction and myths of European antiquity, such as those of Artemis and Acteon or Circe and Odysseus.[28] Poulton also links Kyōka to modern global literature, writing that Kyōka's "adolescent readings of popular European literature," including Verne and Andersen, and possibly Hugo and Dumas, "exerted a profound influence on his early fiction."[29] Poulton's statement, among others, inspired my search to discover the sources and networks of Kyōka's global influences, as well as the elements of his fiction that have given readers the impression that Kyōka's work is somehow timeless, global, or universal in quality.

3. Theory of Literature of the Fantastic

Like studies of literature of the fantastic the world over, this study builds on literary theories formulated in French and English-language scholarship. In the West, literature of the fantastic is often treated as a distinctive genre of modern fiction that introduces elements of the supernatural into the setting of the real world and that features common themes, such as those of phantoms, vampires, magic, illusions, dream states, and haunted houses. It has long been a basic tenet in scholarship of the fantastic, by scholars ranging from Roger Caillois[30] to Tzvetan Todorov[31] and from Rosemary Jackson[32] to Claire Whitehead,[33] that an appreciable difference exists between literature of the fantastic as a genre that incorporates elements of fantasy into realistic settings, and popular fantasy literature that depicts heroic adventures in fairytale worlds, termed genre fantasy, formula fantasy, or quest fantasy, although these forms of writing also have overlapping features. In literature of the fantastic, elements of the supernatural confront the story's narrator or characters with unlikely or impossible situations that disturb their ordinary reality and force them to question the limits of their knowledge and experience of the world. In genre fantasy, authors generally construct secondary or parallel worlds inhabited by a combination of humans and supernatural creatures, such as monsters, ghosts, aliens, or talking animals. These creatures are not considered surprising to the stories' characters because they are naturally integrated into the story world. It is productive and illuminating to study literature of the fantastic and genre fantasy alongside each other, as scholars such as Farah Mendlesohn[34] and Brian Attebery[35] have done in their work.

However, to clarify the terms of the present study, it is useful to present definitions of "the fantastic" from the outset.

In common with most writing on literature of the fantastic, this study builds on the theories of Tzvetan Todorov, as established in *The Fantastic: A Structural Approach to a Literary Genre* (*Introduction à la littérature fantastique*, 1970). In Todorov's frequently referenced formulation, the fantastic in fiction results when a character hesitates in deciding between a natural or supernatural explanation for an occurrence that contravenes the known laws of nature, and when the reader is similarly left in doubt as to the most likely explanation.[36] If the occurrence turns out to be explicable by such causes as "dreams," "drugs," "tricks and prearranged apparitions," "illusion of the senses," or "madness," then the work belongs to the genre of "the uncanny" (*l'étrange*), whereas if the occurrence is credited to something completely beyond any possible explanation in the real world, it enters into the genre of "the marvelous" (*le merveilleux*).[37] As Todorov acknowledges, most literature of the fantastic falls on the borders of such genres. Thus, a work of detective fiction that treats the theme of hypnosis might be considered a work of "the fantastic-uncanny," whereas a story about characters who have possibly stepped through a portal into an alternate reality might be termed "the fantastic-marvelous," if not "fantasy" or a "fairytale." Todorov considers "the fantastic" to be a genre with identifiable historical boundaries, beginning with the work of writers such as Jacques Cazotte (1719–1792) and Jan Potocki (1761–1815) circa the late eighteenth century in France, and ending with "the last aesthetically satisfying examples of the genre" in the work of Maupassant in the early 1890s.[38] Other scholars find origins for "the fantastic" in the work of figures such as Hoffmann,[39] Sir Walter Scott (1771–1832),[40] or Joseph Addison (1672–1719),[41] and most consider the genre to still be operative, even if in different forms than its historical configurations. Another major figure in the origins of the fantastic as a literary concept is author Charles Nodier, who popularized the term *le fantastique* as the preferred description of tales with supernatural themes by writers such as Hoffmann, Scott, Tieck, and Charles Perrault, and who thereby played a key role in the adoption of "the fantastic" as a technical literary term over the more general "fantasy," or *fantaisie*.[42]

Although Todorov is often credited with initiating modern theories of the fantastic, and his formulation is precise enough to justify such views, it is important to note that Todorov's theory of *le fantastique* builds essentially on the work of several French scholars who preceded him, including Pierre-Georges Castex, Roger Caillois, and Louis Vax. The scholarship of these authors is particularly useful for the study of Kyōka's literature, because they treat many of the same texts, writers, and themes that influenced Kyōka. For example, French writers from Nodier to Todorov have repeatedly identified the *Arabian Nights* as a key text in the history of the fantastic imagination in Europe,[43] and French scholars have frequently upheld Mérimée and Maupassant as representative writers of the genre in the modern world.[44] Such scholars also propose theories of the fantastic that resonate with Kyōka's writing: for example, they describe the primary affective qualities of the fantastic as fear and estrangement, they emphasize the importance of image and visuality in the production of the fantastic, and they insist that modern writers often looked to popular traditions of storytelling for their materials, but clarify that they treated such materials from a temporal and cultural distance. For these scholars, "the fantastic" often represented a desire to be frightened just for the pleasure of it, and to believe in something beyond the natural world, whether in magic, the supernatural, or some hidden facet of life.

Useful definitions of the fantastic can be found in the writings of these French theorists, whose work provided a basis for Todorov's later theories. Louis Vax, for example, writes, "The fantastic narrative . . . likes to introduce people who are like us, inhabiting the real world as we are, with the sudden presence of the inexplicable."[45] Vax describes this effect with an example:

> We are, first of all, in our own world, clear, solid, reassuring. An event occurs that is strange, frightening, inexplicable; then we know the particular thrill that is provoked by a conflict between the real and the possible. It cannot be that a criminal passed through the walls, and yet he did. The fantastic is linked to scandal. It makes us believe the unbelievable.[46]

Marcel Schneider, another major scholar of the fantastic, describes *le fantastique* as a genre with "a taste for mystery and disorientation."[47] In reference to the themes of the fantastic, Schneider provides a list that touches on the more abstract content of the genre, rather than particular imagery from European folklore, as is common in scholarship on the subject. Due to their abstraction, Schneider's themes resonate with Kyōka's literary concerns in the context of modern Japan. He writes, "Some are more interested in the nocturnal part of our existence, in dreams, reveries, presentiments, intuitions, delusions, phantasms, chimeras, in irrational manifestations such as signs, augers, omens, etc., than what we do in all reason and consciousness."[48] One might also identify these as major concerns of Kyōka's work, particularly the themes of dreams, delusions, phantasms, and signs of fate.

4. Izumi Kyōka: Biography, Works, and Reception

Kyōka was born and raised in the snowy, atmospheric city of Kanazawa, the provincial capital of Ishikawa prefecture (formerly known as Kaga province) on the north coast of Japan, a place that has long been closely tied to the author's literary imagination. Kyōka was raised in a family with feudal roots in the artisan class in a city renowned for its historic artistic traditions, from local Nō theater to poetry to goldsmithing. Kyōka's father, Izumi Seiji, was a goldsmith and crafter of artisanal objects, including rings, hairpins, blade handles, cups, and incense burners.[49] Kyōka suggests a certain pride in his artisan-class background, as well as in his father's profession, by featuring gold engravers as characters in his fiction.[50] Kyōka is also said to have been influenced by his mother, Izumi Suzu (née Tanaka Suzu), who belonged to a family of Nō actors and musicians from the Kadono school of Nō theater in Tokyo.[51] In a sign of reverence toward his mother, Kyōka often references Nō plays or features Nō drums in his fiction. Suzu was also responsible for introducing Kyōka to *kusazōshi* through her meticulously assembled personal collection. During his youth, Kyōka was educated at an international English-language school run by American missionaries in Kanazawa, and he later decided to move to Tokyo to pursue a career as a writer after encountering the work of one of the most popular authors of the Meiji period, Ozaki Kōyō, who would eventually become his mentor. During the career that followed, Kyōka experienced early years of poverty and struggle in Tokyo, then a quick rise to critical and commercial success, followed by a long period of increasing estrangement from the literary establishment (while still experiencing popular success), only to be recognized as a towering figure of modern Japanese literature in later decades.

When Kyōka began his career in Tokyo in the 1890s, tales of magic, monsters, adventure, and quests for revenge, which had been popular in Japan during previous centuries, were being replaced by realistic novels that described the ordinary lives of modern people, under the influence of European writers such as Zola and Maupassant. During his early career, Kyōka oscillated between literary styles, beginning with his debut, *Kanmuri Yazaemon* (1892), an old-school tale of martial bandits exacting revenge against a corrupt local official, and works like "The Night Patrol" ("Yakō junsa," 1895) and "The Surgery Room" ("Gekashitsu," 1895), known as *kannen shōsetsu* ("idea novels"), which explored social themes such as homelessness, urban policing, and modern medicine in a relatively realistic mode. Kyōka's career began to take a turn early on with stories that described journeys into the mountains

Fig. 1. Portrait of Izumi Kyōka, 1898. (Photograph courtesy of Izumi Kyōka Kinenkan Museum.)

and encounters with ghostly figures or magical women, such as "Shrine of Wonder" ("Tae no miya," 1896) and "Mino Valley" ("Minodani," 1896). While gradually building on these themes in subsequent stories, Kyōka established a new career trajectory with his widely acknowledged masterpiece, *The Holy Man of Mt. Kōya*, a novella whose supernatural atmosphere and elegantly structured narrative have made it one of Kyōka's most enduring and popular works. Thereafter, Kyōka's career split into two adjacent paths, one as a writer of tales of the fantastic and ghost stories (historically known as *kaii shōsetsu*) that were enjoyed by his dedicated fans, and another as a writer of tales of geisha and the pleasure quarters (*karyū shōsetsu*) that became especially popular on stage. Even Kyōka's stories about geisha, however, often feature at least

Fig. 2. Izumi Kyōka, 1927–28. (Photograph courtesy of Izumi Kyōka Kinenkan Museum.)

some supernatural content, such as *Nihonbashi* (1914) and *A Woman's Lineage* (*Onna keizu*, 1907).

Kyōka continued to write for decades, but over time his fiction became increasingly surreal as he built on themes established in earlier works without elaborating on their meaning in his newer stories, while also experimenting with more abstract forms of narrative. Kyōka's later works have generally received less attention than his earlier fiction, in part due to the difficulty of their narratives and literary style. Late stories such as "The Count's Hairpin" ("Hakushaku no kanzashi," 1920), "The Mushroom Sermon" ("Kinoko seppō," 1930), "The Votive Light Volume" ("Tōmei no maki," 1933), and "The Sacred Heron Volume" ("Shinro no maki," 1933) are haunting and dreamlike, if not disturbing and grotesque; in their experimental nature, they display Kyōka moving from fantasy into surrealism. Kyōka was always surrounded by a group of close friends and fans of his work, who endeavored to collect and preserve his fiction, and he was often a favorite of other writers who could appreciate his abstract style of storytelling, but he became the kind of author who was more often respected from a distance than embraced by the casual reader. Nonetheless, Kyōka might also be seen as a writer whose fiction has always had the potential for wider appeal due to its popular themes, such as dreamlike journeys, haunted mansions, and erotic fantasies, as well as an assortment of Japanese-style ghosts and monsters.

In scholarship on Kyōka, biographical details have often been emphasized, at times taking precedence over discussion of the global or historical context of Kyōka's fiction. Since biographies of Kyōka first began to appear in the 1940s, much attention has been paid to the author's personal quirks, which were apparently so pronounced that they were noticed by almost anyone who met him. Some of the most commonly related details of his life include that he was highly superstitious, dedicated in his observance of Buddhist and Shinto rituals, extremely fussy about food, married to a woman who shared the name of his mother (Suzu), and a frequent visitor to the geisha quarters. His most frequently cited phobias include a fear of dogs, flies, thunder, lightning, contaminated food, and contagious diseases.[52] The reader is informed in virtually every study of Kyōka that he lost his mother at the age of nine and that he spent the rest of his life seeking replacements for her. He did this variously through the act of writing, relationships with maternal women and older-sister types, and veneration of sacred female figures, such as Māyādevi, the mother of the Buddha.[53]

As readers of Kyōka are well aware, there is significant variation in the narrative structures of Kyōka's work, such that it is worthwhile to read as many of Kyōka's stories as possible, if only to discover the diversity and talent of one of the great modern writers from Japan. Between 1892 and 1939, over a career that spanned nearly five decades, Kyōka wrote over 300 short stories, novellas, novels, and plays. Many of these are among the most acclaimed works in Japanese literature of the fantastic. A list of representative works includes *Noble Blood, Heroic Blood* (*Giketsu kyōketsu*, 1894), *Shining Leaf Theater* (*Teriha kyōgen*, 1896), "A Tale of a Dragon of the Deep" (1896), *Worship at Yushima* (*Yushima mōde*, 1899), *The Holy Man of Mt. Kōya* (1900), *The Order Book* (*Chūmonchō*, 1901), *One Day in Spring* (1906), *A Woman's Lineage* (1907), *The Grass Labyrinth* (1908), *White Heron* (*Shirasagi*, 1909), "A Song by Lantern Light" ("Uta andon," 1910), "Heat Haze Theater" ("Kagerōza," 1913), *Nihonbashi* (1914), *Women of Fate* (*Yukari no onna*, 1919–1921), "A Quiet Obsession" (1924), *Commentaries on the Mountains and the Sea* (*Sankai hyōbanki*, 1929), *Pale Plum Blossoms* (*Usukōbai*, 1937), and "The Cypress Vine" ("Rukō shinsō," 1939).

Although Kyōka was often ignored by critics during his lifetime, he was consistently mentioned as a favorite author by other writers, including by such prominent literary figures as Tanizaki, Kawabata, and Mishima. Such writers regularly referred to Kyōka literally as a genius (*tensai*) in their essays.[54] Tanizaki, one of Japan's most acclaimed modern novelists, wrote one of the most admiring essays on the author, of whom he claimed, "Certainly, Sensei is the greatest writer that our country has ever given birth to, the one most representative of our land, whose unique qualities could not possibly have arisen anywhere outside of Japan. Should we not then face the world and boast of him?"[55] Tanizaki's desire that the world learn of one of Japan's most talented authors, however, has been hindered by limited translations and scholarship outside of the Japanese language.

In Japan, Kyōka continues to be a favorite author of literary scholars, although the general reader is less likely to be familiar with his work, largely due to the difficulty of Kyōka's language. This difficulty can be traced to various features, including Kyōka's use of classical vocabulary, regional dialects, obscure references to popular culture, uncommon *kanji* characters (Sino-Japanese logograms), irregular grammar, and experimental narrative structures. Challenging elements of Kyōka's narrative delivery include suddenly shifting subjects and scenes, stories related out of sequence, and narratives that obscure or only gradually reveal key information. As scholars have frequently noted, Kyōka is one of the most difficult modern writers to understand.[56] In an attempt to convey the experience of reading Kyōka's more complex narratives, scholar Shinoda Hajime compares one of Kyōka's most notoriously difficult novels, *Commentary on the Mountains and the Sea* (1929), to *Finnegans Wake* (1939) by James Joyce (1882–1941).[57] As Shinoda and others affirm, however, one might also describe Kyōka's ornate literary style as one of the pleasures of his work, because with patient review such language yields rewards of deeper and renewed understanding of his carefully structured narratives.

Over the decades, in addition to major novelists such as Kawabata, Tanizaki, and Mishima, appreciators of Kyōka's work have included major film directors Mizoguchi Kenji (1898–1956), Ichikawa Kon (1915–2008), Suzuki Seijun (1923–2017), Terayama Shūji (1935–1983), and Shinoda Masahiro (1931–2025). Kyōka's stories were frequently adapted to film by these and other directors, in works including *Nihonbashi* (1929, no longer extant), *The Water Magician* (*Taki no Shiraito*, 1933), and *The Downfall of Osen* (*Orizuru Osen*, 1935), all directed by Mizoguchi; *Shirasagi* (1940, no longer extant), directed by Shimazu Yasujirō; *Nihonbashi* (1956), directed by Ichikawa; *The Demon*

Pond (*Yasha-ga-ike*, 1979), directed by Shinoda; *Kagerōza* (1981), directed by Suzuki; and *The Grass Labyrinth* (*Kusameikyū*, 1983), directed by Terayama. Additional movies are either lost or difficult to access due to the state of the film reels.

Other prominent admirers of Kyōka's fiction have included foundational Japanese ethnographer Yanagita Kunio (1875–1962), pioneering manga writer and artist Mizuki Shigeru (1922–2015), and leading kabuki actor Bandō Tamasaburō V.[58] Kyōka has also been a favorite author of numerous prominent women writers, many of whom have written literature in the genres of fantasy or romanticism, including Mori Mari (1903–1987),[59] Yoshiya Nobuko (1896–1973),[60] Kōno Taeko (1926–2015),[61] Tsushima Yūko,[62] Kanai Mieko,[63] Ogawa Yōko,[64] and Matsuda Aoko.[65]

In recent years, interest in Kyōka's literature has been revived due to the adaptation of his work in manga and illustrated books, as well as the publication of new anthologies and translations of his stories. In popular culture, Mizuki Shigeru, creator of the manga and anime series *GeGeGe no Kitarō*, a foundational series of monster manga, was particularly familiar with Kyōka's fiction. He adapted two novels to manga, along with a biography of the author in 2015.[66] The collection includes an adaptation of *The Holy Man of Mt. Kōya* alongside an early novel titled *The Black Cat* (*Kuroneko*, 1895), whose obscurity is evidence of Mizuki's deep familiarity with Kyōka's fiction. In his detailed rendition of Kyōka's biography and novels, Mizuki displays an academic level of knowledge of the author and his work that would qualify him as a scholar of Kyōka's literature. In the last decade, new illustrated editions of Kyōka's works have been adapted by popular illustrators and artists such as Uno Akira (Aquirax Uno),[67] Yamamoto Takato,[68] Nakagawa Gaku,[69] Honojiro Towoji,[70] and Kanaida Etsuko.[71] These books showcase surreal, fantastic, erotic, and grotesque visual styles that resonate with the contemporary world of manga and other popular media from Japan. In an unusual inversion of life and art, a fictionalized version of Kyōka has become one of the most popular characters in the manga series *Bungo Stray Dogs*, by author Asagiri Kafka and artist Harukawa Sango, although Kyōka is transformed in the series into a young woman with magic powers.[72] Kyōka also appears as a female character in *Thus Spoke Rohan Kishibe*, a spinoff of the popular manga and anime series *JoJo's Bizarre Adventure* by Araki Hirohiko, perhaps reflecting a widespread perception among Japanese speakers that the name Kyōka appears to be feminine.[73] On a global level, Kyōka's fiction is finally being translated into foreign languages with regular frequency, with recent collections appearing in Spanish,[74] Italian,[75] and Chinese.[76]

Kyōka's importance as one of Japan's essential authors of fantasy and horror literature lives on in the Izumi Kyōka Prize for Literature (*Izumi Kyōka Bungakushō*), the top prize in Japan for literature of the fantastic, awarded by the city of Kanazawa for works of literature that evince a dreamlike, surreal, or ghostly atmosphere. In addition to being one of Japan's most prestigious literary awards, the Kyōka prize is notable for having been awarded to many of Japan's leading female writers, including Takahashi Takako (1932–2013), Kurahashi Yumiko (1935–2005), Mori Mari, Tsushima Yūko, Kanai Mieko, Yoshimoto Banana, Yū Miri, Tawada Yōko, Kirino Natsuo, Ogawa Yōko, and Kawakami Hiromi. This list suggests that women have been particularly successful in writing literature of the fantastic and related genres in Japan, and also that they have been central in carrying on many of the qualities of Kyōka's work, such as elements of fantasy, dreamlike atmospheres, and a focus on narrative and character. This situation accords with circumstances in Western countries, where women have also found success in literature of the fantastic and related genres.[77]

5. Scholarship and Translation

Previously, three scholarly books have been published on Kyōka's fiction in English. The earliest was *Similitude of Blossoms: A Critical Biography of Izumi Kyōka (1873–1939), Japanese Novelist and Playwright* (1998) by Charles Shirō Inouye.[78] This book provides details of Kyōka's life, work, and major themes of his fiction, with a focus on the visual elements of Kyōka's narratives and the literary images that structure his work. Inouye has also translated two volumes of Kyōka's stories, *Japanese Gothic Tales* (University of Hawai'i, 1996)[79] and *In Light of Shadows: More Gothic Tales* (University of Hawai'i, 2005).[80] These volumes feature major stories such as *The Holy Man of Mt. Kōya*, *One Day in Spring*, "A Song by Lantern Light," and "A Quiet Obsession." In *Spirits of Another Sort: The Plays of Izumi Kyōka* (2001), scholar Cody Poulton examines Kyōka's work in theater, while providing translations of three major plays, *The Demon Pond* (*Yasha-ga-ike*, 1913), *The Sea God's Villa* (*Kaijin bessō*, 1913), and *The Castle Tower* (1917).[81] As Poulton shows, Kyōka's plays are distinguished by their settings in fantastic locations, such as the Dragon King's palace under the sea and a haunted version of Japan's most famous medieval fortress, Himeji Castle, as well as by their large casts of fantastic creatures. Another major study of Kyōka is featured in *Dangerous Women, Deadly Words: Phallic Fantasy and Modernity in Three Japanese Writers* (1999) by Nina

Cornyetz.[82] Cornyetz's book examines the work of three authors who wrote literature of the fantastic: Kyōka, Enchi Fumiko (1905–1986), and Nakagami Kenji (1946–1992). Cornyetz examines Kyōka's fiction from the point of view of psychological theory and feminist critique and presents the argument that Kyōka's literary depictions present women as destabilizing forces in the rational order of the Meiji period. Building on Cornyetz's work, I address gender in Kyōka's depiction of female characters throughout his fiction, including female heroes, sacred feminine figures, and characters who are by turns dangerous, erotic, and maternal.

Unlike the situation in English, scholarship on Kyōka in Japanese is extensive. In fact, Kyōka might be included among the modern authors who have been written on most frequently by scholars in Japan. Overall, around 100 scholarly books have been published on Kyōka. The first biography of Kyōka in Japanese was *Hito: Izumi Kyōka* (1943), written by the author's onetime literary pupil, Teraki Teihō (1883–1972). The first essential scholarly book on Kyōka is generally considered to be *Izumi Kyōka* (1954; revised 1966) by Muramatsu Sadataka, a scholar who befriended the author over the course of his research, late in Kyōka's life, and thereafter devoted a decade to organizing the inaugural full-length study of his fiction.

In Japan, critical approaches to the study of Kyōka's fiction have been diverse. For example, scholar Yoshimura Hirotō, who was trained as a psychologist, diagnosed the author with obsessive compulsive disorder and various phobias based on readings of his fiction, but he later turned his attention to the visual aspects of Kyōka's literary style, in work that compares Kyōka's literature to Buddhist visual art, such as mandalas and Zen ink painting. In the 1980s, Kasahara Nobuo wrote extensively on eroticism as a defining feature of Kyōka's fiction, while Waki Akiko introduced the term *gensō* into studies of Kyōka's work. In 2006, Tanaka Takako pointed out that little attention had been paid to traditional elements of horror (*kaii*) in Kyōka's stories, in a book that examines the cultural and literary lineage of monsters that appear in the author's stories.[83] As examples of the depth and diversity of Kyōka scholarship in Japan, recent books on Kyōka include a study of visuality and religion in Kyōka's fiction by Tominaga Maki,[84] a study of Kyōka's work in theater by Suzuki Aya,[85] a book of essays on themes including Kyōka and Indian philosophy and Kyōka and Shizuoka prefecture by Matsumura Tomomi,[86] and a book on Kyōka's former home in Tokyo, including a survey of his extensive collection of rabbit figurines, tobacco pipes, and traditional household items, edited by the Izumi Kyōka Kinenkan Museum in Kanazawa and the Izumi Kyōka Research Society (Izumi Kyōka Kenkyūkai).[87]

6. The Chapters

In chapter 1, "Visual Landscapes: Elements of Kyōka's Literature of the Fantastic," I examine Kyōka's use of visual language to construct realistic landscapes set in modern Japan, where supernatural elements intrude into the lives of his characters. In theories of the fantastic by scholars such as Roger Caillois and Farah Mendlesohn, descriptive writing is discussed as a primary method for producing convincing portrayals of the fantastic, whose writers aim to draw their readers deep into their story worlds. I argue that Kyōka developed his distinctive visual style by studying literature from Japan, Asia, and Europe in an educational environment that was modern and global. I examine the visuality of Kyōka's language, in part by exploring the dense visual landscapes, supernatural imagery, and erotic themes of Kyōka's fiction, as well as evaluations of Kyōka's work that compare his literary style to modern genres of visual art, such as impressionism and surrealism.

In chapter 2, "*Kusazōshi* and the Japanese Marvelous: Kyōka as a Collector of Picture Books," I examine one of the most important influences from Japanese literature on Kyōka's literary imagination, picture books known as *kusazōshi*. I argue that Kyōka's modern stories draw on images of monsters, magic, and heroes from the premodern world of *kusazōshi* for inspiration. As literature of the fantastic that shares traits with modern fiction from Europe, Kyōka's stories feature protagonists who experience fear and hesitation when confronting the supernatural. In this chapter, I explore elements of fantasy in *kusazōshi*, Kyōka's personal collection of picture books, and images of female heroes and supernatural beings that Kyōka transposed from premodern media into his modern fiction.

In chapter 3, "Literature in Translation: The Global Fantastic," I argue that Kyōka's stories of the fantastic were developed in part as a response to his reading of European fiction and other global literature in translation, particularly the *Arabian Nights*, *The Improvisatore* by Hans Christian Andersen, and *The Sunken Bell* by Gerhart Hauptmann. I argue that Kyōka drew various elements of his approach to the fantastic from the *Arabian Nights*, including the frequent use of complex frame narratives as a literary structure and literary images of metamorphosis, supernatural beings, eroticism, and elaborately described settings. I argue that *The Improvisatore* influenced Kyōka's approach to the fantastic by alternating between realistic description of modern Italian cities and landscapes and dreamlike sequences that suggest the workings of magic and fate. Kyōka was also influenced by *The Sunken Bell*, a fantasy play featuring a cast of supernatural creatures, such as elves, sprites, and fairies.

The influence of this work can be seen in Kyōka's depictions of *yōkai* and traditional Japanese ghosts and monsters in his plays and prose fiction.

Chapter 4, "Kyōka and Maupassant: Modern Ghost Stories," compares tales of the fantastic by Kyōka and Maupassant. In Japan, Maupassant had a significant influence on modern writers as one of the most widely translated and discussed European authors of the Meiji period. Despite his primary reputation as a naturalistic writer, Maupassant was also a major figure in the development of literature of the fantastic in Japan, based on his stories with supernatural themes such as ghosts, hypnosis, and invisible monsters. In this chapter, I argue that Kyōka and Maupassant each display distinctly modern approaches to the fantastic, particularly by considering the roles of science, psychology, superstition, and worldview in experiences of potentially supernatural events.

Chapter 5, "Kyōka and Mérimée: Tales of Magic and Ghosts," examines connections between Kyōka and his favorite European author, Prosper Mérimée. Mérimée is best known as the author of "Carmen" (1845), a romantic tragedy featuring a Roma woman in Andalucía, Spain. Mérimée also wrote ghost stories that are treated in scholarship as exemplars of major themes of literature of the fantastic, such as metamorphosis, phantasmal visions, and living statues. Mérimée's approach to supernatural fiction might be referred to as the "scholarly fantastic," because Mérimée frames his narratives of ghosts and monsters with real scholarship, drawn from his professional experience as a scholar of languages and a national inspector of monuments, thereby giving his tales an impression of veracity. Kyōka, in his late fiction, similarly experiments with a scholarly mode, based on his interests in ethnography, folklore, popular religion, and traditional Japanese literature, while experimenting with the portrayal of ghosts and other supernatural elements of his work.

One

Visual Landscapes

Elements of Kyōka's Literature of the Fantastic

1. Visuality and Fantastic Imagery

One of the most famous statements on Izumi Kyōka was made by scholar and translator of German literature Tanemura Suehiro, who wrote of the author, "Kyōka was new. He was so new that he was too new to be thought of as new."[1] In this chapter, I argue that the novelty of Kyōka's literature can be identified as a combination of its distinctive visual style and modern approach to depictions of the fantastic. Specifically, visuality in Kyōka's fiction may refer to the following major features of his writing: elaborately detailed landscapes, complex layering of visual elements, erotic imagery, and fantastic imagery of monsters and supernatural beings transposed into realistic settings. Kyōka developed his unique visual style by combining literary influences that he absorbed from an early age, including readings of traditional Japanese and Chinese literature, modern Japanese novels, the *Arabian Nights*, and global literature published in translation in the *Yūbin hōchi shinbun* (*Postal Report Newspaper*). Such influences shaped Kyōka's literary expression of a world of the fantastic that is convincing because it blurs the lines between the real, modern world and vividly imagined worlds of fantasy set in various urban and natural landscapes. As scholars have suggested, the style that Kyōka developed displays aesthetic qualities and formal traits that resemble modern genres of visual art, from pre-Raphaelite painting to impressionism and surrealism. As I will show, Kyōka evokes such genres through the use of literary techniques including intensive description, obfuscation of key narrative details, and superimposition of subjects in ways that produce surreal and ghostly effects.

In scholarship on the fantastic in the West, scholars have suggested that the quality of the fantastic in literature is produced in part by the development of intricately detailed settings or elaborate visual landscapes that give form and depth to the story world. Farah Mendlesohn, for example, notes that authors are often particularly concerned with providing meticulous descriptions of landscapes in genre fantasy, or quest fantasies. They do so by giving precise detail to every visual element of a story's setting, in a manner comparable to a landscape painter or a pre-Raphaelite artist, so that they can lead the reader deep into the imaginary worlds of fantasy that they have carefully constructed.[2] Roger Caillois argues that in literature of the fantastic, the world evoked by the language of the text must be realistic and grounded in images of the world inhabited by the reader, so that the terrifying appearance of the supernatural can be effective. He writes, "This is why, among the incontestable masters of the genre, there figure novelists and storytellers attached to plainly describing the most ordinary realities: Balzac and Dickens, Gogol and Maupassant. It is because it is first necessary to accumulate circumstantial proofs of the veracity of an improbable story, a backdrop necessary for the irruption of a shocking event that will first frighten the hero."[3] In common with such authors, Kyōka created convincing tales of the fantastic because he introduced the supernatural directly into vivid and realistic settings in the modern world.

In addition to its detailed landscapes, the visuality of Kyōka's fiction is expressed by the presentation of fantastic images, including images of supernatural creatures and erotic images of female ghosts and sacred feminine figures. Tzvetan Todorov points out that literature of the fantastic in the West has often been defined by recurring images and themes, such as those of vampires, phantoms, and werewolves.[4] On the centrality of monsters to the imagination of the fantastic, Marcel Schneider observes that countless people the world over can identify images of Count Dracula and Frankenstein's monster, even if they are unfamiliar with the names of Bram Stoker (1847–1912) and Mary Shelley (1797–1851). He writes, "Such is the power of the image, the force of the visual narrative, the fascination exerted by certain archetypes."[5] Considering such famous European references, one might ask what is the case for literature of the fantastic in Japan. Roger Caillois poses a beguiling question in this regard. According to Caillois, traditional Chinese and Japanese tales of the fantastic may feature ghosts and vampires, but not gnomes and fairies. Caillois questions if this difference might not point to "the proper limits of the fantastic" itself.[6]

In Kyōka's fiction, one encounters many ghosts (*yūrei*), arguably an occasional fairy (*yōsei*), and creatures that might be referred to as goblins (*henge* and *yōkai*), but probably nothing that could be called a gnome. Properly speaking, one encounters supernatural creatures including *onibaba* (demon hags), *nopperabō* (faceless demons), *karyōbinga* or *kechō* (bird-human hybrids), and even an occasional *kappa* (mischievous water spirits with beaks and shells). One also encounters erotic images, often of women who are in some way connected to the supernatural, either because they are ghosts or because they wield supernatural powers. Such women are often described in scenes of erotic encounter, usually at a point in the narrative when the protagonist must decide whether to continue chasing the supernatural deeper into a world of illusions, or otherwise turn back to a familiar world.

Alongside abundant supernatural imagery drawn from traditional sources, Kyōka's fiction also features imagery that clearly situates his work in the modern world, including references to modern technology and global cultures. Such images include trains, cars, telephones, electric lighting, modern medical offices, Western clothing, Western people in Japan, Christianity, and international school. These modern themes of Kyōka's fiction might be traced to the author's lifelong experience of reading global literature in translation, and to his experience of being educated in an international environment, where he encountered diverse modern literary and cultural traditions. Although Kyōka never left Japan, through his prodigious early reading of literature from various times and places, he developed techniques to evoke seemingly distant worlds and settings.

A further element of visuality in Kyōka's fiction is the generous inclusion of illustrations (*sashi-e*), frontispieces (*kuchi-e*), illustrated endpapers (*mikaeshi*), and elaborate book designs (*sōtei*) in publications of his work, although this topic is too extensive to cover in this study and could easily serve as the subject of a separate book.[7] Throughout his career, Kyōka worked closely with some of the most famous and acclaimed artists and illustrators in Japan, including Komura Settai (1887–1940), Kaburaki Kiyokata (1878–1972), Hashiguchi Goyō (1880–1921), Hirezaki Eihō (1880–1968), Ikeda Shōen (1886–1917), Okada Saburōsuke (1869–1939), and over a dozen others, to provide his literature with images of geisha, ghosts, traditional Japanese architecture, and romantic urban and natural environments.[8] Such artwork often recalled the art and literature of the Edo period through the use of traditional themes and techniques, while also featuring avant-garde elements that paralleled Kyōka's literary experimentation. In this book, only a few exemplary works of illustration are presented, particularly where they reflect elements of fantasy and horror that are central to Kyōka's visual imagination. Building on the themes and atmosphere of Kyōka's writing, such images visually express the combination of eroticism, romanticism, tradition, and modernity that defines Kyōka's literary style.

2. Metaphors of Visuality: From Ukiyo-e to Surrealism

Scholars have frequently referred to Kyōka as a distinctly visual writer, often by drawing on visual metaphors to describe Kyōka's literature, or by comparing Kyōka's writing to various genres of visual art, from ukiyo-e to surrealism. When considered as a whole, such evaluations suggest recurring thematic and formal elements of "visuality" in Kyōka's fiction. For example, comparing Kyōka's work to ukiyo-e highlights the author's depiction of imagery with roots in Edo-period arts and culture, such as images of violence, eroticism, and traditional fashion, whereas evaluations that compare Kyōka's work to surrealist painting emphasize its modern elements, such as multilayered narratives based on a progression or transformation of images. This combination of visual metaphors thus suggests the experimental qualities of Kyōka's style. Unlike modern, realistic fiction, which might be compared to portrait or still-life painting, Kyōka's work emerges as a new kind of literature that sets the themes and images of traditional Japanese art into the dreamlike sequences and deconstructed landscapes of surrealist painting.

Scholars have previously described visuality as one of the most significant traits of Kyōka's writing on various levels. Charles Shirō Inouye, for example, describes Kyōka's literature as "pictocentric," or based on images and figural language, rather than "logocentric," as was much of the modern European literature imported to Japan during the Meiji period.[9] Inouye elaborates on Kyōka's use of archetypal imagery throughout his fiction, including images relating to water, death, bloodshed, women, and the colors white and red.[10] Nina Cornyetz directs attention to Kyōka's written language at the level of his printed text, writing that Kyōka was "attentive to the pictographic power of the word-as-sign" and describing the author as being constantly aware of the tactility and appearance of words on the page.[11] Summarizing critical opinion, Cody Poulton writes of Kyōka's visuality, "Whenever Kyōka has been singled out for praise, it has always been for his rich and intensely visual style."[12]

Historically, Kyōka's work has often been compared to ukiyo-e, or "images of the floating world," due to the author's focus on describing elements of his stories that were frequently the subjects of Edo-period art, such as fashion, theater, and graphic or sensational imagery. Ukiyo-e were popular images from the Edo period that celebrated the ephemeral pleasures of life, such as kabuki, fashion, travel, and the culture of geisha and the pleasure quarters; they were most commonly woodblock prints. Some ukiyo-e also featured fantastic imagery, such as *yōkai* and supernatural beings, or erotic content.

Connecting Kyōka's work to ukiyo-e, author and fellow Kanazawa native Tokuda Shūsei (1871–1943) wrote that Kyōka's literature was "all mixed up" with the woodblock-printed pictures of Toyokuni, which might refer to either Utagawa Toyokuni (1769–1825) or Utagawa Kunisada (1786–1865), also known as Toyokuni III, who was one of Kyōka's favorite artists.[13] On a similar note, author Nagai Kafū (1879–1959) compared Kyōka's literary description of a snowy urban landscape in his novella *The Order Book* (1901) to winter scenes in ukiyo-e by Utagawa Hiroshige (1797–1858), due to similarities in the atmospheres and visual details of their work.[14] Drawing a figural connection between text and image, Kafū equated Kyōka's brushstroke with the visual expression of a woodblock print. Later critics have often compared Kyōka's literature to the genre of *bijinga* ("images of beautiful women"), a variety of ukiyo-e highlighting women's fashion and lifestyles, by artists including Kunisada, Utagawa Kuniyoshi (1797–1861), Katsukawa Shunshō (1726–1792), and Kitagawa Utamaro (1753–1806), because some of Kyōka's most detailed passages of text involve descriptions of women's clothing, from kimonos to overcoats and from sashes (*obi*) to hairpins (*kanzashi*).[15] Kyōka's fiction has also frequently been compared to the decadent art of late ukiyo-e, due to the author's occasional fondness for garishness and excess, such as in scenes of extreme violence or torture, thereby recalling the work of artists such as Kunisada, Kuniyoshi, and Tsukioka Yoshitoshi (1839–1892).[16]

Writers who compare the author's work to modern genres of visual art, such as symbolism and impressionism, give a different impression of Kyōka's fiction, highlighting its elements of novelty. Scholar Ikuta Chōkō, for example, refers to Kyōka literally as an "Impressionist" (using the English-language word) whose "Impressionism should be considered as the pride of Japanese literature."[17] Mita Hideaki, linking Kyōka's impressionistic literary style to cinema, writes that Kyōka's literature makes use of "a generous assemblage of impressions" that "succeed each other, one by one, like scenes reflected in the lens of a movie camera set in motion."[18] Author Kawabata Yasunari, using a striking metaphor, describes Kyōka's work as a "train ride through an ukiyo-e."[19] Although Kawabata does not refer by name to Kyōka as an "impressionist," his metaphor suggests the impressionist technique of attempting to capture the observation of a landscape in real time. Kawabata's description also presents a fantastic scenario that evokes Kyōka's mixture of classical and modern elements in his supernatural fiction.

Other writers have connected Kyōka's visual style to even later developments in European painting, particularly surrealism, thereby emphasizing its most experimental qualities. Mishima Yukio, for example, describes Kyōka's literary style as "surrealism" (*chōgenjitsu shugi* or *shūrurearizumu* in different essays) and states forthright that Kyōka was an "avant-garde" (*zen'eiteki*) and "extremely visual" (*hijō ni bijuaru*) writer.[20] Terayama Shūji similarly characterizes Kyōka as a writer of "surrealistic" fiction, one whose visual style of narrative, based on progressions of related images, translates easily to cinema.[21] On many occasions Kyōka's work has also been compared to cutting-edge art by major visual artists from Europe. Specifically, Kyōka's work has been compared to the decadent illustration of Aubrey Beardsley (1872–1898);[22] the symbolist paintings of Gustave Moreau (1826–1898),[23] Arnold Böcklin,[24] and Gustav Klimt (1862–1918);[25] and the surrealist paintings of Giorgio de Chirico (1888–1978),[26] Max Ernst (1891–1976), and Salvador Dalí (1904–1989).[27] The description of Kyōka's literature as "surreal" seems particularly appropriate when considering that his narratives often mix dreams with reality, daydreams with nightmares, and the ordinary with the inexplicable. Kyōka's fiction might also be characterized as surrealist due to the experimental nature of his narratives, which are often delivered by narrators who are haunted or bewildered by their dreams, or who seem to have fallen under spells of insomnia, feverish mental states, or temporary madness. Kyōka's narratives often unfold like recurring dreams, whose familiar elements are recombined to produce new impressions and effects, in a manner similar to the paintings of Klimt or Dalí.

3. Literary Images: Eroticism, Horror, and Fantasy

Kyōka is known to have structured his literary world on a set list of recurring images. Such images include natural motifs, Buddhist icons, traditional Japanese architecture and material culture, erotic images, monsters, and animals. Repeating images can be found across Kyōka's 300 or so stories, including images of natural features and phenomena, such as forests, mountains, flowers, rivers, the ocean, waterfalls, floods, and fires, as well as images drawn from traditional Japanese culture, including blades, mirrors, combs, theatrical stages, hairpins, kimono sashes, kimono sleeves, woodblock prints, woven handballs (*temari*), and Nō hand drums (*kotsuzumi*).[28] Kyōka's literature also features repeating images of animals, *yōkai*, gods, buddhas, bodhisattvas, sacred feminine figures, and erotic females. Together, such images impart an element of mysticism and otherworldliness to Kyōka's fiction, while also creating a sense of continuity and interconnection in his narrative universe. Combining such themes with carefully selected images to represent the modern world, such as cars, trains, and telephones, Kyōka creates the foundation for the modern imagination of the fantastic in Japan.

If Western literature of the fantastic is shaped by images of vampires, werewolves, fairies, and elves in settings such as dark forests and haunted castles, then Kyōka's vision of the fantastic might be defined by the appearance of *yōkai* and *yūrei* in settings such as deep mountain landscapes, lonely huts in the wilderness, rustic mansions, and the hidden alleyways and backstreets of Tokyo. Some of Kyōka's representative *yōkai* include *nobusuma* (vampiric flying squirrels), *hihi* (monkey demons), *nyūdō* (demon monks), *tōrima* (spirits of misfortune who must be ignored as they pass one by), *ubume* (bloody spirits of women who died in childbirth), *onibaba*, *nopperabō*, *datsueba* (a demonic old woman who steals sinners' clothes and leaves them naked in hell), and *gozu mezu* (the ox-headed and horse-headed guardian demons of hell). It should be noted that some of these creatures are more or less common in Japanese folklore or religion, but they are not likely to be recognized as the most representative *yōkai*, such as *kappa*, living umbrellas, shape-shifting foxes, or multi-tailed cats.[29] The unusual gathering of Kyōka's typical *yōkai* results in a cast that quickly becomes familiar to readers of his fiction and that gives his work a distinctive atmosphere of dark and haunting fantasy. Kyōka's literature also features repeating images of animals, such as snakes, crabs, owls, herons, cats, and butterflies. Such creatures are often shown to exist at the borders of the supernatural, and they occasionally transform or use human language, in ways that recall the goblins or changelings of European fairytales and folklore. In his use of religious imagery, Kyōka similarly draws on a unique group of gods and bodhisattvas, often those with deep ties to his hometown of Kanazawa, where they are venerated at various temples and shrines, or otherwise those connected to Nichiren Buddhism, the sect of Japanese Buddhism that Kyōka belonged to throughout his life. Such figures include Māyādevi, the mother of the Buddha; Shirayama Hime, the goddess of Mt. Hakusan; Kishimojin, a guardian protector of children; Kannon, a popular bodhisattva of compassion; and Benzaiten, the goddess of music, poetry, rivers, and wealth.

In addition to supernatural imagery, some of the defining images of Kyōka's fiction are of an erotic nature. Scholars have frequently noted a prevalence of scenes of bondage and erotic torture in Kyōka's fiction, often of beautiful young women who are tortured by older women or by demons. This kind of content might be traced to the traditional Japanese literature that inspired

Kyōka; it can be found throughout the pages of *kusazōshi*, as well as in popular ghost stories, folktales, and even fairytales and nursery rhymes, as Kyōka points out in his essay "My Disposition" ("Yo no taido," 1908).[30] Another major image of Kyōka's fiction is that of the older female, either an aunt or older sister type, who exposes her breasts or naked body to the male protagonist. Kyōka almost always describes such women by referring to their large, white breasts, which are one of the most frequent images of his fiction. Scholars have even interpreted the depiction of erotic imagery as the main point of Kyōka's literature, such as Katsumoto Seiichirō, who writes, "I believe that the objective lying in the deepest recesses of the best of Kyōka's stories is to capture the density of the mature flesh of the Japanese woman, which has normally been kept hidden under layers of kimono. The sheer density of his depictions is unparalleled."[31] Scholar Kasahara Nobuo, in his book on Kyōka and eroticism, similarly writes, "Kyōka's literature originates with the image of swollen, pendulant nipples that show through thin fabric. The visual eroticism of white breasts emerging from beneath the elegant colors of thin fabric composes the foundation of Kyōka's literature and gives rise to its peculiar shapes."[32]

Forming a sinister counterpoint to Kyōka's depictions of the erotic older female are his portrayals of a monstrous elderly woman known as the *onibaba*, or "demon hag," who is a common figure of terror not only in Kyōka's literature, but in Japanese culture more widely. The legend of the *onibaba* is a popular folktale and religious narrative that has been adapted to literature and the arts, from votive images in temples to the classic horror movie *Onibaba* (1964) directed by Shindō Kanetō (1912–2012). The basic narrative can be found in different versions throughout Japan, but the most famous version comes from Adachigahara, in present-day Nihonmatsu, Fukushima prefecture.[33] In the legend from Adachigahara, a wet nurse is sent by a wealthy noble to find a pregnant woman so that she might extract the fetus from her womb and remove its liver, because this was believed to be the only cure for the noble's ailing daughter. The old woman eventually succeeds in finding a pregnant woman in the fields of Adachigahara, whom she proceeds to kidnap and disembowel, only to find, to her horror, that the woman was her own daughter. She thereafter becomes a demon hag who haunts the fields and captures travelers unfortunate enough to venture into her hut.

Demon hags are one of the most common images in Kyōka's fiction and are featured in story after story, from Kyōka's debut work of fiction through to his final works.[34] Kyōka's fascination with the *onibaba* is demonstrated by his reference to an infamously gory and sadistic print of the demonic figure by ukiyo-e artist Yoshitoshi, known as *Picture of the Lonely House at Adachigahara in Ōshū* (*Ōshū Adachigahara hitotsuya no zu*, 1885), referenced by name in "The Mushroom Sermon" (1930), a late short story depicting grotesque monsters and hallucinations.[35] In Yoshitoshi's woodblock image of the *onibaba*'s hut, the old woman appears bare-chested as she sharpens a butcher's blade. She faces a pregnant woman who is depicted naked from the waist up, bound, and suspended upside-down from the ceiling of her hut. The bound woman's furrowed eyebrows and look of anticipating pain, combined with the *onibaba*'s menacing scowl and reserved pose, create an atmosphere of chilling horror. For art historians of nineteenth-century Japanese art, the image represents the peak of decadence and gory interests seen in late ukiyo-e, by artists such as Kuniyoshi and Yoshitoshi. It is also one of the most gruesome images associated with Kyōka's literature, and one that appears to have had a deep impact on the author's imagination. Although Kyōka does not always mention the *onibaba* by name, he makes frequent allusions to the demon throughout his fiction by use of the word *hitotsuya*, which references the popular legend, and Yoshitoshi's print in particular.[36]

4. Fantastic Landscapes of the Modern World

In addition to recurring supernatural and erotic imagery, one of the most prominent elements of Kyōka's visuality is the level of detail he pours into describing the settings or landscapes of his fiction. This element of Kyōka's work might be traced to his lifelong interaction with a diverse range of literature from Japan, China, Europe, and the Middle East from an early age. Texts as varied as the *Arabian Nights* and the novels of Jules Verne feature detailed descriptions of landscapes, both real and imagined, from countries of the modern world to magical cities and kingdoms. Such literature introduced Kyōka to cultures, landscapes, and images from distant or invented places, thereby broadening his imaginative horizons. In his own fiction, Kyōka created romantic settings for his stories that he described in extensive detail, such as the deep forests and treacherous mountain passes of central Honshū in *The Holy Man of Mt. Kōya*, the rustic seaside villages of the Shōnan coast in *One Day in Spring* and *The Grass Labyrinth*, and dense networks of alleyways, canals, bridges, and teahouses in Tokyo in urban stories such as *The Order Book*, *Nihonbashi*, *Celestial Kabuki* (*Hoshi no kabuki*, 1915), and *A Peony Song* (*Shakuyaku no uta*, 1918). Although these works are all set in Japan, Kyōka's imaginative descriptions turn such settings into unfamiliar and enchanted spaces, or seemingly distant "other worlds" (*takai*) hidden in modern landscapes.

Kyōka's perspective on the modern world, including the world beyond Japan, has not often been described in scholarship, which tends to picture Kyōka as an author who existed in a hermetic cultural environment, as though oblivious of the world around him. In a way, such characterizations are understandable, particularly when one compares Kyōka to some of his peers, whose experiences were more markedly international than his. For example, Mori Ōgai studied in Germany from 1884 to 1888 and translated dozens of works of European literature from German throughout his career,[37] Natsume Sōseki studied in England from 1900 to 1902 and wrote extensive treatises on English literature and literary theory,[38] and Nagai Kafū traveled across the United States from 1903 to 1907, then lived in France for one year, and then became an acclaimed translator and scholar of French literature.[39] Kyōka, by contrast, spent his entire life in Japan, and mostly in Tokyo and Kanazawa, with occasional travel to nearby regions. However, as a youth in Kanazawa, Kyōka was educated at an English-language school, Hokuriku Eiwa Gakkō (Hokuriku English Conversation School) from 1884–1887, where he studied geography and history textbooks in English and read world literature in translation in newspapers the school subscribed to. Moreover, Kyōka was apparently proficient in English and even considered becoming an English teacher as his first career choice. In a record of Kyōka's educational history given by Muramatsu Sadataka, Kyōka is said to have passed an English exam with full points when trying to enter Ishikawa-ken Senmon Gakkō (Ishikawa Prefectural Technical School), although he was unable to pass the math exam required for entry.[40] He also found employment as a substitute English teacher at a local tutoring school in Kanazawa, and even briefly opened his own private English school with a friend between 1888 and 1889, apparently at the age of fifteen or sixteen, which suggests that he was reasonably proficient in English at one point in his life.

Kyōka's reading of global literature in translation, as well as history and geography textbooks in English, introduced him to locations and landscapes that enriched his literary imagination. One of Kyōka's favorite texts during his youth was the *Arabian Nights*, a collection of fantastic tales featuring imagery of genies, magic spells, and beautiful princesses set in the Middle East, North Africa, Persia, India, and places across the Asian continent, as well as in enchanted cities, islands, and palaces whose imaginary settings are described in extensive detail. Another work of classical world literature that influenced Kyōka during his youth was *The Golden Ass* by Apuleius, a second-century text written by an author from North Africa in Latin that features imaginative depictions of magic, witches, and metamorphosis in the landscapes of ancient Greece. A minor character in early episodes of *The Golden Ass*, Pamphile, has the power to transform men into animals, a feature that has been linked to Kyōka's depiction of the witch of Mt. Kōya.[41]

At school, Kyōka read global literature in the *Yūbin hōchi shinbun*, including stories that were translated by Morita Shiken (1861–1897), one of the most prominent translators of French literature during the Meiji period, who was known especially for his translations of fiction by Jules Verne and Victor Hugo. During Kyōka's time at Hokuriku Eiwa Gakkō, Morita published translations of several stories by Verne in the *Yūbin hōchi shinbun*, including "The Blockade Runners" ("Les forceurs de blocus," 1865), *Michael Strogoff* (1876), *Off on a Comet* (*Hector Servadac*, 1877), and *The Begum's Fortune* (*Les cinq cents millions de la Bégum*, 1879).[42] He also translated global stories whose sources are unknown, including "Tale of Charuma, the Indian Prince" ("Indo Taishi Charuma monogatari," 1886) and "Tale of an English Military Officer" ("Eikoku shikan no monogatari," 1887), in addition to episodes from *The Golden Ass* by Apuleius (translated as *Kinroba*, 1887). Morita's translations are set in richly imagined locations all over the world. They include settings and reference to places such as Angola, India, Singapore, Siberia, England, Scotland, the Cascade mountains, Civil War–era South Carolina, and Islamic Spain. One story even takes place on a comet flying through the solar system.

The only translation by Shiken that Kyōka mentions reading by name is *Michael Strogoff* by Jules Verne, translated by Shiken as *The Blind Emissary* (*Mekura no shisha*, 1887).[43] However, Kyōka indicates that, during his school years, he was far more interested in reading translations in the *Yūbin hōchi shinbun* than in his assigned school readings, thereby suggesting that he probably read other translations by Shiken. Works such as *Michael Strogoff* would have expanded Kyōka's awareness of the vastness of the world around him, while also supplying his imagination with fantastic themes. *Michael Strogoff* is an imaginary tale of an emissary of the czar of Russia who is dispatched to Siberia to attempt to prevent a troop of allied Turkic forces from the emirate of Bukhara and the steppes of Central Asia from taking the Siberian cities of Omsk and Irkutsk.[44] In the novel, Verne strives to relate the vastness of the Russian empire and to capture its landscape with accurate geographic detail, from the cities of European Russia through the central Ural mountains and into the immense plains, forests, swamplands, and lakes of Siberian Russia, while also describing the regional cities, cultures, and peoples of Russia, Siberia, and the Turkic world. The result is the account of an epic landscape, where heroes struggle against an unforgiving environment, elite warriors, and even, at one point, a troop of wolves that chases them across ice floes on a frozen river that is set ablaze with chemical fire. Shiken's title for his translation refers to a sequence in the novel where Michael Strogoff is captured by the emir of Bukhara and his eyes are supposedly seared by a heated sword, although the effect of the searing is averted by the hero's tears; he is revealed by the story's conclusion to have feigned his blinding to gain an advantage over his enemies in battle. Kyōka writes that the novel was serialized "day after day" in the *Yūbin hōchi shinbun* and that he found it to be "extraordinarily interesting."[45] One can only imagine the impression that the fantastic account of an exotic landscape made on the young reader.

In addition to encountering distant lands in works of fiction, Kyōka learned of the broader world around him through his textbooks in English, many of which were centered on the study of geography and world history. According to a chronology included in the original edition of the *Complete Works of Izumi Kyōka* (*Kyōka zenshū*), published by Shun'yōdō in 1925, Kyōka studied from the following books during his school years: the *Reader of the School and Family* series by Marcius Willson; *Peter Parley's Universal History, on the Basis of Geography: For the Use of Families, Illustrated by Maps and Engravings* (1838) by Samuel G. Goodrich (penname Peter Parley), Nathaniel Hawthorne, and Elizabeth Manning Hawthorne; *Special History of the New England States* (1879) by George Payn Quackenbos; *Mitchell's Geographical Reader: A System of Modern Geography, Comprising a Description of the World with its Grand Divisions, America, Europe, Asia, Africa, and Oceanica, Designed for Instruction in Schools and Families* (1840) by Samuel Augustus Mitchell; and *Handbook of Japanese-English Etymology* (1880) by William Imbrie.[46] These textbooks would have presented Kyōka with a vision of a vast, unknown, and unreachable world, which he could experience only through literary descriptions and illustrations. As a sign of the impact that such readings made on Kyōka, this list of his textbooks was published long after his school days, in 1925, raising the question of whether the author had held on to his schoolbooks for nearly four decades, or if his memories of them were sufficiently vivid to recall them after so many years. In several stories, described later in this book, Kyōka presents characters who study subjects such as world history and geography, thereby reinforcing the impact of his early education on his literary imagination.

5. Lover's Treatment

The combination of local and global literature that inspired Kyōka's visual imagination can be gleaned from his essay "Lover's Treatment" ("Iro atsukai,"

1901), as well as early stories that depict Kyōka's school days in Kanazawa. Scholars often present this essay, one of Kyōka's most frequently cited, as evidence of his traditional literary education, but without paying attention to the essay's diversity of details. Considered alongside Kyōka's early stories, the essay suggests that he was supplied with wide-ranging literary sources from his youth, from which he was able to craft literary worlds that combined elements of traditional Japanese aesthetics, European romanticism, modern realism, and global fantasy. As detailed in such work, Kyōka was raised on an array of literature and media that included woodblock-printed picture books, typeset books, textbooks, newspapers, classical East Asian literature, and modern European fiction in translation.

In "Lover's Treatment," Kyōka describes the first books that he encountered during his childhood as *kusazōshi* (a topic treated in detail in the following chapter), including popular series that were part of his mother's picture-book collection. After early days of childhood spent immersed in *kusazōshi*, which often centered on themes of magic and adventure, Kyōka found his desire to read such fiction challenged by his father, who redirected his son's attention to more "serious" literature. As Kyōka relates, his father was strict in matters of education and endeavored to pass on traditional Confucian values to his son. For this reason, after Kyōka learned to read, he spent his days studying classical Chinese texts, such as the *Analects of Confucius* and the writings of Mencius.[47] His father encouraged him to read martial epics that described heroic feats of bravery in ancient China, and thus he immersed himself in tales of military heroes from the Warring States Period such as General Wu Zixu (d. ca. 484 BC) and Duke Ai of Qin (r. 536–501 BC). Kyōka relates that he grew to enjoy such literature, particularly for its ostentatious style of storytelling. From these historical texts he moved on to some of the most famous and influential novels in East Asia, the Ming vernacular novels, such as *The Water Margin* and *Romance of the Three Kingdoms* (Chinese: *Sanguo yanyi*; Japanese: *Sangokushi engi*), whose accounts of powerful martial artists wielding special weapons captured his imagination.

As the essay continues, Kyōka describes his later connection to another foundational author of modern Japanese literature, Higuchi Ichiyō (1872–1896), whose hybrid literary style both resembled and differed from his own. As Kyōka writes, as a youth, when he was caught reading noneducational materials, his father would lock him in a closet, an experience that Ichiyō could apparently relate to. As Kyōka conveys, Ichiyō was similarly punished by her parents with confinement, but the place of her confinement, a storeroom outside of her family home in Tokyo, was stacked with books. Due to her fondness for reading, Ichiyō intentionally sought punishment by playing pranks so that her parents would send her to the storeroom, where she could spend her time reading books in solitude. Kyōka, as a young author, was deeply influenced by Ichiyō, with whom he became acquainted after moving to Tokyo. Such influence can be seen in Kyōka's approach to describing the inner neighborhoods, backstreets, and brothels of Tokyo in meticulous detail, although his work diverged from Ichiyō's thoroughly realistic fiction by its inclusion of supernatural elements.[48]

As a child at Hokuriku Eiwa Gakkō, Kyōka was exposed to a wider world of literature—in particular, he mentions reading Shiken's translation of *Michael Strogoff* by Jules Verne. In the classroom, works of fiction were prohibited, so Kyōka was forced to read them in secret. He recalls hiding *Recent Accounts of Handsome Youths* (*Kinsesetsu bishōnenroku*, 1829–1848) by Takizawa Bakin (1767–1848), a *yomihon*, inside one of his textbooks, *Outlines of the World's History: Ancient, Medieval, and Modern, with Special Relation to the History of Civilization and the Progress of Mankind* (1874) by William Swinton, in his English class.[49] He writes that he would rush to conceal the book in a panic whenever his teacher approached his desk, but his attempts at concealment sometimes failed, and thus some of the books he borrowed from the lending library were confiscated. Kyōka's account of hiding Bakin's work of fiction inside his geography textbook might be interpreted as a symbolic anecdote about the meeting of literary worlds that took place in the English-language classroom in Kanazawa, due to the incongruity of the content and format of these books. Bakin's *yomihon* was a softcover book printed with woodblocks and illustrated with traditional ukiyo-e-style images by Kunisada. It relates a historical tale of samurai battles and love affairs between handsome young men (*bishōnen*) and beautiful young women (*bishōjo*) in sixteenth-century Japan.[50] Swinton's textbook, according to its lengthy subtitle, was one that purported to relate "the history of civilization and the progress of mankind."

By the time that Kyōka began committing the "evil deeds," as he puts it, of selling his textbooks to pay for his confiscated library books, he had fallen in love with fiction, hence the title of the essay, "Lover's Treatment." He would stop by the book lender while heading out to the oil vendor as a pretense, lie to his teacher that he was out washing his loincloth while sneaking a read down by the river, and slip home barefoot, so as not to make a sound, with books hidden beneath his kimono sash. He compares books to geisha, prostitutes, and beautiful women of the pleasure quarters, whom he longs to spend the night with, if only he had the money to pay the fee for a day's accompaniment. He later compares them to aristocratic women who give in to his pleading for affection, writing, "When night falls, they sink deeper into my body, the books that I've fallen in love with, I hug them as I fall asleep. There is a clamor and I feel rushed, like a stubborn servant or jealous patron, I want to meet all of the noble wives and elegant young women, if only I could engage in secret love affairs with every hidden tome."[51]

After having described his earliest "love affairs" with classical Japanese literature, Kyōka turns to his experience with modern literature from Japan, which he refers to, plainly, as "new works" (*atarashii mono*). The texts that he mentions represent a transitional literary style, mixing the language and themes of Edo-period fiction with literary techniques and references drawn from modern, global literature. Kyōka claims that the first modern work of Japanese literature that he can remember reading was *A Mirror of Marriage* (*Imo to sekagami*, 1885–1886) by Tsubouchi Shōyō (1859–1935), the story of an up-and-coming bureaucrat, Misawa Tatsuzō, who marries a woman from a lower social class, Otsuji, but later comes to regret his decision when he becomes involved in a public scandal. Misawa, who is unhappy with his marriage, begins visiting a geisha in the pleasure quarters, supposedly because the geisha was owed money by his father, which arouses the jealousy of his wife. Otsuji has a public confrontation with the geisha's sister that is overheard by a journalist, who reports the scandal in the local newspaper. Misawa, as a public official, is shamed and forced to divorce Otsuji, who takes her life.

As a "new work," *A Mirror of Marriage* is considerably old-fashioned in terms of its literary style and plot, thereby serving to highlight the modern elements of Kyōka's own fiction. Featuring a bare minimum of descriptive writing, most of the novel consists of dialogue, along with didactic exposition, as was common in literature of the Edo period that was modeled on theater or traditional storytelling arts such as *rakugo* and *kōdan*. Shōyō was a prodigious scholar and translator of English literature, including the work of William Shakespeare (1564–1616), Sir Walter Scott, and Edward Bulwer-Lytton (1803–1873), and his translations of authors such as Scott into Japanese feature detailed passages of scenic description, yet his own fiction was modeled on traditional Japanese literature to a much greater degree than Kyōka's work. The main parts of Shōyō's novel that stand out as being modern are its didactic passages, mainly because of Shōyō's references to English literature. In the novel, Shōyō references work by Shakespeare, Bulwer-Lytton, Benjamin Disraeli (1804–1881), and Thomas Otway (1652–1685), particularly in relation to the theme of marriage in the Western world. In a comparative note on global cultures, Shōyō describes customs of courting and marriage in England, France, and Japan, and concludes that Japan most closely resembles

France among Western nations, due to the central role taken by parents in mediating marriage in both countries, as well as the widespread custom of keeping mistresses.[52]

Despite the traditional style of Shōyō's novel, Kyōka recognized elements of the work that diverged from traditional Japanese literature, particularly by identifying the quality of hesitation in its narrative. Specifically, Kyōka characterizes premodern narratives as being related with certainty or bravado, as opposed to the indecisive position of the modern narrator. He writes, "If people from the past read the novels of today, they would be confused by the hesitation of the protagonist, because they expect the narrator to say something like 'There was once a wandering samurai,' or 'He sustained his life to the age of eighty.' It impressed my youthful mind and made me realize that, ah, there are other ways of thinking."[53]

Kyōka goes on to describe his encounter with the work of the modern Japanese author who would inspire him to become a writer, Ozaki Kōyō, his future mentor. As a modern author, Kōyō was deeply influenced by a combination of traditional East Asian literature and modern European novels and was known as a prodigious adaptor and translator of European fiction, from English-language versions. Kōyō's fiction changed in style throughout his career, although some of his writing featured elaborately detailed descriptions of settings and landscapes, including his mainstream literary debut, *Two Nuns' Confessions of Love* (*Ninin bikuni irozange*, 1889). Kyōka writes that he read this work while he briefly ran an English-language tutoring school with a friend.[54] This novella was Kōyō's breakthrough work as a popular author, although he had already developed a considerable following among young authors and educated readers as the editor of literary magazines such as *Garakuta bunko* (*Rubbish Heap Library*), *Edo Murasaki*, and *Bunko* (*Library*), in which he published his early fiction. Kyōka nostalgically recalls his experience of encountering Kōyō's debut novel:

> I had rented a room on the second floor of a poor tenement house with a friend, where I had taken on a few students, to whom I was teaching English. The building next door was a weaving factory and you could look down from the mountain into the valley below and see girls as pretty as Seki-no-Koman [a famous prostitute from songs and plays of the Edo period] putting laundry out to dry. While listening to the factory girls sing an old song, I sat at my nice desk in the sunlight and read the newly published book. It was our Sensei's famous *Two Nuns' Confessions of Love*.[55]

Although *Two Nuns' Confessions of Love* relates a largely traditional tale of fated encounter and military honor in a medieval Japanese setting, it also includes elaborate descriptions of landscape, such as in opening passages that present a rustic mountain dwelling in detail. Around the same time that Kyōka read *Two Nuns' Confessions of Love*, he also read another novel by Kōyō, one set in the modern world, *Kyoto Doll* (*Kyō ningyō*, 1888). As Kyōka puts it, he read the novel "over and over again," more times than he could count. He read it so many times, in any event, that he could still remember lines spoken by a female student, such as "Away from here, Satan," and "Front row, forward"; these odd quotations suggest the strong influence of Western literature on Kōyō's early work, while also hinting at Kyōka's attention to Western themes. Although Kyōka claims that living in Kanazawa made it difficult to access the latest Japanese fiction, he adds that some novels from Tokyo were so popular that one simply had to try to read them, such as Kōyō's *Two Nuns' Confessions of Love* and *The Elegant Buddha* (*Fūryūbutsu*, 1889) by Kōda Rohan, another of the most notable works of supernatural fiction written during the Meiji period. It was novels such as these, most of all, that convinced Kyōka to move to Tokyo and try his hand at becoming a modern author. Drawing on these diverse influences, he followed on the work of writers such as Rohan and Kōyō in developing atmospheric modern tales suffused with elements of fantasy.

6. Early Fiction and Landscapes of the Fantastic

Kyōka's development as a visually oriented writer of supernatural fiction can be traced across a sequence of early stories that depict his childhood in Kanazawa and his school years at the Hokuriku Eiwa Gakkō, an arc which gradually acquires more fantastic details and settings with each story. In works including *Volume One* (the "Ichi no maki" series, 1896–97) and "The Story of a Famous Princess" ("Meienki," 1900), Kyōka describes his early years in Kanazawa in ways that emphasize the international nature of his upbringing, while also providing romantic descriptions of his hometown and its landscape. In *Volume One*, Kyōka showcases his ability to write modern, realistic fiction with detailed settings, but with minimal elements of fantasy. It is a story that almost seems as though it were written by a different author, because it describes the modern world in starkly realistic terms, and thereby suggests a direction that Kyōka might have taken had he been more interested in following mainstream literary trends. In a subsequent story about his school days, "Story of a Famous Princess," Kyōka introduces supernatural imagery into his narrative in references to the *Arabian Nights* and *The Golden Ass* by Apuleius and in frame tales about magical creatures. Kyōka begins to move fully into a world of fantasy in early stories that shift from the setting of the classroom to the mountains outside of Kanazawa, specifically in "Shrine of Wonder" ("Tae no miya," 1896) and "Mino Valley" ("Minodani," 1896), where he expands on his ability to evoke otherworldly landscapes. These stories set up his development of the deep mountain setting of *The Holy Man of Mt. Kōya*, a work that showcases Kyōka's full development as a writer of the fantastic in portraying a vividly imagined world of romantic natural landscapes, magic, and eroticism.

Volume One was published in the *Bungei kurabu* literary magazine from May 1896 through January 1897. The prestige of the journal, one of the most important of the Meiji period, provides evidence of Kyōka's early rise in the ranks of the literary establishment. The *Volume One* series was published in seven installments, as "Volume One" ("Ichi no maki") through "Volume Six" ("Roku no maki"), concluding with "The Promise Volume" ("Chikai no maki"), but it essentially functions as a single novel that is often referred to by Japanese scholars simply as *Ichi no maki*. Although *Volume One* does not feature overt elements of fantasy, it might be seen as a first step toward the fantastic in its turn to the space of childhood, as Kyōka began to experiment with romanticism in increasingly nostalgic tales.

Volume One is notable for providing a detailed description of Kyōka's hometown of Kanazawa in a story that relates an autobiographic account of the author's education in the international environment of an English-language school. The story provides details of Kyōka's experience with foreigners in his hometown, as well as his youthful love for an American woman. The woman in the story, Ms. Milliard, was modeled on Francina Porter, an American teacher and Christian missionary who taught English at Hokuriku Eiwa Gakkō.[56] The story is related in classical, literary Japanese, or *bungotai*, and thus might initially give the impression of being a traditional literary text, but the content of the narrative clearly marks the story as modern. This shift can be seen thematically, for example, in Kyōka's descriptions of Kanazawa and Tokyo as globalized, modern cities, or at the narrative level in sustained descriptions of daily life in a realist or naturalist mode. *Volume One* opens with passages of description of the hills and forests outside of Kanazawa, introducing elements of romanticism and ghostliness that would pervade the rest of Kyōka's fiction. Providing a literal bird's-eye view of the landscape, Kyōka writes:

> A slight breeze blew by as paper kites sailed across the blue skies and butterflies flitted across the face of the valley. As the joys of spring reached their height, people begin drifting out of their homes, away from the city, to scramble up slopes in the hillside. Many groups of people rendezvoused throughout the day, here and there, at outlooks in the hills, at a temple of the Nichiren sect, in the valley of Ōgi-ga-hara, and at the peak of Tobi-ga-mine. They spread out woven mats, unfurled carpets, opened wooden lunchboxes, and tilted back drinking cylinders. Above the heads of old and young, men and women, black kites [birds of prey] spread their wings, and while dancing circles through the sky, they surveyed lakes, rivers, bridges, villages, the castle, and the city, all entering their vision as they traversed the skies and looked down upon the land below. Contrasting with this tranquil beauty was a single standing grove of pine and cedar trees, growing thick with melancholy. Ah, a field of graves, cold even in the spring.[57]

At the graveyard, the boy, Shinji, finds that his mother's gravestone has been overturned by mischievous children. As he mourns in solitude, a tall, pale woman appears to help him put the stone upright, foreshadowing overlapping images of maternal, romantic, and ghostly female figures throughout the story, and in Kyōka's fiction more broadly.

The romantic idyll of the hills is later contrasted with descriptions of the modernizing aspects of Kanazawa, including descriptions of electric lighting, the English-language school, and Christian missionaries (*senkyōshi-ra*). When the narrator's father, a gold engraver, sends him to deliver a gold ring to a customer, he passes by electric poles to the glass-fronted store of a clockmaker. At school, Shinji is instructed by an American woman, whom he describes admiringly:

> Ms. Milliard was responsible for conversation time at school. She was a young, beautiful woman from America. Her speech was lively, her dress and appearance were stylish, and her heart was kind. After living in our country for four or five years and becoming accustomed to it, she learned to say "Good morning," "Goodbye," and the like with no problem.[58]

The modernity of the narrative is also reflected in the vocabulary of the text, which features transliterated words from English. These include words such as table (*tēburu*), handkerchief (*hankechi*), class (*kurasu*), next (*nekkisuto*), strawberry (*sutoroberī*), and Sunday school (*Sandē sukūru*), as well as references to Western goods, such as a "Western lamp" (*yōtō*, glossed as *akari*), Western clothes (*yōfuku*), and a pipe organ (*yōkin*, glossed as *orugan*). To this list of foreign words might be added the name of the character of Ms. Milliard, whose name appears as *Miriyādo* throughout the narrative, in the *katakana* syllabary used to transliterate foreign words into Japanese, thereby giving the work a foreign atmosphere even at the level of the printed text on the page. The combination of English-language loan words, *bungotai* grammar, details befitting a realistic, autobiographic narrative, and the setting of an international school thus creates a mixed literary expression of modernism and romanticism that draws on the past while remaining rooted in the historical context of the Meiji period.

A major element of Kyōka's visual style that he establishes in *Volume One* is his use of erotic imagery, particularly as relating to older female figures, in this case Ms. Milliard. Early in the narrative, Ms. Milliard is depicted as showing favoritism to Shinji when she tries to help him with questions for an exam. In the incident, Shinji is supposed to remember the English word "strawberry," but he is unable to recall it. Ms. Milliard hints, "It's small, it's beautiful, it's red, it's red." She fumbles with a button near her breast as she says, "Like this size."[59] The suggestion is that she is gesturing toward her nipple, whether intentionally or by mistake. This reading is supported later in the story when Ms. Milliard holds Shinji as an adult against her "warm, soft, white breasts," which leads the narrator to remark that he was "unable to withstand the excitement."[60]

As an adult, Shinji follows Ms. Milliard to Tokyo, where his former teacher provides him with financial support in exchange for reading her pages from the *Tokyo eiri shinbun* (*Tokyo Illustrated Newspaper*). Ms. Milliard chooses a boarding house for Shinji in the Azabu neighborhood of Tokyo, an affluent part of the city where other foreigners live. As the two grow closer, Ms. Milliard reveals to Shinji that, like him, she lost her mother at an early age. Taking pity on Shinji, Ms. Milliard offers to serve as a replacement mother for him. In a tragic plot twist that might be considered typical of contemporary melodrama, Ms. Milliard falls ill and nears death just as the couple finally declare their love for each other. The final scene of the novel, however, displays Kyōka's development of one of his own characteristic themes—that of the eroticized and sacred maternal figure. Ms. Milliard asks Shinji, "Are you not listening to me? Who do you think that I am?" In response to her ardent question, Shinji replies, "Mother."[61]

A teacher modeled on Francina Porter appears again in "Story of a Famous Princess" (1900), but this time around the atmosphere of Kyōka's autobiographical narrative has been transformed into something darker, more reminiscent of a dream or nightmare of childhood, full of bizarre and haunting imagery, rather than a realistic recollection. As such, the story takes a definitive step into the world of the fantastic. The "famous princess" of the story's title is a reference to Shahrazad, the "princess" or storyteller of the *Arabian Nights*, who tells stories to King Shahriyar on a nightly basis for 1,001 nights to postpone her execution.[62] Shahrazad and the *Arabian Nights* are referenced multiple times in the story, providing rare examples of direct references to global literature in Kyōka's fiction. The story might even be interpreted as Kyōka's adaptation of the *Arabian Nights*, one of the author's favorite works of literature. In common with the *Arabian Nights*, "Story of a Famous Princess" is related through a series of complex frame narratives or embedded tales that start, are abruptly interrupted, and are reintroduced and concluded later in the work. Kyōka also enhances the story's romantic environment by describing its setting in greater detail than in his earlier work, particularly by providing picturesque descriptions of a lonely forest and an isolated mansion, the kinds of spaces conducive to evoking an atmosphere of fantasy.

Hinting at the fantastic quality of the work from its opening page, Kyōka gives the American teacher in "Story of a Famous Princess" the unusual and fairytale-like name of Lilika (Ririka), in contrast to the more realistic-sounding American name of Ms. Milliard from *Volume One*. The work opens with a strange and frightening tale being told by Lilika to the narrator, a Japanese student at her school. Lilika tells the boy that in her hometown in America there is a variety of snake that can play an instrument with the tip of its tail. She claims that among countless numbers of snakes that inhabit the place where she lives, some are large, some are poisonous, some have beautiful colors, and some have kind personalities. One type of snake even has the ability to reassemble itself after being split into multiple parts.[63] Lilika leaves her story unfinished, but, like Shahrazad, resumes it later in the narrative. She tells the narrator a story about a man in France who collected approximately 3,000 different kinds of snakes, including some that were poisonous, and locked them all together in a box. The snakes eventually escaped the box and created a scene, in Lilika's words, that was worse than hell or a South American rainforest where the native people cannibalize intruders.[64] Kyōka's technique of beginning the story in the middle of an embedded narrative introduces fantasy imagery into a modern, realistic setting, while also momentarily disorienting the reader, until the characters and setting of the work are more clearly established. It is a technique that he uses repeatedly throughout his fiction, which occasionally opens with embedded fairytales, songs, or nursery rhymes, before switching to modern prose narratives that continue to borrow imagery and themes from these other genres.

Due to Lilika's penchant for telling scary stories, she is compared by the narrator directly to Shahrazad, the famous storyteller of the *Arabian Nights*. The narrator remarks that he read the *Arabian Nights* at school, a text that he claims "completely captured his attention," and he describes Lilika as making up her own stories, just like the "famous princess" of the collection.[65] The narrator recalls that he was required to listen to lectures on the political novel *Plum Blossoms in the Snow* (*Setchūbai*, 1886), by Suehiro Tetchō (1849–1896) in class, but that he preferred reading works of literature in translation in the *Yūbin hōchi shinbun* subscribed to by his school. He mentions reading a story about a character named Lucius who is transformed into a donkey after imbibing the wrong magic potion and who must eat a rose to resume his human form, a reference to scenes from *The Golden Ass* by Apuleius. The student also enjoys listening to Lilika's invented tales. On the effect of listening to her stories, the narrator remarks:

> As a youth with strong curiosity, at the time, I imagined that Lilika was the princess who told stories in the *Arabian Nights*. These brought comfort to a child of this country, as though they were mysterious tidings told by a female mystic who descended from heaven and honored me with her presence. Her beauty, her nobility, I thought that these qualities in her surpassed those of other people.[66]

In this quote, Kyōka's vision of a sacred maternal figure takes on increasingly mystical aspects, in a passage that includes heightened elements of fantasy. Not only is the woman compared to Shahrazad, she is described as a celestial being and as a female mountain immortal (*sen'en*) from the world of Chinese legends.

As in *Volume One*, the narrator develops a romantic attraction to his foreign teacher and begins to visit her as often as possible. Unlike in the earlier text, however, the teacher does not move to an urban residence in Tokyo, but rather lives in the unlikely abode of a Western manor hidden in a forest in the narrator's hometown. Kyōka's description of the setting displays the further development of his picturesque literary style, which provides extensive visual detail of the landscape, while establishing a romantic or fairytale-like atmosphere for the narrative. Kyōka writes:

> She had told me "Come over to my house to play some time" almost every Sunday, but I felt as though I needed to go with a string of yarn attached to my parents' hands, or even a treasured sword at my side, to that Western manor that I knew nothing about. I felt somewhat afraid to go by myself and hesitated to go until that day. The mansion was built directly on the ruins of a castle gate of this mountain country, a three-story manor rising like a tower in the middle of a forest. . . . I had no way of opening the rigidly shut and locked gate, and so I started to leave, but then I went around to the back of the manor. Within a grove, a wooden fence ran parallel to a twisting and meandering path, but it was lonely and no people passed by.
>
> From the front gate that was hidden by the forest, I could look up and see part of the outer wall. From my position, I could furthermore see a window, light yellow-green curtains, and a balustrade in front of the window. There was a grove behind the manor, which made everything look dreary, and there was no sign of any people around. Suddenly, in the window of the magnificent building, as though having descended from heaven, a figure in purple appeared . . .[67]

Overcoming his fear, the narrator enters the manor in the woods and begins taking private lessons in English conversation and writing from Lilika. As in *Volume One*, this leads to a romantic relationship. The narrator remarks, "as I intimately received Lilika's instruction, my feelings of love grew ever deeper and stronger."[68]

"Story of a Famous Princess" ends with a haunting scene that displays Kyōka's developing penchant for portraying elements of horror and fantasy. In the conclusion, the boy informs Lilika that he has been searching for a snake that can play an instrument with its tail in the forest, just like the snake that she told him about in her story at the beginning of the narrative. The boy tells her that he searched for a spot in the forest where a Christian girl had been buried in an urn, because he figured that would be the kind of area likely to be inhabited by snakes, but he was unable to find any snakes there or anywhere else. Lilika turns pale, trembles, and cries as she listens to the boy's story. She had hoped to convince the boy to be baptized, but on hearing that he has been searching for snakes in the forest, she fears that he is drawing close to demons. She explains to him that she had simply been telling interesting stories for his entertainment, and in an apparent attempt to dispel any evil influences, she makes the sign of the cross on his chest.

In two more stories from early in Kyōka's career, "Shrine of Wonder" (1896) and "Mino Valley" (1896), the author moves from the setting of the school building and the foothills of Kanazawa to hidden spaces located deep within the mountains, which provide a fitting setting for his early explorations of fantasy. Such settings might even be equated to the space of fairytales or the marvelous, because their landscapes appear to exist beyond the borders of the ordinary world. They can only be entered through hidden passageways or in dreamlike states, therefore existing as hermetic spaces or alternate worlds inhabited by mystical animals and otherworldly beings. Both stories also introduce the element of a sacred maternal figure into the space of the fantastic, although the presence of the mother in the first story, "Shrine of Wonder," is only hinted at by a discarded sash tied around the railing of a shrine.

"Shrine of Wonder" is an experimental early story that reads as though it is an account of a dream, in part due to the obscurity of its setting and plot. The short story is simple: a young military officer climbs a staircase to a shrine and discovers that his pocket watch went missing along the way. When he reaches the shrine at the top of the staircase, he finds an abandoned baby who somehow has acquired his watch. As he tries to take the watch away from the baby, he notices a red sash tied to the railing outside of the shrine. The story has no resolution, but might be interpreted as a narrative of abandonment by a missing mother, a reflection on the past, or a feeling of having lost time.

Part of the appeal of "Shrine of Wonder" is its obscure and dreamlike scenery, composed of series of layered images that all appear to symbolize or gesture toward some deeper psychological or metaphysical meaning, but without establishing clear correspondences to underlying ideas. The story opens near a bridge over a river near the mountains northeast of an unnamed town, where a youth is climbing a hill to the shrine. The approach to the shrine is apparently dangerous, but the source of danger and the reason for the climb are left unspecified. Kyōka writes, "The day before yesterday someone, yesterday someone else, altogether five of the officer's friends had approached with hearts full of courage, but not a single one of them had returned without incident."[69] The path is dark, lined with trees, and full of spiderwebs. There are no people around and the only sign of life is a waterwheel rotating by a thatched-roof hut with no lights on. There are 216 steps to the top of the stairs, but the shrine is located even deeper in the mountains. After losing his watch, the youth sees strange plants and animals, such as leaves that scatter and seem to turn into a batch of spider hatchlings, two crabs that face him with claws held up as though on guard, and a snake that crosses the path to the shrine before slithering up the trunk of a cedar tree. At various points in the story, the narrator describes moonlight shining down on treetops, the dark mountain path, and the old shrine. The overall impression created is one of quiet tension and a vaguely menacing landscape. The images of the narrative would seem to merit a comparison to the work of artists such as Moreau or Dalí, whose paintings depict dreamlike scenes in mysterious landscapes that suggest hidden or symbolic meanings.

Kyōka moves even deeper into the fantastic in "Mino Valley," a story that details the meeting between a young boy and a woman in the mountains who appears to be some kind of fairy, goddess, or guardian spirit of nature. "Mino Valley" builds on Kyōka's narrative pattern of an encounter between a young boy and a sacred, erotic mother, but in this story the woman no longer appears human. She is also no longer purely maternal, but has become frightening and forbidding. Rather than giving the narrator comfort, she offers him an embrace that is literally chilling, before banishing him from her territory for life.

"Mino Valley" opens abruptly in a setting removed from the real world with the vision of an enchanted female figure by the basin of a waterfall in the mountains. The story begins: "Facing a waterfall that looks cool enough to give one goosebumps, her back was turned to me, presumably that mysterious princess. The fireflies of Mino Valley have a master, one who does not allow people to hunt them recklessly. That master was a beautiful goddess, as my mother always told me."[70] We soon learn that the narrator is a boy who lost his way in the mountains while chasing a firefly and becoming separated from his companions. He has wandered into a remote area, where an otherworldly woman appears to preside over nature. Both the setting and the woman are described in ways that emphasize a sense of foreboding and lack of connection with the outside world. Kyōka describes the setting at length, with reference to traditional Japanese imagery such as a shrine and Buddhist statues, but with a degree of visual detail that suggests the painterly mode described by Farah Mendlesohn as a hallmark of modern genre fantasy:

> The waterfall descended from the treetops, where tree upon tree overlapped and grew thickly. From around its middle, the waterfall hit a boulder and flowed in three levels. There was a small shrine to the left. Ivy and vines were tangled vertically and horizontally and the shrine was tightly shut and padlocked. The drops of water that rushed down the boulder sprinkled the roof of the shrine, leaking through rotten openings in the wood and trickling onto the earth. To the side were sacred statues of Jizō [a bodhisattva] of one foot to two feet in height, the one on the right being the tallest, and each one next to it smaller,

> one by one in a single line, seven of them standing in all. Not only the waterfall, but more so the boulders, and more so the earth—water bubbled up and gushed out everywhere, forming puddles here and there, sacred water overflowing, in the space between pebbles, striking branches, glimmering like a white snake. The sound of water flowing below was not unlike the sound of whispering, it wove the branches of dense groves together and enveloped all in deep luxuriance . . .[71]

The level of detail included in Kyōka's description of the landscape suggests that the author desires the reader to fully inhabit the story world. Then, from within realistic scenery, an erotic and supernatural figure appears. Kyōka describes the goddess of the forest as wearing a wet, transparent garment and "a sash that holds in her bulging breasts."

Although the sacred woman is erotic, she is also frightening, and not quite of this world. The firefly that the boy was chasing flits through her loose clothing and her body is described as cold, wet, and lit by the light of the firefly. Kyōka writes, "The firefly passed under her armpit, then crawled out from the back of her sleeve, then suddenly it crawled around her neckband, its blue light flickering, passing through the wet garments that she wore, her pure white breasts visible through the fabric."[72] In a scene that is more chilling than inviting, the woman hugs the boy, but when she does, the narrator feels a "cold that passes into his bone marrow as his body seems about to turn into ice." After the embrace, the woman warns the boy to never return to the basin. The narrator remarks that he complied with the woman's order, but that he would sometimes pass by the forest and could still hear the sound of water flowing deep within. He adds that the basin is a "place of haunting" (*masho*) and that the local people avoid prying into the surrounding forest. With his detailed description of an inaccessible forest hidden deep in the mountains, in "Mino Valley," Kyōka appears to have found the perfect setting for evoking a mysterious atmosphere and suggesting an encounter with the supernatural. It is a formula that he would use to even more spectacular effect in his magnum opus, *The Holy Man of Mt. Kōya.*

7. The Holy Man of Mt. Kōya

The Holy Man of Mt. Kōya (1900) is one of the most famous and critically acclaimed works of fantasy literature from Japan. The theme, that of a man who encounters a dangerous woman with supernatural powers in the mountains, resembles several traditional Japanese narratives, such as those of the *yamamba* (mountain witch), the serpent-woman of Dōjōji, or, less directly, tales of the *onibaba*. However, Kyōka's novella is a distinctly modern story that blends traditional themes and motifs with a modern literary style, characterized by intensive visual description of the landscape, a setting in the modern world, richly imagined fantasy sequences, and a complex narrative structure expressed through multiple levels of framing. Scholars have described *The Holy Man of Mt. Kōya* alternately as mythical, traditional, romantic, fantastic, supernatural, modern, and avant-garde in reference to its literary style and artistic vision. Perhaps the most outstanding feature of the work, however, is the impression that it has often given readers of being somehow ahead of its time, or otherwise timeless, as though it belongs to a shared world of global fantasy and storytelling, and not just to the literary environment of Meiji-period Japan. On this note, Hinatsu Kōnosuke (1890–1971), a major romantic poet, scholar, and translator of English literature, referred to *The Holy Man of Mt. Kōya* as "the pinnacle of Meiji-period Romanticism" and suggested that it should rightfully be included among the best works of a similar kind from England, France, or Germany.[73] In reference to the work's layered fantasy imagery, exemplified by the central female figure of the text, Nina Cornyetz writes, "The woman living isolated deep in the mountains in *Kōya hijiri* evokes the medieval archetype of the *yamamba* or mountain hag, who pounced on and devoured those hapless male travelers who strayed into her domain. . . . In Kyōka's narratives, she is displaced from her fixity and set afloat in a plurality that eroticizes her and mixes her up with Shinto shamanesses, archaic serpent-demons, and the bird-woman deities of folklore and fairytales."[74]

Scholars have often attributed the fantastic qualities of *The Holy Man of Mt. Kōya* to the influence of classical sources from both East and West, including *The Golden Ass* and the *Arabian Nights*,[75] as well as *Tales of Moonlight and Rain* by Ueda Akinari and the Nō play *Yamamba*.[76] Other scholars have emphasized modern elements of the work, such as Miri Nakamura, who discusses the preoccupation of the story's protagonist with pollution and hygiene.[77] As Nakamura points out, the modernity of *The Holy Man of Mt. Kōya* is apparent from its opening phrase, "the map compiled by General Staff Headquarters" (*sanbō honbu hensan no chizu*), a modern topographic survey map that the monk references on his travels, although he is unable to find his way using the map. The specificity of the map mentioned in the opening lines of the text clearly situates the story in the space of modern Japan, while the monk's inability to locate the path on the map suggests a journey into a timeless space of fantasy.[78]

The Holy Man of Mt. Kōya relates the story of Shūchō, a mendicant monk from Mt. Kōya, a vast temple complex and the center of Shingon Buddhism in the mountains of western Japan, who loses his way in the deep mountain ranges of central Honshū, on a mountain pass in the Hida mountains (also known as the Japanese Alps). The story is related as a complex series of frame narratives: the main narrator of the story is a student who relates a tale told to him by the monk Shūchō at an inn near a train stop in the city of Tsuruga, where the monk describes his adventures in the mountains from many years earlier, including tales told to him by local people whom he met on his journey. The student meets Shūchō on a train while traveling home to Wakasa, on the north coast of Japan, while Shūchō is on his way to visit Eiheiji, the head temple of the Sōtō Zen school of Buddhism, in a mountainous region northeast of Tsuruga. Shūchō relates that he was once passing through the mountains of central Japan when he decided to take a little-used mountain path at a fork in the road to avoid a flooded area, and also to chase after a foul-mouthed medicine peddler whom he believed might be in danger for having taken the wrong path.

In the mountains, the monk observes a series of increasingly eerie and seemingly supernatural phenomena. On the path, the monk encounters giant snakes that block his way, and he imagines that the forested slopes of the mountains are inhabited by mischievous nature spirits, or *chimi mōryō*. Further up the mountain, he wanders into a forest with trees crawling with leeches, who drop from the branches, suck his blood, and leave his body bruised. In a strange apocalyptic vision, the monk imagines that the end of the world will be brought about by leeches, who will cover the earth in muck and blood, rather than by a tearing of the earth's crust, in a scene that suggests that Kyōka's early education included study of geology. Deep in the mountains, the monk finds a solitary hut whose sole inhabitant appears to be a mentally impaired man (referred to literally as an "idiot," or *baka*, by the narrator), who is toying with his strangely extended bellybutton, until the man's beautiful wife appears to greet the monk. The wife offers the monk lodging and brings him to a river whose waters are reputed to have magical healing properties, where she disrobes both him and herself so that she can bathe him, in a scene of erotic encounter that is one of the most famous scenes in Kyōka's literature. The monk feels tempted by lust as the woman washes him, but he ultimately resists his lustful urges. In the area around the river and the hut, the monk encounters a succession of animals, including a monkey, a toad, bats, rabbits, snakes, and a horse, who appear to be attempting to communicate their distress to the woman, who in turn hushes them and tells them that she is busy with a visitor. Shūchō then spends a restless night in the woman's hut, chanting protective prayers and spells as he hears strange beastly sounds in the space around him. He imagines that he has descended into the Buddhist hell of animals (*chikushōdō*) and that the house is haunted by supernatural creatures. The next day, after leaving the hut, Shūchō meets a traveling vendor who relates that the woman has magic powers, including the power to turn men into animals, heal wounds, and control the weather, and that she transformed the medicine peddler into a horse, who the vendor sold at the market in exchange for a carp. The man reasons that Shūchō was saved by his faith, and at the conclusion of the narrative, Shūchō exits the mountains and lives to tell the tale to the narrator.

Throughout the narrative of *The Holy Man of Mt. Kōya*, Kyōka appears intent on conveying as clear and detailed an image of the story's landscape as possible, often in terms that border on naturalism. In a pivotal moment in the narrative, before the story takes a turn into the realm of the fantastic, the monk must choose between two branches of a forked path in the mountains. The monk relates details of the landscape to the narrator:

> The road split into two paths. One path ascended a steep hill and had thick grass growing on both sides. By the side of the road was a giant hinoki tree with a trunk that was four, no, maybe five arms' lengths in circumference. Behind the tree were two, three, four giant boulders lined up in a meandering formation that looked as though they had been quarried and left there. The twisting path that ascended behind the tree did not appear to be the one that I had planned to take. Surely enough, the wide, gently sloping road that I had followed up until that point appeared to be the main route. Roughly five miles ahead the road climbed into the mountains, and the mountain pass followed beyond.[79]

Similar passages of careful topographic description follow throughout the story's pages, as Shūchō travels across mountain slopes and through forests to the isolated dwelling. Once Shūchō reaches the lonely hut in the mountains, many pages of description of travel deep into the story's mysterious landscape have primed the reader for an encounter with the otherworldly woman.

Another major element of the visuality of *The Holy Man of Mt. Kōya* is its erotic imagery, particularly the famous bathing scene at the center of the narrative. Kyōka relates the scene as follows:

Fig. 3. Kajita Hanko, *The Holy Man of Mt. Kōya*, woodblock frontispiece from *Shinshōsetsu* magazine, 1900. (Courtesy of Kanagawa Museum of Modern Literature.)

At some point, the woman had finished washing rice and her kimono had come loose, so that her breasts were faintly visible. As she stood up, her large breasts bounced. With pursed lips and a prominent nose, she turned her eyes up in ecstasy toward the peak of the mountain, where the moon shone down directly on a mass of boulders.

"When you look up like this, it seems scary," she said as she crouched back down and started washing her arms. "Hey, you, if you keep standing there on ceremony your robe will get wet. It won't feel good. Strip down completely naked and take a bath. I'll wash you."

"No."

"Not no. Look, look, your sleeves, they're all wet already," she said as she suddenly moved in behind me and put her hands in my sash.

> As I squirmed and shrunk back, she became strict and stripped me completely naked . . .
>
> You would think the water would chill me to the bones, but that wasn't the case. It's true that it was still hot outside, but that wasn't the reason. I felt as though my blood were boiling. The woman's warmth and the water that washed over me felt good and sank into my body . . .[80]

The eroticism of the scene relies in part on the physical description of the woman, whose body is described as voluptuous and who acts "strictly" (*jaken rashiku*) in forcing her guest to strip naked and accept her touch, while revealing her own naked body to the visitor. It is a scene that might even be identified as presenting one of the core themes of Kyōka's fiction, the revelation of the erotic maternal figure, who is alternately a source of danger and comfort, and who awaits at the endpoint of so many of his adventures, beckoning the wary protagonist onward. The importance of the bathing scene in *The Holy Man of Mt. Kōya* was highlighted in an illustration by woodblock-print artist Kajita Hanko (1870–1917) included in *Shinshōsetsu*, a major literary magazine, which depicts the woman bathing the monk. Hanko's image emphasizes the eroticism of Kyōka's story, although the artist hesitates in following the author all the way to the revelation of the nude female figure at the center of the work.

Scholar Katsumoto Seiichirō identifies the bathing scene in *The Holy Man of Mt. Kōya* and its expression of erotic visuality as the center not only of this novel, but of Kyōka's entire literary universe. He emphasizes the novelty of Kyōka's visual representation of the woman's naked body by describing its departure from traditional varieties of eroticism in Japanese literature, particularly in its details of the woman's fleshliness. He writes:

> Kyōka's literary works are constructed like the intricately detailed, giant Buddhist mandalas created by the Shingon sect during the Kōnin era [810–824], but with the central figure of worship overlaid with the image of a young naked woman through the process of double exposure. Kyōka places an offering of fragrant, smoldering incense before the central image, which emerges from the depths of the mandala like a living Buddha called forth into the material realm. From within the middle of a suspiciously insensate structure of various natural phenomena, the undeniable truth of the human body—of the flesh of a woman's body—flickers in and out of view within the deepest layers of

> the image. The result is a reflection given density. *The Holy Man of Mt. Kōya* is literally a Buddhist icon.[81]

One might add to this description the fact that Kyōka's erotic women are often not young women, but rather older women. In his depictions of such women, Kyōka combines maternalism, eroticism, and the supernatural, thereby transforming his female characters into literary icons. Such figures move within richly described landscapes that harbor supernatural powers and otherworldly beings, all as part of the elaborate visual tapestry of Kyōka's literature. In *The Holy Man of Mt. Kōya*, Kyōka demonstrates the full development of a narrative pattern that he would alter and expand on throughout later works. In story after story by Kyōka, the protagonist wanders through mountains, forests, caves, seashores, swamps, alleyways, and backstreets, where magical women, monsters, and other supernatural beings emerge against backdrops of intricately described visual landscapes.

Two

Kusazōshi and the Japanese Marvelous

Kyōka as a Collector of Picture Books

1. *Kusazōshi* as Literature of Magic and the Marvelous

One of the genres of Japanese literature most often credited with inspiring Kyōka's literary imagination was a variety of illustrated fiction from the Edo period known as *kusazōshi* ("grass books"). *Kusazōshi* are a premodern genre of Japanese literature of the marvelous that is transformed in Kyōka's fiction into a ghostly icon of tradition. In this way, *kusazōshi* might be compared to fairytales and folk stories in Europe, which were similarly subsumed into the modern genre of the fantastic. In scholarship from Europe, the fantastic is often distinguished from earlier genres of literature, such as legends, fairytales, and fables, referred to by scholars such as Roger Caillois, Tzvetan Todorov, and Louis Vax variously as the marvelous (*le merveilleux*), fairytales (*conte de fées*), or fairytale-like (*la féerie, le féerique*).[1] The difference between these genres and the fantastic is often attributed to the emotions or attitudes of the characters when confronted by the supernatural, for while characters in the modern fantastic are disturbed by supernatural intrusions, the heroes of the marvelous and fairytales bravely confront monsters and intentionally embark on perilous adventures. Kyōka, in his own way, appears to have realized the difference between premodern and modern narrative modes, for in "Lover's Treatment" he distinguishes the heroes from literature of the past, who acted without hesitation, from the protagonist of the modern novel.[2] In his fiction, Kyōka draws on the supernatural content of *kusazōshi* for inspiration, but he introduces fear and hesitation into narratives that treat premodern picture books as haunted artifacts and sources of phantasmal illusions.

Kusazōshi have been described by scholars variously as "the strongest influence" on Kyōka's writing,[3] "the seedbed of his literary endeavors,"[4] and "the womb of his work."[5] Despite the strength of such claims, in scholarship there remains an overall lack of specific details on connections between *kusazōshi* and Kyōka's literature. As Kyōka indicates in his fiction and essays, he was deeply familiar with several of the most popular series of *kusazōshi* from the nineteenth century. These series, listed alongside their original writers and illustrators, with subsequent contributors given in the notes, include the following: *The Life of Shakyamuni in Eight Phases: A Japanese Library* (*Shaka hassō Yamato bunko*, 1845–1871), written by Mantei Ōga (1818–1890) and illustrated by Utagawa Kunisada;[6] *The Tale of Shiranui* (*Shiranui monogatari*, 1849–1885), written by Ryūkatei Tanekazu (1807–1858) and illustrated by Kunisada;[7] *Fake Murasaki, Rustic Genji* (*Nise Murasaki inaka Genji*, 1829–1842), written by Ryūtei Tanehiko and illustrated by Kunisada;[8] *The Tale of Brave Jiraiya* (*Jiraiya gōketsu monogatari*, 1839–1868), written by Mizugaki Egao (1789–1846) and illustrated by Kunisada;[9] and *Beautiful Tale of Northern Snow: A Mirror of the Times* (*Hokusetsu bidan jidai kagami*, 1855–1883) written by Tamenaga Shunsui II (1818–1886) and illustrated by Utagawa Kunisada II (1823–1880).[10] Evidence of Kyōka's abiding passion for the art form is attested to by his personal library of *kusazōshi*, preserved at Keiō University in Tokyo. It is one of the most extensive and complete collections of the genre in Japan to have been assembled by an individual collector.

Contemporary writers first noted the association between Kyōka and *kusazōshi* during the author's own lifetime. However, early critics often claimed that *kusazōshi* had a largely negative influence on Kyōka's work, and it was only later in the twentieth century that scholars began to identify picture books as a major source of inspiration for Kyōka's unique visual style. Looking closely at the themes of Kyōka's fiction, one finds that *kusazōshi* influenced Kyōka's depictions of the supernatural, horror, violence, eroticism, and tales of adventure. They also influenced his diverse depictions of women, including female heroes and women who wield magic powers.

2. Critical History of Kyōka and *Kusazōshi*

One of the first evaluations of the supposedly negative influence of *kusazōshi* on Kyōka's writing was by Natsume Sōseki, in a review of Kyōka's early novel *Silver Poem Strip* (*Gin tanzaku*, 1905). In his review, Sōseki describes the novel as a combination of "ideas drawn from the era of *kusazōshi* and ideas drawn from the Meiji period."[11] For Sōseki, however, the result is unsatisfying. He writes: "Fantasy [*mugen*] as fantasy is interesting. Breathing in the atmosphere of the Meiji period, and then reproducing that atmosphere, is also interesting. But this patchwork cloak fails to evoke the feeling of a complete outfit." Nevertheless, Sōseki concedes in his review that Kyōka is a "genius" (*tensai*). He claims, cryptically, "If only this person attains enlightenment, his work will be peerless under heaven." To attain enlightenment, however, it would seem that Kyōka would need to abandon his attachment to the outdated world of *kusazōshi*. Another early critique of the influence of *kusazōshi* on Kyōka's work was made by Osanai Kaoru (1881–1928), an influential playwright and theatrical reformer. Osanai wrote in the *Yomiuri shinbun* in 1908, "The lines that Kyōka's characters speak, their actions and behavior, and the overall structure of his narratives are all drawn straight from the musty world of *kusazōshi*."[12] Replacing the character for "grass" (*kusa*) in *kusazōshi* with "foul-smelling" (also *kusa*), Osanai renders *kusazōshi* as "stinky books" rather than "grass books," thereby underscoring his poor opinion of the medium. Like Sōseki, he implies that the Edo-period influence on Kyōka's literature held the author back from reaching his full potential as a modern author.

In later evaluations of Kyōka's fiction, scholars have described *kusazōshi* as a positive influence on the author's work, often suggesting that Kyōka's writing captured the magic and excitement of the detailed illustrations found in the pages of the medium. Scholar Okitsu Kaname, for example, writes:

> It is as though numerous colorful illustrations from the world of *kusazōshi* had been waiting in Kyōka's imagination since his younger days, only to awaken and climb his brush as he plotted new ideas in succession. The result was picture books written in words, which took a medium that had once been little more than a popular pastime for women and children and had been consigned to a forgotten corner of literary history. Kyōka took these *kusazōshi* and sublimated them into an artistic form.[13]

Scholar Asada Shōjirō describes the influence of illustration on Kyōka's stories in a similar manner, with emphasis on the fantastic depictions in such images:

> Kyōka begins with the content [of *kusazōshi*] such as magic and monsters, then he draws on their literary expression, which he uses to approximate the kinds of scenes that one sees in illustrations. . . . He even adapts the forms and ideas of *kusazōshi*, coloring them in to

create careful structures that recall the regional products of his hometown, Kanazawa.[14]

In English-language scholarship, Jean Akemi Funatsu first explored the influence of *kusazōshi* on Kyōka's fiction in *Through the Colored Looking Glass of Izumi Kyōka: Reflections of the Kusazōshi* (1972), a dissertation representing the earliest scholarship on Kyōka in English. In her dissertation, Funatsu argues that Kyōka adapted certain narrative elements of *kusazōshi* in his work, such as a focus on character, complex plot structures, and the building of suspense.[15] In more recent scholarship, Charles Shirō Inouye argues that illustrations from *kusazōshi* provided the initial motivation for Kyōka's literary career, beginning with the author's experience of tracing pictures from the pages of *kusazōshi* during his childhood. As Inouye notes, according to Izumi Kyōka's younger brother, Izumi Shatei (the penname of Izumi Toyoharu, 1880–1933), as a child Kyōka would often trace the illustrations that he found in his mother's collection of *kusazōshi* in "vivid detail," including one of "a pitiful young maiden who was bound, hung from a tree, and beaten."[16] Of this experience, Inouye writes, "Kyōka's life as a writer began with this act of tracing. Eventually, the impulse to reaffirm the power of these and other images would lead him to produce verbal images that would reconfigure the world of his mother's illustrated texts."[17] In the estimation of scholars such as these, rather than leading Kyōka to produce stories that were stale or outdated, *kusazōshi* supported the author's development of a vivid literary world unique in modern literature.

While *kusazōshi* have long been recognized as a major source of inspiration for Kyōka, much work remains to be done in tracing specific influences from the premodern genre in his fiction. Writing on this subject, scholar Yoshida Masashi comments that references to *kusazōshi* in Kyōka's literature, including allusions and direct references, are "too numerous to count."[18] Yoshida begins this work, however, by identifying several references to specific *kusazōshi* titles in Kyōka's fiction, with a focus on *The Life of Shakyamuni in Eight Phases*. Yoshida also traces the adaptation of certain fantastic images in Kyōka's stories, such as those of Kishimojin (Hārītī), a protector of children in Buddhism who was once a demon and devourer of children, before being enlightened by the Buddha, and various types of avian-human hybrids, including *amatsu otome*, celestial maidens who perform concerts on heavenly clouds, and *karyōbinga* (*kalavinka*), angelic creatures who appear in various human-bird forms, as found in Buddhist and Hindu iconography.[19] In this chapter, I emphasize the influence of another pivotal series on Kyōka's imagination of the fantastic, *The Tale of Shiranui*, while also exploring Kyōka's adaptation of fantastic images of female heroes, religious icons, magic, monsters, gore, and eroticism in his fiction. In addition, I provide an account of the content of Kyōka's personal collection of picture books.

As Yoshida points out, Kyōka includes a detailed summary of an episode from a late volume of *The Life of Shakyamuni in Eight Phases* in his magnum-opus novel *Women of Fate* (*Yukari no onna*, 1919–1921), thereby demonstrating his intimate familiarity with the long-running series, while also suggesting the depth of his interest in *kusazōshi* as a source of fantastic imagery for modern fiction. *Women of Fate* is a modern novel that describes the return of a native of Kanazawa to his hometown to visit his mother's grave to deal with the impending demolition of the graveyard where his mother is buried. The episode from *The Life of Shakyamuni in Eight Phases*, summarized by Kyōka in the novel, relates the origin story of Kishimojin by mixing elements of traditional religious narratives with fairytale-like elements.[20]

In author Mantei Ōga's version of Kishimojin's origin story, Kishimojin is married to a hunter named Gusoku Yasha, who goes out hunting for a *shōjō*, a monkey demon similar to the more widely known *hihi*. Gusoku Yasha falls into a river and is saved by an obscure mythical creature called a *seidaku*, who is described as having the white face of a woman, eight blue wings, and one leg. After saving him, the *seidaku* makes Gusoku Yasha promise to never reveal her location. When Gusoku Yasha returns home, he finds that his wife, Kishimojin, is preparing to kill and eat a kidnapped prince. The Buddha arrives on the scene, stops Kishimojin from killing the prince, and then instructs and enlightens her, but the prince falls ill, and it is revealed to his mother in a dream that only the feather of a *seidaku* can cure him. Gusoku Yasha ignores the warning of the *seidaku* and reveals her location, and as a result he is cursed and transformed into a cat. As a fantasy narrative, it is difficult to imagine a more typical example of the marvelous. With its details of metamorphosis, cruel punishment, and hybrid animal monsters, Ōga's story would hardly be out of place in texts such as the *Arabian Nights* or *The Golden Ass*.

Alongside images of supernatural beings, Kyōka also draws on *kusazōshi* as a source of popular imagery of women, including imagery that is by turns sacred, heroic, erotic, and violent. Such images include those of powerful female heroes, women with supernatural powers, women wielding swords and other weapons, erotic depictions of women, and sacred images of female deities. In Kyōka's fiction, *kusazōshi* are related to a feminine realm, and particularly to the author's mother and the females around whom he was raised, because these women often collected and read *kusazōshi*, as described by

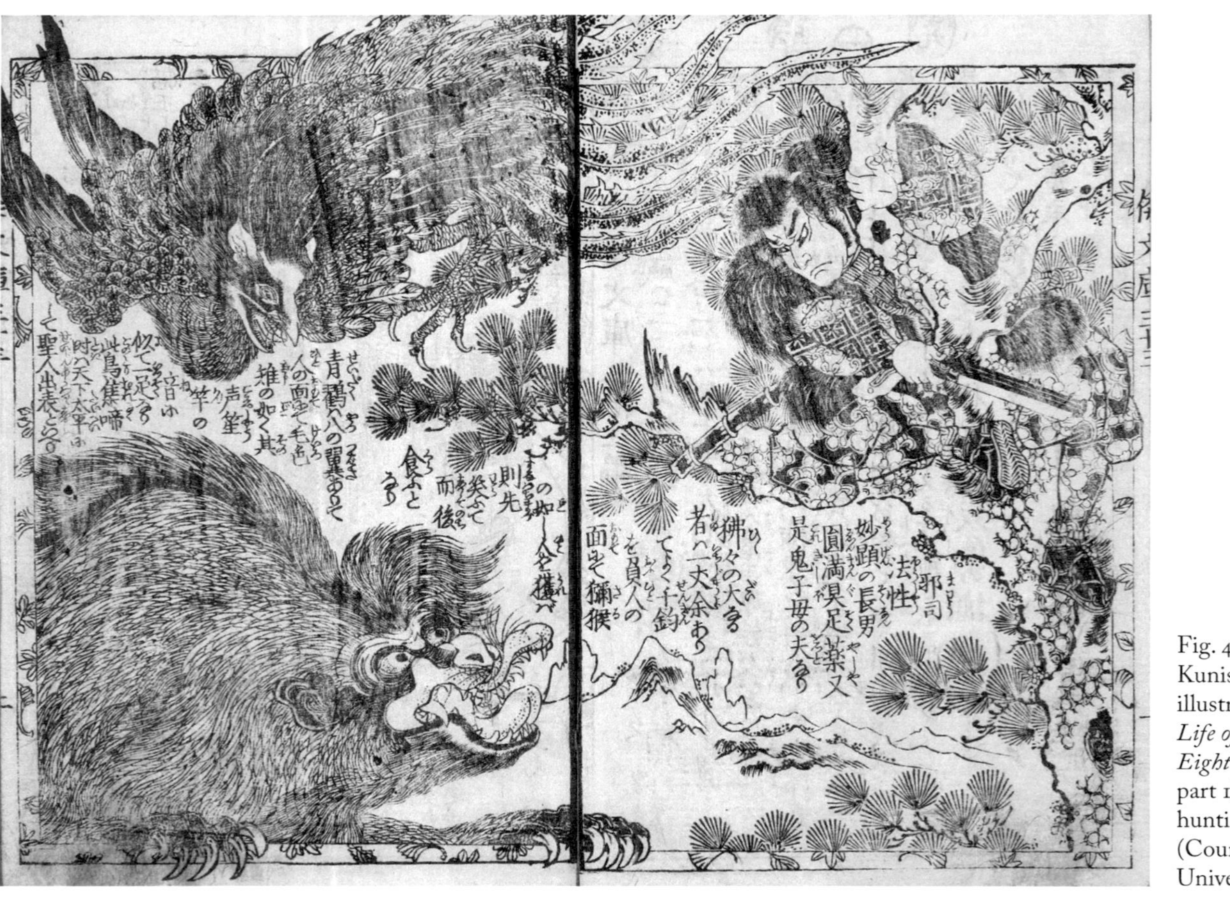

Fig. 4. Utagawa Kunisada II, an illustration from *The Life of Shakyamuni in Eight Phases* (vol. 33, part 1): Gusoku Yasha hunting monsters. (Courtesy of Waseda University Library.)

Fig. 5. Utagawa Kunisada, illustration from *The Tale of Shiranui* (vol. 7, part 2): Princess Wakana vs. Toriyama Akisaku I. (Courtesy of Waseda University Library.)

Fig. 6. Utagawa Kunisada, cover illustration from *The Tale of Shiranui* (vol. 17, parts 1 and 2): Princess Wakana vs. Toriyama Akisaku 2. (Courtesy of Waseda University Library.)

Fig. 7. A votive statue of Maya Bunin from Gyōzenji, a temple in the city of Hakusan, formerly known as the village of Mattō. (Photograph provided by Takeo Satoshi, Groovy Inc., reprinted courtesy of Bussi-en and Gyōzenji.)

Kyōka in his stories and essays. In his writing, Kyōka references images of popular female characters from *kusazōshi* series, including Princess Wakana, the protagonist of *The Tale of Shiranui*, and Māyādevi, the mother of the Buddha, as featured in *The Life of Shakyamuni in Eight Phases*.

Much has been written on Kyōka's devotion to Māyādevi, or Maya Bunin in Japanese, a Buddhist figure who Kyōka venerated throughout his life, and whose image features prominently in his fiction. The connection of Kyōka to Maya Bunin might be traced to his upbringing in Kanazawa, where images of Maya Bunin can be found at several local temples, despite the relative rarity of her images in Japan. In his later years, Kyōka is known to have kept a Buddhist altar dedicated to Maya Bunin at his home in Tokyo.[21] Kyōka wrote several stories about Maya Bunin and associated her image with his mother, due to the appearance of the religious figure as a character in the opening

Fig. 8. Izumi Kyōka's votive statue of Maya Bunin, from his personal Buddhist altar at his former home in Tokyo. (Currently in the collection of Shōchiku Co., Ltd. Photograph courtesy of Izumi Kyōka Kinenkan Museum.)

chapters of *The Life of Shakyamuni in Eight Phases*, one of his mother's favorite series, and also because his father took him to pray before an image of Maya Bunin at a temple in Mattō, a village near Kanazawa, following his mother's passing.[22] Kyōka was also a devotee of Kishimojin, a popular Buddhist deity who is referenced in his fiction, although she is too monstrous to be associated with his mother. The horrific aspects of Kishimojin are emphasized in *The Life of Shakyamuni in Eight Phases*, with illustrations by Kunisada that depict her as an *onibaba*.

While drawing on *kusazōshi* as a source of images of monsters, supernatural beings, and sacred women, Kyōka also treats the illustrations found throughout the pages of *kusazōshi* as enchanted pictures in themselves. As Yoshida notes, in *Celestial Kabuki* (1915), the narrator describes the illustration of a flood in a work of *kusazōshi* as acquiring lifelike qualities. Kyōka writes, "If you look at the water drawn in the picture, it's difficult to resist the desire to drink it. The moon, the snow, a flower in the grass, because they are pictures, they are more real than the real thing. One desires them, one is captivated by them."[23] Kyōka again describes the illustrations of *kusazōshi* as living images in his essay "Ukiyo-e of the Past and Images of Beautiful Women Today" ("Mukashi no ukiyo-e to ima no bijinga," 1911). He writes that the reader feels a sense of unrequited love (*okabore*) when looking at pictures of women in *kusazōshi* and describes feeling that such characters must be real—that they "simply must exist."[24]

Although Kyōka adapts the supernatural creatures of *kusazōshi* to his fiction, in the context of his stories, such creatures become haunting apparitions, or icons of a traditional past, rather than beings who appear clearly to the story's characters. This disparity recalls Caillois's description of the difference between the monsters of fairytales and the marvelous and the phantoms of the fantastic. Caillois writes, "The courageous man can fight and vanquish a dragon spitting flames or a monstrous giant. He can kill them. But his bravery is worth little in the face of a specter . . . because the specter comes from the other side of death."[25] In the premodern genre of *kusazōshi*, the supernatural is a physical force. Characters cast spells and wield enchanted weapons to defeat giant monsters. In Kyōka's fiction, the supernatural has become more elusive. Ghosts and monsters appear in the dark corners of rooms or in dreams, or even manifest as extensions of psychological states of fear, anxiety, distress, or guilt. Even when Kyōka's ghosts are treated as being more "real," they tend to shift out of sight when made the subject of excessive scrutiny.

3. A History of *Kusazōshi*

A discussion of Kyōka and *kusazōshi* begins by necessity with an overview of the history, terminology, and themes of the medium, which has become obscure over time. *Kusazōshi* are comparable in many ways to modern fantasy literature, including genre fantasy and quest fantasy, due to prominent themes of monsters and magic, while also resembling modern illustrated media such as comic books and manga because of their extensive use of images. *Kusazōshi* might be thought of as premodern comic books, due to several factors. Like modern comic books or manga, *kusazōshi* were illustrated on every page, serialized over years or decades, and created by teams of writers and artists who handed over popular series to their proteges. Also like these modern media, *kusazōshi* tended to feature sprawling casts of characters, multiple interweaving storylines, and plots that centered on themes such as hunting monsters, training for battle, defeating enemies, seeking revenge, recovering treasured items, and courting romantic interests. *Kusazōshi* also tended to include at least occasional scenes of graphic violence, in common with modern comics.

According to scholar Andrew Lawrence Markus, the reputation of *kusazōshi* could be such that one publisher, Tsutaya Jūzaburō, sent a letter to writer Takizawa Bakin in 1808 advising him to avoid depictions of "cremations, drowned corpses, female and child brigands, the spontaneous combustion of adulterers, and the rolling about of lopped heads."[26] Later, in 1821, writer Ryūtei Tanehiko denounced the most vulgar elements of *kusazōshi*, which he listed as "vendettas, first of all, human prodigies; sorcery; tales of the supernatural . . . dream oracles from gods or buddhas; self-disembowelment, self-immolation, [and] drawn swords."[27]

A history of *kusazōshi* must begin with the name of the genre itself, which already leads to a complicated issue. The books that Kyōka almost always refers to as *kusazōshi* scholars commonly refer to as *gōkan* ("collected volumes") as the proper genre designation, to differentiate them from several distinct genres included under the general name of *kusazōshi* as an umbrella term for Edo-period picture books. Specifically, *gōkan* refers to the most elaborately illustrated variety of *kusazōshi*, which was developed during the nineteenth century. *Gōkan* feature many more pages and volumes than earlier varieties of *kusazōshi*, along with greater development of plot and character and a stronger focus on themes of adventure and epic quests for revenge. Due to their popular content, *gōkan* were one of the most widely consumed genres of fiction in nineteenth-century Japan. I refer to *kusazōshi* and *gōkan* interchangeably, with a preference for the term *kusazōshi*, because this is the word used by Kyōka himself, as well as by most scholars of Kyōka's fiction. However, the term *gōkan* is useful for specifying differences when making comparisons to related genres of picture books. The literal translation of *kusazōshi* is "grass booklets," a term of uncertain etymology. Markus suggests that the word "grass" (*kusa*) refers to the "ephemeral or trivial character" of such books,[28] whereas Adam Kern suggests that this is a reference to "squiggly-looking 'grass' (*kusa*) script" featured in the genre.[29] Other terms that have been used in history to refer to the same medium include *ehon* ("picture books") and *ezōshi* ("picture booklets").

During the Edo period, *kusazōshi* were one of the most prominent forms of media used to publish stories with supernatural themes. The origins of *kusazōshi* can be traced back to the early years of the publishing industry in the city of Edo in the seventeenth century, and specifically to the genre of fiction known as *akahon* ("red books"). These early picture books featured tales of ghosts and monsters related primarily through images, and flourished in Edo from the Hōei era (1704–1711) to the Kyōhō era (1716–1736).[30] In common with the genres that followed, they were identified primarily based on the color of their covers. *Akahon* in turn gave rise to the *kurohon* ("black books") and *aohon* ("blue books"), two genres that flourished from the Enkyō era (1744–1748) through the An'ei era (1772–1781) and that were nearly indistinguishable from each other in terms of their themes. The *kurohon* and *aohon* continued to showcase stories of ghosts and heroes, but they also featured more sophisticated narratives that drew content directly from classical Japanese and Chinese sources.[31] The black books and blue books were eventually replaced by the *kibyōshi* ("yellow covers"), a genre of *kusazōshi* that was published mainly between 1775 and 1806 and that featured humorous tales that were variously satirical, parodic, or didactic and often concerned the pleasure quarter and their residents.[32] During the early nineteenth century, the most intricately illustrated variety of *kusazōshi*, known as *gōkan*, was developed by combining multiple ten-page booklets or fascicles (*kan*) into longer books. *Gōkan* are thus named after this publication format of "combined booklets." These volumes were published annually or semi-annually over years, or even decades, to form continuous series. The most popular series might reach somewhere between thirty and fifty volumes in length, or thousands of pages in a few cases.

The woodblock-printed illustrations of *kusazōshi* were one of the main attractions of the medium and likely contributed to their success with readers. Such illustrations transformed the literary medium into a genre of popular entertainment, full of vivid images of heroes, supernatural creatures, and beautiful women who move through intricately detailed environments. Suzuki Jūzō, a leading scholar of *kusazōshi* and Edo-period print culture, praises the cultural and artistic value of the illustrations of *kusazōshi* and suggests that they rival modern print media in terms of their technical accomplishment. He writes, "Famous ukiyo-e artists applied their brushes to these diverse illustrations. There is no small possibility that they would meet expectations for visual entertainment and be appreciated in modern times."[33] The illustrations of *kusazōshi* are often precisely detailed, creatively structured, and usually fill much of the page. Detail is often concentrated in clothing, whose folds and patterns are designed with tremendous care, while the most lavishly illustrated *kusazōshi* feature depictions of entire rooms or buildings and include minor details throughout the image. Text is fitted into the blank space around the images and consists of a combination of narrative and dialogue. The placement of text and image on the page was often coordinated by the author and illustrator of a story, with some authors, such as Tanehiko, providing outlines and instructions for the desired outcome of the artist's work.[34] The illustrations of *kusazōshi* were created by many of the most popular and talented artists of the late Edo period, such as Toyokuni, Kunisada, Kuniyoshi, Utagawa Toyohiro (1773–1828), and Keisai Eisen.[35] Their illustrations for picture books might be included among their most elaborate and skillfully produced work.

Relying on a combination of detailed illustration, sensational content, and fantastic storylines, *kusazōshi* were one of the most widely read forms of literature in nineteenth-century Japan. As Markus finds, Bakin recorded that his most successful *kusazōshi* sold between 4,000 and 8,000 copies, whereas numerous scholars have estimated that copies of *Fake Murasaki, Rustic Genji* sold between 10,000 and 15,000 copies per volume, at a time when a print run of 5,000 copies for a woodblock-printed book would be considered a solid success.[36] *Kusazōshi* were so lucrative that they were written by almost every one of the most famous authors of the nineteenth century, including writers as prominent as Santō Kyōden, Shikitei Sanba, Jippensha Ikku, Tamenaga Shunsui, Bakin, and Tanehiko.[37] Markus estimates that the total number of *kusazōshi* published during the Edo period amounts to around 3,000 titles, including standalone titles and individual volumes in longer series.[38]

In terms of their primary audience, *kusazōshi* were often referred to as literature for "women and children."[39] While it might seem odd that a genre featuring scenes of graphic violence and horror made such books suitable for women and children, one might also interpret this designation as a way of excusing content of monsters, supernatural beings, and storylines that might be considered inappropriate for adult male readers. However, it appears that *kusazōshi* were enjoyed beyond their described target demographic. A more accurate description of the situation might be that *kusazōshi* were promoted as books for women and children, and were probably enjoyed by such readers, who made up a key part of their audience, but evidence suggests that they were appreciated beyond these demographics. As Markus finds, the most popular *kusazōshi* were read by everyone from the shogun in Edo to daimyo and merchants in the provinces, and from the shogun's wife and concubines in the apartments of the inner palace to the maids employed in their service.[40] Also, the sales numbers of *kusazōshi* suggest that they were supported by a large reading public whose occupations allowed them to afford the relatively expensive picture books.[41] At the same time, *kusazōshi* continued to be associated with female readers in the modern period, in part due to later memoirs by modern authors who describe women as the primary audience for *kusazōshi*.

As scholar Maeda Ai has written, during the Meiji period, the reading of literature was often divided along gendered lines, with works of history,

Confucian philosophy, and classical Chinese literature and poetry being considered essential reading for men, and *kusazōshi* being associated with female family members, such as mothers, grandmothers, and sisters.[42] Maeda notes descriptions of this tendency throughout the memoirs of authors raised during the Meiji period, including Shibusawa Eiichi (1840–1931), Emi Suiin (1869–1934), Taoka Reiun (1870–1912), Ōgai, and Rohan.[43] In addition to suggesting common patterns of readership, such authors describe historical approaches to reading texts that differ from modern ones. As Maeda notes, during the Edo period, reading was often not a solitary practice, but instead took place in groups.[44] Some authors indicate that women would read the text of *kusazōshi* aloud while enjoying their illustrations as part of the reading experience. They also suggest that women would improvise narratives that took the content of the illustrations into account, along with previous knowledge of the stories, in a reading practice known as *etoki* ("explaining the pictures"). Kyōka provides an account along these lines, of women reading *kusazōshi* in group settings. In "Lover's Treatment," Kyōka relates that he first gained knowledge of the content of *kusazōshi* by overhearing his older female relatives reading the texts aloud, or otherwise explaining the details of their illustrations, in a manner of reading that he refers to specifically as *etoki*.[45]

4. Princess Wakana and the Character Type of the Female Hero

In addition to historical evidence of women reading *kusazōshi*, their content also suggests a focus on female readers. Such content includes detailed and extravagant depictions of contemporary fashion and dress, storylines involving women who are skilled in combat, and a large number of women who are featured as main characters, in both the narratives and their illustrations. Such characters might be equated with the heroes of fantasy literature or the marvelous, for they show little hesitation in confronting even the most terrifying monsters. In *kusazōshi*, female characters are frequently portrayed fighting enemies using swords, daggers, knives, spears, *naginata* (halberds), magic spells, or even wrestling throws. In *The Life of Shakyamuni in Eight Phases*, for example, the aunt of the Buddha, Kyōdonmi, defends the future mother of the Buddha, her younger sister Maya, by fending off an unwanted suitor with a sword, although she later attempts to curse her younger sister with a spell when they compete for the affection of an emperor. In *The Tale of Shiranui*, one of the main characters, Princess Wakana disposes of her enemies using magic spells in scenes of gruesome violence. Far from making her a villain, this appears to have been part of her appeal to nineteenth-century

readers. Kyōka was inspired by characters such as Princess Wakana in his diverse depictions of women, or characters who range from talented geisha to successful actresses, mysterious witches to adventurous maids, and violent murderers to heroic defenders of the weak.

In "Lover's Treatment," Kyōka describes Princess Wakana from *The Tale of Shiranui* as his favorite character from the world of *kusazōshi*. *The Tale of Shiranui* was one of the most popular and longest-running series of Edo-period fiction, published between 1849 and 1885 in ninety volumes and running to over 3,000 pages.[46] In addition to being one of the most successful series of *kusazōshi*, *The Tale of Shiranui* was also one of the most imaginative and outlandish in terms of its fantasy content. Like other *kusazōshi*, it features more characters and plotlines than can be summarized neatly. New characters,

Fig. 9. Utagawa Kunisada, illustration from *The Tale of Shiranui* (vol. 4, part 2): Princess Wakana summons a giant earth spider, who bites off the head of a prostitute. (Courtesy of Waseda University Library.)

including heroes and villains, are introduced in almost every chapter of the series from the opening pages of the work, and their adventures overlap and diverge as the series progresses. One of the main storylines in the series, however, is that of Princess Wakana, a fictionalized daughter of historical daimyo Ōtomo Sōrin (1530–1587) of Kyushu. Princess Wakana is depicted as a magic-wielding princess who establishes various mountain fortresses and gathers warriors together to plan revenge attacks against the Kikuchi clan, who once betrayed her father. Most of Princess Wakana's abilities involve summoning spiders, who provide her with support in battle. These spiders bite and poison enemies, steal hidden treasure, shoot webs that freeze enemies in place, and weave webs that lift her up into the trees to evade enemy attacks. In one of the most stunning episodes from the series, Princess Wakana summons a giant shapeshifting "earth spider" (*tsuchigumo*) to bite off the head of a prostitute, whose form it then assumes so that it can invade enemy territory undetected. In his essay "The Disposition of the Women of Edo as Featured in *Kusazōshi*" ("Kusazōshi ni arawaretaru Edo no onna no seikaku," 1911), Kyōka recalls his favorites episodes from *The Tale of Shiranui* as being those that highlight Princess Wakana's combination of bravado and gentility. In an unusual detail of the narrative for the time, one of Princess Wakana's powers is her ability to transform into a man, who is known as Minister Shiranui (Shiranui Daijin). While disguised as a man, Princess Wakana courts another female character, who swoons over her charm and gallantry. This surprising power might be compared to the gender-bending content of today's media and might be considered as further evidence that *kusazōshi* were targeted toward a female audience.

In an episode that Kyōka describes at length, Princess Wakana transforms from a man back into a woman after succeeding in cornering her enemy. She summons spiders to bind her enemy to a tree with spiderwebs before stabbing her to death with a bamboo spear. When a geisha she had been courting is shocked by her sudden change in appearance, Princess Wakana responds by boldly reassuring her, "There's nothing to fear, come here by my side."[47] Kyōka elaborates on his interest in the tough fighting women of Edo fiction by writing, "To put it bluntly, I like a woman who wields a dagger and keeps a short sword hidden in her breast pocket."[48] He praises the traditional women of Edo particularly for their qualities of *hari*, or toughness, a term that literally means "tautness" and might be thought of as resilience or sprightliness, and *ikuji*, "resolve," or a determination to stand one's ground and fight, or otherwise to push ahead and see matters through to the end.

Kyōka's interest in strong female characters may come as a surprise to readers familiar with his stories that feature women primarily in conservative social roles, such as housewife, mistress, geisha, or prostitute, or that depict women driven into positions of suffering and powerlessness, from public humiliation to suicide. Such an understanding is not entirely inaccurate, because these types of characters are common in Kyōka's fiction, as they were in the Edo-period fiction that inspired him, but this is only a partial understanding of his work. Rather than attempting to completely overturn this reading, I wish to point out that the figure of the tragic geisha or prostitute is only one among many character types in Kyōka's fiction that is derived from the arts of the Edo period. Kyōka's fiction also features some of the most diverse depictions of female characters from his time, including women who exemplify the qualities of *hari* and *ikuji* displayed by the

Fig. 10. Utagawa Kunisada II, illustration from *Tale of Shiranui* (vol. 27, part 2): Princess Wakana stabs an enemy with a wooden spear. (Courtesy of Waseda University Library.)

brave women of *kusazōshi*. In addition to geisha, the female characters in Kyōka's fiction include nurses, teachers, students, scholars, small shop owners, madams, maids, writers, painters, actresses, traveling performers, witches, fortune-tellers, thieves, murderers, and gang leaders.[49] Like the women of *kusazōshi*, these female characters are defined by their toughness and occasional cruelty, but also by their accomplishments in the arts, entertainment, business, martial arts, and scholarship. One of Kyōka's most famous female characters, the witch from *The Holy Man of Mt. Kōya*, is so intriguing because her true nature, whether as hero or villain, is open to interpretation. This character must be acknowledged, at the very least, as one of the most alluring characters in Kyōka's fiction, just as Princess Wakana was one of the most appealing characters to nineteenth-century readers of *kusazōshi*.

5. Kyōka's Collection of *Kusazōshi*

Evidence for the importance of *kusazōshi* to Kyōka's literary imagination can be found in his essays on collecting picture books, his extensive personal collection of *kusazōshi*, and references to *kusazōshi* that appear throughout his fiction, from his early days as a writer through his late career. Details of Kyōka's initial meeting with *kusazōshi*, including his encounter with Princess Wakana, can be found in "Lover's Treatment." Toward the beginning of the essay, in a section describing his earliest literary experiences, Kyōka writes:

> My mother came from Tokyo with a doll box that she used as a box for books, in which she kept collections of *The Tale of Shiranui*, *The Life of Shakyamuni in Eight Phases*, and *A Mirror of the Times* shut inside. Ten volumes, five volumes, eight volumes of various *kusazōshi* were stacked with the cut ends of the pages lined up. My mother valued the collection and kept it in shape, and when she had a break she would remove one, but not read it. When I was three or four years old, she would line the chapters in rows for summer airing, their covers with beautiful pictures, some with splendid warriors, others with pretty girls . . .[50]

Over time, Kyōka came to learn details of the characters' backgrounds by listening to his female relatives read *kusazōshi* in the *etoki* style. He discusses various characters from *The Tale of Shiranui*, with a focus on Princess Wakana. He writes, "Princess Ōtomo Wakana was by far my favorite character. . . . Princess Wakana was so great that I can hardly explain myself. She was so outrageous that I thought she was on the side of the villains."[51] Kyōka had

Fig. 11. Portrait of Izumi Kyōka reading *kusazōshi* in front of a folding screen (*byōbu*) decorated with cut-out frontispieces by Kunisada from *Fake Murasaki, Rustic Genji.* (Photograph courtesy of Izumi Kyōka Kinenkan Museum.)

mistaken the protagonist for a villain, perhaps due to her occasional acts of cruelty, but he adds that he was not alone in considering her to be one of the most popular characters in the series. To prove his point, he recalls a frontispiece from a later volume of *The Tale of Shiranui* that presents the character as "Everybody's favorite, Princess Wakana."[52] He thereby suggests that there was a fan base of readers during the Edo period who were interested in depictions of female heroes like Princess Wakana, many of whom were probably women themselves.

Toward the end of "Lover's Treatment," Kyōka reminisces over the images of beautiful female heroes in *kusazōshi* in ways that gesture toward content of eroticism and fantasy. Following Kyōka's detailed account of his early experiences with modern literature, he references a rare and antique picture book by Tanehiko, *Woodblock-Printed Words: Dolls of the Past* (*Moji tezuri mukashi ningyō*, 1813), from which he describes a scene that depicts a partially disrobed female warrior in battle. He writes, "While grappling and throwing an enemy soldier who advances toward her, she tosses her armor aside, leaving her forearm guards and shin guards on. [Tanehiko writes] of the armor, 'The trembling threads of her red undergarments on her thin waist are almost transparent, how lovely.' Beautiful, is it not?" Kyōka ends "Lover's Treatment" by treating *The Tale of Shiranui* as a ghostly relic of the past, or a variety of enchanted media, in a short fantasy sequence. He writes, "Yes, even now I still enjoy *kusazōshi*. I have many nostalgic mementos from my mother and father, such as books by Kyōden, and when I am sad I place them by my pillowside. I see Princess Wakana use her spider magic just like in those pictures, as though watching an illusion. It is much better than watching theater."[53]

In two essays written years later, Kyōka indicates that he continued to collect *kusazōshi* and enjoy their illustrations as an adult. In "Those Days" ("Sono koro," 1908) and "Ukiyo-e of the Past and Images of Beautiful Women Today" (1911), Kyōka describes a period of fanatically collecting *kusazōshi* during his early years in Tokyo. In his account, he reveals that he was concerned with completing series of *kusazōshi* in his collection, and that he sought quality used items. He also suggests that he appreciated the illustrations of *kusazōshi* as one of their most memorable aspects. In both essays, Kyōka relates that he would search through secondhand goods shops and used bookstores in Tokyo with his friend, Hirezaki Eihō, a contemporary illustrator of popular fiction and an accomplished painter of *bijinga*.

Kyōka begins his short essay "Those Days" by thanking readers for reading and collecting his stories and by discussing the various magazines available at the time for publishing fiction, including *Shinshōsetsu*, *Bungei kurabu*, *Taiyō*, *Chūō kōron*, *Bunko*, *Shinchō*, and *Shinsei*. He adds that literary magazines did not exist when he was younger, with the exception of *Miyako no hana*. In the second half of the essay, he hints that reading and collecting *kusazōshi* was a pastime that might have been frowned upon as an eccentric hobby by the reading public in 1908. He begins his account of collecting picture books by writing, "As for hobbies, mine is kind of strange. I like to collect *kusazōshi*."[54] He compares this hobby to a common pastime of his own era, collecting picture postcards, perhaps as a way of providing context for his "strange" habit. As he puts it, like the novice collector of postcards, a collector new to the art of *kusazōshi* tries to buy everything at once, regardless of the condition of the items or the quality of the printed pages of the work. A more seasoned collector, however, is able to select the best works and later sells books that are no longer needed.

In "Ukiyo-e of the Past and Images of Beautiful Women Today," Kyōka describes the rarity of *kusazōshi* series as one of their more appealing qualities. As he puts it, some series are commonly available at used bookstores, such as *The Life of Shakyamuni in Eight Phases* and *The Tale of Shiranui*, whereas other series are difficult to find, such as *Dreamlike Tales of the Provinces* (*Kantan shokoku monogatari*, 1834–1856), written by Tanehiko and illustrated by Kunisada,[55] or *Grasses of Learning: The Characters of Wives* (*Oshiegusa nyōbō katagi*, 1847–1868), written by Santō Kyōzan (1769–1858) and illustrated by Kunisada.[56] Narrating his search for rare series such as these, Kyōka writes that he would wander around the city with Eihō and that they would grow dizzy with excitement as they sought used picture books. They would even stop in front of houses that looked like they had been built during the Edo period and would consider knocking on their doors to inquire if the owners had any *kusazōshi* for sale. Kyōka suggests that he was more careful than Eihō in selecting books to purchase. He writes that he would aim to buy complete series in good condition, whereas Eihō would buy *kusazōshi* in any condition, even stained books or single issues from the middle of a series. Kyōka adds that Eihō's approach to collecting *kusazōshi* had its advantages, because it led him to discover rare books with unforgettable illustrations.

According to a posthumous list of Kyōka's *kusazōshi* collection made in 1942, at one point, Kyōka's library contained over one hundred different series and probably thousands of individual volumes of *kusazōshi*. A large part of this collection, however, has been lost. Two lists of items featured in the collection exist, one created during World War II, in 1942, and one after, in 1976.[57] The lists show considerable variation in the items listed, with many items appearing in the first list that do not appear in the second. In between the creation of both lists, the majority of Kyōka's library was destroyed by fire during World War II.[58]

The *kusazōshi* list from 1976 provides details of the volumes that Kyōka owned from each series and indicates that many of the series that Kyōka collected were either complete or near completion, whether three, five, twelve, fifteen, or dozens of volumes in length, thereby demonstrating his thoroughness as a collector. According to the list, Kyōka owned the complete series of *A Mirror of the Times*, at 48 volumes, 42 of 43 volumes of *The Tale of Brave Jiraiya*, 54 of the 58 volumes of *The Life of Shakyamuni in Eight Phases*, and 29 of 38 volumes of *Fake Murasaki, Rustic Genji.* In addition to volumes of *Fake Murasaki, Rustic Genji* contained in the collection, Kyōka famously cut out frontispieces from the same series and pasted them all over a folding screen (*byōbu*) that he kept in his house, thereby bringing the colorful world of *kusazōshi* illustration directly into his living and working space.[59] As for *The Tale of Shiranui*, one of Kyōka's favorites series, the extant collection features only volumes 1–18 and 29–38, out of a total of 90 volumes published; later volumes of the series, published during the Meiji period, are extremely rare.[60] Other series in the collection are far too numerous to list here. A very brief sample of series includes *The Water Margin with Courtesans* (*Keisei Suikoden*, 1825–1835), written by Bakin and illustrated by Utagawa Toyokuni II (1777–1835);[61] *The Water Margin in Japanese* (*Kanagaki Suikoden*, 1830–1851), written by Tanehiko and illustrated by Kuniyoshi;[62] *A Library of Japanese Syllabary* (*Iroha bunko*, 1859–1866), written by Ryūentei Tanehisa (active ca. 1850s–1860s) and illustrated by Utagawa Kunimori II (active ca. 1850s–1860s);[63] *Saigyō's View of Edo* (*Edo mi Saigyō*, 1838–1850), written by Kyōzan and illustrated by Kunisada; *Grasses of Learning: The Characters of Wives* (1847–1868), written by Kyōzan and illustrated by Kunisada; *Wayside Shrine of the Rat: Tale of the Vigil* (*Nezumi no hokora tsuya monogatari*, 1867–1875), written by Ryūtei Senka and illustrated by Kunisada II;[64] and *Nursery Rhyme: Wheels of Wondrous Wonder* (*Warabeuta myōmyōguruma*, 1855–1867), written by Tanekazu and illustrated by Kunisada II.[65]

The most heavily represented writer in Kyōka's collection is Tanehiko, with 33 individual series in the list, while the most heavily represented artist is Kunisada, with 46 series. While one might take this to mean that these two individuals were Kyōka's favorite creators of *kusazōshi*, his collection also reflects the reality of their positions as leading figures in nineteenth-century *kusazōshi* publication.[66] Following Tanehiko, the most heavily represented writers in the original collection are Ryūtei Senka (14), Santō Kyōzan (11), Santō Kyōden (10), Shikitei Sanba (8), and Tamenaga Shunsui II (7). The second most represented artist in Kyōka's collection is Kunisada's pupil, Kunisada II, with 24 titles illustrated. The majority of the remaining artists represented in the collection are other members of the Utagawa school of woodblock printing and illustration, including major figures such as Toyokuni (11), Kuniyoshi (11), and Yoshitoshi (1), and many artists about whom little is known, such as Utagawa Kuniaki, Utagawa Kunikiyo, and Utagawa Yoshitsuna. Other artists of note whose work is found in the collection include Kitao Shigemasa (1739–1820), Yanagawa Shigenobu (1787–1832), Keisai Eisen, Kawanabe Kyōsai, Adachi Ginkō, and Toyohara Chikanobu. Altogether, the collection presents a nearly complete image of *kusazōshi* production and publication in nineteenth-century Japan.

6. Stories About *Kusazōshi* and Ukiyo-e

In several of his stories, Kyōka treats *kusazōshi* as enchanted literary objects whose images come to life to haunt the present. Such stories present vivid narratives of the fantastic that take shape at the borders of realism and worlds of illusion, hallucination, and magic. Most of Kyōka's stories about *kusazōshi* were written late in his career, in the 1920s and 1930s, demonstrating that his interest in the genre continued throughout his life. These stories include "Blessings of the Holy Mother" ("Bunin rishōki," 1924) and "Picture Books in the Springtime" ("Ehon no haru," 1926). An earlier story, "Illustrated by Kunisada" ("Kunisada egaku," 1910), centers on a collection of woodblock prints of beautiful women (*bijinga*), rather than *kusazōshi*, although such images are attributed to the most famous and prolific illustrator of *kusazōshi*, Kunisada. A late story, "The Votive Light Volume" ("Tōmyō no maki," 1933), brings the world of *kusazōshi* directly into the space of the modern novel with the reproduction of an illustration by Kunisada that was printed on the endpapers of one of the final collections of Kyōka's fiction published during his lifetime.

"Illustrated by Kunisada" (1910) showcases Kyōka's ability to work in a realistic mode, with elements of fantasy integrated seamlessly into the narrative in surreal or dreamlike sequences, in a manner reminiscent of magical realism. On one hand, it is a realistic story centering on the mundane theme of a financial transaction, or a negotiation to purchase a collection of woodblock prints by Kunisada. On the other hand, the realistic narrative incorporates references to fantastic images drawn from the worlds of Edo-period folklore, media, and woodblock-printed art that color the reader's impression of the story world. In a direct nod to premodern media, the title of the story, "Kunisada egaku," or "Illustrated by Kunisada," takes the form of a traditional phrase used to identify illustrators in *kusazōshi*, in which illustrators' names regularly appeared followed by the verb *egaku* ("illustrates" or "draws") in the closing pages of each volume.[67]

"Illustrated by Kunisada" describes the return of Tatsuta Oriji, a resident of Tokyo, to his hometown, modeled on Kanazawa, where he tries to buy back woodblock prints by Kunisada from a former neighbor that were previously owned by his family. The story begins in the modern world, in a provincial post office, where the narrator, Oriji, is frustrated by the slow processing of a money order. After leaving the post office, Oriji wanders through the streets of his hometown, where he notices modern changes in the urban landscape, such as a new glass-fronted bakery on the former site of a *misemono*, or circus sideshow. Oriji's memory of the *misemono* evokes images of a world of magic, monsters, and cruel tales that he once knew as a youth, upon which the narrative begins to blur the lines between fantasy and reality. When Oriji was young, he would visit a *misemono* run by the so-called *kumo otoko* (literally the "spider-man"), who had a physical deformation in his legs that caused him to walk in an unusual manner, which the narrator likens to a spider walking across webs. Also performing at the *misemono* was a group of dwarf women, who could usually be found frequenting the local public bath. The bath once featured curtains with images of mythical warriors, such as Fujiwara no Hidesato, who was depicted fighting a giant centipede, although such curtains had been replaced with glass doors by the time of the narrative. When Oriji was young, his mother warned him that the *kumo otoko* had kidnapped the dwarf women and forced them to serve him as entertainers in the sideshow, a frightening account that left a lasting impression on the boy. While reminiscing on the legends and tales of his youth, Oriji recalls that traveling mountain ascetics, or *yamabushi*, used to stop by the outskirts of town, where they recited narratives of magic and horror, such as the tale of Princess Takiyasha, a sword-wielding princess with the power to summon frogs to her aid in battle. In a scene of cruelty that Oriji remembers vividly many years later, a female character named Himematsu is bound and hung over a smoldering fire of pine needles by her enemies. Oriji recalls that he handed over all of his allowance to the *yamabushi* to hear the tale of Princess Takiyasha, but adds that the *yamabushi* disappeared one rainy night without finishing the story.

In the scene following the *yamabushi*'s disappearance, Kyōka introduces elements of surrealism into the narrative with the description of a dreamlike illusion. Oriji relates:

> I stood blankly by the crossroads, lamenting the rain of the night before, and looked up at the sky. The clear, luminous light of a band of the Milky Way was cast from the edge of the mountains nearby, like a jeweled bridge, toward the rooftops of the townhouses. Above that, I could see a pure white shape and a faint golden outline with a hint of transparent lapis lazuli, a kimono sash loosely tied, a figure seen from behind, the shape of a woman like clouds stood up and walked swiftly before the light of the moon, then disappeared.[68]

Within a single sentence, Kyōka evokes the supernatural image of a woman traversing the skies, then negates the fantastic nature of the image by suggesting that the scene is little more than a daydream or a wishful thought evoked by the shape of the clouds.

The image of the ghostly woman is echoed later in the text in a sequence that mixes varying temporal and spatial settings, in ways that further demonstrate Kyōka's surrealistic technique. In the passage, the adult Oriji is watching a married woman in a kitchen who suddenly reminds him of his mother. He is thereby transported to the past in a narrative shift that occurs without warning. Kyōka writes:

> From within shadows, against a faintly glimmering light in the distance, in a thin blueish-green kimono, she leaned directly against the wooden door . . . there she stood, a woman.
>
> With a single glimpse, young Oriji saw a shape that no longer belonged to this present world. He was not surprised, although he felt as though he had suddenly shrunk in stature.
>
> A noble face of pure white looked back toward the child, then, like snow, suddenly disappeared. A creaking sound was made—it came from a hexagonal enclosure near the kitchen, within an inner well partitioned by a well curb of crossed wooden beams; it was the sound of a pulley ringing out. This was followed immediately by a clattering of small plates.
>
> By the sink, pale blue-green hairbands, from time immemorial, striking through clouds and trickling down like thick moonlight, loose strands of black hair straggled along the sides of a face with a high-bridged nose seen faintly in profile . . .[69]

In this passage, Kyōka juxtaposes clauses that the reader must piece together to form a coherent image (*nagashi no tokoro ni, asagi no tegara ga, toki narazu, kumo kara sasu, koi tsukikage no yō ni chira chira shite, kurokami no okurege hara-hara to kakaru* . . .). The loose grammatical structure produces the surreal image of an ephemeral, ghostlike figure, who disappears among the shifting subjects of the sentence.

Returning to the present time of the narrative, Oriji stops by the home of Heikichi, a former friend of his family, who once secretly purchased a collection of 200 woodblock prints by Kunisada that Oriji's mother had been forced to sell to a used bookstore. As Oriji relates, his mother had sold the prints so that she could purchase a set of science textbooks for him, but she later regretted the decision after realizing the value of the prints, including both their sentimental value and their price on the market. In a rush to buy a set of modern textbooks, the family had sold the antique prints at far too low a price, without realizing that their value would only compound in the years to follow. As Heikichi puts it, in the present time of the narrative, a single print by Kunisada was worth the price of 200 prints in the past, and thus he refuses to return the prints without receiving a just return on his investment.

In a metaphor that once again gestures toward fantasy, Oriji personifies the prints by Kunisada as his "older sisters" (*anesama*), while describing the textbooks as demons who have driven his older sisters into captivity. Kyōka writes, "That's the prestige of science. My young eyes had been blinded by the power of the science textbooks, whose black covers beat, bashed, and expelled my beautiful older sisters. Thinking back on it now, they were demons."[70] Back in the present time of the narrative, Oriji meets Heikichi's wife (the woman by the sink), who is nearly thirty years younger than her husband, and who greets the narrator with a lustful expression in her eyes. Oriji imagines that Heikichi is a kidnapper who has had a long and successful career in kidnapping, beginning with the abduction of his "older sisters," the prints by Kunisada, and continuing with his "kidnapping" of the young woman who had become his wife. At the conclusion of the narrative, Oriji announces his firm decision to buy back the woodblock prints, thereby demonstrating his dedication to recovering the mementos of his childhood, while also suggesting Kyōka's endeavors to evoke the visuality of Edo-period art in modern fiction.

In a later story, "Blessings of the Holy Mother" (1924), Kyōka combines references to the popular, erotic, and religious imagery of *kusazōshi* while conveying his abiding interest in Buddhist iconography as a key source of his literary imagination. The story centers on images of Maya Bunin, the mother of the Buddha, as represented in votive images in temples in Kanazawa, as well as in the *kusazōshi* series *The Life of Shakyamuni in Eight Phases*. The story also suggests the visual nature of Kyōka's writing process. At the conclusion of the story, Kyōka writes, "I have attempted to transcribe the sacred image of Maya three times before, in *The Ashoka Tree* [*Muyūju*, 1906], *The Tea House Suicides on Mt. Maya* [*Minejaya shinjū*, 1917], and 'Hall of the Sacred Mother' ['Bunindō,' 1911]. Even though I try again here, I am afraid that my clumsy effort is unable to evoke even the shadow of the shadow of her figure."[71] With this closing passage, Kyōka suggests that his stories begin with a central image, around which the narrative is structured, all with the purpose of leading the reader toward the image hidden within the story's depths.

In "Blessings of the Holy Mother," Kyōka relates the story of Kijima, a resident of Tokyo who returns home to pay respects at his mother's grave in Kanazawa. At a temple in Kanazawa, Kijima discovers a series of *oshi-e* ("raised-cloth images") modeled on illustrations from *The Life of Shakyamuni in Eight Phases*, whose opening episodes the narrator summarizes, providing descriptions of both the story and its illustrations. Later in the narrative, Kijima places an order for a votive image of Maya Bunin, with the request that her face be modeled on illustrations by Kunisada from the series. At the conclusion of the story, the statue of Maya Bunin arrives at Kijima's residence in Tokyo, where damage to the statue's hand is interpreted as a sign of its miraculous power.

The Life of Shakyamuni in Eight Phases, the *kusazōshi* series referenced at length in Kyōka's story, is often characterized as a religious or didactic work of literature, because it relates details of the life of the historical Buddha, along with moral lessons, although it was also a popular work of fiction that included liberal scenes of combat, magic, and romance, thereby transforming a religious narrative into popular entertainment. Illustrations by Kunisada, and later Kunisada II, contribute to developing an atmosphere of fantasy that pervades the work, with many creative depictions of fearsome monsters and demons, whom the Buddha and his followers confront using a combination of force, magic, and enlightening lessons. The narrative also includes many deviations from traditional hagiographies, including an early focus on the figure of the mother of the Buddha. In the opening chapters of the work, Maya Bunin is presented to the Emperor (Mikado) of the Kingdom of Magadha in ancient India (Tenjiku) along with her sister, Kyōdonmi, as potential consorts. The Emperor favors Maya Bunin, and thus Kyōdonmi attempts to curse her sister through a magic ritual involving the burial of an effigy, but she eventually relents in her attacks. Following a three-year pregnancy, Maya Bunin gives birth to the Buddha in a garden through her side, a variation on the theme of the Buddha being born through her sleeve, as is more commonly depicted in Buddhist art, and she dies shortly thereafter.[72] It was this tragic figure, the protagonist of the opening volumes of *The Life of Shakyamuni in Eight Phases*, that Kyōka sought to depict in his story.

"Blessings of the Holy Mother" exemplifies Kyōka's picturesque literary style, featuring extended passages of scenic description and dense layering of parallel imagery. In the story, the sacred and maternal figure at the center of the work is revealed via a sequence of images that appear in successive stages of the narrative, including the following images: memories of the departed mother of the protagonist, the appearance of the beautiful wife of a local priest, a photograph of the same woman found in a temple, a votive statue of Maya Bunin, woodblock illustrations of Maya Bunin by Kunisada, and *oshi-e* reproductions of the same illustrations. By combining these visual referents,

Kyōka layers descriptions of traditional and modern forms of visual art and media, from woodblock printing to photography, in ways that parallel his mixing of narrative techniques drawn from premodern and modern literature. The narrative takes place in a series of richly imagined settings, including verdant hills, city outskirts, Buddhist temples, a graveyard, a sculptor's studio, and a house in Tokyo, where the protagonist discovers series of related images that are superimposed onto the central image of Maya Bunin.

Kyōka opens "Blessings of the Holy Mother" with an extended description of the story's landscape. The opening passages of the story are quoted here at length, as a demonstration of Kyōka's visual style, although the diffuseness of Kyōka's narrative can only be partially captured in translation. Elements of Kyōka's style that appear in the quoted passage include superimposed and overlapping subjects, obscure presentation of characters and images that are only clarified later in the text, and sudden shifts from passages of realistic description to sequences of fantasy. In addition to these elements, Kyōka makes creative use of punctuation, with dashes and ellipses highlighting visual moments in the narrative. Kyōka writes:

> There she stood under clear lapis lazuli skies, within a grove of trees, in the center of a shadow cast by a hanging temple bell, its round mouth splayed open like that of a dragon, an incredible beauty—somebody's wife—when he saw the photograph, Kijima's blood ran cold . . . . . .
>
> Right at that spot, water that welled up from the roots of the mountain trickled down into a sluice and then turned into a stream. A bell tower cast its shadow upon shimmering waters, and thus the place was known as the Clear Spring of the Temple Bell.
>
> Kijima traveled along narrow roads through the city and its outskirts as he made his way to the foothills at the northern edge of town. Looking up once again toward the mountains, he began his ascent up a winding slope. In the lower reaches of the hills, near the edge of a shallow valley, the stream broke into a gentle flow. Opposite the stream stood the small cliff of a hill, where the bell tower was perched high. Even though it was already late autumn, the area was dense with bushes, and from within the middle of dry rustling leaves, one could almost spot the midday moon, or stars that appeared to be reflected on the bell. Still, it was not some famous spot, or the kind of place that merits a commemorative inscription . . .
>
> On one side of a narrow path, where small houses faced the water, backyards were planted with radishes and onions. Purple hyacinths

bloomed warmly through gaps in roughly woven bamboo gates, while dragonflies flew lazily in the space between the flowers. From their wings . . . . . . No, riding on their wings, shimmering air, heat haze, luminous spectral illusions, just like at the height of spring, drift and play . . . . . .

It had happened an hour earlier—under the heat of direct sunlight, Kijima had taken a seat on a crumbled embankment in the fields behind the houses—the photograph I was mentioning before—that was her true form.[73]

Throughout this passage appear sudden jumps in subject and perspective, such as the shift from a wide panoramic view of the landscape to a close-up of a dragonfly's wings, or from the past to the future of the narrative, hinging on the image of the woman's photograph. It is a passage that is difficult to understand on first reading, but it is clarified once the reader attains a wider picture of the story.

As the story continues, it is revealed that Kijima has returned home to Kanazawa to pay respects at his mother's grave at a local temple, Akamon Dera (modeled on Zenshōji temple in Kanazawa).[74] After commissioning prayers from an elderly priest, he decides to visit a temple that his mother would take him to when she was still alive, Rengyōji (modeled on Shinjōji), where he plans to pray before an image of Maya Bunin. On his way to the temple, Kijima is distracted by a beautiful woman washing laundry by a river, who gives him directions. At the temple, Kijima finds a statue of Maya Bunin, along with photographs of women with babies that have been offered in gratitude by female parishioners whose prayers for fertility and safe childbirth had been granted. Included among the photographs is one of the woman whom he met by the river, who is later revealed to be the wife of a local priest. This is the photograph mentioned in the opening passage of the story.

As Kijima wanders around the hallways of the temple, he finds a series of woven images modeled on illustrations by Kunisada from *The Life of Shakyamuni in Eight Phases* decorating the temple walls. Describing the *oshi-e* in detail, and in turn images from the *kusazōshi* series, Kyōka demonstrates his intimate familiarity with the text and its illustrations:

Written by Mantei Ōga, illustrated by Kunisada. That series of *kusazōshi*, printed by Kinjūdō, published during the Edo period, the series of picture books that rose like a storehouse of knowledge for the world, *The Life of Shakyamuni in Eight Phases: A Japanese Library*. From

Fig. 12. Utagawa Kunisada, illustration from *The Life of Shakyamuni in Eight Phases* (vol. 1, part 1): Lady Maya bathes while Kyōdonmi applies makeup. (Courtesy of Waseda University Library.)

among the illustrations found in the series, the women had selected pictures that displayed the sacred countenance of Lady Maya and had made them into framed *oshi-e*. Weaving *habutai* and *yūzen* silk together with threads of twill and brocade, they inlaid the images with bits of coral, putting flesh on the raised-cloth images . . .

Among the pictures, there's one of Lady Maya sitting before a full-length mirror, her hands poised on a washbasin that is painted black with lacquer. Naked from the waist up, her holy breasts are woven with

> white silk, like pearls wrapped in snow. Her shoulders, back, and upper body are all completely exposed, right down to the skin.
>
> Other images display the following scenes: Lady Maya descends from the clouds, from her residence in Tushita heaven, riding on the back of a white elephant with six tusks. Lady Maya appears in a dream robed in white, standing by the pillowside of one fast asleep. In one especially large frame, lotus blossoms bloom by the pond in Lumbini Garden. Beneath the Ashoka Tree, whose flowers emit a marvelous fragrance, Lady Maya reaches out her right hand, garlanded in Ashoka flowers, and from her sleeve is born the Great Sage Shakyamuni.[75]

As described further on in this chapter, Kyōka references a variation of the illustration of a woman in the bath by Kunisada in another story, "The Votive Light Volume." Additional variations of the same image by Kunisada can be found in *Fake Murasaki, Rustic Genji* (volume 12, part 2) and *The Tale of Shiranui* (volume 19, part 1), each time depicting a different character. In a manner similar to Kunisada's illustrations, Kyōka repeats variations of sacred and erotic images throughout his fiction, using language as his medium.

Kyōka references *The Life of Shakyamuni in Eight Phases* once again toward the conclusion of the narrative, when Kijima places an order for a votive statue of Lady Maya. Kijima initially asks a local sculptor and priest to model the face of the statue on Kunisada's illustrations from the series of *kusazōshi*. He then makes a mischievous request by asking the priest to model the face of the votive image on that of the priest's own wife—the woman from the photograph. The final incident of magic, or otherwise paranoid coincidence, occurs at the end of the story, when Kijima receives the statue of Lady Maya through the mail at his home in Tokyo. In the days prior to the delivery of the statue, Kijima had nearly lost two of his fingers in a door jamb. When he opens the package, he is stunned to find that the statue of Lady Maya is missing the same two fingers that he nearly lost. He is further disoriented on recognizing that the face of the statue does not resemble that of the priest's wife, but rather that of his own departed mother. It is a skillful conclusion to a story that centers on the transposition of images across media, with a suggestion of the intrusion of the supernatural.

Kusazōshi continue to haunt Kyōka's fiction in a story written two years later, "Picture Books in the Springtime" (1926). In this work, Kyōka again draws images from the pages of *kusazōshi* into the space of the modern short story, but this time around he emphasizes images of horror and gore, as well as the character type of the supernatural woman. Like many of Kyōka's sto-

Fig. 13. Utagawa Kunisada II, illustration from *The Life of Shakyamuni in Eight Phases* (vol. 37, part 1): Shakyamuni encounters his mother in Tushita Heaven. (Courtesy of Waseda University Library.)

ries, the work opens in Kanazawa and is related as the recollections of the narrator. At the beginning of the story, a younger version of the narrator walks down an alleyway in his hometown. During his walk, he catches sight of a sign advertising "book lending" (*kashihon*) through tree branches in the yard of an abandoned manor. As a fan of *kusazōshi*, he is intrigued by the advertisement, but he is afraid to trespass into the unknown territory.

While the narrator stares at the sign advertising *kashihon*, he notices a woman walking down the alleyway on her way back from the public bath, as indicated by her wet hair and washcloth. The boy is frightened and remarks that the woman looks like a *kechō*, a bird changeling, or a *tengu*, a long-nosed trickster deity with avian features, but then he recognizes her as a local fortune teller, whom he refers to as "aunty" (*obasan*). As the narrator relates, "aunty" was a famous fortune teller with supernatural powers. She once died and came back to life after three days, following a descent into hell, in a clear parallel to Christian accounts of the death and resurrection of Christ. Leaving open the possibility of alternate explanations, however, it is also said that she had simply fallen into a coffin in a drunken stupor. In any event, after she tore the lid off of her coffin, she had acquired the supernatural ability to accurately tell fortunes, and so she set up shop by the river, where she told fortunes from behind curtains adorned with images of stars and the moon. In addition to her supernatural abilities, the woman was highly educated. She practiced Zen Buddhist meditation and studied the Chinese classics of history, poetry, and Confucianism; many dozens of books lined the shelves of her fortune-telling shop. On encountering the boy in the alleyway, the woman invites him back to her shop by the river. At the shop, the boy relates news of the sign that he found in the yard of the manor, although he claims that the sign just appears in the evenings, only to disappear during the day. The woman warns him to stay away from the manor, then describes the background of the abandoned building. The story that she relates is a variation of the tale of the *onibaba*.

According to the fortune teller, the manor was once occupied by a feudal lord who became ill, and who was informed that the only cure for his illness was the fresh liver of a woman who had been born on the year, month, day, and hour of the snake. The lord spent an extravagant amount of money to purchase a slave woman matching the requirements. He then stripped her naked, nailed her to a rain shutter used as an impromptu cutting board, and had her white belly sliced open, so that her liver could be extracted. The woman then died in the garden of the manor. The lot became a scene of death once again during the fortune-teller's own lifetime. As she relates, she can still remember the incident of a man who collapsed in the yard as he suffocated on a scarlet silk bag filled with rice bran, the kind of item used for scrubbing and washing in the bath. As the town residents later learned, the man had followed a woman on her way back from the bath, accosted and tried to kiss her, but the woman defended herself by shoving her wash bag down his throat and suffocating him to death, in a scene of violent bravado from a female character that evokes the action of *kusazōshi*.

The boy continues to stare at the sign marked *kashihon* in the evenings until, one day, a ghostly woman grabs him by the hand and leads him to a shrine on the manor grounds. Opening the door to the shrine, the boy finds a single volume of *kusazōshi* set before a votive candle. The woman offers to read him the book by asking, "Shall I explain the pictures to you? [*etoki o shiteagemasu ka*]," after which Kyōka inserts an author's aside: "Note: *etoki* is when a mother, aunt, etc. shows a work of *kusazōshi* to a young listener and describes the story."[76] The boy then rushes home with the *kusazōshi* tucked into his kimono breast pocket, in an effort to conceal the book from his father. On the way home, he is shocked when he finds a passage depicting a woman born during the year, month, day, and hour of the snake, just like in the fortune-teller's story.

In a dreamlike scene toward the conclusion of the story, Kyōka unleashes a torrent of imagery that superimposes common visual elements of his work, in a literary sequence that is so abstract that it requires deep familiarity with Kyōka's literature to parse. In the scene, a storm releases a nest of vipers that flows through the streets of Kanazawa, along with the flooded waters of a local river. The narrative then unfolds as a sequence of transforming images: "Suddenly, before one's eyes, ah, a Shimada bun flows . . . a cut of scarlet-dappled cloth unravels and floats, with another glimpse, a single line of pure red snake. In a stack piled as thickly as a hand box, wrapped up in the variegated woodblock-printed covers of booklets—it flows like tumbling hand drums . . ."[77] The sequence ends with another surreal vision, that of hundreds of snakes nesting on a beach, all of which raise their sickle-shaped heads in unison and look up at the sky, in a haunting scene that is vaguely phallic in nature, thereby suggesting the nightmarish landscapes of surrealist painting.

In one of the final collected volumes of Kyōka's fiction, *To Hear Auspicious News* (*Yoki koto kiku*, 1934), Kyōka suggests the lingering presence of *kusazōshi* in his work by including the reproduction of an actual illustration by Kunisada directly on the endpapers of the book. It is an illustration from *Miraculous Devotion: Jizō's Journey* (*Kimyō chōrai: Jizō no michiyuki*, 1832) by Tanehiko and Kunisada, and also a variation of the illustration of Maya Bunin in the bath from *The Life of Shakyamuni in Eight Phases*, this time used to depict a celestial maiden. Kyōka's decision to print this particular image in his late collection of stories visually reinforces the impression of the erotic, maternal, and supernatural woman at the center of his narratives. Kyōka's reference to the illustration appears in the first part of a two-part novel, "The Votive Light Volume" ("Tōmyō no maki," 1933) and "The Sacred Heron Volume" ("Shinro no maki," 1933), included in the collection. The work is a modern, experimental novel in many senses, particularly because of its oscillation between the styles of a realistic modern travelogue, a naturalist novel, a tale of fantasy or horror, and a surrealist work of fiction that nearly collapses under the weight of recurring and transforming images.

In the early part of the novel, the narrative relates a visit by modern haikai poet Ogata Bonhai to a graveyard in an isolated area of Miyagi prefecture, in rural northeastern Japan, or the Tōhoku region. Ogata stops in the graveyard after visiting Sendai, the capital of Miyagi, and Matsushima, an archipelago of small islands covered in pine trees that is one of the most popular natural tourist sites in Japan. Kyōka hints at his own provincialism and lack of travel experience beyond the borders of Japan by describing a visit to Matsushima as "excessively ordinary" (*bon sugiru*).[78] As the narrator indicates, Matsushima is a site deeply rooted in Japanese tradition, because the same islands were visited by the preeminent haikai poet Matsuo Bashō and described in *The Narrow Road to the Deep North* (*Oku no hosomichi*, 1702), one of the most famous collections of haikai poetry and travel narratives in Japanese literature.[79] Ogata relates that, in contrast to himself, his friends all travel to distant locations around the world, such as Germany, France, Marseilles, Hamburg, and even Abyssinia (or Ethiopia). One of his friends even went island-hopping across the islands of the Pacific, where he witnessed whales in the open ocean. Ogata's travels, by contrast, bring him only as far as Sendai at the northeastern corner of Tōhoku. Still, Ogata is a modern traveler, because rather than being restricted to travel by trains and rickshaws, he continues his journey by renting a car. Kyōka is also a modern writer, with an awareness of the world around him, as evidenced by references to global cities in the story, from Marseilles to Moscow.[80]

Kyōka continues "The Votive Light Volume" by describing Ogata's visit to a rural temple and a shrine hidden in a cave deep in the wilderness of Miyagi prefecture. At the temple, Ogata finds a handbag (*handobaggu*) that he recognizes as belonging to a waitress from Tokyo named Osei. Naturally, he is shocked to come across the item in an isolated temple located so far from the capital city. As he ruminates on the modern culture of Tokyo, Ogata

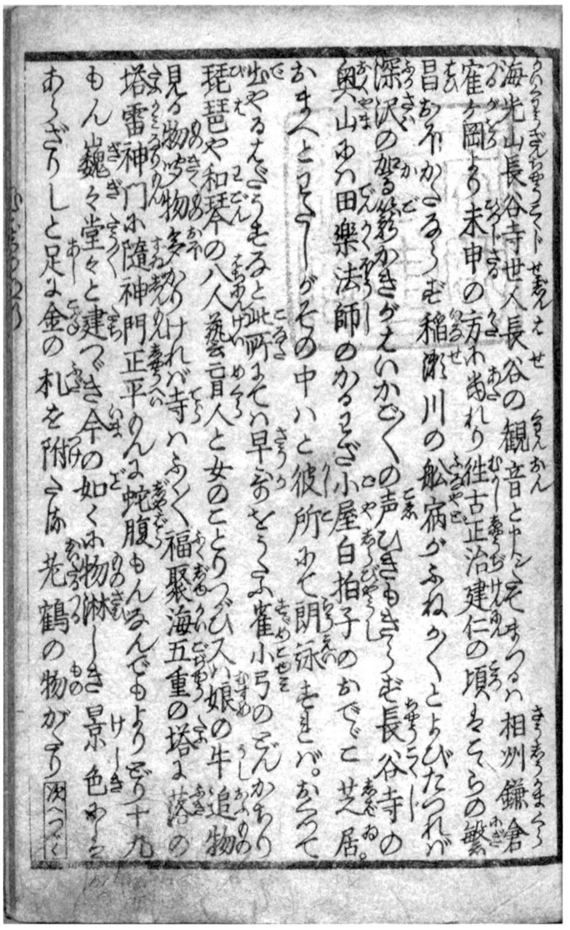

quotes a line of Edo-period slang from *Miraculous Devotion: Jizō's Journey*, an obscure *kusazōshi* that relates a fantastic tale of votive images (*ema*) that come to life at night in the Sensōji temple in Asakusa. The narrator describes an illustration of a celestial maiden in the bath, while also quoting a line of dialogue spoken by the animated image in the narrative. The line is delivered in exceptionally slurred, mimetic language of the Edo period, making it a difficult passage to understand within an already obscure reference. Kyōka quotes Tanehiko as follows:

> The angel from the painting on the ceiling of Sensōji temple strips down and applies makeup within a lotus-shaped basin and exclaims,

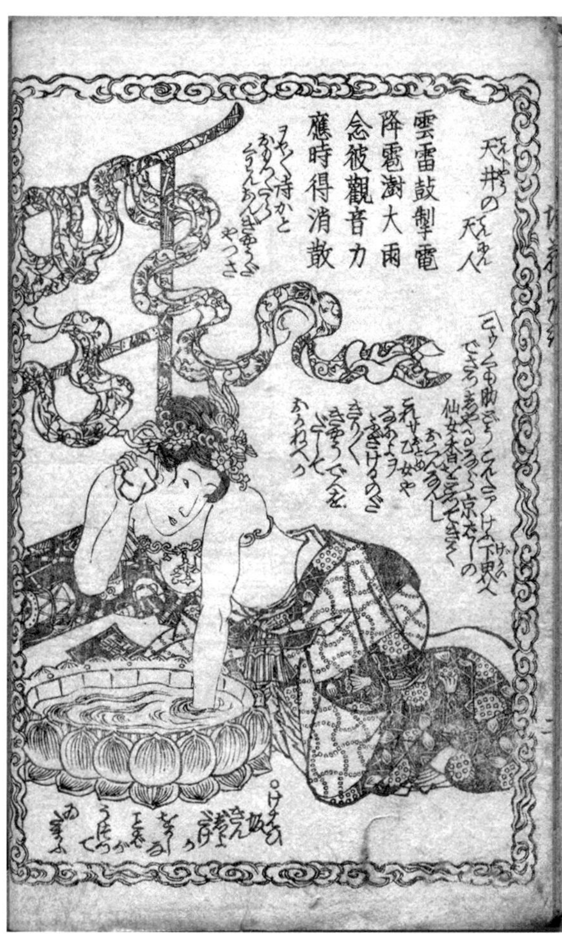

Fig. 14. Utagawa Kunisada, illustration from *Miraculous Devotion: Jizō's Journey* (*Kimyō chōrai: Jizō no michiyuki*, 1832): a celestial maiden from Sensōji temple bathing. (Courtesy of National Diet Library, Japan. Digital Library: https://dl.ndl.go.jp/pid/8929461/1/5)

> "Hey, Kumosuke, listen up, are you heading down to the world below the clouds today? If so, can you pick up some Senjokō makeup from Kyōbashi? Young women these days can't mess around. Can you hurry up and get me some today?"[81]

As a sign of the commercial nature of *kusazōshi*, as well as their implied female audience, the line serves as an advertisement for a real brand of white face powder that was sold during the Edo period.[82]

As "The Votive Light Volume / The Sacred Heron Volume" continues, the narrative becomes increasingly difficult to follow. Like the *kusazōshi* referenced in the text, the novel revolves around a logic of images, which seem to

Fig. 15. Komura Settai, cover design of *To Hear Auspicious News* (*Yoki koto kiku*, 1934). (Courtesy of Izumi Kyōka Kinenkan Museum.)

morph into other images every few pages. Many of these images are familiar from Kyōka's oeuvre, including references to the print of *Picture of the Lonely House at Adachigahara in Ōshū* by Yoshitoshi, Kishimojin, a votive statue of Kannon, white herons, poisonous tiger beetles, and a woman wielding a spear. In summary, Ogata proceeds to a cave where there is supposedly a hidden statue of a heron deity. The cave is guarded by a living votive image that possesses a *naginata* that is rumored to fall on the heads of intruders. On entering the cave, Ogata is attacked by a woman with a *naginata*, who turns out to be Osei, the waitress from Tokyo. She is pregnant and has come to the distant shrine with the intention of stabbing herself in the stomach, so that she might kill the baby within her womb. While relating this story, the narrator weaves in a related story about an ornithologist and a hunter who shot a white heron that transformed into a woman. As the story grows increasingly surreal, the *naginata* flies into the sky and becomes a crescent moon, while Osei disrobes and enters into a lake poisoned by tiger beetles. In an erotic passage that hints at the imagined sexual practices of Western cultures, Kyōka writes, "In the West, actually, even here in recent times they do things like this . . . it wasn't as though he tried to kiss her toes."[83] The story ends with a rapid sequence of disparate images, including references to a wooden statue of Kakinomoto no Hitomaro (the famed seventh-century poet), an elderly female medium from Niigata, the city of Moscow, a *kechō*, and Osei's eventual miscarriage, all within a chaotic outpouring of visual imagery in a loose string of seemingly random sentence clauses.

In *To Hear Auspicious News*, the print by Kunisada from *Miraculous Devotion* makes a direct appearance on the back endpapers of the collection. The book was designed by Komura Settai, a pioneering graphic designer and groundbreaking modern artist responsible for the design of many of Kyōka's books, who was also a close friend of Kyōka. Settai's emblematic illustrations and designs for Kyōka bring out further aspects of the visuality of Kyōka's literature, in part by highlighting the ghostly atmosphere and otherworldly imagery of his narratives.[84] For the design of *To Hear Auspicious News*, Settai illustrated the cover of the collection with a series of overlapping decorative surfaces, including layered imagery of seashells on a beach, a giant peony flower with yellow butterflies, and repeating figures of cranes against a blue background. The natural imagery of the design recalls the classical, poetic themes of Kyōka's fiction, while the overlapping surfaces display a sleek art-nouveau design that resonates with the modern elements of Kyōka's writing. Settai's reproduction of the woodblock print by Kunisada on the endpapers of the collection brings the world of *kusazōshi* directly into the pages of Kyōka's fiction, while assisting Kyōka with visually guiding the reader toward the image hidden at the center of his work.

In the preface of *To Hear Auspicious News*, Kyōka directs readers' attention to the illustration printed on the endpapers by inviting them to engage in a game of finding hidden pictures. He writes:

> As you read this collection, I ask you to find where the image of the half-naked, seductive heavenly maiden in the back endpapers comes from. This is not a picture hunt [*e-sagashi*], nor is it a ploy to force you to read through the entire book. It is merely a diversion for young boys and girls on long spring days. It is not the kind of thing that distinguished men of letters or moody authors might do, but is rather the kind of amusement that a writer of stories enjoys.[85]

By directing the reader's attention to an illustration from a work of *kusazōshi* printed just over 100 years prior the publication of his collection, Kyōka suggests that *kusazōshi* are still a major source of inspiration for his fiction. The image that he references encapsulates several of the themes that Kyōka

Fig. 16. Komura Settai, back endpapers of *To Hear Auspicious News*, a copy of a print by Kunisada from *Miraculous Devotion*. (Courtesy of Yale University Library.)

adapted from *kusazōshi* throughout his stories of the fantastic, including images of supernatural beings, Buddhist iconography, living votive images, and erotic portrayals of women. It is featured in a story that also functions on a logic of images, or in a modern literary mode that pushes the ability of language to function in a visual capacity. While building on the supernatural imagery of a premodern medium, Kyōka created distinctively modern works of fiction, whose fantastic images constantly overlap, transform, come to life, and shift out of sight.

Three

Literature in Translation

The Global Fantastic

1. Kyōka as Global Author

Kyōka rarely mentioned any Western authors or texts by name in his writing. Moreover, he seems to have intentionally distanced himself from Western cultures in his public persona. He famously wrote a *tanka* poem that appears to encapsulate his repudiation of the West, with the words, "It is my good fortune to owe nothing to the likes of Rodin or Tolstoy."[1] He furthermore appears to have made good on his claim to "owe nothing" to Western authors based on the books he acquired for his personal library. As widely noted, a 1941 list of Kyōka's library includes only three items from beyond East Asia: the *Arabian Nights* and two volumes of writings by Russian romantic author Mikhail Lermontov (1814–1841).[2] Based on such evidence, it is easy to see why scholars have often been quick to characterize Kyōka as an author who rejected or avoided global influences. As I show throughout this book, however, Kyōka clearly read many more texts of Western and other global literature than this list suggests. Three of the works of literature that most influenced Kyōka's approach to the fantastic were global in origin—the *Arabian Nights*, *The Improvisatore* (*Improvisatoren*, 1835) by Hans Christian Andersen, and *The Sunken Bell* (*Die versunkene Glocke*, 1896) by Gerhart Hauptmann. Such works contributed to Kyōka's creation of an elaborate literary world of fantasy, influencing his depictions of supernatural beings, eroticism, magic, and detailed romantic settings. These texts also represent different degrees or varieties of the fantastic, from the light, romantic fantasy of *The Improvisatore*, to the gory and erotic fairytales of the *Arabian Nights*, to the thoroughly magical world of goblins and fairies of *The Sunken Bell*. Kyōka's fiction reflected similar transformations in categories of the fantastic, from the uncanny to the marvelous, or from romanticism to fantasy and surrealism, in literary experiments inspired in part by his continued readings of world literature in translation.

In this chapter, I connect Kyōka's development of the fantastic to global literary networks by situating his work within the historical environment of translation and global influences that prevailed in the world of modern literature in Japan. As I have shown, Kyōka was raised reading global literature of the fantastic, such as the *Arabian Nights*, *The Golden Ass* by Apuleius, and novels by authors including Jules Verne in translation, in the *Yūbin hōchi shinbun*. Kyōka's interaction with foreign literature continued during his early years as a writer, when he apprenticed under Ozaki Kōyō, who was known to lecture his pupils on topics such as European literature, the English language, and the *Arabian Nights*;[3] Kyōka also appears to have been familiar with Kōyō's work in translation and adaptation. Kōyō was one of the first authors in Japan to translate Western fairytales, including stories by Andersen and the Brothers Grimm (Jacob Grimm, 1785–1863, and Wilhelm Grimm, 1786–1859), both translated while Kyōka lived with Kōyō as an author-in-training. Kyōka was also influenced early in his career by the translations of Mori Ōgai, who, in addition to being one of the most famous authors of the Meiji period, was one of the most prolific and influential translators of Western fiction in modern Japan. Scholars have claimed that Kyōka changed his literary style and themes after reading Ōgai's translation of *The Improvisatore*, a novel set in Italy that mixes elements of realism, fantasy, and travel writing. Kyōka also continued to be influenced by the *Arabian Nights*, one of his favorite works of literature throughout his life. Kyōka's admiration for the *Arabian Nights* connects him to the fantastic as a global literary genre, because the same text was one of the most influential works on the development of literature of the fantastic in Europe, and particularly in France.

Another crucial work on Kyōka's development as a fantasy writer was *The Sunken Bell* (translated as *Chinshō* in 1907), a fairy play (*märchendrama*) credited to Kyōka as a co-translation with Tobari Chikufū, a prominent scholar of German literature. Technically speaking, Tobari was the actual translator of the text, whose manuscript Kyōka heavily edited to match his vision of the narrative, dialogue, characters, and atmosphere of the work, but as the editor of Tobari's translation, Kyōka became intimately familiar with the fantastic content of the play.[4] *The Sunken Bell* was tremendously influential on Kyōka's later stories of the fantastic, particularly in deepening their supernatural elements.

Although Hauptmann was known primarily for writing naturalist dramas, his play *The Sunken Bell* delves fully into a world of fantasy, starring a cast of supernatural beings including a fairy, a water sprite, a wood sprite, and a witch, in the narrative of a bell-maker who defies conventional religion by building a pagan temple in the mountains. Following Kyōka's translation of Hauptmann's play, Kyōka began to feature monsters and other supernatural beings as major characters with talking parts throughout his work in theater and in his prose fiction. Kyōka's signature fantasy plays, including *The Demon Pond* (1913), *The Sea God's Villa* (1913), and *The Castle Tower* (1917), all clearly display the influence of Hauptmann's fairy play, as scholars have previously shown, but one can also see such influence in prose works of fantasy such as in *The Grass Labyrinth* (*Kusameikyū*, 1908), one of Kyōka's most explicitly supernatural novels.

This chapter traces different strains of global influence in Kyōka's fiction in three of his masterpieces of literature of the fantastic, *Shining Leaf Theater* (*Teriha kyōgen*, 1896), *The Grass Labyrinth*, and *The Castle Tower*, while also exploring the world of global literature in translation in Japan that influenced Kyōka's work, particularly the translations of Kōyō and Ōgai. Kyōka's stories examined in this chapter display the author's development from a writer of romantic tales to a definitive founding figure of fantasy literature in Japan. They also suggest the confluence of global influences that met in Kyōka's development of *gensō bungaku*. Combining elements such as the cruel pessimism of fairytales and nursery rhymes, the rhythmic structures and ghostly revelations of Nō plays, and the magic and richly imagined settings of tales of the supernatural from Europe and the Middle East, Kyōka created stories of the fantastic of unparalleled depth and vision in twentieth-century Japan.

2. Kōyō, Kyōka, and the *Arabian Nights*

In rare examples of direct references to global fiction in his oeuvre, Kyōka references content from the *Arabian Nights* in two texts, his early romantic tale, "Story of a Famous Princess" (1900), and his literary essay, "As Though I Knew" ("Shitta furi," 1907). Kyōka was preceded in these references by his literary mentor, Kōyō, who produced some of the first adaptations of the *Arabian Nights* in Japan. Kyōka directly references a lecture given by Kōyō on the *Arabian Nights* in "As Though I Knew," thereby demonstrating his familiarity with Kōyō's adaptations of the classical text. By adapting the *Arabian Nights*, Kōyō and Kyōka became connected to a lineage of writers of literature of the fantastic on a global scale, in a tradition spanning from the Middle East to France to Japan.

The global influence of the *Arabian Nights* can be traced to the famous translation made by Antoine Galland (1646–1715) from Arabic into French in the late seventeenth century. As a text of ancient provenance, the origins of the *Arabian Nights* are lost to time. References to a Persian text called *Hezar Afsaneh*, or *A Thousand Stories*, survive from the tenth century, while scholarly reconstructions have posited the existence of Sanskrit progenitors from as far back as the eighth century.[5] The earliest surviving manuscripts in Arabic are from much later, however, from around the late fifteenth century, and are speculated to have diverged significantly from earlier versions, accruing many new details of monsters, erotic encounters, and fantastic adventures in the intervening centuries.[6] The *Arabian Nights* was introduced to European audiences based on Galland's translations of the fifteenth-century text, as well as translations of tales related to Galland by a Syrian storyteller named Hanna Diyab. These include two of the most famous works from the collection, "Aladdin" and "Ali Baba," which are known as "orphan stories" because no original Arabic version remains.

As scholars have long observed, the *Arabian Nights* exerted a major influence on the development of literature of the fantastic in Europe. This influence can be seen in the Orientalist themes and atmospheres of early stories of the fantastic set in places such as southern Spain, with an emphasis on the region's historical connections to North Africa and the Middle East. Works that scholars such as Pierre-Georges Castex, Tzvetan Todorov, and Marcel Schneider describe as the earliest examples of modern literature of the fantastic fall into this category: *The Devil in Love* (1772) by Jacques Cazotte, and *The Manuscript Found in Saragossa* (1804–1805), written by Polish novelist Jan Potocki in French.[7] In the century and a half following the publication of Galland's translation of the *Arabian Nights*, numerous collections of fantastic tales imitated its title and content. Examples include *A Thousand and One Quarter Hours: Tatar Stories* (*Les mille et un quart-d'heure: contes Tartares*, 1715–1717) by Thomas-Simon Gueullette (1683–1766); *A Thousand and One Hours: Peruvian Stories* (*Les mille et une heure, contes Peruviens*, 1733) by Gueullette; *A Thousand and One Follies: Stories to Sleep Standing Up To* (*Les mille et une fadaises: contes à dormir debout*, 1742) by Cazotte; and *A Thousand and One Ghosts* (*Les mille et un fantômes*, 1849) by Dumas.[8]

Although the *Arabian Nights* remains widely known around the world based largely on popular media adaptations, particularly in works for children that feature magic and genies, the content of the original work is often gory, erotic, and sensationalistic in ways that are clearly not intended for children. The *Arabian Nights* features stories of men who kill their wives for sleeping with slaves, jinn who torture and kill humans who free them after responding to the jinns' requests to be freed, and women who transform people into animals, either as acts of revenge or simply because they can. The fantastic world of the *Arabian Nights* is full of sorcery, spells and counter-spells, trapdoors, dungeons, hidden palaces, abandoned cities, deserted islands, and supernatural creatures. In scenes of fantasy and horror, beautiful princesses invite unsuspecting travelers to magical feasts with erotic entertainment, only to threaten to kill their guests by the end of the night. Some of these details will probably sound familiar to readers of Kyōka's *The Holy Man of Mt. Kōya*, a text scholars have frequently compared to the *Arabian Nights*.[9] Indeed, it was precisely the most salacious content of the *Arabian Nights* that captured Kyōka's imagination, and the attention of writers including Kōyō, Tanizaki, and Akutagawa.[10]

As scholar Sugita Hideaki describes in his major study of the translation and reception of the *Arabian Nights* in Japan and around the world, the *Arabian Nights* was one of the first works of global, non–East Asian literature translated into Japanese during the Meiji period; it was also one of the most widely read and influential global texts during this time. A small part of the collection was first translated into Japanese in 1875 as *Kaikan kyōki: Arabiya monogatari* (*Unraveling Scroll, Astounding Mystery: Arabian Nights*) by Nagamine Hideki (1848–1927), based on a censored English-language version translated by George Fyler Townsend (1814–1900) for young readers.[11] The next translation of the *Arabian Nights* into Japanese was far more influential than the first. It was given an eye-catching but beguiling title, *The Greatest Astounding Text in the Entire World* (*Zen sekai ichidai kisho*), with the phrase *Original Title: Arabian Nights* (*Genmei Arabiyan naito*) appearing only as an inner title within the covers of the book. This is the book that Kyōka kept in his personal library, according to the list from 1941. The *Arabian Nights* was translated by Inoue Tsutomu (1850–1928) between 1883 and 1885 in ten volumes, then collected in a single-volume edition of just over 600 pages in 1885.[12] Inoue's translation was based on an unidentified English translation that was in turn based on Galland's French-language translation. This translation was so influential in Japan that the *Arabian Nights* was regularly referred to as the *Kisho*, or the *Astounding Book*, into the early twentieth century.[13]

One of the first adaptations of the *Arabian Nights* in Japan was written by Kōyō as his debut work of literary adaptation. According to author Yamagishi Kayō (1876–1945), who apprenticed under the famous author, Kōyō was a constant promoter of the *Arabian Nights*—he often carried around a copy of the collection and offered lectures on its stories.[14] Kōyō's adaptations of the

Arabian Nights present the work as a sensational collection of stories with oftentimes gory content, while also making connections between the *Arabian Nights* and literature from around the world, in early examples of comparative literary writing from modern Japan. The stories that Kōyō adapted center on the theme of jealous husbands who kill their wives, although Kōyō includes moral lessons in his adaptations on the perils of jealousy.

Kōyō's first adaptation of the *Arabian Nights* was of "The Husband and the Parrot," a frame narrative told on night 579 out of 1,001 in the latest English-language translation of the collection by Malcolm C. Lyons with Ursula Lyons.[15] In the tale from the *Arabian Nights*, a man who suspects his wife of adultery buys a parrot to report on his wife's nightly activities. To show her husband that the parrot's reports are unreliable, the woman simulates a fake thunderstorm, which the parrot describes to the man on the following day. Because no thunderstorm took place on the preceding night, the man doubts the parrot's reliability and decides to kill it, but he later catches his wife cheating with a younger man. He reacts to this discovery by slitting his wife's throat.

Kōyō adapted the narrative of "The Husband and the Parrot" as "The Japanese Wang Zhaojun" ("Yamato Shōkun," 1889), a confusing title that includes the name of one of the four great beauties of ancient China with a traditional place name used to refer to Japan, thereby mixing Japanese and Chinese references in the adaptation of an Arabic story.[16] Further complicating the cultural nuance of the adaptation is its setting, because Kōyō partially sets the narrative not in Persia or Arabia, but rather in the Netherlands, seemingly as a generic representation of a distant land. In Kōyō's adaptation, an elderly retainer in the Edo period purchases a Dutch parrot to spy on his wife. The bird vendor informs the retainer that the parrot's mother, back in the Netherlands, caught the wife of its owner in an act of adultery, thereby proving the reliability of its offspring as an informer; upon receiving the parrot's report of his wife's infidelity, the husband in the Netherlands shot and killed her. Convinced by the bird vendor's information, the Japanese man buys the parrot and takes it back to his home, where the parrot overhears the man's son and maid wishing that he would stay away from the house. The man mistakes the parrot's report as information originating from his wife and kills her with a sword. Unlike the wife in the original story, however, the woman was entirely innocent of the suspected act.

Kōyō's second adaptation of the *Arabian Nights* appeared in 1900, more than a decade after the first. This second adaptation was not actually a written text in the traditional sense, but was rather a lecture on the *Arabian Nights* that was transcribed and printed in the *Yomiuri shinbun* and later published as a book by Shun'yōdō in 1902.[17] Like the first adaptation, it features an exotic and confusing title: "The Famous Incense of Musashi, the Apples of Arabia: The Short-Tempered Blades of East and West" ("Musashi no meikō, Arabia no ringo: tōzai tanryo no yaiba," 1900). The word *tōzai* in the title indicates a comparison of East and West, and thereby suggests that Kōyō is categorizing the *Arabian Nights* as a "Western" text. Kōyō's lecture compares one of the better-known stories from the *Arabian Nights*, "The Three Apples" (nights 19 through 20 and night 25 in the Lyons translation), with an obscure work of Edo-period fiction, *The Hundred Samurai Families of Our Country* (*Honchō shoshi hyakkaki*, 1709) by Nishiki Bunryū, both as stories about false rumors that lead men to kill their innocent wives. In Nishiki's story, a misplaced box of incense leads a father to suspect his daughter of infidelity to her husband. The man beheads his daughter and sends her head in a box to his son-in-law, who brings the head to the man who spread the false rumor. The widowed husband then kills the man, before killing himself. In the story of "The Three Apples" from the *Arabian Nights*, a man travels from Baghdad to Basra and pays a large sum of money to buy three apples for his ailing wife. After he returns home, one of the apples goes missing, but later turns up in the hands of a slave, who secretly stole the apple from the man's son. The slave lies and says that the apple was given to him by the man's wife, whom he falsely claims is his lover. Enraged, the man kills his wife, beheads her, wraps her corpse in a carpet, places her corpse in a chest, and throws the chest into the Tigris River. When the man's son appears, crying because he is unable to find his mother, the man learns the truth about the stolen apple and realizes that he murdered an innocent woman.

In the conclusion of the lecture, Kōyō presents a scholarly theory on historical connections between these works that represents an early attempt to link global fiction in Japan. He conjectures that Nishiki's *The Hundred Samurai Families of Our Country* was directly influenced by the *Arabian Nights*, which he speculates was first imported to Nagasaki during the Edo period, then transported by a merchant to Osaka, where it was acquired by Nishiki and used as a basis for his own story. Although the theory is wild, it suggests that Kōyō recognized a degree of resonance between the *Arabian Nights* and the sensationalistic fiction of Edo-period Japan. In response to such theories, scholars have described Kōyō's lecture as one of the earliest examples of comparative interpretation of literature from Japan and the Middle East.[18]

Following Kōyō's example, Kyōka produced two adaptations of the *Arabian Nights* in the early twentieth century. The first of these adaptations,

"Story of a Famous Princess" (1900), is discussed in chapter 1 in relation to Kyōka's literary education at an English-language school in Kanazawa. As the reader will recall, in "Story of a Famous Princess," Kyōka compares his American teacher Lilika to Shahrazad from the *Arabian Nights*. Drawing on the literary structure and supernatural themes of the *Arabian Nights*, Kyōka uses multiple frame narratives to relate embedded stories of the fantastic, such as that of a snake that can play instruments with its tail and a man in France who finds himself in a hell of snakes. At the conclusion of the narrative, the narrator learns to tell scary stories after listening to Lilika, a development that might be equated with the lessons that Kyōka learned from reading the *Arabian Nights* from an early age.

Kyōka's second adaptation of the *Arabian Nights* takes the form of an essay, "As Though I Knew" (1907), and makes direct reference to Kōyō's lecture, "The Short-Tempered Blades of East and West," as a source of inspiration for its global literary framework.[19] In common with Kōyō's work, Kyōka's essay foregrounds the theme of jealousy and concludes with a remonstrance against excessive jealousy of one's wife. The essay is structured as a comparison of tales from Arabia, India, and China, supposedly as works with related themes. As such, it is another early example of comparative writing on global literature in modern Japan inspired by the *Arabian Nights*, and also a rare example of literary scholarship by Kyōka.

In "As Though I Knew," Kyōka compares tales of the fantastic from the *Arabian Nights*, a Chinese collection of strange tales known as *Xu qixieji* (*Zoku seikaiki*) by Wu Jun (469–520), and *Kuzō hiyukyō*, a sutra from the Indian Pāli Canon of Buddhist writings, translated by Kang Senghui into Chinese during the Three Kingdoms Period (220–280).[20] Kyōka describes episodes from the Indian and Chinese texts of people who produce food or other people from within their mouths. He compares these bizarre tales to a story in the *Arabian Nights* of a jinn who keeps his mistress locked in a box, as found in the opening frame narrative of the collection. In the story from the *Arabian Nights*, King Shahriyar and his brother Shah Zaman encounter a woman who has been released from a box, where she has been imprisoned by a jinn. She reveals to them that she is an expert in adultery. As evidence, she shows them seventy rings that she has collected from her seventy secret lovers. While the three narratives hardly seem related, Kyōka concludes "As Though I Knew" by remarking that the "three countries" (*sangoku*) of China, India, and Persia are like three old friends from the city of Edo who meet in Nagasaki and shake hands upon recognizing each other.[21] In his conclusion, Kyōka indirectly alludes to Kōyō's unlikely argument about the *Arabian Nights* being imported to Nagasaki during the Edo period, while also suggesting cultural connections between the three countries, or four including Japan, as friendly nations of the East.

Beyond simply referencing the *Arabian Nights*, in "As Though I Knew," Kyōka suggests the depth of his interest in the work by describing multiple translations of the text available in Japan, including in English, in a rare demonstration of his cosmopolitan interests. At the beginning of the essay, he remarks that he only has access, at the time of writing, to a censored English-language version of the work that is for use by schoolteachers. Based on the lines of the text quoted by Kyōka in English in his essay, "It is written in the chronicles of the Sassanian monarchs . . . ," scholars have identified the version that Kyōka was referring to as the translation by Townsend from 1865, titled *The Arabian Nights' Entertainments*.[22] Kyōka laments that the Townsend translation is missing the scene of the woman with the rings from her secret lovers, but he assures the reader that he has read such a scene before. He even claims to have sent an acquaintance to Maruzen bookstore, famous for its section of imported fiction, to check an alternate translation and confirms that his contact found an edition of the book that includes the lewd episode, although he does not identify the version in his reference.[23]

Following Kyōka, modern writers who were influenced by the *Arabian Nights* include Akutagawa and Tanizaki, both of whom recognized the fantastic and erotic content of the collection. Akutagawa, in an early story titled "Magic" ("Majutsu," 1920), referenced belief in "djinn" from the *Arabian Nights*, and he later wrote about the explicit sexual content included in the version of the work translated by Sir Richard Francis Burton into English from 1885 to 1888.[24] This was, until the recent Lyons translation, the only translation of the complete and uncensored text into English. It became famous in Japan following Akutagawa's description, and Tanizaki referred to it as "an obscene book" in a letter to a friend.[25] Tanizaki references the *Arabian Nights* in several stories, including "The Secret" ("Himitsu," 1911), "From Lahore" ("Rahōru yori," 1917), "The Mermaid" ("Kōjin," 1920), and *Some Prefer Nettles* (*Tade kuu mushi*, 1929).[26] Thus, three of the major Japanese writers of stories of the fantastic from the modern period, Akutagawa, Tanizaki, and Kyōka, were all known to be fans of the *Arabian Nights*, one of the most influential collections of literature of the fantastic on a global level.

3. Kōyō, Kyōka, Adaptation, and Translation

While Kōyō and Kyōka clearly shared an interest in the *Arabian Nights*, it is likely that Kōyō introduced Kyōka to other works of global literature during Kyōka's lengthy apprenticeship as a live-in student in Kōyō's home, from

October 1891 to February 1895, or for roughly three and a half years.[27] During this period, Kōyō translated and adapted fiction by authors including Molière, Zola, and Giovanni Bocaccio (1313–1375), in addition to fairytales by Andersen and the Brothers Grimm.[28] The likelihood of Kyōka having close familiarity with Kōyō's work in translation is suggested by a comment Kyōka makes in one of his essays, in which he describes assisting with the manuscript of a translation by Kōyō. In "Kōyō-sensei's Gatekeeper" ("Kōyō-sensei no genkanban," 1909), Kyōka writes that he personally prepared the final manuscript (*seisho shita*) for Kōyō's translation of *The Miser* (1668) by Molière, a play that Kōyō translated as *Short Sleeves in the Summer* (*Natsu kosode*, 1892) from an English-language version.[29] In preparing the final manuscript, or clean copy, of the work, Kyōka would have gained intimate familiarity with the details of Molière's play.

Many of Kōyō's own publications were adaptations or translations of Western fiction, including around thirty stories that have been positively identified as such. As scholar Sakai Miki finds, Kōyō relied on English-language translations of European literature from various languages, as well as the assistance of scholars of French and Russian literature, to translate and adapt work by authors including Andersen, the Brothers Grimm, Lessing, Bocaccio, Molière, Zola, Maupassant, Hugo, Turgenev, Tolstoy, Pierre de Marivaux (1688–1763), Fyodor Dostoevsky (1821–1881), and Anton Chekhov (1860–1904).[30] His translations of Grimm and Andersen represent some of the earliest translations of Western fairytales in modern Japan, particularly from Denmark and Germany. Such fairytales are notable for their dark and even morbid subject matter, which might have influenced Kyōka's own production of stories that combine elements of traditional fairytales with horror and grotesque imagery.

Around the turn of the twentieth century, Kōyō was one of the most popular and influential authors in Japan. Today, he is known mostly for his novel *The Gold Demon* (*Konjiki yasha*, 1897–1903), a popular novel about a student who becomes a loan shark after his fiancée leaves him for a wealthy suitor. As has been widely discussed in scholarship, *The Gold Demon* was one of the most widely read and frequently reprinted novels in early-twentieth-century Japan.[31] Kōyō was once known, however, for many additional works of literature that were enthusiastically received by readers and critics alike during his lifetime, such as *Two Nuns' Confessions of Love* (1889), *Three Wives* (*San'nin zuma*, 1892), *Darkness of the Heart* (*Kokoro no yami*, 1893), and *Great Passion, Great Sorrow* (*Tajō takon*, 1896).[32] He was also renowned as a translator and adapter of global literature, who was partially responsible for introducing the work of authors such as Zola and Molière to the Japanese reading public.[33] Many of Kōyō's adaptations, however, drastically altered the content of the works that he adapted, to the point that some of his "adaptations" are practically unrecognizable as such.[34] Oftentimes, it appears that Kōyō borrowed little more than an image or an idea as the kernel for his new stories. Other works, however, can be referred to as largely faithful translations.

Like Kyōka, the only foreign language that Kōyō had proficiency in was English, although he became interested in French and Russian later in life and he frequently worked with scholars of these languages. For his translations of Russian literature, Kōyō often worked with scholar and translator Senuma Kayō (1875–1915), one of the most prominent female translators of European fiction during the Meiji period. Together, they worked on short stories by Chekhov and Turgenev, as well as a partial translation of Tolstoy's *Anna Karenina* (1875–1877), published in 1902.[35] For French literature, Kōyō worked with various scholars, including Matsui Tomotoki, a native of Kanazawa who was introduced to Kōyō by Kyōka.[36] As one of his final literary projects, Kōyō worked with scholar of French literature Osada Shūtō (1871–1915) on a co-translation of *The Hunchback of Notre-Dame* (*Notre-Dame de Paris*, 1831) by Hugo.[37] According to author Uchida Roan (1868–1929), Kōyō spent the final days of his life reading an English-language translation of Hugo's novel in bed as he pressed for the completion of the project.[38] Scholar Kashiwagi Takao suggests that Kyōka was also familiar with *The Hunchback of Notre-Dame* based on similarities between Kyōka's early novel, *Tale of the Owl* (*Fukurō monogatari*, 1898), and Hugo's novel, most convincingly in the detail of a character with a physical deformity who is dropped off at a temple as a child and who becomes the caretaker of the temple's bell tower.[39]

The work in translation by Kōyō that Kyōka most clearly knew intimately was *The Miser* by Molière, due to his involvement in preparing the final manuscript. The play is a comedy that depicts the follies of an avaricious father who competes with his son for a much younger love interest and who suspects all of his servants of stealing a box of money that he had buried in his yard. In the unlikely conclusion of the play, in a scene that borders on fantasy, a suitor asking for the hand of the miser's daughter is revealed to be a nobleman from Naples who was lost at sea as a boy, rescued by a Spanish vessel, and who reencountered his father in Paris, thereby regaining his claim to nobility. Kōyō translated another play by Molière during the same year, *The Doctor Despite Himself* (*Le médecin malgré lui*, 1666), as *Love Sickness* (*Koi no yamai*, 1892). Another comedy, *The Doctor Despite Himself* is a play about a drunken woodcutter who is mistaken for a doctor and who uses his new profession, among other things, as an excuse to insist on examining the breasts of a wet nurse. With its bawdy humor and satirical examination of social behavior, Molière's plays might be compared to the work of Ihara Saikaku (1642–1693), a Japanese author of the seventeenth century, who was one of Kōyō's favorite writers.

Kōyō's translation of a story by Andersen, undertaken during the period of Kyōka's residency at his home, represents one of the first translations of a fairytale by the Danish author into Japanese. The story that Kōyō translated was "Little Claus and Big Claus" ("Lille Claus og store Claus," 1835), translated as "The Two Mukusukes" ("Ninin Mukusuke," 1892). Kōyō's choice of a fairytale must be described as one of Andersen's more bizarre and gruesome works, even when considered as part of a genre that often presents young audiences with dark themes. The fairytale tells of a bitter rivalry between Little Claus and his neighbor Big Claus that escalates to acts of grotesque violence.[40] At the beginning of the story, Little Claus kills and skins a horse. While wandering through a forest, Little Claus happens on the home of a farmer, whose wife is entertaining a sexton with a fine meal in the farmer's absence. When the farmer returns home, the sexton hides in a box, and the farmer invites Little Claus in for dinner. Little Claus tells the farmer that he has a conjurer in his bag (referring to the horse skin) and he has his "conjurer" produce a fancy meal, while actually revealing the meal that has been hidden by the farmer's wife in the oven. The farmer then asks Little Claus if he can conjure the devil, and he happily agrees. Little Claus then reveals the sexton hiding in the box. As a reward, the farmer purchases Little Claus's supposedly magical horse skin with a bushel of gold.

When Little Claus returns home, he informs Big Claus that he has made a fortune by selling his horse skin, so Big Claus kills his own horses and attempts to sell their skins, but finds that they are not as valuable as he had been led to believe. Later, Big Claus accidentally mutilates the corpse of Little Claus's grandmother while attempting to murder Little Claus. Thereafter, Little Claus convinces Big Claus to murder his own grandmother, whose corpse he attempts to sell to an apothecary. Having grown sick of Little Claus's tricks, Big Claus ties him up in a bag and prepares to throw him into a river, but Little Claus escapes from the bag and convinces an old man to take his place and forfeit his life, so that the old man might finally achieve his goal of reaching heaven. At the end of the story, Little Claus convinces Big Claus to let himself be tied up in the bag and thrown into a river, with the promise of a fantasy world of sea cows and sea maidens at the bottom of the river. Throughout the translation, Kōyō sticks close to the details of

Andersen's narrative, but he alters cultural markers, such as by transforming a Christian church into a Buddhist temple, and European household furnishings into more familiar Japanese ones.

The other fairytale translated by Kōyō during the period of Kyōka's apprenticeship was "The Devil with the Three Golden Hairs" ("Der Teufel mit den drei goldenen Haaren," 1812) by the Brothers Grimm.[41] It was first published by Kōyō as "Three Strands of Hair" ("Misuji," 1892) in the *Yomiuri shinbun* and later collected as *Ukigimaru* (1896), using the name of the protagonist of the Japanese version for its title. Like "Little Claus and Big Claus," "The Devil with the Three Golden Hairs" features morbid imagery and themes. In the story, a poor boy who marries a princess after presenting a forged letter to the king is sent by the king to collect three hairs from the head of the devil. On his way to hell, the boy encounters three people who ask for their problems to be solved, including a ferryman who is unable to stop from rowing his boat back and forth on a river. In hell, the devil is absent, but the boy encounters the devil's grandmother, who transforms him into an ant and tells him to hide in her dress. When the devil returns, the devil's grandmother plucks three hairs from his head, while procuring answers to the problems of the people who the boy met along the way. At the conclusion of the story, the boy becomes rich by solving the three problems that he faced, while the king is cursed with taking over the job of the ferryman. Again, Kōyō sticks close to the outline of the original fairytale, but he greatly expands its length, while also adapting many of its details to a Japanese cultural setting, such as by changing the devil into a "mountain man" (*yamaotoko*), a traditional Japanese ogre, and the devil's grandmother into a "mountain woman" (*yamaonna*). The macabre and imaginative details of these fairytales are echoed in the occasionally bizarre and morbid content of Kyōka's stories of the fantastic. As such, these tales might be included among the larger archive of fantastic stories, from traditional Japanese fairytales (*otogibanashi*) to European fairytales and the *Arabian Nights*, that influenced Kyōka's literary imagination.

4. Kyōka and *The Sunken Bell*

Along with the *Arabian Nights* and *The Golden Ass*, one of the other works of global literature of the fantastic that most clearly influenced Kyōka was *The Sunken Bell* by Hauptmann. Although little read today, Hauptmann was once one of the most famous and critically acclaimed writers in Germany. He was known primarily for his naturalist dramas, such as *Before the Dawn* (*Vor sonnenaufgang*, 1889) and *Lonely People* (*Einsame menschen*, 1891). *The Sunken Bell*, however, was written in the genre of the fairy play. *The Sunken Bell* relates the tale of Heinrich, a bell-maker, whose masterwork in bell-making is sabotaged when a wood sprite damages a cart carrying a church bell and sends it tumbling to the bottom of a lake. While traveling in the mountains, Heinrich falls from a cliff and is tended to by a forest nymph named Rautendelain, who lives in the company of elves, nature sprites, and a witch named Wittikin. After Rautendelain revives Heinrich, he forsakes his wife and children, throws himself into a passionate relationship with the nymph, and begins work on a bell intended for a pagan temple in the mountains. He later learns that his wife has taken her own life by throwing herself into the lake and he hears her ghost toll the bell from beneath its waters. The town vicar attempts to persuade Heinrich to abandon his blasphemous work, but he drinks wine offered to him by the witch and abandons his life to Rautendelain and pagan adoration of the sun.

Scholars have long identified *The Sunken Bell* as one of the most influential works of Western literature on Kyōka's literary imagination. Muramatsu identifies such influence in Kyōka's "combination of the world of humans and the world of fairies" in his plays.[42] Cody Poulton examines the colloquial style of Kyōka's edited version of the play, writing, "The translation of *Glocke* laid the groundwork for further experiments in Kyōka's own fairy plays, in which the fabulous prodigies of the author's imagination are made to utter comical dialogue that is informal and colloquial."[43] Scholars have found evidence of the influence of Hauptmann's play throughout Kyōka's theatrical writing, including in *The Demon Pond*, *The Sea God's Villa*, and *The Castle Tower*. The last of these three works, *The Castle Tower*, has long been treated as one of Kyōka's masterpieces, and even as one of the masterpieces of Japanese literature of the fantastic, because of its deep elements of fantasy and horror.

The Castle Tower relates the story of a visit from the fairy princess of Inawashiro Castle in Aizu, northeast Japan, to the fairy princess of Himeji Castle, also known as White Heron Castle, in Himeji in southwest Japan, followed by the narrative of the intrusion of a handsome young samurai into the upper reaches of Himeji Castle, where humans are forbidden. The play opens with a scene of fairy maidens fishing for flowers from the upper levels of the castle. Although they are only positioned on the fifth floor of the castle, the impression given throughout the play is that they practically inhabit the heavens, because they are able to fly through the sky, people below appear as small as ants, and an image is suggested of the Milky Way (*ama no kawa*) flowing below.[44] The maidens and their master, Princess Tomi, are visited by Princess Kame and her supernatural retainers, Shu no Banbō, a demon

Fig. 17. Komura Settai, back endpaper illustration from *The Red Plum Blossom Collection* (*Kōbaishū*, 1918): a living lion's-head mask (*shishi no kashira*). (Courtesy of Izumi Kyōka Kinenkan Museum.)

with a red face and a rhinoceros horn, and Shitanaga Uba, a woman with a long, snaking tongue, both variations of traditional *yōkai*. The visitors present Princess Tomi with a gruesome gift, the severed head of the master of Inawashiro Castle, but find that it has become messy during transportation. The long-tongued old woman slurps blood and juices from the head to clean it up before offering it to a living lion mask who rules over the fairy world within the castle. Back on the veranda of the castle, Princess Tomi tricks the falcon of the lord of the castle into venturing into her domain and holds it captive. A young samurai, Himekawa Zushunosuke, then appears on the upper floors of the castle to retrieve the falcon. Princess Tomi tells him to leave the forbidden area of the castle and never return, but she also feels compelled to retain the young man, having fallen in love with him on first sight. The man battles a giant monk demon (*ōnyūdō*) when he attempts to descend to the lower floors and is eventually confronted by other samurai, who accuse him of stealing an ancestral helmet, which was actually stolen by Princess Tomi.

At the conclusion of the play, the fairies in the castle are all blinded when the warriors stab the eyes of the lion mask, but their sight is restored when a master sculptor appears and carves new eyes for the mask.

Considering the mainstream of realist and naturalist fiction that dominated the literary scene of early-twentieth-century Japan, *The Castle Tower* feels like a story from another time and place. As Muramatsu and others have pointed out, its supernatural beings are drawn from Japanese folklore, although the overall structure and atmosphere of the play seem to draw on the fairy world of *The Sunken Bell*, as well as Kyōka's own lavish imagination. In reference to the gruesome scene of the severed head offered as a gift to a princess, Muramatsu speculates that Kyōka might have been influenced by the play *Salomé* (1893) by Oscar Wilde.[45] Although there is no direct evidence that Kyōka read or watched the play, Muramatsu makes a convincing case for influence by comparing grotesque details in the scenes of severed heads from both stories, particularly details of kissing or licking the severed head and describing it as overripe or juicy. Muramatsu also notes that Japanese theatergoers and critics of the time showed tremendous interest in Wilde's play. As he writes, *Salomé* was translated by Kobayashi Aiyū (1881–1945) in the major literary magazine *Shinshōsetsu* in 1909, and again by Mori Ōgai in *Kabuki* during the same year.[46] It was first staged in 1913 and was widely discussed throughout major newspapers and literary magazines, making it likely that Kyōka, a regular playwright and theatergoer, would have been familiar with the work, either in text or on stage. Regardless of this particular influence, *The Castle Tower* appeared as a work unlike almost anything else in Japanese theater of the time. Shibusawa Tatsuhiko credits part of the success of the play to the fantastic setting and unusual vertical structure of the castle tower, writing, "A beautiful dream such as this, with its scenes of surrealism, *The Castle Tower* occupies an honorable position within the history of Japanese drama, which has never attempted to jump beyond the boundaries of the earth in this way before, and never will again."[47] The fantastic cast and cosmic scale of *The Castle Tower* are echoed in Kyōka's later works of prose fiction, such as *The Grass Labyrinth*, a work that features an otherworldly ending that is staged across heavenly space, as described further on in this chapter.

5. Kyōka, Ōgai, Andersen, and *The Improvisatore*

One of the most influential works of global literature on Kyōka's development as a modern author was *The Improvisatore* (1835) by Hans Christian Andersen, a novel that combines realism with light touches of fantasy and elaborate descriptions of the landscapes of modern Italy. *The Improvisatore* was famously translated as *Sokkyō shijin* (*The Improvisational Poet*) by Mori Ōgai from a German translation of the Danish-language original between 1892 and 1901.[48] *Sokkyō shijin*, as the work is generally called in Japan, has long been treated by scholars as a masterpiece in literary translation that influenced a generation of writers with its elaborate prose style, including novelists such as Shimazaki Tōson (1872–1943), Tayama Katai (1871–1930), Oguri Fūyō (1875–1926), Nagai Kafū, and Kyōka, along with poets such as Yosano Akiko (1878–1942), Yosano Tekkan (1873–1935), Ishikawa Takuboku (1886–1912), and Kitahara Hakushū (1885–1942).[49] It was discussed by Kyōka with deep fondness many years after its serialization and has been treated by scholars as a novel that transformed Kyōka's literary style. Muramatsu characterizes Kyōka's encounter with *The Improvisatore* as one that set him on a new literary trajectory, essentially transforming him from an author of social novels written in terse, academic prose to an author of nostalgic tales written in flowing romantic language.[50] *The Improvisatore*, in turn, is only one part of the much larger translation project by Ōgai, a project that Kyōka appears to have followed throughout his formative years as a writer. Although Ōgai is best known today for writing some of the first works of modern literature in Japan, and for his literary essays and historical fiction, during his lifetime he was also known as one of Japan's most influential translators, if not the preeminent translator of European fiction of his era. As scholar Yoshida Seiichi points out, at least one third of Ōgai's entire literary output consisted of translations, including translations of stories by dozens of European authors.[51] Yoshida suggests that Ōgai was even more valued as a translator than as a writer of original fiction.

Ōgai's work as a translator is too extensive to describe in more than summary form here. Such work deserves a book-length study to trace the transformative effect of Ōgai's translations on the modern literary establishment in Japan. In Japanese scholarship, an entire book is devoted only to his translations of works originally written in Scandinavian languages, including major translations of works by authors such as Andersen, Ibsen, and August Strindberg (1849–1912).[52] In common with his other translations, Ōgai translated the work of these authors from German versions. Ōgai's translations introduced the work of major European and American writers to Japanese audiences, including the work of Hoffmann, Poe, and Rainer Maria Rilke (1875–1926). In his selection of Western authors for translation, Ōgai seems to have aimed for coverage, including of geographic region, time period, and genre, while also attempting to discover up-and-coming authors, or authors who appeared to be in the vanguard of their literary scenes. An example of Ōgai's trendsetting work can be found in the collection *Tales from Various Countries* (*Shokoku monogatari*, 1915), a collection featuring work by Poe, Rilke, Tolstoy, Dostoevsky, and Henri de Régnier (1864–1936). Ōgai's most influential translations include *The Improvisatore* by Andersen, *Faust* (1808–1832) by Johann Wolfgang von Goethe (1749–1832), and *Salomé* by Wilde, in addition to work by Rilke, Strindberg, and Ibsen. As a sign of his prescience and taste, Ōgai was one of the first critics in the world to realize the value of Rilke's poetry.[53]

Overall, Ōgai was considered to be something of a pathfinder or a national instructor when it came to introducing European and American literature to Japan. Muramatsu describes the literary establishment as eagerly awaiting his every translation and as refraining from translating the same authors that Ōgai was working on.[54] Author Satō Haruo (1892–1964) describes one of Ōgai's early collaborative works in translation, *Vestiges* (*Omokage*, 1889), a collection of short poetic excerpts from longer works by authors such as Lord Byron (1788–1824), Shakespeare, and Goethe, to be "an upper level textbook" of poetic composition.[55] Both Satō and Akutagawa treated Ōgai's translations as essential reading for the modern author.[56] Kyōka confirms the character of Ōgai as an instructional figure in an essay, while also including himself as one of Ōgai's national pupils.

Kyōka's reference to Ōgai's work in translation can be found in a memorial essay that he wrote in August 1922, one month after Ōgai's passing. The essay, titled "On *Foam on the Waves Collection*, etc." ("*Minawashū* no koto nado"), recounts Kyōka's interactions with Ōgai as part of the Useikai (Voice of the Rain Gathering), a short-lived literary meeting of prominent Japanese writers inaugurated in 1917 that also included such major authors as Kōda Rohan, Shimazaki Tōson, Tayama Katai, Kunikida Doppo, and Tokuda Shūsei, in addition to Ōgai and Kyōka.[57] The title of the essay refers to Ōgai's early volume of collected European and American literature in translation, *Foam on the Waves Collection* (*Minawashū*, 1892), which Kyōka references in an anecdote related in the essay, although most of the essay focuses on another work in translation by Ōgai, *The Improvisatore*. In his essay, Kyōka reveals that he was fanatically devoted to *The Improvisatore*, a work that he read in multiple editions and apparently memorized passages from, while also suggesting that Ōgai's other work in translation, such as the *Foam on the Waves Collection*, was considered required reading by the literary establishment.

Kyōka begins his anecdote about the *Foam on the Waves Collection* by relating that, as a matter of course, all members of the gathering had responsibly purchased the collection and added it to their personal libraries (*kokoroete hizō shite*) when it was first published. He later revealed to Ōgai, however, that he was forced to pawn his copy of the book a few years after purchasing it.[58] While this detail might appear to indicate that Kyōka did not value the collection seriously, it is worth noting that Kyōka purchased the book in 1892, at the fairly high cost of forty sen, during a time in his life when he often suffered from poverty and relied on friends for food and lodging. According to Kyōka, the collection sold out shortly after it was published and became a prized commodity on the book market, going for close to its original price at the pawnshop. Kyōka attempted to defend his action to Ōgai by explaining that, on pawning the book, he was finally able to afford food, a haircut, and a bath. Kyōka relates that Ōgai responded to his confession with some surprise, remarking, "Really? They gave you that much for it?" and that he looked away while forcing a bitter smile. Kyōka, apparently embarrassed, complains that Ōgai had probably never in his life had occasion to visit a pawnshop.

Although Kyōka ultimately pawned Ōgai's collection of translations, the fact remains that he purchased the *Foam on the Waves Collection* on its original publication, when his resources were limited, and while he was attempting to enter the ranks of the literary establishment in Tokyo. It thus seems likely that he would have become familiar with at least part of the content of the collection. As one of the most influential collections of translated global fiction in 1890s Japan, the book served as a capacious and enlightening introduction to world literature, primarily European and American literature of the eighteenth and nineteenth centuries, as it does even today. The collection features translations of short stories, novels, and plays by many European and American authors, including Lessing, Hoffmann, Kleist, Turgenev, Tolstoy, Alphonse Daudet, Aloisia Kirschner, Washington Irving, Brett Harte, and Pedro Calderón de la Barca, among others. This is in addition to three stories by Ōgai himself: "The Dancing Girl" ("Maihime," 1890), "A Tale of Foam on the Water" ("Utakata no ki," 1890), and "The Courier" ("Fumizukai," 1891), all set in Germany and based on Ōgai's experience of studying abroad.

Highlights from the *Foam on the Waves Collection* suggest something of the experience of distant lands and cultures that it presented to its readers, as well as the literary themes that defined Ōgai's early work as a writer. Such themes include those of civilization and progress (*bunmei kaika*), justice, violence, traveling musicians, and the value of art to society. The collection is also notable as a snapshot of the genres considered most valuable by the literary establishment in Meiji-period Japan. In common with most of Ōgai's work in translation, the majority of the stories in *Foam on the Waves Collection* feature realistic settings and plots, with almost no elements of overt fantasy or supernatural content. The only exceptions are "Rip van Winkle" (1819) by Irving and an excerpt from "Visions: A Phantasy" (1872) by Turgenev. This tendency to avoid fantasy might be seen throughout Ōgai's work as a writer and translator, although two of his most famous and influential translations, *The Improvisatore* and *Faust*, break this pattern.

Summaries of works that Ōgai included in his collection suggest the larger concerns of the book, which might be considered as a literary guidepost or milestone for contemporary writers. The earliest translation in the *Foam on the Waves Collection*, in multiple senses, is of *The Mayor of Zalamea* (*El alcalde de Zalamea*, ca. 1642) by Calderón, a play from seventeenth-century Spain translated by Ōgai together with his younger brother, Miki Takeji (1867–1908); an odd detail for an author who had minimal interaction with Spanish literature throughout the rest of his career.[59] In addition to being the oldest work in the collection chronologically, it was also Ōgai's first work in translation, translated as *High-Toned Melody: A Composition for Guitars* (*Shirabe wa takashi: gitarura no hitofushi*, 1889). *The Mayor of Zalamea* is a play about crime and vengeance, in which a troop of soldiers stays in the small town of Zalamea, in rural Extremadura, Spain, where a military captain sexually assaults the daughter of a local man. After the local man is unexpectedly elected mayor by the town's citizens, he orders the execution of the army captain. The reference to the guitars in Ōgai's title is to the scene of a serenade played by La Chispa, a gallant woman in the military regiment who intermittently sings and plays guitar and castanets in the play. Similar themes of violence and justice can be found in *Emilia Galotti* (1772) by Lessing, a play set in the Emilia-Romagna region of Italy. In the play, the eponymous character is kidnapped by a corrupt regional prince, who has his henchman murder the woman's fiancé on her wedding day. Rather than marry her fiancé's murderer, the prince, Emilia convinces her own father to kill her. At the conclusion of the play, her father agrees to meet justice at the hands of the corrupt prince for the murder of his own daughter.

A major romantic writer featured in the collection is Kleist, although Ōgai chose to translate relatively realistic works of fiction by the German author. The two short stories by Kleist translated by Ōgai, "The Earthquake in Chile" ("Das Erdbeben in Chili," 1807) and "The Betrothal in Santo Domingo" ("Die Verlobung in St. Domingo," 1811), present violent and exotic tales of societies beset by racial and religious turmoil at the farthest reaches of the Spanish and French colonial empires ("The Betrothal in Santo Domingo" is actually set in Haiti, on the island of Hispaniola). "The Earthquake in Chile" depicts a zealous and intolerant Catholic society in seventeenth-century Spanish Chile, in which a woman and her lover are condemned to death for having sexual relations at a Carmelite convent. Following an earthquake, the couple manages to escape, but they are caught in a riot in a church that ends with the brutal murder of a child. In "The Betrothal in Santo Domingo," black slaves turn against white slaveowners and kill the white inhabitants of Haiti during the revolt that led to the nation's independence. One former black slave, Toni, tries to protect a Swiss resident of the island, Gustav von der Reid, from the revolting slaves, but when Gustav mistakenly believes that Toni is planning to deliver him into the hands of his enemies, he kills her with a pistol. After realizing his mistake, he turns the gun on himself.

One of the most extensive and significant translations in *Foam on the Waves Collection* is *The Story of a Genius* (*Die geschichte eines genies*, 1884), a realistic novel by Aloisia Kirschner (a.k.a. Ossip Schubin). Kirschner, an Austrian writer from Prague, has become a largely unknown author, about whom only a bare minimum of information is available. However, her representative novel was once popular in Japan, based on Ōgai's translation.[60] *The Story of a Genius* relates the narrative of a violinist of Roma, Hungarian, and Flemish descent who is raised in the backstreets of Brussels, where he is discovered by a famous composer, who eventually steals both his fiancée and his music. The protagonist's genius goes to waste when he ends up wandering the backstreets of Paris, where he plays music for children and is cared for by a mother who works for the circus. Ōgai revisits the theme of an itinerant musician in his translation of "Lucerne" by Tolstoy, a standout work of naturalistic fiction from the collection. In "Lucerne," Tolstoy describes the scene of a traveling guitarist from northern Italy at a resort town in Switzerland. The guitarist displays uncommon talent when he plays music for the tourists, but they refuse him any support when he begs for money during his performance. The narrator of the story, modeled on Tolstoy, is outraged by the cruelty of the crowd, because they fail to acknowledge the joy that the itinerant musician has brought to them by his performance.

The most important and influential writer of literature of the fantastic featured in the *Foam on the Waves Collection* is Hoffmann, although Ōgai once again chose to translate a relatively realistic story by the author, "Mademoiselle de Scudery" ("Das fräulein von Scuderi," 1819). As a sign of Ōgai's literary values, in the introduction to the collection, Ōgai even claims that Hoffmann is not entirely to his taste and clarifies that he was urged to translate "Mademoiselle de Scudery" by newspaper editors.[61] Nevertheless, "Mademoiselle de Scudery" features haunting imagery associated with literature of the uncanny, such as hidden passageways that are opened by operating switches found in statues and a murderer who prowls the shadows of a labyrinthine city. "Mademoiselle de Scudery" relates an elaborate detective story about a goldsmith who murders his customers and takes back his handiwork because he is unable to stand the idea of parting with his prized jewelry. The novella portrays the society of Paris as being completely engulfed in fear due to constant thefts, poisonings, stabbings, and murders in its streets, as well as unjust trials, detentions, and executions by the authorities. Hints of fantasy find their way into Ōgai's translation, including a reference to the print of a devil sold in "picture book stores" (*ezōshiya*) in Paris, representing demonic powers aligned with criminal organizations, and descriptions of the practices of superstitious Parisians, who wear amulets and douse themselves in holy water as protections against misfortune.[62]

If "Mademoiselle de Scudery" borders on the fantastic, two other works in the collection enter fully into the realm of fantasy. One is "Rip van Winkle" (1819) by Irving, a story that might be referred to as a fairytale. In the popular American tale, a Dutch colonist wanders into the Catskill Mountains of New York, where he encounters a group of elflike creatures playing ninepins. They give him a strange drink, he falls asleep, and when he returns to his village, he finds that twenty years have passed in what seemed like the span of a night. Although Rip van Winkle is reasonably shocked at the discovery, he quickly adjusts and makes this new, unfamiliar home his own. The other story of the fantastic in the collection comes from "Visions: A Phantasy" (1872) by Turgenev. However, Ōgai excerpts only a few pages from the story, so that it is difficult to imagine the larger context of the work. In the passage that Ōgai translates, a character who has been flying across Europe in a kind of dream state encounters the flying head of Julius Caesar.

While Ōgai appears to have made a considerable impact on the literary scene with the *Foam on the Waves Collection*, such that it was almost immediately bought up by many aspiring writers in Japan, one of his most influential translations was his next project, a nearly decade-long translation of *The Improvisatore*. Ōgai translated the novel from 1892 to 1901, although with a long pause between 1894 and 1897. *The Improvisatore* has been discussed as the most significant romantic novel translated into Japanese during the Meiji period, although it might furthermore be described as a novel bordering on the fantastic, or one that exists at the borders of genres, somewhere between realism and fantasy. In relation to its hybridity, John Timothy Wixted characterizes the work as "a fairy-tale, a *Bildungsroman*, a picaresque novel, and a travelogue,"[63] whereas Nagashima Yōichi describes it as combining "dreamy realism" with a "fairy-tale world."[64] In Japan, *The Improvisatore* is almost always referred to by the title of Ōgai's translation, *Sokkyō shijin*, and is practically treated as though it were a work by Ōgai himself. This tendency can be seen in Kyōka's essay, which does not even mention the name of the original author of the text, Andersen. On this phenomenon, Nagashima writes, "Its fame and popularity has been so enormous that it is considered to be one of the classics of modern Japanese literature. Allured by Ōgai's superb translation into an elegant and flowing literary language, many readers in Japan have expressed their admiration, saying that Ōgai's translation, *Sokkyo shijin*, is 'better' than Andersen's original, *Improvisatoren*."[65]

Nagashima explains that Ōgai's translation of *The Improvisatore* departs from the original in its transformation of such key elements of the text as its narrative perspective and linguistic register or by rendering the text into *gabuntai* ("elegant prose"), which hides the position of the first-person narrator and turns prosaic passages into quasi-classical Japanese poetry.[66] Nevertheless, even though it has been radically modified in places, Ōgai's rendition is still based closely on Andersen's *Improvisatore*. One has only to compare Ōgai's translation to versions of the text in other languages (I have to rely on the most recent English-language translation, by Frank Hugus, due to my inability to read either Danish or German) to find corresponding passages of descriptive prose, names of people and places, and matching stylistic choices in terms of vocabulary and grammar. As Nagashima points out, it was "the exotic scenery of Italy" described in the text that most "caught the heart of young Japanese for many decades."[67] Ōgai himself recognized the exotic scenery and romantic atmosphere of the story as its major attractions, referring to the text as a balance between realism and romanticism and remarking that it allowed the reader to leave behind the "dusty industrial metropolis" and "enter into a picturesque other world of mountains and water."[68] Far from avoiding romantic elements of the narrative, Ōgai includes passages of fantasy throughout his translation.

The Improvisatore tells the story of Antonio, a boy from Rome who is orphaned at an early age, cared for by a wealthy Roman family, and provided with a private education. He rejects his life of comfort and sets off on a journey across the Italian peninsula after becoming involved in a duel over a Spanish opera singer named Annunziata. Antonio makes his living during his journeys as an *improvisatore*, an improvisational poet, singer, and guitar player, a career that brings Antonio modest fame and financial stability. Over the course of his travels, Antonio arouses feelings of love and admiration in numerous women, including married women and noble daughters, who vie for his affection. Although *The Improvisatore* is a relatively realistic novel that features extensive description of travel through real Italian cities and rural landscapes, it is also full of improbable details that belong more to the world of fantasy than to a novel modeled on real life. Alongside realistic descriptions of places and culture, *The Improvisatore* features details of fortune-telling, folk magic, dreamlike experiences in crypts and grottoes, and constant prayers to the Virgin Mary. The overall structure of the novel is one of fortuitous encounters with familiar people across Italy and a life that seems to be guided by fate, as though in answer to Antonio's prayers. True to the fashion of literature of the fantastic, the interpretation of any of the miraculous events in the novel is left to the reader, although the constant succession of improbable meetings eventually pushes the boundaries of plausibility.

It is almost a rule of the *Improvisatore* that characters met in one city will be encountered again in another distant city during a moment of need, in chapter after chapter. The suggestion throughout the novel is that Antonio's entire life is guided by fate, either because he chooses to believe in fate and interprets events accordingly, or because fate is an operative force in his life. Toward the beginning of the novel, Antonio witnesses the scene of an eagle that drowns while trying to catch a fish. When his mother dies shortly afterward, he interprets the scene as having been a prophecy of her death. On the same occasion, Antonio's future fortune as a traveling musician is foretold by a wise old woman who cooks up poisons and love potions in the mountains. Later in the novel, in a scene of horror, Antonio encounters the woman's head on the spike of a city gate, where it has been placed as a warning against allying with thieves. Of course, most of the characters who Antonio re-encounters throughout the novel are still alive when they meet again.

In the latter part of *The Improvisatore*, Antonio's fate becomes tied to a blind girl named Lara, who begs for money among the ruins of Greek temples in Paestum in southern Italy. Lara reappears to Antonio during the most otherworldly scene in the novel, in a cave called the "Blue Grotto" (Grotta Azzurra) on the island of Capri, where Antonio awakens after a shipwreck. Andersen writes of her appearance: "She was a ghostly apparition. Everything was a ghostly apparition, I felt, and not the dream images of my imagination."[69] When Antonio later awakens in a hotel room back in Naples, his rescuers ask him about the incident in Capri, but none of them believe his story about the girl who appeared to him in the grotto. Antonio's reaction foregrounds the question of whether such events are even possible: "They all said that it was my imagination, a feverish dream in the night air. I almost had to believe that myself, and yet I couldn't. It stood out much too vividly in my mind."[70] While Antonio wonders about the reality of his experiences, the workings of fate bring him back to Lara, this time in Venice, where she has regained her sight after eye surgery and has taken on the name of Maria. Lara, now Maria, informs Antonio that she had a dream of a woman who prophesied that she would regain her sight in the Blue Grotto in Capri, where she met Antonio for the second time.

Throughout *The Improvisatore*, Antonio inhabits a world of fantasy that is halfway between the real world and a world of illusions, depending on one's interpretation. At one point, he is told to improvise a song about the "fata morgana," a famous mirage that appears over the horizon in the Strait of Messina. He writes:

> Then I was given "fata morgana." I hadn't seen this beautiful aerial display either, which Naples and Sicily possess, but I was well acquainted with the beautiful fairy called Fantasy who inhabited those splendid castles. I could describe my own dreamworld. Her gardens and castles floated in it as well. And life's most beautiful fata morgana did in fact live in my heart.[71]

When he wanders the ruins of Herculaneum, he remarks, "I felt that I had stepped out of our own age in this place and that I had wandered like a ghost into remote antiquity, the way we imagine that vanished generations can enter into the activities of our lives as spirits."[72] Such comments capture aspects of the fantastic, a genre that prizes hesitation and indirectness as a way to evoke fantasy as something that is fleeting to the perceptions.

With the content of *The Improvisatore* in mind, it is not difficult to imagine why Kyōka would have been so intrigued by the novel. In his essay "On *Foam on the Waves Collection*, etc." he relates an anecdote about a meeting with Ōgai in which he embarrassed himself by revealing the depth of his familiarity with the translation. According to Kyōka, during the seventh or eighth meeting of the Useikai, he informed Ōgai that he found a typo on line 2 of page 210 of volume 1 of the standard, *kikuban*-sized edition of Ōgai's translation of *The Improvisatore* (1902), but adds that the typo was amended in the compact *shukusatsu* edition (1914).[73] As he related to Ōgai, in the standard edition, the phrase "*sayō ka*?" ("is that so?") was misprinted as "*yō ka sa*," a nonsense phrase. According to Kyōka, Ōgai responded to this display of obsessive attention to his translation by remarking, "Oh really? Was there something like that in there?" He then lightly nodded his head, said "It's a misprint, it's a misprint," and laughed softly to himself.

Kyōka returns to his discussion of *The Improvisatore* toward the end of the essay, following his anecdote about the *Foam on the Waves Collection*. He transitions back to the topic of *The Improvisatore* by noting that he is writing his essay in the middle of the summer heat, and then recalling that he once read Ōgai's translation on hot summer days many years earlier. He claims to have read it every day around the period of its early serialization, writing, "I would even go so far as to say that, in spring and in fall as well, I would hardly let a single day go by without reading it."[74] He explains that the descriptions in the text were so vivid that he wanted to drink the watermelon juice and lukewarm wine described in its pages.

Kyōka relates that he still thinks with longing of the landscape of the Roman campagna, or countryside, described in the early chapters of the novel. He describes picturing the scenery of the novel while sipping imported curaçao, a French liqueur that author Minakami Takitarō (1887–1940) had recently introduced him to. While drinking curaçao, Kyōka suggests the global vision that Andersen's novel presented him with. He writes, "I look upon the vast wilderness of the campagna in the distance, in ecstasy, I think of the peaks of the low clouds and the forms of red-eyed water buffaloes, a crisp coolness erases the blazing heat of the height of summer, and in gladness I give thanks."[75]

When describing the setting of *The Improvisatore* in the campagna, Kyōka quotes various passages of descriptive writing by Andersen, as translated by Ōgai, presumably from a copy of the novel that Kyōka had on hand. His quotations correspond to the following passages from the English-language translation by Frank Hugus:

> The sun burned hotter with each passing day. Its rays were a sea of flame flowing across the campagna. . . . The sun blazed straight down. I thought that my shadow was trying to hide from it beneath my feet. The buffalo lay like lifeless masses on the scorched grass or, seized by madness, raced around in great circles with the speed of an arrow. . . . Every single swamp had dried up. Tepid yellow water trickled drowsily down the Tiber. The melon juice was warm, and even the wine tasted sour and half boiled, despite the fact that it had been buried beneath stones and gravel. And not a cloud, not a single cloud, appeared on the horizon. Day and night the sky was always that eternal, endless blue. . . . Only the sirocco fanned us with waves of hot air for two very long months.[76]

In his focus on landscape, Kyōka identifies one of the main attractions of the novel, as noted by Ōgai himself. Romantic descriptions of the landscape are also emphasized throughout the novel, such as when the narrator relates, "Italy is the land of the imagination, of beauty: twice blessed is he who greets it again."[77]

6. Fantasy: From the Uncanny to the Marvelous

Muramatsu has suggested that Kyōka was influenced by his reading of *The Improvisatore* in the writing of two early novellas, *Volume One* (discussed in chapter 1) and *Shining Leaf Theater* (1896). These works marked new directions in Kyōka's fiction and anticipated his development as a writer of *gensō bungaku* circa the early twentieth century. According to Muramatsu, Kyōka's earliest stories were written in a stiff, scholarly style of classical Japanese that resembled the translations of Morita Shiken in the *Yūbin hōchi shinbun*, a variety of writing that he refers to as *kanbun kuzushi*–style, or literary Chinese rendered into Japanese, which resulted in prose that was distant from the modern spoken language.[78] Following Kyōka's encounter with *The Improvisatore*, Muramatsu claims that the author's style switches to flowing prose in modern Japanese. Noguchi Tetsuya notes a similar shift, from the meticulous and calculated prose style of Shiken's translations to a modern style that was freer, more elegant, and closer to Ōgai's.[79] Such scholars also note a shift in subject matter. Kyōka's early *kannen shōsetsu* (idea novels) were concerned with larger social ills, whereas *Volume One* and *Shining Leaf Theater* shift to the perspectives of individuals recollecting scenes of childhood in a hometown modeled on Kanazawa, where they were once defended by older-sister-type characters.[80] Such elements of fantasy would only become more prominent in Kyōka's later works, such as in *The Grass Labyrinth*, long considered to be one of the masterpieces of Kyōka's fiction, alongside works such as *The Holy Man of Mt. Kōya* and *The Castle Tower*.[81]

Shining Leaf Theater strikes a skillful balance between realism and fantasy, like Andersen's *The Improvisatore*. While falling on the side of realism, the novella features references to fairytales, nursery rhymes, folklore, supernatural creatures, circus sideshows, and a Nō play about ghosts. Such references are integrated into a realistic narrative set in the modern world, thereby creating a nostalgic and dreamlike atmosphere that seems to constantly border on a realm of fantasy. As such, the story might be thought of as "the fantastic-uncanny," in Todorov's classification system, or as a variety of the fantastic that suggests rational explanations for strange occurrences.[82] This stands in contrast to *The Grass Labyrinth*, one of the most overtly supernatural works of fiction in Kyōka's oeuvre, if not the entire canon of modern Japanese literature of the prewar period. It is a work that would easily qualify as "the fantastic-marvelous," if not outright genre fantasy. In *The Grass Labyrinth*, Kyōka lets his imagination run wild as he depicts elements of fantasy such as ghosts, goblins, levitation, phantasmagoric transformations, supernatural omens from the heavens, and a cast of supernatural characters including girls with animal faces, a giant demon king, and a host of celestial maidens. In its wildly imaginative depictions of fantasy, *The Grass Labyrinth* appears to draw inspiration from a range of works with supernatural themes that Kyōka encountered throughout his life, including *The Sunken Bell*, the *Arabian Nights*, Nō plays, *kusazōshi*, and traditional Japanese ghost stories.[83] A comparison of *Shining Leaf Theater* to *The Grass Labyrinth* reveals the deepening and intensification of Kyōka's depictions of the supernatural during the middle of his career.

Although *Shining Leaf Theater* is light on supernatural elements, it evokes an atmosphere of fantasy right from the beginning of the narrative, based on its setting in a world populated almost exclusively by women, as related by a narrator who recounts his idyllic past as a child in Kanazawa. The narrator, Mitsugi, describes his childhood neighborhood as being inhabited by "beautiful mistresses, wealthy widows, and serious young girls who passed their days peacefully like a dream."[84] Mitsugi lives with his aunt, because his mother has passed away, and he spends his days listening to nursery rhymes and fairytales told by "aunties" (*oba*) and playing with dolls with his "older sister" (*nē-san*), a beautiful neighbor named Hirooka Yuki. The only other significant male character in the story is a local bully, a child from a wealthy samurai family, whom Yuki defends Mitsugi from. As a pastime, Mitsugi attends performances at a local circus sideshow (*misemono*) whose performers are all women. The women at the circus perform *kyōgen*, or short plays that are shown during intermissions in Nō theater and that often feature comical or supernatural themes. The all-female cast of performers includes Kochika, Shigeko, Komatsu, Akiko, Shinobu, Komitsu, Koina, and Koroku. Kochika is Mitsugi's favorite, particularly when she dresses as the male hero Ushiwaka-maru, a mythologized youthful version of twelfth-century warrior Minamoto no Yoshitsune, and also when she carries around a sword or a spear. Although it might not be considered particularly unusual that there are so many women in Kyōka's narrative, it is noteworthy that the male presence is minimal in this particular novella. The work depicts a world seen

Fig. 18. Suzuki Kason, woodblock frontispiece of *Shining Leaf Theater* (*Teriha kyōgen*, 1900): Mitsugi and Yuki with theatrical costumes. (Courtesy of Izumi Kyōka Kinenkan Museum.)

through the eyes of a juvenile protagonist, whose "older sisters" care for him and entertain him with folkloric songs, local legends, and *kyōgen* plays all day.

Kyōka frames *Shining Leaf Theater* with a nursery rhyme and a fairytale at the beginning of the narrative and a Nō play at the end. Although the events of the narrative are realistic, this frame has the effect of creating an atmosphere of fantasy, theatricality, or a folkloric past that pervades the work. At the beginning of the story, a local "auntie" and maid ask Mitsugi to sing a *temari uta*, or a handball song, a song that resembles a nursery rhyme or counting song sung to the rhythm of a bouncing, woven ball known as a *temari*. Mitsugi surprises them with a song related from the perspective of a girl who is sexually assaulted by a monk. The women praise Mitsugi's song, but they also note with surprise that his version is much darker than the version they are familiar with. The maid then proceeds to relate to Mitsugi another dark story: a fairytale about an evil stepmother who tortures her stepdaughter, Ogin. In the story, the stepmother decides to expel Ogin from home and leave her in the mountains, and so Ogin's younger sister, Kogin, gives her older sister sesame seeds to mark the path to the place where she will be abandoned. Kogin follows the trail of sesame seeds and finds that her sister has been locked inside a covered well. Ogin cries for help because the water is rising, and Kogin comes back to visit day after day, but she is unable to assist her older sister, who eventually stops crying for help, presumably because she has died. With its elements of cruelty, Kyōka's fairytale recalls those of Andersen and the Brothers Grimm, but also traditional Japanese fairytales, such as *otogibanashi* and *temari uta*, whose content could often be dark. As Kyōka notes in his essay "My Disposition" (1908), *temari uta* often featured frightening imagery, such as snakes and centipedes, and morbid subject matter, particularly in tales of young women met by cruel fates.[85]

Another element of fantasy woven into the narrative of *Shining Leaf Theater* is a reference to a *yōkai* known as a *nobusuma*. The *nobusuma* is a kind of flying squirrel that resembles a vampire bat, because it sucks the blood of humans. Kyōka describes the *nobusuma* as an aged bat with multiple tails, a description that combines features of the *nobusuma* with those of various other supernatural creatures from Japanese folklore, such as the multitailed fox or cat. He describes the *nobusuma* as follows:

> It has a wingspan as wide as that of a black kite. Bats that live past the age of one hundred become *nobusuma*. The paper fan-maker next door, who is over sixty, said that he used to see them every night, but now he only sees them three times a year, or once every three months, and sometimes they don't appear before peoples' eyes at all. It has not only one tail, but two or three. It's not one of the usual, small creatures. It only appears at times such as summer evenings, moonlit nights, lantern-lighting time, or twilight. Once evening has fallen, it spreads its wings and covers peoples' faces. It feels like a soft, cold folding cloth that covers one's mouth as it drinks blood from one's chest. They glimmer under eaves like illusions and they scrape past the torii gates of Shinto shrines, before going into hiding once again.[86]

Mitsugi was warned to stay away from the *misemono* by his mother, who told him that such places were haunted by *nobusuma*. After his mother passed away, his aunt allowed him to go the circus. Mitsugi's fear of the *nobusuma* continues, however, and one night he believes that he has been attacked by a *nobusuma* when he feels a creature sucking on his cheek. A geisha's apprentice named Some offers to cast a spell (*majinai*) for protection and then thinks that she notices blood on Mitsugi's cheek, but it turns out to be lipstick, presumably from one of the older women who has smothered Mitsugi with kisses.

Mitsugi approaches a world of fantasy again toward the end of *Shining Leaf Theater*, when he returns to his hometown eight years later, after having joined a traveling circus himself. As he recounts tales of the past with Kochika, he relates to the reader, "As I spoke, I began to see illusions. The sky was blue, the sun shone brightly, and in the thick green leaves of the maple tree, butterflies made out of silver paper and gold paper flapped their wings and shook in the breeze . . ."[87] It is a light and impressionistic touch of fantasy that recalls the romantic literary style of Andersen's *The Improvisatore*. The tree that Mitsugi sees is a vision of a tree from his childhood, which has been washed away, along with his childhood home, by a flood. When Kochika drops her tobacco pipe in pain during their conversation, Mitsugi becomes worried that she might be suffering from rheumatism. This detail then leads to a bizarre anecdote about an actress named Koroku, who became virtually paralyzed after developing rheumatism. Because she was no longer able to perform, Koroku sold her body, in a literal sense, to a magician, who employed her in a "crucifixion" (*haritsuke*) show, or who tied her to a cross and prodded her paralyzed body with spears to elicit cries that entertained his audience. In the closing scene of *Shining Leaf Theater*, Mitsugi climbs a hill in the outskirts of Kanazawa, where he hears itinerant actors performing the Nō play *Matsukaze*, a standard of Nō theater that relates the tale of a wanderer who encounters two sisters mourning for an absent lover on a windswept beach. In a plot twist typical of Nō, both sisters are revealed at the conclusion of the play to be ghosts. Beyond simply referencing a Nō play, Kyōka's novella evokes the larger *jo-ha-kyū* rhythmic structure of Nō theater, or a basic rhythmic pattern that begins with a long, slow sequence, proceeds to a shorter and mid-paced middle section, and ends with a quick-paced conclusion, often involving the revelation of a ghost or supernatural being. The final reference to *Matsukaze* adds a touch of otherworldliness to an overall realistic narrative, which borrows scenes from fairytales and traditional Japanese theater to create an atmosphere of fantasy in the modern world.

In *The Grass Labyrinth*, a novel written over a decade after *Shining Leaf Theater*, Kyōka demonstrates a total transformation of style, as well as his narrative approach to the fantastic. If *Shining Leaf Theater* was influenced by the romanticism of *The Improvisatore*, then *The Grass Labyrinth* was influenced by the deep fantasy of *The Sunken Bell*, *Arabian Nights*, and traditional Japanese ghost stories, whose themes and forms are recombined into a radi-

Fig. 19. Okada Saburōsuke, frontispiece of *The Grass Labyrinth* (*Kusameikyū*, 1908): a girl with a *temari* and Akira with a translucent veil, in the style of Western painting (*yōga*). (Courtesy of Izumi Kyōka Kinenkan Museum.)

cally experimental work of fiction. *The Grass Labyrinth* is a notoriously difficult novel, whose layered and meandering narrative, sudden leaps in logic and narrative perspective, and bizarre accounts of supernatural phenomena make it one of Kyōka's more difficult works to understand.[88] It is the type of novel that would seem to support the characterization of Kyōka's work by later critics as "impressionistic," "surrealistic," "avant-garde," or "too new to be thought of as new."[89] The dense visuality and proto-surrealist qualities of the novel are suggested by its adaptation into modern forms of art, including the surrealist film *The Grass Labyrinth* by Terayama Shūji, a loose cinematic adaptation of the work, and a recent illustrated version of the novel (2014), whose illustrator, Yamamoto Takato, adapts the narrative's fantastic imagery into a modern manga style that is at turns idyllic, grotesque, and reminiscent of popular fantasy art.

One of the greatest difficulties of *The Grass Labyrinth* is its meandering introduction, which presents loosely layered images and anecdotes across the span of around seventy pages, before the novel picks up pace and switches to a quicker tempo nearly midway through. As an experimental novel, the work is built, in part, on the rhythmic structures of traditional Japanese art forms, particularly *temari uta* and Nō theater, but the short, songlike narratives of these artistic traditions are expanded to the length and scope of the modern fantasy novel. From *temari uta*, Kyōka adapts structures of repeating parallel images and narrative sequences, as typical of counting games and nursery rhymes. From Nō theater, he adapts the *jo-ha-kyū* rhythmic structure, as well as narrative details of an itinerant monk on pilgrimage, a petition for the exorcism of local ghosts, and a gradual revelation of supernatural powers as the rhythm of the narrative intensifies. The specific supernatural imagery of *The Grass Labyrinth*, however, is unprecedented in Japanese literature, as exemplified by an ending fantasy sequence that depicts illusions and hallucinatory visions on a cosmic scale.

The Grass Labyrinth begins by quoting lyrics from a *temari* song, whose meaning is obscure, because the song follows the rhythmic logic of a counting game:

A snake stands in the small marshland across the way,
The village elder of Hachiman, his younger daughters,
How skillfully they stand,
How skillfully they plot,
With two jewels in hand,
And golden shoes on their feet,

Calling here and calling there,
Sunset on the mountain, sunset in the fields . . .[90]

Following this quotation, the subject and setting shift repeatedly, and often without notice, thereby leading to potential disorientation for the reader. Kyōka begins the main part of the narrative with a dreamlike scene of bathers on the Shōnan coast who drown after refusing to heed voices that call out from heaven and urge them to return home. He then establishes the first major setting of the novel, a section of narrow coastal path perched atop a cliff in the vicinity of the village of Akiya, which drops straight into the ocean on the outer side of the path. The setting of the cliffside and surrounding caves and beaches is described at length, with geographic precision, like the deep mountain paths of *The Holy Man of Mt. Kōya*.

After establishing the setting of the novel, Kyōka introduces the first of its main characters, an itinerant monk named Kojirō, who stops by a roadside tea hut and listens to a long series of anecdotes told by an elderly proprietress. The tea vendor begins her stories by recommending that the monk visit a local landmark called the "Birthing Stone" (*koumi ishi*), a stone purported to have the power to grant women's requests for successful pregnancy and safe labor, but the monk insists that, as a lone pilgrim in the world, he has no need for such a visit. The *koumi ishi* introduces the central image of the narrative, that of a sphere, which appears in variations throughout the narrative, first as the birthing stone, and later as a *temari* handball, a hairpin jewel, a watermelon, a severed head, the moon, and a mother's breasts.[91] After the old woman tells Kojirō about the *koumi ishi*, she relates an extended background narrative about a local young man named Kakichi who had an excessive fondness for alcohol and who lost his mind after hearing a mysterious shrine maiden sing a *temari uta*. After finding Kakichi tied to a cart and thoroughly hung over, the shrine maiden offered him a blue jewel from her hairpin to help him to repay his debts, but when she began singing a *temari* song about the "narrow road to Akiya," a village and mansion deep in the mountains, Kakichi went insane. The old woman's story then grows more fantastic as she relates that the local children have developed a strange habit of cutting holes for eyes and mouths into taro leaves and wearing them as masks. The children resemble foxes, *tanuki*, or *ubume*, a popular *yōkai* that takes the form of a grieving spirit of a woman who died in childbirth and who is stained in blood from the waist down.

Following this sequence of anecdotes, the old woman relates the legend of the haunted Akiya Manor (Akiya Yashiki). As the woman relates, the manor was built by the son of a local aristocrat who returned to his home village from Tokyo so that his wife could give birth in peace and seclusion. Despite his hopes, however, the man's wife died in childbirth, along with his child, and he subsequently committed suicide by throwing himself down a well. Ever since then, people have rarely dared to enter the mansion. The old woman then begs the monk to pray for the repose of the spirits in the Akiya Manor, and so he decides to take up lodging in the haunted mansion.

Over seventy pages into the novel, the protagonist of the story and the main setting of its action are finally introduced. Chapter 21 opens inside Akiya Manor, where the monk Kojirō meets Hagoshi Akira, the protagonist, a young man from the town of Kokura in Buzen province (present-day Fukuoka prefecture) in Kyūshū, who has traveled throughout the provinces and cities of Japan collecting *temari* songs as he searches for a song that his departed mother once sang to him when he was young. The rest of the novel unfolds within the space of the haunted mansion and might be characterized as a rapidly intensifying sequence of supernatural occurrences and fantastic imagery. The hauntings begin on the level of the vaguely paranormal, with details of levitating tatami mats and rotating lamps. The novel takes a turn into surreal and kaleidoscopic horror, however, when a levitating watermelon is described as transforming into the head of a blind masseur, then the severed head of a demon monk (*nyūdō kubi*), then the severed head of a woman (*onna no namakubi*), and finally the moon.[92]

Akira and Kojirō spend days in the mansion, where they repeatedly encounter apparitions and otherworldly beings. One evening, Akira provides a background narrative that deepens the fairytale-like atmosphere of the story. As Akira relates, his mother used to sing a *temari* song along with three of her friends, all girls from his hometown. One of the women died during doll festival (Hina Matsuri), one went missing, and one was now married to a jealous husband who refused to allow Akira to question his wife about the song. Akira claims that the woman who disappeared was "hidden away by the gods" in a miraculous instance of *kamikakushi*, or "spiriting away." As he relates, in his hometown, on the year, month, day, and hour of the ox, young women sit in front of mirrors and await to see visions of their future lovers. The woman from his hometown, however, saw a supernatural being who hid her earthly form. Akira believes that he will encounter the woman in the haunted mansion, and that she will be able to fulfill his request of singing the *temari* song that he has long sought for.

Toward the conclusion of the novel, Kyōka sets the stage for one of the most virtuosic passages of writing in his oeuvre, a thirty-page crescendo of fantastic imagery that reaches from hell to the cosmos. On a night of heavy rainfall, the outline of a figure formed of leaking water on the mansion's inner wall becomes animated and emerges from the shadows. The figure is a demon king (rendered variously as *ma'ō*, *daima*, and *kijin*), or "a passing spirit of misfortune" (*tōrima*), who, in his stature and fierce nature, resembles the genies of the *Arabian Nights*. The demon king asks Kojirō to remove a Buddhist statue that he has installed in an alcove so that he may pass unimpeded through the space of the mansion. The giant introduces himself as Akuzaemon, and when Kojirō murmurs "Aku . . ." (meaning "evil"), the giant responds, "Yes, 'evil' as in 'good and evil' [*zen'aku*]."[93] The demon king claims to inhabit the space of darkness and span of time of the blink of the human eye and remarks that humans are only harmed by such spirits when they accidently glimpse them. Confronted by the *ma'ō*, Kojirō asks in dismay, "Am I . . . am I . . . am I in hell [*meido*]?"[94]

Throughout the scene of Kojirō's confrontation with the demon king, Akira sleeps in the corner. As the giant informs him, Akira is currently in mortal danger, because he has been drinking poisonous well water that was secretly dripped into his water pitcher by a maiden with a dog face. The implication appears to be that Akira has been searching too intently for the *temari* song, and by extension for his mother who died long ago, and has thus approached the realm of death himself. He is saved from danger, however, by the married woman, one of the three who knows the *temari* song, who appears to the monk and announces her intention to save Akira and teach him the song. As the woman relates, Akira's mother desires nothing more than to reach down from heaven and feed her child milk from her pale white breasts. In a scene of cosmic drama, the author describes the mother's appearance in the heavens to save her son:

> Unable to bear the misery, the mother's affection for her child turns to love and, overstepping the rules of heaven and breaking the divine law, she leans over the jeweled railing of the great tower in the clouds, grabs onto the branches of a *katsura* tree, and departs the heavenly manor. As her body floats down from the sky and descends from the middle of the moon to the world below, her cloud flips upside down and turns into a waterfall one hundred thousand million billion meters high that rumbles monstrously as it plummets from the infinite sky to the bottomless earth below. Upon the waterfall descends a single hem like a trail of fine mist—it is his mother, braving danger as she clings perilously to a shaking branch of *katsura*.[95]

The mother becomes terrified that her son has wandered into a "*hitotsuya*" (the lair of the *onibaba*) and that he will become guilty of having an affair with a married woman. As Akira embraces the married woman, he suddenly finds that he has descended into an infernal realm—the walls turn into red lotuses, the tatami turn into mats of needles, snakes bind his arms, lizards bite at his knees, and his body turns as cold as ice. In a passage of baroque language, the woman exclaims, "Over there is heaven, and here is hell. Do not be mistaken, it is all a beautiful dream. . . . Child, return to your past, seek out the breasts of your mother . . . awaken . . ."[96]

Having layered this sequence of supernatural imagery about as densely as one could imagine, Kyōka ends the novel with one final scene of fantasy. As Akira awakens, the demon king knocks over a bucket of well water that flows through the garden, prompting the novel's final spectacle:

> Thereafter the water ran, the white clouds of dawn rose early, and within rain puddles that flowed through the garden like smoke, the moon sank and turned into a boat, its prow pointed forward as it passed over white flowers, gliding smoothly along the way. The sleeves of the demon king turned into a sail and a beautiful woman, hidden behind the sail, sang, "What narrow road is this? What narrow road? This is the narrow road of Tenjin [a Shinto god].[97] The narrow road. Won't you let me pass?" The song is so painfully nostalgic. Gusts of wind burst through dense groves, tree leaves, and the green rapids quicken . . . a horizontal cloud, over there, a horizontal cloud . . .[98]

Incorporating a *temari uta* into the ending sequence, Kyōka demonstrates the full flowering of his imagination of the fantastic. It is an imagination that drew heavily on Japanese fairytales and traditional ghost stories for its imagery, while also building on Kyōka's experience with global literature of the fantastic, such as the *Arabian Nights*, *The Improvisatore*, and *The Sunken Bell*, to create a vision of fantasy that is unprecedented in its modern expression, romantic language, and experimental form. Overall, *The Grass Labyrinth* is so complex and heavily layered with fantastic imagery that it seems to anticipate later forms of literature, such as surrealism or even the genre fantasy novel. In common with *The Castle Tower*, almost no other work of fiction is similar to it from early-twentieth-century Japan.

Four

Kyōka and Maupassant

Modern Ghost Stories

1. Modern Approaches to the Supernatural

In two essays written in 1908, "Romanticism and Naturalism" ("Romanchikku to shizenshugi") and "My Disposition" ("Yo no taido"), Kyōka discusses the state of modern Japanese literature and relates his ideas on literary genres and the influence of European fiction in Japan. In the essays, Kyōka laments the seemingly unquestioned adulation of certain European authors, while also criticizing the tendency of critics to judge all works of literature according to the generic distinctions of naturalism and romanticism. These essays appear to offer more evidence for those who would see Kyōka as a traditionalist who rejected developments in modern literature; they also offer evidence, however, that Kyōka was not simply opposing modern trends in fiction, but that he was seriously considering the demands of the modern novel, the value of literature to society, and his own relationship to European writing. In both essays, Kyōka breaks with his reticence to comment on European fiction and mentions a story by a European author he finds to be particularly engaging and well-structured, "Mademoiselle Fifi" (1882) by Guy de Maupassant, a work he even refers to as "dazzlingly brilliant."[1] Although Kyōka's comments on Maupassant are brief, they constitute a literary intersection between representative writers of literature of the fantastic from France and Japan, both of whom wrote distinctly modern ghost stories by reflecting on contemporary knowledge and worldviews, while also featuring avant-garde depictions of eroticism, gore, and psychological horror as defining elements of their work. Comparing Kyōka and Maupassant reveals Kyōka's modern mindset and the innovative elements of his fiction. In common with Maupassant, Kyōka experimented with the form of the modern tale of the fantastic by considering the intersecting roles of science, psychology, religion, and superstition in perceptions of the supernatural.

In this chapter, I explore resonances in the stories of Kyōka and Maupassant, authors who had more in common than it may initially appear, while also examining the influence of Maupassant on the wider development of literature of the fantastic in Japan, including through the depiction of content that is uncanny, erotic, grotesque, and supernatural. As in the West, Maupassant was received in Japan as a representative writer of both naturalism and literature of the fantastic. Maupassant is frequently mentioned in histories of Japanese literature alongside writers such as Zola, Flaubert, Chekhov, and Turgenev as one of the most influential writers in the development of naturalism, or *shizen shugi*, in Japan.[2] As such, he is discussed as an author who supposedly influenced Japanese writers to concentrate on objectively recording what they saw and heard during their daily experiences, without overt literary adornment or the excessive use of figural or poetic language. However, Maupassant's work was also recognized in Japan early on for its sensationalism, skillful plotting, and forays into the fantastic. Although Maupassant was widely known for writing literary sketches of daily life in France, much of his fiction also deals with lurid and risqué themes, including prostitution, adultery, sexual depravity, madness, and murder. More than a literary sketch artist, Maupassant was a storyteller who mastered the techniques of creating suspense and shocking the reader with plot twists and surprise endings, all within tightly structured narratives that seem almost effortless in their delivery.

In some senses, Maupassant was hardly a naturalist at all, unless one considers real life to consist of a constant series of scandals and astonishing events, with the occasional haunting and bout of madness. If anything, Maupassant's reception as a "naturalist" in Japan reveals a peculiar understanding of the term, because Japanese writers interpreted Maupassant's naturalism as being fundamentally linked to depictions of lust and shocking stories of human sexuality.[3] His most ardent fans included many foundational figures of modern Japanese literature, such as Ozaki Kōyō, Tayama Katai, Kunikida Doppo, Shimazaki Tōson, and Nagai Kafū, all of whom adapted or translated the author's work.[4] Kyōka can also be included in this group of modern writers influenced by Maupassant, due to both his personal reading of the author's work and because of the wider influence of Maupassant's fiction in the literary establishment. Maupassant's influence on Japanese literature was overwhelming, if one considers the centrality of sex, confession, and scandal in many of the most popular and influential Japanese novels of the modern period.

In addition to the influence of his naturalistic narratives, Maupassant was also one of the first European authors whose stories of the fantastic were translated into Japanese. These include signature works such as "On the Water" ("Sur l'eau," 1881), "The Hand" ("La main," 1883), "Fear" ("La peur," 1884), "The Dead Girl" ("La morte," 1887), "The Inn" ("L'auberge," 1886), and "The Horla" ("Le Horla," 1887).[5] Tales of the fantastic formed only a portion of Maupassant's literary output, which, overall, included 300 or so stories, 6 novels, 3 books on travel, and an assortment of plays and poetry.[6] However, Maupassant's tales of horror and nightmarish fantasy have consistently been among his most popular stories and frequently discussed works in literary scholarship. Overall, stories of the fantastic amount to around a tenth of Maupassant's work, or around thirty stories, depending on how strictly one defines the fantastic as a genre. Some of these are among the most famous stories of the fantastic from nineteenth-century France, such as "The Horla," "On the Water," "The Apparition" ("Apparition," 1883), and "Night: The Nightmare" ("La nuit: cauchemar," 1887), works that continue to haunt readers today with depictions of horror, madness, and despair that still feel groundbreaking. These stories are particularly disturbing because of their depiction of the tormented psychological states of their modern subjects, who are unable to ascertain if they are genuinely being haunted or if they have simply lost all touch with reality due to extreme states of anxiety and fatigue, if not the degradation of their mental faculties and sensory organs.

At first glance, Kyōka's approach to the fantastic might appear to have little in common with Maupassant. Scholars have often characterized Maupassant as a writer whose literature of the fantastic rarely features content that is overtly supernatural, being closer to the uncanny in nature, and whose approach to the fantastic and the "other side" of life was rooted in skepticism, pessimism, and a search for rational explanations for mysterious phenomena.[7] Kyōka, by comparison, wrote stories full of ghosts, monsters, and supernatural beings. His stories also feature reverential allusions to Buddhist sutras, bodhisattvas, deities, and religious ideals. In life, Kyōka had a reputation for religiosity and superstition that was considered eccentric or unusually fervent by his peers. He was known to begin every day with prayers, devotions, and offerings before his Buddhist altar and portraits of his parents and his literary mentor, Kōyō.[8] While writing, he would dip his pens in incense smoke and mix his ink with water kept in an offertory sake bottle, like those found at the altars of Shinto shrines, as though to bless or purify his work.[9] He carefully preserved any paper with writing on it, including manuscript pages and even scraps of paper, and he saved all of his pens, which were eventually buried in a *fudezuka* (pen hill), in rituals that signaled a traditional East Asian sense of reverence for the written word.[10] He was known to bow and pay respect every time he passed by a Buddhist temple or a Shinto shrine, even if this meant interrupting a conversation with a companion.[11] For reasons such as these, Kyōka often appeared to critics as either a living relic who had somehow managed to hold on to premodern beliefs and religious attitudes with an inexplicable tenacity, or an eccentric who clung to belief as a creative force.[12] Such characterizations of both Kyōka and Maupassant, however, draw on limited biographical details and anecdotes that obscure certain elements of their work.

Although Maupassant has often been read as a skeptic and a trenchant realist, it is entirely possible to read his work, without in-depth knowledge of his biography, and get the impression that he is a writer of the fantastic and the supernatural in a strict sense. While his stories lack the colorful cast of supernatural creatures seen in Kyōka's fiction, they feature vivid descriptions of ghosts, nightmarish reveries, and phenomena that can only be described as supernatural, or as lying outside of the realms of science or the known laws of nature. Maupassant also leaves open the possibility of an "other side" to life, particularly in stories of invisible beings and powers that cause his protagonists to question the limits of their abilities to perceive reality.[13] In this way, Maupassant might be compared to Kyōka, a writer who has been characterized as almost naïve in his traditional and religiously oriented worldview, but who also drew on modern ideas and experiences in experimental ghost stories. In common with Maupassant, Kyōka considers the roles of psychology, medicine, and modern perspectives on belief and religion in experiences of the supernatural. These are elements of his fiction that have rarely been commented on, although they can be found throughout stories that suggest that physical and mental states such as fatigue, illness, and paranoia facilitate the appearance of ghosts. Many of Kyōka's stories also feature doctors and references to medicine and disease in their accounts of the supernatural.[14] Kyōka shares with Maupassant an ability to frighten and disturb readers with horrific images drawn from the modern world, while suggesting that the forces that govern human life are fundamentally imperceptible or invisible. Both writers, each in his own way, treat human life as frightening and fragile, or as constantly under threat from forces that are only dimly perceived and barely understood.

2. The Themes of Maupassant's Fiction

Before comparing Kyōka and Maupassant, it is useful to review the themes of Maupassant's fiction, because readers today may have limited familiarity with parts of the author's oeuvre, and particularly his contributions to literature of the fantastic as a genre. Maupassant was one of the most popular writers in late-nineteenth-century France, whose work spanned the genres of realism, naturalism, the fantastic, and horror. The major themes of Maupassant's fiction include peasant life in rural Normandy, commercial life in coastal Normandy and the northern cities of Rouen and Le Havre, the glamorous and seedy sides of urban life in Paris, boating on the Seine river, violent conflict in the Franco-Prussian War of 1870–1871, ghosts, madness, murder, prostitution, and adultery. Much of Maupassant's fiction might be described as naturalist, due to his realistic depictions of modern life in France, as well as intricate descriptions of clothing, material culture, cityscapes, and natural landscapes. While most of Maupassant's stories are set in Normandy and Paris, a significant number of works take place in adjacent locations around the Mediterranean, including Cannes, the French Riviera, Corsica, and North Africa. At least two stories are set in Switzerland, and one takes place in India, the only place in this list that Maupassant did not personally visit.

Although Maupassant's tales of the fantastic form only a portion of his larger body of fiction, they are among his most famous and critically acclaimed works. They were also part of his literary endeavors throughout his career. While Maupassant would probably be remembered as one of the most successful writers of late-nineteenth-century France based only on his realistic fiction, his stories of the fantastic have broadened the appeal of his work for literary critics, as well as for fans of horror and fantasy literature, and have done much to bolster the author's reputation and encourage continued interest in his work. In this way, Maupassant's stories of the fantastic might be compared to those of Kyōka, as work that secured the writer's reputation and the interest of future generations of readers. As evidence of the continued ability of Maupassant's fiction to enchant and frighten readers, a collection of his darker stories, published in 1989, bears this endorsement by major horror and fantasy novelist Clive Barker: "One of the best collections of horror tales that I've ever read."[15]

The themes of Maupassant's stories of the fantastic include ghosts, invisible beings, nightmares, night terrors, madness, visits to the graveyard, and living body parts. Additional themes that emphasize Maupassant's distinctly modern approach to the fantastic include "mesmerism, hypnotism, magnetism, spiritualism, and even vampirism," themes described by scholar and translator Siân Miles as "buzzwords" in Parisian society during Maupassant's lifetime.[16] Miles links these themes in Maupassant's fiction to the author's distrust of modern methods and instruments for measuring human perception. Some of Maupassant's dark tales contain clear examples of supernatural phenomena, such as haunting or telekinesis, although others stick closer to the real world and are more easily grouped into horror fiction or literature of the uncanny, with a focus on murder and madness. Maupassant's interests were occasionally morbid in the extreme, in the case of such graphic narratives as "Châli" (1884), "The Diary of a Madman" ("Un fou," 1885), "The Case of Louise Roque" ("La petite Roque," 1886), and "The *Lull-a-Bye*" ("L'endormeuse," 1889). Among the most disturbing themes that one finds in Maupassant's fiction are child murder, rape, and graphic depictions of suicide. His work is also disturbing, however, on an existential level, because of its incessant exploration of themes of death, suicide, depression, and failure, and because of its general pessimism. Maupassant's work has often been treated as scandalous due to its sexual content, including constant depictions of adultery and prostitution, as well as occasional depictions of sexual violence and incest. Maupassant's most morbid tales are so graphic that they are likely to shock readers even today. In the introduction to his translation of Maupassant's dark stories, Arnold Kellett suggests that such work might even come with "a health-warning."[17]

Maupassant's representative tale of the fantastic is "The Horla," a masterpiece of bizarre nineteenth-century fiction that famously treats several major themes of modern literature of the fantastic, including those of an invisible monster, a terrifying threat that cannot be named or defined, hallucination, mass insanity, and pseudoscientific theories of hypnosis and magnetism.[18] "The Horla" was translated into Japanese by major scholar and translator Uchida Roan (1868–1929) in 1905, and it was one of the most radically experimental works of literature of the fantastic available in Japan at the time.[19] Titling his translation "Uyamuya no ki" ("An Account of the Indefinable"), Uchida signaled his understanding of the central interest of the story as lying in its descriptions of a vague, invisible menace. Another author who encountered "The Horla" early on was Tayama Katai, who indicated his interest in the work by circling its title in a collection of English-language translations of Maupassant's fiction that he personally owned.[20]

"The Horla" has frequently been interpreted as a firsthand, real-life account of Maupassant's own mental demise and experience of hallucinations.[21] Maupassant enjoyed a quick rise to celebrity status during the 1880s in France, publishing most of his prodigious output of fiction between 1880 and 1891, but he thereafter suffered a rapid descent into madness and death in an asylum, in 1893. This collapse appears to be reflected all too convincingly in stories such as "The Horla." In this way, "The Horla" might be compared to "Cogwheels" ("Haguruma," 1927) by Akutagawa, a short story that is similarly read, almost unavoidably, in an autobiographic manner, due to its vivid and chilling first-person narrative of hallucination and madness. "The Horla," an invented word meaning something like "from beyond," is the name of an unidentified invisible being in Maupassant's story who is described, in diary format, as a creature that relentlessly follows the narrator. The invisible monster haunts the narrator by drinking water and milk from his nightstand at night, sucking his breath and pressing down on his chest while he sleeps (thereby suggesting a night terror), moving the pages of a book as though by telekinesis, and effacing the narrator's image from a mirror by standing in between him and the mirror's reflecting surface. The narrator comes to believe that the Horla is an advanced life form, possibly from another planet, who has come to replace humanity, and that humanity will be enslaved and exterminated by this new species. As evidence that he is not insane, the narrator claims that his neighbors and household employees have suffered from symptoms similar to his own. He even points to evidence in a newspaper printed in Brazil that the citizens of the state of São Paulo have experienced similar phenomena, leading to mass panic. He connects this to his sighting of a ship from Brazil, mentioned at the beginning of the story, and believes that the invisible being may have entered France from the same ship. At the conclusion of the story, the narrator burns down his own house in an attempt to kill the Horla, trapping his servants within, and then settles on suicide as the only possible means of escape from this terrifying being.

Maupassant treats themes of invisible powers only dimly known to science in other short stories, such as "Magnetism" ("Magnétisme," 1882) and "Was He Mad?" ("Un fou?" 1884). In "Magnetism," guests at a dinner party in Paris are described as treating the recent "science" of magnetism as a religious doctrine and are described as "falling back into superstitions, beliefs, clinging to these last remnants of the marvelous, becoming devotees to this mystery of magnetism."[22] In "Was He Mad?" the narrator tells the story of a recently deceased patient of an asylum, who demonstrated his supernatural abilities to the narrator by telekinetically drawing a paper knife to his hand. Maupassant's interests in magnetism and hypnotism were not limited to his fiction, but rather extended to personal studies and observations of pseudoscientific experiments, as he searched for the existence of hidden or metaphysical truths in a modern world that seemed to be devoid of deeper meaning.[23]

Pessimism and skepticism have been interpreted as core elements of Maupassant's modern approach to the fantastic, such as by scholar Pierre-Georges Castex. Of Maupassant, Castex writes, "As a disciple of Schopenhauer, he discovered universal illusion. . . . As a disciple of Flaubert, he observed with bitterness the stupidity of man."[24] Other scholars, however, question the vison of Maupassant as an extreme skeptic and pessimist. Didier Philippot concedes that Maupassant's approach to the fantastic appears to be pessimistic, referring to his approach as "crepuscular" and writing that scholars have described his work as "the fantastic without significance, fundamentally skeptical, non-affirmative, deprived of all profundity and all revelatory scope."[25] Philippot presents an alternative reading of Maupassant, however, by asserting the importance of mystery in his work. According to Philippot, by refusing dogmatic positivism and suggesting the limits of knowledge and the senses, Maupassant opens a space of "metaphysical depth" and "irreducible mystery" that is not purely psychological and that resists any attempt at explanation.[26]

While stories such as "The Horla" present the intersection of science, psychology, and the fantastic in avant-garde modern literature, other stories by Maupassant express more traditional images of ghosts and haunting. Some stories, such as "The Apparition" and "On the Water," even recall the content of traditional Japanese ghost stories, because of their vivid depictions of female ghosts who return from death to haunt the living. In "The Apparition," the narrator is sent to an abandoned manor with an overgrown garden to retrieve some documents from a room where a woman had died. In the room, the man confronts a ghost: "A tall woman dressed all in white stood watching me, behind the armchair where I had been sitting just before."[27] The ghost hands the man a tortoiseshell comb and asks him to brush her long black hair. It is a scene that one might even expect to find in a story by Kyōka, whose work often features female apparitions with long black hair, as well as imagery of tortoiseshell combs and hairpins. While such elements suggest universal qualities of the fantastic, the man's reaction to the ghost suggests the modern mindset of a writer based in late-nineteenth-century France. In search of a rational explanation for his experience, the narrator remarks, "For an hour, I anxiously wondered if I hadn't been the victim of a hallucination. I surely must have had one of those incomprehensible nervous attacks, one of those panics in the mind that are the source of miracles, moments that endow the Supernatural with so much power."[28] His skepticism is challenged, however, when he finds strands of the woman's hair entangled in the buttons of his coat.

"On the Water," translated into Japanese in 1905, the same year as "The Horla," deals with themes of invisible beings and a nervous and excitable imagination as the source of supernatural experiences, while leaving open the possibility that the work can be read as a straightforward ghost story. In the short story, a man goes canoeing on the Seine, whose nighttime scenery strikes him as haunted. He sees the river at night as "a fairy-tale world of mirages and spectres" and feels as though "some invisible force or being was slowly dragging [his] boat to the bottom of the river."[29] As night deepens, the narrator remarks, "I began to imagine all sorts of supernatural things. I imagined that someone was trying to climb onto the boat—that I could no longer see—and that the river, hidden in this dense fog, was filled with strange beings swimming all around me."[30] The reader familiar with Japanese ghost stories is likely to imagine a riverscape teeming with *kappa*, mischievous goblin-like creatures, or other river-dwelling *yōkai*. The work's resemblance to a Japanese ghost story is only strengthened by the ending, in which the canoer pulls up the body of an old woman who had thrown herself into the river with a stone tied around her neck. The idea of a location haunted by the ghost of a woman who died in grief, either by murder or suicide, is common in Japanese tales of the supernatural, while belonging to the larger category of the phantom, one of the most common themes in literature of the fantastic globally. In his modern approach to representing ghosts and the supernatural, Maupassant resembles Kyōka, who similarly contributed to the establishment of the fantastic as a global literary genre by bringing new perspectives to traditional themes.

3. The Reception of Maupassant in Japan

According to the research of scholar Ōnishi Tadao, Maupassant was the most frequently translated European author in Japan from the Meiji period through the Taishō period (1912–1926). Total translations of his stories amount to over 200 works, compared to around 70 for Alphonse Daudet, 53 for Zola, 28 for Flaubert, 13 for the Goncourt brothers (Edmond de Goncourt, 1822–1896, and Jules de Goncourt 1830–1870), and 3 for Joris-Karl Huysmans (1848–1907).[31] Maupassant's popularity as an author for translation can be attributed to multiple factors, including the brevity of many of his stories, the concision and relative simplicity of his language in both their original French editions and in English-language translations, and the sensational and erotic content of his narratives. A number of the earliest stories by Maupassant to be translated into Japanese were four to eight pages long, as were many of his works, although his longer stories are several dozen pages long, and his novels range from over 100 pages to nearly 400 pages. Maupassant was also popular because of his skillful and humorous storytelling. In Japan, as in America and in other countries, Maupassant's most frequently translated and popular stories include such works as "The Necklace" ("La parure," 1884), "The Umbrella" ("Le parapluie," 1884), and "The Jewels" ("Les bijoux," 1883), which are biting naturalist sketches that satirize contemporary Parisian society, the materialistic obsessions of the bourgeoisie, and the institution of marriage. They are also known for the skillful use of surprise endings, often of a darkly humorous nature. Beginning in the 1890s, Maupassant became one of the most influential European writers in Japan, based in part on his naturalistic fiction, but also due to the translation of sensationalistic stories of eroticism, madness, and the supernatural, which offered alternatives to the mainstream of realist or naturalist fiction in the modern literary environment.

Maupassant was so popular in Japan that his work could be found throughout the pages of influential literary journals, including *Bungei kurabu*, *Kokumin no tomo*, *Waseda bungaku*, *Myōjō*, *Taiyō*, *Shinshōsetsu*, *Shinsei*, *Shinchō*, *Chūō kōron*, *Geien*, *Bunko*, *Subaru*, and *Seitō*.[32] His stories were also frequently featured in the *Yomiuri shinbun*, one of the most widely circulated newspapers in Japan. Among modern writers who read Maupassant, the most heavily influenced by his work were Kōyō, Katai, Doppo, Kafū, and Tōson, all of whom read Maupassant's fiction extensively and translated or adapted his stories. One of the first major fans and promoters of Maupassant in Japan was Kyōka's mentor, Kōyō. According to authors including Tokuda Shūsei and Tayama Katai, Kōyō constantly praised Maupassant's "light touch" and endeavored to adapt elements of the author's literary style.[33] Kōyō also translated one short story by Maupassant, "The Colonel's Ideas" ("Les idées du colonel," 1884), with the help of translator Matsui Tomotoki.[34] The story, published as "Onna" ("Woman") in 1902, is a humorous sketch describing the romantic disposition of French men and their historical inclination to be led into battle by women.[35] Tōson, who Katai referred to as "the Japanese Maupassant," wrote essays on Maupassant's literature and Maupassant's theory of the novel; he even wrote an essay on Tolstoy's essay on Maupassant.[36] Katai wrote some of the earliest critical essays on Maupassant in Japan and translated several of Maupassant's stories as some of his first publications.[37] Kafū adapted Maupassant's short stories in his early fiction, translated Maupassant's travel writings in 1909, and wrote an essay comparing Maupassant to haikai poet Matsuo Bashō in 1945.[38] The depth of interest in Maupassant by some of the most influential Japanese writers throughout the modern period is revealed by the ubiquity of translations of his stories in major print publications and the constant production of reviews of his work, such that his influence became a nearly unavoidable reality of the literary environment of modern Japan.

The origins of Maupassant's influence in Japan can be traced to a partial translation of his theory of the novel in an article by Tōson, published in *Jogaku zasshi* in 1893. In the article, Tōson quotes from "The Novel" ("Le Roman," 1888), Maupassant's treatise on naturalism and modern literature included as a preface to his novel *Pierre and Jean* (*Pierre et Jean*, 1888), and compares it to Zola's theory of the novel, "The Experimental Novel" ("Le roman expérimental," 1879). Tōson describes Zola as more objective than Maupassant, while describing Maupassant's brand of naturalism as being concerned especially with "things that are frightful and shameful."[39] An emphasis on the place of sex in Maupassant's work, as well as a recognition of his pessimism, can be seen in an article published in 1893 in *Kokumin shinbun*, likely written by novelist Tokutomi Roka (1868–1927). The article reads, "Both in his own life and in his works, Maupassant was primarily concerned with matters of lust and desire. . . . He held on to the idea that humans are led on by fate, of which they know nothing, only to end in death."[40]

A struggle to separate Maupassant as a representative writer of naturalist fiction and an author of lurid and grotesque literature can be seen in an article by translator Ueda Bin (1874–1916), published in *Teikoku bungaku* in 1897, the year in which translations of Maupassant finally began to appear in Japanese. Ueda writes:

> [Maupassant] made his name with short stories that people compare to instant photographs. . . . Their beauty lies not in skillful dramatization, but can rather be found in the sublime rhythm of his literary style. It is relaxed and transparent, without the slightest poetic adornment and not despising elegant simplicity. . . . Although Maupassant's literature may occasionally be stained with spots that one should not show to youth or students, the path of his brush is normally elegant, refined, clean, and the height of purity.[41]

In his attempt to preserve a clean image of Maupassant, Ueda presents a distorted image of his work, which often features skillful narrative structuring and poetic adornment and is rarely describable as clean and pure.

The reception of Maupassant following the translation of his work into Japanese, including both his naturalist fiction and his shocking short stories, is encapsulated in the early career of Katai, which mirrors the wider development of a deeper understanding of Maupassant's work in Japan. Katai first encountered Maupassant's work in a book that has acquired almost legendary status as a singular volume that exerted tremendous influence on a circle of writers that included Katai, Doppo, Masamune Hakuchō (1879–1962), and Yanagita Kunio, all of whom borrowed the book from Ueda Bin.[42] The book was a volume of Maupassant's short stories translated into English by Jonathan Sturges and titled *The Odd Number: Thirteen Tales by Guy de Maupassant* (1888).[43] *The Odd Number* was the first widely available volume of translations of Maupassant's work in America and featured an introduction by American-British author Henry James, who had a major influence on the development of literature of the fantastic in the English-speaking world and beyond. The collection contains signature stories such as "Happiness" ("Le bonheur," 1884), "The Wolf" ("Le loup," 1882), "Mother Savage" ("La Mère Sauvage," 1884), "The Wreck" ("L'épave," 1886), "The Apparition" (translated as "The Ghost"), and "The Necklace," whose content ranges from the quotidian to the fantastic. The collection has also been described by scholar Artine Artinian as being "carefully selected in order not to offend sensitive souls," and as being "enthusiastically received by the critics,"[44] a situation that might be compared to that in Japan, where the collection presented a relatively safe image of Maupassant to enthusiastic readers of his work. Such readers included Katai, who was one of the first translators of Maupassant into Japanese, but whose image of the writer was radically altered by his subsequent readings.

In common with his peers, Katai's first encounter with Maupassant was through *The Odd Number*. Shortly after reading the collection, Katai translated two short stories into Japanese, "Two Soldiers" ("Petit Soldat," 1885) and "Happiness." "Two Soldiers" is a romantic tragedy about a soldier who falls into a river and drowns after his friend becomes involved with a woman whom he loves. "Happiness" is, appropriately enough for its title, a rare work by Maupassant with a happy ending; it relates the story of a French woman from a high-class background who moved to Corsica and accepted a life of hardship and toil so that she could spend her life with her true love. Katai later related that his initial impression of Maupassant was that he was an author of romantic fiction, if occasionally tragic stories, but his impression was altered on reading Maupassant's most celebrated novels, *Pierre and Jean* and *Bel-Ami* (1885).[45] Of *Pierre and Jean*, Katai wrote that he did not have the same pleasant feeling that he had when he read the short stories in *The Odd Number*, perhaps because the novel presents the scandalous story of a woman who has raised a son, Jean, who was fathered by an adulterous lover. Pierre and Jean's mother accepts a fortune left by her lover to care for Jean, while her legitimate son, Pierre, is left with nothing. When Pierre discovers his mother's secret, he berates and shames his mother, but rather than react with contrition, his mother proudly displays her lover's photograph on the home mantelpiece in full view of her family, while her ineffectual husband quietly accepts his fate, in part due to the fortune that it will bring to his household (the theme of shameful passivity by a husband in return for financial gain is repeated in numerous stories by Maupassant).

Katai was more deeply shocked by *Bel-Ami*, a novel that describes a constant series of extramarital affairs in detail. *Bel-Ami* is a vivid and realistic novel that presents the story of an increasingly successful journalist who sleeps with one colleague's wife after another, while also making such shameless decisions as trading a mother for her daughter as lovers or asking for the hand of a friend's widowed wife just hours after his friend has died, while the corpse of his friend lays in a bed in the same room. Katai writes:

> *Bel-Ami* is a truly extreme novel. It boldly drags its protagonist into sexual situations, as though this were the most natural thing in the world, adultery after adultery, immorality after immorality. Moreover, it describes in detail the passionate emotions that arise in these situations, skillfully taking as its territory the extreme debauchery of the French upper classes. The effect is such that the reader will doubt that such people are even human.[46]

Katai was even more deeply disturbed by his continued readings of Maupassant, particularly after he acquired an eleven-volume set of Maupassant's short stories translated into English, *The After Dinner Series*, translated by R. Whitling.[47] Katai related in *Taiheiyō* magazine that the content of some of the stories was shocking and abysmal, including stories that include details of rape and incest. Katai's response of disgust in the press, however, was contradicted by his subsequent translation and publication of one of Maupassant's most infamously morbid stories, "The Case of Louise Roque," in 1901. The work describes the rape and murder of a preadolescent girl by the mayor of a provincial town, who jumps from the parapet of his manor and is smashed against the rocks below after nightly visits by the ghost of the girl.

Other early translations of Maupassant in Japan suggest that readers gravitated toward his more salacious and grotesque stories. In "Old Amable" ("Le père Amable," 1886), translated by Katai in 1901, an elderly man hangs himself in despair following the death of his son and the remarriage of his daughter-in-law. In "The Dead Girl," translated twice in 1902 and 1903, skeletons rise from the grave and reveal their hypocrisy and pettiness to a man visiting the grave of a lover. At the conclusion of the narrative, an apparition of the man's lover reveals that she died from a cold that she caught while having an affair. Two stories translated by scholar and translator Baba Kochō in 1902 feature themes of accidental incest. In "The Hermit" ("L'ermite" 1886), a philanderer accidentally sleeps with his daughter, whose existence he never acknowledged, whereas in "In Port" ("Le Port," 1889) a man accidentally sleeps with his sister, who had become a prostitute in the years that they had been separated. Other early translations of Maupassant focused on his exotic fiction based in foreign lands, including stories that are steeped in orientalist imagery. Such works include "Allouma" (1889) and "One Evening" ("Un soir," 1889), both set in Algeria, "Happiness" and "The Corsican Bandit" ("Un bandit corse," 1882), both set in Corsica, and "Châli," set in India. In "One Evening," a short story translated by Katai in 1902 and again by Kochō in 1903, the narrator summarizes an extended romantic description of the landscape of Algeria by comparing it to the enchanted world of the *Arabian Nights*, thereby suggesting a source of inspiration for Maupassant's stories of the fantastic. Maupassant's reference to the *Arabian Nights* thus links him in an additional way to Kyōka, as modern writers who were both inspired by one of the most influential texts in modern fantasy literature on a global level.

4. Kyōka and Maupassant

Kyōka's references to Maupassant appear in two essays from 1908, "Romanticism and Naturalism" and "My Disposition." Both essays present Kyōka's response to criticism of the unrealistic content of his own fiction, and particularly his decision to write ghost stories at a time when the trend of naturalism was at its height in Japan. Overall, the essays present evidence of Kyōka's dissatisfaction with modern literary genres and trends, but they also suggest his enthusiastic approval of certain modern writers and texts from Europe. As evidence, in "My Disposition," Kyōka positively evaluates the fiction of Maupassant and Turgenev, while questioning the widespread enthusiasm for Ibsen and Zola among modern Japanese writers and critics. Furthermore, his comments on Maupassant in "Romanticism and Naturalism" include specific reference to a collection of translations by Baba Kochō, *Collection of*

Famous Works of Western Literature (*Taisei meichoshū*, 1907), whose content he was apparently familiar with. The collection includes three short stories by Maupassant, as well as a story by Turgenev, thereby suggesting that Kyōka had this specific collection in mind when relating his admiration for both authors. Kyōka's singling out of a specific story by Maupassant for praise, "Mademoiselle Fifi," reveals affinities of Kyōka's fiction with the modern literary style of Maupassant, particularly in the qualities of intensive descriptive detail, well-structured and suspenseful narratives, and pronounced elements of gore, sensationalism, and eroticism.

Kyōka's essay "Romanticism and Naturalism" represents a rare attempt by the author to interject his opinion directly into contemporary literary debates in Japan. The essay presents Kyōka's theory of modern literature, thereby placing the author in the company of writers such as Shōyō, Ōgai, and Futabatei Shimei (1864–1909), all of whom wrote earlier treatises on the novel in response to their readings of modern European fiction and literary theory. Kyōka's essay takes the form of a defense that questions the right of critics to judge works of art according to the imagined standards of naturalism, while also presenting the argument that supposedly "realist" or "naturalist" fiction requires some degree of artistry to produce. In the essay, Kyōka questions the possibility of objective observation as a method for writing literature, whose essence he describes as "technique," or *gikō*.[48] He compares the naturalist writer to an archer who jams an arrow into its target, while comparing the truly artistic author to an archer who demonstrates skill with a bow. Kyōka criticizes the tendency of naturalist writers to want to expose shameful truths and portray what is ugliest in life, although this part of his essay is contradicted by his praise of Maupassant, and particularly by the story that he praises. Ironically, Kyōka condemns the cruelty and perversity of modern writers, despite the frequent depictions of eroticism and cruelty throughout his own work. He also condemns the gory interests of Edo-period artists, despite personally owning and referencing such artwork in his own literature. Reaching a middle ground in his argument, he suggests that eroticized depictions can be valuable as art, but only when portrayed skillfully through *gikō*. He also reveals a surprisingly modern value by praising the Western art of nude painting (*rataiga*), which intellectuals had criticized throughout the Meiji period.[49]

As an example of the successful meeting of eroticism and technique in modern literature, Kyōka discusses "Mademoiselle Fifi" by Maupassant, a work that he describes encountering in *Collection of Masterpieces of Western Literature*. Kyōka's selection of this story for praise reveals something of his literary interests and tendencies as an author, because it is the most clearly erotic and violent story in the collection. Overall, the translations by Kochō are of naturalistic or realistic literary sketches that seem to prize evenness and simplicity as aesthetic values. In "Biryuk" by Turgenev, a short story from *A Sportsman's Sketches* (1852), a groundskeeper berates an illegal logger before taking pity on the impoverished thief and setting him free. In "The Recruit" ("Le Réquisitionnaire," 1831) by Balzac, a woman hopes that her son will escape from prison and return home, but she dreams that he has been killed, and so she decides to take her own life. In one of very few scenes of fantasy in the collection, the reality of her dream is confirmed by the death of her son at the moment of her dreaming. In "The Lighthouse Keeper of Aspinwall" by Henryk Sienkiewicz, an elderly lighthouse keeper who has experienced adventures around the world, from Hungary to California to the Amazon, settles down to a stationary life on a tiny island in the harbor of Aspinwall, Panama (present-day Colón). One day, while he is reading a collection of poetry by Adam Mickiewicz (1798–1855), a representative poet from his native Poland, the lighthouse keeper forgets to light the guiding lantern, and a ship gets wrecked on a sandbar at the entrance to the harbor.

These stories in *Collection of Masterpieces of Western Literature* might be compared to the three works by Maupassant found in the same collection, which show a greater predilection for drama and erotic content. In "Moonlight" ("Claire de Lune," 1882), one of two completely different stories by Maupassant published in France during the same year with the same title, and both translated by Kochō and featured in the same collection of translations, a woman is influenced by a dreamy scene of moonlight to cheat on her husband with a complete stranger in the resort town of Lucerne in Switzerland. The other story titled "Moonlight" ("Claire de Lune," 1882) describes the jealousy a priest feels when he catches his niece in a romantic embrace with her lover on a moonlit night. Another story in the collection, "Debt," is also attributed to Maupassant, but is in fact a forgery.[50] Although it reads like a work by a different author, it is useful as a text that indicates the general perception of Maupassant's work around the world, because it features descriptions of prostitution, sex, insanity, and death. "Mademoiselle Fifi," a work correctly attributed to Maupassant, departs from the relatively calm atmosphere of the other stories by Maupassant in the collection with graphic descriptions of prostitution, violence, and murder. Thus, ironically, *Collection of Masterpieces of Western Literature* is mostly a collection of incidental sketches, and even a forgery, with only one story that would probably be recognized as a major work of European fiction, "Mademoiselle Fifi."

"Mademoiselle Fifi" is one of Maupassant's best-known tales of the Franco-Prussian War, a category that includes one of his longest and most famous novellas, "Boule de Suif" (1880). Both works combine cynicism, dark humor, and descriptions of prostitution with accounts of pragmatic choices and hypocritical decisions made by French citizens in a state of war. "Mademoiselle Fifi" describes the occupation of a French country manor by a troop of German soldiers, who demonstrate their lack of civility by destroying antique furniture and fine works of art in the manor. One officer is nicknamed Mademoiselle Fifi due his effeminate character and habit of saying "*fi fi donc*" in French, a phrase indicating dismissiveness or contempt. He regularly engages in destructive behavior, such as smashing drinking glasses, shooting out the eyes of a portrait, and blowing up a statue of Venus with a makeshift bomb. After days of boredom, the soldiers decide to send a dispatch to a brothel in town to summon a group of prostitutes for a party. The prostitutes are accustomed to German soldiers, because they regularly have sex with them at the brothel, as the narrator relates plainly. At the manor, the prostitutes indulge in heavy drinking and coarse jokes with their clients. Mademoiselle Fifi, however, grows violent with a prostitute named Rachel. He blows cigar smoke into her mouth, pinches her roughly, and bites down on her lips while they are kissing, thereby drawing blood. Rachel vows revenge for the bite and is finally pushed into action when the German soldiers claim they own all of the women of France, whose men were too cowardly to defend them. In response, Rachel stabs Mademoiselle Fifi in the throat and then escapes out a window. She hides in a church bell tower, where the priest continues to ring the bell to conceal its hidden occupant, until the German soldiers end their search for her. In an unusually happy ending, Rachel eventually leaves the bell tower and marries a respectable French citizen, who is not bothered by her former profession as a prostitute.

Kyōka recounts the major details of "Mademoiselle Fifi" in "Romanticism and Naturalism," including the shooting of the portrait, the party with the prostitutes, and the bloody kiss. He acknowledges that these are scenes of sexuality and violence, but argues that they are related skillfully, in a manner that sublimates them into artistry. He was particularly moved by the image of the bell tower in the narrative, which is emphasized in the Japanese version of Maupassant's story, because Kochō rendered the title in Japanese as "The Sound of the Bell" ("Kane no oto"). Kyōka writes that the theme of the resounding bell "thinly envelopes the story in colors of sublimity, a kind of mysticism."[51] He would appear to have in mind a passage referring to the bell tower that describes the bell as seemingly ringing of its own accord in the middle of the night; this leads the townspeople to fear that the bell tower is inhabited by demons who would possess those who wandered too close to it. In the translation, Kochō refers to the demons as *chimi* (nature spirits or goblins), opting for a traditional Japanese translation to describe the spirits who would possess the local people if they wandered too close to the mysteriously tolling bell.[52] Such language is reminiscent of Kyōka's writing, because Kyōka often refers to mischievous or dangerous nature spirits as *chimi mōryō,* and writes of spirit-possession and mysterious temple bells in many of his stories. In "Mademoiselle Fifi," the bell tower offers safety for the concealed prostitute, serving as a place of refuge in an environment of war and violence. Kyōka reiterates his positive impression of "Mademoiselle Fifi" in "My Disposition," an essay published three months after "Romanticism and Naturalism." In the latter essay, he refutes critical writing that describes the work of authors such as Turgenev and Maupassant as presenting somehow artless (*mugikō*) or unadorned impressions of reality. He specifically refers to "Mademoiselle Fifi" by Maupassant as a work "rich in technique and dazzlingly brilliant," thereby underscoring his appreciation for a story that sublimates violence and eroticism with poetic descriptions and thoughtful dramatization.[53]

Unfortunately, it is impossible to positively identify other stories by Maupassant that Kyōka read, although his references to Maupassant, Turgenev, and *Collection of Masterpieces of Western Literature* in the essays from 1908 suggest that he read through the wider collection by Kochō, and thus would have encountered the two stories titled "Moonlight" and the forgery "Debt." With their themes of adultery, prostitution, sex, violence, and romantic descriptions of temple bells and moonlit evenings, these works would have appealed to Kyōka's aesthetic sensibilities. It is also likely that Kyōka would have become familiar with Maupassant earlier in his career, while studying under Kōyō, because of Kōyō's promotion of Maupassant and his work. Moreover, the sheer frequency with which Maupassant's stories appeared in translation in magazines, newspapers, and collected volumes throughout the Meiji and Taishō periods would make it likely that Kyōka would have encountered the author's work in other contexts. The very fact that Kyōka even discusses Maupassant, as one of very few European authors whose work he mentioned in his writing, is evidence of the far reach of Maupassant's reputation. It is as though one simply could not be a modern writer in Japan and remain ignorant of Maupassant. His influence permeated the literary environment, and his tastes for erotic storytelling and unflinching depictions of moral corruption were reflected in the work of many of the most successful authors of the early twentieth century.

5. Kyōka's Modern Ghost Stories

Like the work of Maupassant, Kyōka's fiction features depictions of gore, eroticism, psychological horror, and unconventional sexual behavior that situate his work in a modern literary paradigm. While it is true that graphic sexual content can also be found in Japanese literature from the Edo period, as in the work of Saikaku and similar writers, the erotic nature of Kyōka's fiction differs from premodern literature. In particular, Kyōka frequently depicts relationships between young male characters and older female characters, many of whom prefer their younger lovers to older, ineffectual husbands, and, it is often implied, take on the role of "older sister," "aunt," or "mother" to a degree that borders on incestuous role-playing. Kyōka also frequently describes the exposure of maternal, female bodies, as well as scenes of women being bound and tortured, often with erotic overtones. Such content is difficult to imagine without the influence of writers such as Maupassant and Zola, who encouraged Japanese writers to unleash the darker parts of their imaginations in depictions of human sexual behavior in its various aspects.

Beyond the issue of direct influence, Kyōka and Maupassant can also be productively compared as representative authors of literature of the fantastic in their respective countries, Japan and France, who wrote modern ghost stories that vividly reflected their social and historical contexts. In *The Fantastic in Modern Japanese Literature*, Susan J. Napier raises the question of whether there exists "a distinctively Japanese fantastic."[54] She answers the question with a qualified "yes," but adds, "individual authors and specific periods give rise to particular uses of the fantastic, but it would be reductive to say that these treatments are somehow uniquely 'Japanese.'" In the case of Kyōka and Maupassant, the convergences and deviations in both authors' work are so pronounced that they suggest aspects of Japanese and French culture and society that fostered diverse approaches to the fantastic. Kyōka's literature is rarely as pessimistic or skeptical as Maupassant's, suggesting that the author's adherence to traditional cultural practices and values, particularly as grounded in Buddhism and Japanese religion, resulted in a different vision of the fantastic. One finds in Kyōka's fiction a technique of deferral, whether to religious authorities, doctors, or scientists, and an intellectual position of ignoring any need to explain the mechanisms of supernatural phenomena. Whereas Maupassant's fiction implies a desperate search for answers to life's questions in the invisible forces described by pseudoscientific studies, such as magnetism and hypnotism, Kyōka's work stops short when the search becomes too protracted, or seems unlikely to produce positive results.

Still, modern science appears as a haunting presence in Kyōka's fiction, or as a reminder that, even if the author can refrain from speaking too strongly about the relationship between psychology, physiology, and ghosts, he cannot escape the influence of modern systems of knowledge in his life and art.

Some of Kyōka's most incisive writing on the complications of belief in the modern world can be found in one of his most famous and critically acclaimed stories, *One Day in Spring* ("Shunchū" / "Shunchū gokoku," 1906). In the two-part novella, a nameless protagonist living in the resort town of Zushi, on the Shōnan coast southwest of Tokyo, sets out to visit a local Buddhist temple, Gandenji, to venerate a famous image of the bodhisattva Kannon. At the temple, the protagonist spots a poem attributed to the famous Heian-era poet Ono no Komachi that has been copied onto a pillar of the temple by a beautiful married woman named Tamawaki Mio. On noticing the visitor's interest in the poem, the temple priest relates the story of a previous visitor to the area who lost his life in romantic pursuit of the woman. During the visit, the priest also discusses with the protagonist religious iconography and the role of Buddhism in modern Japanese society. As the narrative continues, the protagonist begins to identify increasingly with the former visitor to Zushi and enters into a dreamlike realm of ghostly illusions, coming dangerously close to death after becoming entangled with the mysterious married woman.

Early in the novel, the state of belief in supernatural powers in modern Japan is described by the Buddhist priest of Gandenji, who presents the matter as a crisis of faith that affects the mental health of young people. The priest is surprised by the relative youth of the narrator, given the average age of the usual visitor to his temple, and he relates to the narrator his vision of religion in the modern age:

> The tenets of the faith have gradually fallen into decline. I am not certain what sect you belong to. Recently, my visitors are all people who are falling apart with age. Young people, today's students, hardly believe in salvation. These days, they don't even believe in Kannon. . . . In the worst cases, they even look at a painting of hell and can barely resist saying something like, "That looks like a good outcome." . . . Some young people, on the other hand, aspire to become leaders of their own sects. They writhe in agony as they struggle to attain peace of mind. Among these, some even go insane or commit suicide. . . . Speaking seriously, within the world of ideas that emerged during the great restoration [of 1868], some people saw God, some encountered

> buddhas who appeared before their very eyes, and some even believed themselves to be the savior. Groups like the Divine Wind in Kumamoto incited rebellions, as was heard about from time to time. In any event, these are matters for elevated debate and serious academic research, priests like me are simply here to guard idols . . . like these.[55]

The priest then relates that young visitors to temples are more likely to treat Buddhist statues as specimens of fine art and sculpture than as votive images. Although both the priest and the visitor present themselves as believers in such images and the beings that they represent, a comment made by the visitor suggests that he also reserves room for modern interpretations of religious veneration. After arguing that one would be happy to meet a loved one even in dreams, the visitor proclaims, "Even if they are only illusions, I would like to meet the gods and buddhas. Are not the very forms of Shakyamuni, Manjushri, Fugen, Seishi, and Kannon something to be thankful for?"[56] The visitor's skillfully worded response appears to support the priest's dogmatic interpretation of the power of religious images, while leaving open the possibility that religions are collections of archetypal images that reassure people in search of a symbolic order to reality.

Kyōka's fictional depiction of a religious debate in *One Day in Spring* might be compared to statements made in an essay he wrote the following year, in 1907, "Some Comments on My Love of Ghosts and My Debut Work" ("Obakezuki no iware shōshō to shojosaku"). Like the visitor in his narrative, Kyōka suggests a basic affirmation of the tenets of Buddhism, while simultaneously presenting a modern mentality that reserves questions about religion. He opens the essay by claiming, "I am an extremely superstitious person [*boku wa zuibun na meishinka da*]," thereby welcoming various interpretations of the comments that follow.[57] After introducing himself as superstitious, Kyōka claims, "I firmly believe that there are two major supernatural powers in this world. If I am forced to designate them, one is the power of Kannon, and the other might be called the power of demons. It is impossible for humans to resist either of these powers." Kyōka then affirms his belief that Buddhist sutras retain supernatural power in their very words, but then, as though reminding himself of his modern audience, he again begins to describe himself as extremely superstitious. He recounts an incident of being entrusted by Kōyō with a manuscript to drop off at a post office box. After depositing the manuscript, he circled around the box multiple times to make sure that he had not accidentally dropped the manuscript on the floor. His account appears to be one of obsession or mania, rather than supernatural power, although he again suggests a religious outlook by describing the reassuring power that Kōyō's words had for him. Relating that Kōyō managed to ease his mind by pointing out the absurdity of his behavior, Kyōka compares his mentor to a missionary who turned him away from superstition.

In his essay, Kyōka writes on the debilitating power of superstition in vivid terms, in a manner that suggests a lucid view of his own condition, while also suggesting an acknowledgment of the blurry borders of belief and perception. He writes:

> When I think back on the time that I fell into the depths of superstition, it gives me chills. It was as though my body or soul were bound tightly and I didn't have a day or even a moment of peace. When I would try to sleep, a demon would sit on my chest and my dreams would shatter into thousands and thousands of pieces. When I tried to stand up, I worried that I might step on insects, and that I would thereby commit the sin of taking the lives of living creatures. In this state, I was unable to separate night from day, I was unable to sleep, I was unable to get up, and my perception of my own self became incredibly vague.[58]

As a result of his struggles, Kyōka admits that he contemplated suicide. Kyōka's essay suggests the author's understanding of a complex relationship connecting psychology and belief. Although he presents his thoughts on this relationship through the language of religion, he also describes psychological phenomena such as compulsive behavior, night terrors, insomnia, and depersonalization in ways that suggest his modern understanding of such themes.

Returning to the narrative of *One Day in Spring*, in addition to its modern take on religious devotion and iconography, Kyōka's narrative expresses its modernity through presenting fantastic imagery that is macabre and surreal. In a central scene of fantasy in the novel, Kyōka displays a visual imagination as dark and avant-garde as that of Maupassant. At one point in the priest's tale, he relates that the previous visitor to Zushi followed the sound of a phantom band into the mountains, where he encountered a supernatural stage:

> To the left and right of the stage, from the sides of the mountain, a single band of white mist hung like a stage curtain. Drawn suddenly toward both sides of the stage, it folded away like whirling smoke. In a crude construction that resembled windows or boxes, thirty to

> fifty women appeared in small, dark, horizontal holes, one by one, in partitioned spaces, all lined up in a row. Some were sitting, some were standing, and some had a single knee propped up while sitting back in a loose position. Some wore only red undergarments. Some had blood dripping down their cheeks. Some appeared to be bound.[59]

With its surreal imagery suggestive of haunting and erotic torture, the passage reads like an account of a nightmare whose space and contours have become unstable. Rather than presenting a clear scenario, Kyōka's impressionistic description of the ghostly stage suggests an attempt to relate an experience of disorientation or insanity itself.

Kyōka once again considers the role of superstition in perceptions of the supernatural in one of his most vivid ghost stories, *The Order Book* (*Chūmonchō*, 1901), a work that reads like a traditional tale of the supernatural on the surface, only to reveal its novelties on closer reading. In this work, Kyōka juxtaposes the traditional, insular world of old Japan with a rising generation of globally oriented students, while using the figure of the ghost as a haunting force that takes revenge on a disbelieving youth. The story depicts a world at the intersections of tradition, superstition, and modern education, while featuring one of the most memorable ghosts of Kyōka's oeuvre. Kyōka's ghost displays popular traits of Japanese ghosts, such as pale skin, long black hair, and a vengeful nature. The ghost of *The Order Book* is also a modern ghost, however, as seen in the ways she morphs throughout the tale, at times appearing as a fleshly, erotic being, and at other times as a cold and fleeting figure. Kyōka's ghost might be compared to those of Maupassant, in stories such as "The Apparition" and "The Horla," because of its alternating appearance as a transparent spirit and a palpable presence, who appears to modern people caught between the forces of superstition and enlightenment.

The Order Book clearly presents its roots in tradition through its setting, the area surrounding the Yoshiwara district, one of the most famous red-light districts in Japan from the Edo period through the mid-nineteenth century. The story's roots in tradition are further reinforced by the occupations of two of its main characters, one of whom is a blade sharpener, the other a mirror polisher. The characters note their own increasing irrelevance in the modern world in a conversation that associates traditional culture with haunting. Gosuke, the blade sharpener, remarks, "If a fox lives one thousand years it turns into a monster, my occupation as a blade sharpener was already old in the Edo period lists of professions, and in a place like this, spirits easily take possession."[60] Sakubei, the mirror polisher, responds, "People like us have already transformed into goblins [*henge*] . . . as the generations in Tokyo change over, we look just like mortuary tablets to the dead Edo period."[61] During their conversation, Gosuke reveals his superstitious nature by conveying that he is terrified by the nineteenth day of every month, because he supposedly loses a customer's blade on the nineteenth without fail. Gosuke is later contrasted with the character of Wakiya Kinnosuke, a young man preparing to head for Germany to continue his upper-level education, who refuses to believe in the superstitions of the older generation. Wakiya's rejection of superstition, however, leads to his haunting and eventual death at the hands of a geisha possessed by a ghost.

The Order Book presents the history of its ghost in a frame narrative told by Sakubei. The character relates the story of a successful military veteran who began to frequent the pleasure quarters and to seek the affections of a geisha named Onui, who became jealous of her married client and attempted to murder him. At the climax of the frame narrative, Onui attempts to stab her lover, but her blade is blocked by a mirror that the man holds against his chest. In frustration, the woman slits her own throat. According to Sakubei, the suicide and attempted murder took place on the nineteenth of the same month exactly eight years prior to the time at which the story is being told. The mirror thereafter became a household treasure, which the veteran's wife intended to give to her nephew, Kinnosuke, as a graduation present, to serve him as a protective talisman.

Returning to the present time of the story, Kyōka introduces the story's ghost in a scene that combines eroticism and gore with vivid images of haunting. In gruesome detail, Gosuke and Sakubei excitedly discuss Onui's appearance as she took her own life, describing the dark red blood, as black as fish guts, that must have spurted out of her throat after she slit it open. Sakubei shows contrition over his indulgence in bloody details and decides to visit a Buddhist temple to pray for the souls of dead geisha. After Sakubei leaves, Gosuke discovers that he has lost a razor blade for a customer, a geisha named Owaka, just as expected, considering the date. As Gosuke searches for the blade, Kyōka presents the ghost of Onui:

> "It can't be on the shelf . . ." [Gosuke] blurted out without thinking. Lifting his head, the panel of the sliding door was open, and at the edge of the threshold was a hem, held up by sleeves just above the waistband, gray sleepwear with a pattern of dappled snow, vibrant eyebrows and a high-bridged nose, loose strands of hair straggling on pure white cheeks, he could see it all clearly. She was so tall it seemed that her bundled-up hair might strike the lintel of the door . . .

> "Gosuke-san," she said with an indescribably thick voice. She opened the lapel of her kimono with her left hand. . . . Her breasts were visible, heavy and luscious, apparently still warm, and from her breast pocket she removed a pale hand and held it straight out to Gosuke. Like the glittering scale of a poisonous snake, she grasped a single razor blade in her hand.
>
> "Is this it?" . . .
>
> The ghostly illusion appeared before his very eyes.[62]

In his description of the ghost, Kyōka combines traditional imagery of *yūrei*, such as pale white skin and messy black hair, and *yōkai*, some of whom have the power to grow taller, with unusual and sensuous details, such as descriptions of a thick voice (*futoi koe*) and ample breasts (*shishitsuki yutaka na . . . chibusa*). Kyōka concludes the passage with a vague phrase, "an illusion all the more before one's eyes" (*maboroshi wa kaette manoatari*), thereby presenting the ghost as both a vivid presence and a fleeting impression at once.

The second part of *The Order Book* focuses on the story of Wakiya Kinnosuke, while reintroducing the ghost in another creative scene of haunting. At the beginning of the section, Kinnosuke heads out for drinks to celebrate his graduation and imminent departure for Germany. His aunt insists that he take the heirloom mirror as a protective talisman, but he refuses to concede to the truth of her superstitions. Due to heavy snowfall and an accident in a rickshaw, Kinnosuke ends up stranded in the Yoshiwara district, where he encounters the ghost of Onui. In the scene, Kinnosuke describes to Owaka his encounter with the fugitive ghost:

> "There was a woman standing there. I thought I would ask her for directions and I ventured to speak to her, but when I approached her she startled and fled like a white heron. I paced briskly forward, but I suddenly felt uneasy and came to a halt. Within the heavily falling snow, her shape disappeared. When I looked again, she had moved to the edge of the drawbridge, so I began running swiftly in her direction again. As I continued walking toward her, she turned around and began heading in my direction, so I came to a halt again, and she brushed past me for the third time, then appeared once again by the drawbridge."[63]

The scene of haunting suggests an optical illusion, presenting a dreamlike scenario of constantly approaching a fleeing figure who can never be reached, and who repeatedly disappears, then reappears elsewhere in space. The other-

Fig. 20. Komura Settai, front endpapers of the *Dyed-in-Love Collection* (*Aizenshū*, 1916): the ghost of Onui on a backstreet in the Yoshiwara pleasure quarters. (Courtesy of Izumi Kyōka Kinenkan Museum.)

worldly atmosphere of the scene is visually captured by artist Komura Settai in the front endpapers of the *Dyed-in-Love Collection* (*Aizenshū*, 1916), which depicts a traditional neighborhood in Tokyo's pleasure quarters on a snowy night. Making use of linear perspective to draw the reader's line of sight toward the ghost in the middle of the alleyway, Settai skillfully evokes the haunted space of Kyōka's fiction.

At the conclusion of *The Order Book*, Kinnosuke's future plans for study in Germany are cut short when Owaka is possessed by the ghost of Onui and murders Kinnosuke with the razor blade. Gosuke witnesses the scene of the murder in a dream, and it is later confirmed by news of Kinnosuke's death delivered by Sakubei. In the dream, Gosuke looks through a glass window into a residence hall for geisha, where he sees Owaka undressing and bathing in a steam-filled bath, a razor blade held firmly in her mouth in preparation to murder her guest. When Owaka looks into a mirror, her face transforms into that of Onui, the vengeful ghost who appeared to Gosuke earlier in the narrative. Gosuke tries to scream and alert the residents of the hall of

Fig. 21. Owaka, possessed by the ghost of Onui, holds a razor blade in her mouth. Tashiro Gyōshū, woodblock frontispiece of *The Order Book* (*Chūmonchō*, 1901, reprinted in *Shinshōsetsu* magazine). (Courtesy of Izumi Kyōka Kinenkan Museum.)

the intrusion, but no sound escapes from his mouth. Once again, the visual impact of the ghostly scene is highlighted in artwork created to illustrate the story, in a woodblock frontispiece by illustrator Tashiro Gyōshū (b. 1870), printed in *Shinshōsetsu* magazine in 1901. In the image, Gyōshū depicts the possessed geisha in the bath with a straight razor held in her mouth as she prepares to murder her guest.

Following the scene of Owaka's possession, the maid witnesses a figure resembling Onui walking around the building, but she finds herself frozen in place and unable to respond. When she finally regains the ability to move, she finds Owaka dead in a blood-splattered room, where Kinnosuke is dying from a mortal wound. Kinnosuke's aunt sends a famous doctor (*ichimei no igakushi*) to attempt to save Kinnosuke, but he arrives on the scene too late. In an odd detail, the doctor is accompanied by a Christian female teacher named Tachibana, a friend of the Wakiya family, who recalls the figures of

Ms. Milliard and Lilika in Kyōka's early stories. Earlier in *The Order Book*, the teacher had agreed with Kinnosuke that the idea of a mirror serving as a protective talisman was only superstition. By the story's conclusion, however, the potential for the mirror to have saved the young man's life, whether by chance or through supernatural power, is suggested as a possibility. In the final scene of the story, Kyōka draws on literary clichés for a highly improbable conclusion. In a sign of his acceptance of his fated meeting with Owaka and subsequent death, Kinnosuke signs a paper declaring his marriage to the geisha, which the gathered witnesses cheerfully applaud as he passes away.

Doctors and medicine take on increasingly central roles in Kyōka's mid-career fiction, particularly in *The Swamp Woman* (*Numa fujin*, 1908) and *Nihonbashi* (1914). In both works, however, Kyōka uses the technique of deferral to avoid fully explaining the psychological and physiological implications of supernatural experiences from a modern cultural perspective, while mixing Buddhist imagery with that of modern medicine in creative ways. *Nihonbashi*, one of Kyōka's most popular works, is not generally considered to be a novel of the fantastic, but it features key scenes with supernatural content and grotesque imagery, as well as one of the most brazenly erotic scenes in Kyōka's fiction. The novel includes a ghost whose presence is made known by the sound of clacking wooden sandals in an alleyway, as is related toward the opening and closing of the novel, framing the modern narrative in an atmosphere of haunting. The protagonist of the story, like the young man in *The Order Book*, is a student with plans to study in Germany. Unlike the character in the earlier narrative, however, his course of study is specified as medicine, and he successfully makes the trip to Europe to continue his studies.

Nihonbashi relates a tale of rivalry between two geisha, Kiyoha and Okō, for the affections of Katsuragi Shinzō, a medical student who, in response to the complications of his love affairs, briefly forsakes his study of modern medicine to wander the country as an itinerant monk. The temporal delivery of the narrative is intricate and complicated (in his film version of *Nihonbashi* from 1956, Ichikawa Kon rearranges and reverses the narrative flow for easier comprehension). In series of frame narratives, flashbacks, and scenes whose relations are initially unclear, the reader learns that Katsuragi was raised in poverty and supported by an older sister, who sacrificed her happiness and married a wealthy older suitor in order to support her family, before disappearing and losing contact with her relatives. As a medical student, Katsuragi seeks the affection of geisha, who remind him of his older sister, and he performs an annual ritual of casting shellfish into the Nihonbashi river as a

Fig. 22. Komura Settai, *Nihonbashi* (cover, 1914): an abstract representation of the Nihonbashi river and warehouse district in central Tokyo. (Courtesy of Izumi Kyōka Kinenkan Museum.)

reminder of the sacrifice his sister made for his family. In a bizarre early scene in the novel, Katsuragi is stopped by a police officer when he is caught throwing shellfish wrapped in newspaper into the river. The officer does not believe Katsuragi when he explains that he is saving the shellfish from a doll stand (*hinadan*), where they were being offered as food to the dolls in a kind of sacrificial ritual, as was the custom in his family. The officer asks Katsuragi's occupation, but reacts with incredulity when the strange young man claims to be a doctor. Later in the narrative, the police officer demands that Katsuragi bring him to his medical facilities to prove his occupation. He discovers that Katsuragi is actually a medical researcher, rather than a doctor, and that his experimental laboratory is housed in a university. Contrary to the nature of such a setting as a rationalized modern space, the scene of the laboratory presents some of the more haunting and fantastic imagery in the novel.

The police officer relates his experience of visiting the university laboratory to Okō, to whom he describes the reason for his visit—to ascertain Katsuragi's identity. He explains:

> Unable to suppress my suspicions, I headed in the direction of Hongō, but not in a great hurry. I had pressed his colleague for information and learned that there was no doctor named Katsuragi Shinzō present. As it turns out, he was not employed in internal medicine, external medicine, or even in women's medicine. In fact, he was involved in research at a physiological sciences laboratory on a university campus.[64]

The police officer proceeds to relate his impressions of fear and awe on visiting the laboratory, whose resident researcher, having proven his identity as a medical scientist, suddenly struck him as imposing. He compares the visit to some of his more frightening experiences in police work:

> Last year I was in Gifu prefecture on service in a rural area in the mountains outside of Hida. In the shadows of a deep mountain valley, tucked away into the sheer cliffsides, I was investigating a case of illegal tobacco production. . . . Not to imply that being an outsider entering into the inner hallways of a university is quite the same thing as venturing into deep mountains.[65]

On entering the laboratory, the police officer demonstrates a newfound respect for Katsuragi, thereafter referring to him as "Sensei."

The police officer continues to relate the awe that he experienced when he was confronted with the accoutrements of Katsuragi's profession. He remarks:

> Like a flash of lightning, my gaze fell upon bookshelves that lined the entire room. The shelves were tightly packed with books, I think in German, whose names appeared in gold letters on their spines. . . . In a neighboring room was a device whose name I don't even know. It was like the mirror used by King Enma in hell to judge good and bad deeds. It seemed as though it could illuminate the interior organs, passing even through bone marrow, and it gave off a bright, flickering light.[66]

The officer's reference would seem to be to an X-ray machine, at the time a relatively recent invention in global medicine, whose presence in Kyōka's novel is somewhat surprising. His comparison of the X-ray machine to a mythical mirror is both darkly humorous and indicative of the officer's reliance on traditional concepts to understand the machines of modern medicine. The incongruity of the comparison is reinforced when Katsuragi provides

Fig. 23. Komura Settai, cover of the *Dyed-in-Love Collection* (1916): Katsuragi's dream of a giant enoki tree, with a view of his older sister on a distant veranda. (Courtesy of Izumi Kyōka Kinenkan Museum.)

evidence to back his story about the shellfish and the dolls. From the drawer of a bookshelf, he produces a set of dolls that "appear to be alive." The eerie scene brings an element of magic into the modern space of a cutting edge university laboratory, in a move that exemplifies Kyōka's treatment of urban space as a setting for modern ghost stories. It is an element of Kyōka's fiction that is highlighted by scholar Chiyoko Kawakami, who writes of Kyōka's urban stories, "the introduction of the uncanny in the Metropolis is a projection of the desire to reinstate a community that embraces a sacred space as part of everyday life, the very site slighted by the newly imported positivistic culture of rationalism."[67]

In another surreal sequence in the novel, Kyōka mixes an account of a dream with an intense scene of eroticism. Early in the sequence, Katsuragi relates to Okō a dream that he had of his older sister following her disappearance:

> Somewhere . . . Facing the second floor of my dormitory, a building of the same height across the single line of a river . . . The single line of a river . . . Perhaps it's a dream? The water flows as steadily as the Edogawa River down below. On the opposite bank stands a two-story building. I can only see the front of the building and a horizontal railing . . . Right in the middle is a giant enoki tree that blocks my view onto the second floor. It seems like there's a lower floor facing the flowing river and a room for entertainment toward the back. Because it's a dream, right? Well, listen . . . Yes, please listen.
>
> Behind the railing, somewhere toward the right, I can see a beautiful sleeve, lithely draped. Propping her chin on her sleeves, or with some forlorn expression, a woman appears to be staring right back at me. I catch a glance of her wrists, white as snow, but her face remains obscured by the enoki.[68]

The implied meaning of the dream, based on the context of the narrative, is that the woman hidden behind a giant enoki tree on a distant veranda is Katsuragi's older sister. The fantastic nature of the dream is reflected in the cover illustration of the *Dyed-in-Love Collection* by Komura Settai, in a design that places the leaves and branches of a giant enoki tree in the foreground, with the figure of the older sister on a veranda obscured in the depths of the image, like a hidden representation of the central female icon of Kyōka's fiction.

Following his account of his dream, Katsuragi relates to Okō that he fell in love with her rival, Kiyoha, because she resembled his older sister. Not to be outdone by her rival, Okō remarks, "When it's dark, don't I look like your older sister? Can't you pretend that I'm your older sister?"[69] Having revealed one of the central impulses of his literary endeavors, Kyōka pushes the scene further into erotic territory:

> If it's not enough for you to play with me as your older sister, then you can play with me as your younger sister. I could be your cousin and we can have fun. I can be your fiancée, your wife, your lover. . . . I can be a demon, a monster, a snake. I can show you anything that you want to see. After all, I'm an artist.

It is a stunningly erotic scene from Kyōka, who is often more reserved in his depiction of erotic themes. Although scenes with similar content appear throughout his fiction, they are rarely related as vividly and clearly as in

Nihonbashi. It is the kind of scene that seems to belong to the modern psychological novel, while also gesturing toward fantasy and a kind of erotic horror. In other words, it is the kind of scene whose production was facilitated by the translation of transgressive and psychologically realistic fiction by modern writers such as Maupassant.

One more ghost story by Kyōka, *The Swamp Woman* (1908), similarly features a doctor as a major character and a medical facility as a main setting. It is one of Kyōka's most conspicuously modern ghost stories and one of the most vivid intersections of science, fantasy, and religion in his fiction. It is also a psychologically chilling ghost story, with central themes of illness, guilt, and suicidal despair. In the opening line of the story, Komatsubara Ryūji, who is staying at a friend's house in a rural area toward the coast outside of Tokyo, cries out, "Oh, Mrs.!" in the middle of the night. He is surprised by his own voice, a detail suggesting corporeal disconnection that would strike a reader of Maupassant as familiar. Ryūji awakens atop a medical examination table, which has been inexplicably offered to him as a bed during his stay. He is lodged in a room with various animal fetuses in bottles of formaldehyde, as well as a skeleton hanging in a glass case. As related by the doctor, it was the skeleton of a female, a detail that causes the narrator to treat the skeleton with deference as a female companion sharing the space of his lodging, until the skeleton appears to come to life and approach him.

The opening chapters of *The Swamp Woman* vividly convey the experience of a narrator who is experiencing medical symptoms such as insomnia, night sweats, night terrors, and vertigo as he falls in and out of dreams on the medical examination table, in part through the use of repeating phrases that punctuate the narrative like a refrain, or like verbal indicators of recurring experiences of déjà vu. At varying intervals, the protagonist cries out, "Mrs.!" (*okusan!*), and "Again, a dream?" (*mata yume ka*), as he observes mysterious phenomena in a doctor's office, such as faces peering through the windows of the exam room and medical remains that seem to come to life. The narrator reveals a traditional mindset that is incompatible with his cold scientific setting, through his personification of the skeleton as "Mrs. Skeleton" (*gaikotsu-san*), and later by his identification of her bodily remains as Buddhist relics or images for worship (*Honzon! Honzon!*). As the night grows deeper, the narrator relates an experience suggesting a night terror, as he feels the skeleton on top of him, grasping him and weighing him down, so that it becomes difficult for him to breathe. He then tells of multiplying physiological and psychological symptoms, remarking,

> I had a hard time distinguishing the border of illusions and reality. Moreover, I felt cold, my head felt heavy, my whole body felt so sluggish that I could hardly stand it. As night deepened, I even began to think that I should wake up the owner of the house and request a medical examination, but my strength left me, even more so than before. The most difficult thing to endure was that it became difficult to breathe, and my ears started to ring, and my heart was beating so furiously in my chest that I nearly fainted.[70]

In a scene combining gore and eroticism, from his frozen position on the medical table, Ryūji witnesses the skeleton take on female flesh, before blood begins to pour from her breasts. He is finally roused out of bed when the cabinet begins rattling, a supernatural occurrence that proves too much for him to bear. Ryūji's doctor friend gives him a bottle of wine to calm his nerves, admitting that wine is not prescription medicine, but remarking that it is effective, as he measures Ryūji's racing pulse. The doctor then diagnoses Ryūji with *kurōshō*, a nervous disposition, and warns him that excessive worry can lead to hallucinations.

In the second part of *The Swamp Woman*, the doctor asks Ryūji to explain a rumor that he had absconded with a married woman and attempted to commit suicide with her. Like a modern psychologist, the doctor informs Ryūji of the ameliorative effect of revealing one's anxieties to a doctor, although, unlike in a modern medical office, both the doctor and the patient proceed to light cigarettes as they converse. As Ryūji explains, he had temporarily moved to the coast in the Zushi area to convalesce from illness, a detail that matches Kyōka's own life—the author similarly moved to Zushi for the same purposes from 1905 to 1909, for four and a half years (hence the setting of works including *The Grass Labyrinth*, *One Day in Spring*, and *The Swamp Woman*).[71] While living on the Shōnan coast, Ryūji became friendly with a woman whose husband was away at war. One day, Ryūji and the married woman went out for a walk in the extensive rice paddies near their area of lodging, leading to the rumored incident of attempted double suicide.

In the scene of Ryūji and the married woman's walk through the rice paddies, Kyōka devotes over a dozen pages to describing the geography of flooded and muddy rice fields, creating a landscape that is at turns naturalistic and romantic, with occasional hints of fantasy. At times, the scenic description is so meticulously detailed with visual observations of natural scenery that it recalls the nature sketches of Doppo or Tōson, or the naturalistic writing of Flaubert or Maupassant; at other times the landscape is romanticized with references to mystical locations in Chinese and Buddhist cosmologies, from Mt. Penglai to Buddhist hell. The naturalistic passages, delivered in clear, modern language, are particularly noteworthy, because they suggest that Kyōka was proficient in the naturalist techniques favored by modern novelists. Kyōka describes the scene as follows:

> The road was bad. The wife's feet glimmered in reflections in occasional puddles. The mud in the middle of the road was so terrible that, even though she could tolerate getting her hem wet, they had to walk through the grass along the sides of the road. The train station was nearby, you see? Piles of coal were visible within a fenced enclosure and gave off a strange white light, as though they would burn blue in the night. The sky above the town was pitch black, stretching from the path where they walked to the mountains, from which the white edges of clouds flowed out, from the railroad crossing toward the rice paddies, breaking into clusters as they flew by. Only the distant edge of the cape embracing the sea still had clear blue skies above.[72]

As the scene continues, the agricultural scenery takes on a darker aspect and is compared to a sojourn into hell, due to the impropriety of the situation. In this way, the scene resembles the *michiyuki* scenes of *jōruri* puppet plays. In the famous plays of Chikamatsu Monzaemon (1653–1725), the *michiyuki* is a climactic scene that describes the journey of lovers toward their place of suicide, often by combining details of real geographic settings with references to realms of the afterlife.[73] In a *jōruri* play, however, such scenes normally continue for three to four pages or so, with an abundance of allusions and poetic phrasing, unlike the dozen or so pages of realistic description found in Kyōka's novella. In another modern twist, at the conclusion of the sojourn, the married woman is struck by a train in what appears to have been an accident.

In the third part of *The Swamp Woman* (whose three-part division and quickening pace again recall the *jo-ha-kyū* structure of a Nō play), the doctor interprets Ryūji's cries of "Mrs.!" throughout the night as an attempt to call out to his former lover. Ryūji suggests that the doctor store his skeleton in a more respectful location, and eventually the doctor's wife convinces him to return the skeleton to the place where the doctor found it, in a swamp. The doctor recruits his rickshaw driver, a religiously devoted villager named Shōkichi, to return the skeleton to the swamp. As a fervent believer in Pure Land Buddhism, who uses charms and spells to cure illnesses, Shōkichi is not afraid of the skeleton's influence. At the swamp, the party tosses the skeleton back into the murky water. Ryūji stays behind, contemplating the scene of death before him, and is visited by the woman's ghost. The ghost then attempts to convince Ryūji to commit suicide by jumping into the swamp, saying to him, "The water of the swamp will cover your bones and become your skin. The water that you suck in as you drown will be none other than the lips of the one you love. Jump in! Jump in! Jump in!"[74] In a scene that suggests fantasy or a hallucination, Ryūji is approached by the married woman from before, who leads him to her lonely hut in the mountains. The scene then recalls the dream of the giant enoki tree from *Nihonbashi*, as Ryūji witnesses a banana tree growing so tall that its leaves block the sky and the light of the moon from view. Ryūji slashes wildly at the branches of the gigantic tree, until the moon shines through. The next day, he is found face down in a swamp, although he is still alive. The concluding lines of the narrative then summarize one of the main themes of the novel: the conflict between modern knowledge and faith. Acknowledging the extreme psychological nature of Ryūji's experience, the doctor remarks, "In the past, this is when you would turn seriously to Buddhism, but you've studied philosophy, so it's no longer an option. I have to say, though, that swamp is truly eerie."[75]

As I have attempted to demonstrate, Kyōka's ghost stories are clearly products of the modern world. They should be considered equivalent to the ghost stories of Maupassant in aesthetic value, emotional power, and the ability to frighten and disturb the modern reader. Although they draw on classical Japanese imagery and narrative structures for inspiration, they feature modern themes of medicine, skepticism, psychology, and eroticism that differentiate them from premodern literature. Moreover, their haunting creatures and imagery are the product of Kyōka's meticulous creation of new ghosts. By mixing Buddhism and modern medicine in narratives describing nightmarish visions, bizarre apparitions, states of distress and anxiety, and haunted medical facilities and instruments, Kyōka creates eerie stories that form the basis of modern literature of the fantastic in Japan.

Five

Kyōka and Mérimée

Tales of Magic and Ghosts

1. Kyōka and Mérimée: Kindred Writers

The most clearly referenced European writer in Izumi Kyōka's fiction is Prosper Mérimée. He is referenced three times, twice by name, in "Shepherd's Purse" ("Nazuna," 1921) and "Signs of the Chinese Calendar" ("Kinoe kinoto," 1925), and once in a clear allusion to Mérimée's most famous literary character, Carmen, in Kyōka's final published work of fiction, "The Cypress Vine" ("Rukō shinsō," 1939). In the years in between, other writers described Kyōka as a major fan of Mérimée. First, in 1925, Akutagawa Ryūnosuke wrote in a letter to a friend that Kyōka described Mérimée as "really great" (*umagasu na*), and in 1938 biographer and scholar Muramatsu Sadataka described Kyōka as "constantly bringing up the supernatural aspects" of Mérimée's fiction and as reciting passages of Mérimée's work aloud.[1] In this chapter, I argue that Kyōka was influenced by Mérimée in late experiments with his literary style and narrative techniques, particularly the use of scholarly frameworks for introducing ghosts into his stories. Kyōka and Mérimée both shared interests in common themes of the fantastic, such as ghosts, living images, popular religion, and the occult, although their treatment of these themes tended to differ. Mérimée's approach to writing ghost stories often involved posing a narrative riddle, while drawing on real scholarship on the local languages, histories, and cultures of Europe to lend an air of veracity or probability to otherwise impossible or inexplicable situations. Kyōka's treatment of the supernatural was often more impressionistic, otherworldly, or entirely fantastic in nature. In some of Kyōka's late stories, however, such as *The River*

Goddess (*Kahaku reijō*, 1927) and *Commentaries on the Mountains and the Sea* (*Sankai hyōbanki*, 1929), Kyōka experiments with his writing in ways that recall the work of Mérimée, as in the use of scholarly frameworks for his fiction and in his treatment of local history, religion, and folklore as central themes of his work.

In the West, Mérimée, who was active during the nineteenth century in France, is known as a representative writer of tales of adventure, vendetta stories, historical romances, and literature of the fantastic. For the general reader, however, he is most likely to be known for his short story "Carmen" (1845), a tragic romance about a Roma woman and a Basque man involved in lives of banditry in Andalucía, Spain; the story was adapted to a famous opera (1875) by Georges Bizet (1838–1875), and thereafter in dozens of movie adaptations in countries around the world, including France, Spain, the United Kingdom, the United States, Brazil, and Senegal.[2] In France, Mérimée is also remembered for his stories of banditry, loyalty, and vendettas on the island of Corsica, including "Mateo Falcone" (1829) and *Colomba* (1840); for "Tamango" (1829), a gruesome story about the revolt of African slaves on a ship in the Caribbean sea; and for "The Storming of the Redoubt" ("L'enlèvement de la redoute," 1829), a story of military bravery and slaughter in the Napoleonic invasion of Moscow (1812).[3] On a global level, recognition of Mérimée is skewed toward his relatively realistic fiction that treats themes of banditry, warfare, and femme-fatale protagonists, although a complete view of Mérimée's oeuvre reveals that much of his fiction also dealt with themes of the fantastic, including ghosts, vampires, the evil eye, supernatural visions, witches, magic spells, living statues, and a werewolf (or more accurately, a werebear). As I will show, Mérimée's approach to such themes was shaped by his professional scholarship, in fields including history, archeology, and comparative languages.

In France and Europe more broadly, Mérimée contributed to the early development of the fantastic as a genre, alongside contemporary French writers such as Théophile Gautier, Gerard de Nerval, and Honoré de Balzac. Early on, he was influenced by Charles Nodier, one of the first writers of the fantastic in France.[4] As an author with a strong grasp of English, he was also deeply familiar with stories of the supernatural in English literature, by writers including Shakespeare, Sir Walter Scott, and Lord Byron, as well as representative writers of the gothic novel, such as Matthew Gregory Lewis (1775–1818), Anne Radcliffe (1764–1823), and Mary Shelley.[5] Going further back into European history, Mérimée was influenced by the classical literature and theater of France and Spain, including the work of Molière, Voltaire (1694–

1778), Diderot (1713–1784), Miguel de Cervantes (1547–1616), Lope de Vega (1562–1635), and Pedro Calderòn de la Barca, as well as by the writings of classical antiquity. Building on a lifelong passion for literature, Mérimée wrote modern ghost stories that were deeply informed by his prodigious reading of European fiction from various eras, from seventeenth-century Spanish and French theater to nineteenth-century English gothic novels, and later by the modern fantastic stories of Ukrainian-Russian writer Nikolai Gogol (1809–1852). During the early twentieth century, Mérimée's erudite approach to the fantastic made its way to Japan, where his work influenced Kyōka as well as Akutagawa and Sōseki.

In Japan, Mérimée was received during the Taishō period through the beginning of the Shōwa period (1926–1989) as a representative European writer of romantic literature, whose popular tales of adventure, heroes, and ghosts suggested alternative directions for modern authors who wished to move beyond naturalism in their work.[6] As in the rest of the world, some of Mérimée's most popular stories in Japan included his comparatively realistic fiction, or stories featuring themes of bandits and female outlaws, such as "Carmen" and *Colomba*, although Mérimée was also widely perceived in Japan as a writer of the fantastic, due to the early translation of much of his supernatural fiction. As a sign of Mérimée's influence and popularity in Japan, almost all of Mérimée's fiction was translated into Japanese between 1911 and 1939, making him one of the most widely translated European writers of fantastic literature available in Japan during this time. Kyōka's acclamation of Mérimée might be understood as his recognition of a kindred writer from a European country, who helped to validate Kyōka's lifelong pursuit of supernatural themes in modern literature.

2. Mérimée's Themes of the Fantastic

Mérimée wrote stories of the fantastic throughout his career, from his early work in the mid-1820s until his final story of 1870. The themes and scholarly frameworks of Mérimée's supernatural fiction are represented by some of his most famous stories, including "The Vision of Charles XI" ("Vision de Charles XI," 1829), "The Venus of Ille" ("La Vénus d'Ille," 1837), and "Lokis" (1869). In "The Vision of Charles XI," the narrator presents a ghost story traced to a historical document from seventeenth-century Sweden; in "The Venus of Ille," an archaeologist relates an account of a living statue unearthed in French Catalonia; and in "Lokis," a scholar of European languages recounts the story of a hybrid human-bear encountered in Lithuania. These works are framed with descriptions of local history, geography, and folklore, drawing on Mérimée's scholarly interests. Other stories of the fantastic by Mérimée, featuring themes such as phantoms, vampires, magic spells, and mystical visions, include *La Guzla* (1827), *A Chronicle of the Reign of Charles IX* (*Chronique du Règne de Charles IX*, 1829), *Souls in Purgatory* (*Les Ames du Purgatoire*, 1834), "Il Viccolo de Madame Lucrezia" (1847, published posthumously in 1873), and "Djoûmane" (1870, published posthumously in 1873).

Mérimée's modern approach to the fantastic has often been characterized by scholars as cold, carefully plotted, and academic. The author is known for his literary technique of laying out details that suggest the veracity or probability of mysterious events, and as deducible by logical inference, only to undermine the most probable explanations for his narratives with key plot points that suggest the intrusion of supernatural forces into realistic settings.[7] Mérimée's approach to the fantastic should be understood against the background of his other occupations—in addition to being one of the most successful writers of fiction in nineteenth-century France, he enjoyed a long career as a historian, a scholar of languages, an official inspector of historical monuments, and a senator of France. In addition to his native French, he was fluent in English and Spanish and had advanced skills in German, Russian, Italian, Latin, and Greek.[8] He was also familiar with aspects of Romani, Basque, Catalan, Lithuanian, and Sanskrit. Mérimée was one of the foremost experts on Spanish literature, theater, and culture in France, and one of the most familiar with the real landscape of Spain during his era, based on years of travel to the country. He was also partially responsible for introducing Russian literature to France through translations of the work of Gogol and Alexander Pushkin (1799–1837).[9]

Beyond his work in fiction, Mérimée produced work as a historian, archeologist, and scholar of antiquities. His scholarly works include a partial history of the Roman Empire (*Études sur l'histoire romaine*, 1844), a history of Pedro I, king of Castile (*Histoire de Don Pèdre I*er *roi de Castille*, 1847–48), an essay on medieval religious architecture in France (*Essai sur l'architecture religieuse au moyen âge, particulièrement en France*, 1837), several works on the history and archeology of the various regions of France, numerous essays on Russian literature and history, and writing on the history of Ukraine and the Cossacks.[10] His academic knowledge was complemented by frequent travel to the places he studied and wrote about, including six visits to Spain between 1830 and 1864, a visit to Corsica and Italy in 1839, and a visit to Italy, Greece, and Turkey in 1841, in addition to constant travels throughout the regions of France, for the purposes of inspecting monuments for preservation and repair.[11] His most frequent trips abroad were to England, where he had many friends.[12]

Because Mérimée was so often busy with other responsibilities, he produced a limited quantity of fiction during his lifetime, often taking years off before writing a single novella or short story. He almost stopped writing fiction entirely during the later decades of his life, with the exception of a few short stories written around the late 1860s. His most famous stories can easily be collected into a single volume of a few hundred pages, although a more complete accounting of his fiction and other writing would fill several volumes (his complete works in French, including historical studies, is twelve volumes long), much of this with work that is eminently readable and entertaining. Due to his hybrid identity and career as a historian and a writer of fiction, Mérimée has been compared by Japanese scholars to Mori Ōgai.[13] He might also be compared to Kōda Rohan, particularly as writers who combined work in history with the occasional story of the fantastic.

In addition to its scholarly qualities, Mérimée's approach to the fantastic has also been noted for its skepticism and disavowal of religious dogma, if not religion itself, although Mérimée's fiction makes frequent reference to popular religious practices, particularly the veneration of relics and saints, and also shows a frequent fascination with superstition and magic. Pierre-Georges Castex summarizes Mérimée's intellectual attitude as follows: "A rebel against the discipline of dogma, Mérimée was also not a believer in salvation by science: his religious incredulity was accompanied by a reasoned defiance of positivist mysticism. For him, the universe was populated by formidable forces, which popular superstition illustrated, through the childish precision of myth, as a menacing presence."[14] Castex also notes, however, Mérimée's lifelong love of a well-told scary story, writing, "In common with Nodier, he affirms that the storyteller, to achieve the effect that is sought, must know how to abandon himself to a certain extent to the persuasive charm of the story; he admits voluntarily that even the most skeptical of people is at times superstitious."[15] Examining Mérimée's work from a different perspective, scholar Peter Cogman describes Mérimée's literary style as the "playful fantastic," or as a kind of game offering hints, clues, and deceptions that call for the reader's participation in the story, by which suspense, apprehension, and fear are produced.[16] Mérimée's approach to the genre might also be referred to as the "scholarly fantastic," or as a kind of mock scholarship that invites the reader deep into realistic settings, and eventually into a world of the fantastic, while providing real details of history and language, as well as liberal quantities of imagined local color, along the way.

Mérimée demonstrates his scholarly approach to the fantastic in his representative work in the genre, "The Venus of Ille," which was one of his most popular and frequently translated stories in Japan.[17] The story centers on a living statue, a major theme of the genre of the fantastic, according to Roger Caillois, who describes the theme as part of a group of related images, including "the statue, the mannequin, the suit of armor, [and] the automaton that suddenly becomes animated and acquires a dreadful independence."[18] Building on Mérimée's experience as an inspector of monuments, "The Venus of Ille" opens as an account of a scholar visiting the town of Ille-sur-Têt, on the outskirts of Perpignan in French Catalonia, to inspect the ancient and medieval ruins of the surrounding area. In Ille, the narrator is hosted by a Catalan antiquarian, Monsieur de Peyrehorade, who has recently unearthed an unusual statue of Venus. The classically trained inspector from Paris and the local antiquarian debate the provenance of the statue, as well as the meaning of a phrase in Latin inscribed on its pedestal, leading the inspector to adopt a condescending view of the provincial archaeologist and his limited historical knowledge. Attitudes such as these are, it must be noted, a common element of Mérimée's exoticized depictions of "local color" in his fiction, despite the author's intimate, firsthand knowledge of the places, people, and cultures that he depicts. Similar views can be seen in aspects of his depictions of Romani culture in "Carmen," Balkan and South Slavic culture in *La Guzla,* and Corsican culture in "Mateo Falcone" and *Colomba.* The inspector's skepticism and self-assured attitude in "The Venus of Ille," however, are challenged when he becomes involved in what appears to be the case of a living statue. As Todorov has noted, details throughout the story prepare the reader for the animation of the statue, such as its vaguely menacing grin.[19] Of the statue's peculiar expression, Mérimée writes:

> As for the face, it had a strange quality which defies description, and which resembled that of no other ancient statue that I can recall. It had none of that calm and severe beauty of the Greek sculptors, who systematically imparted a majestic immobility to every feature. Here, on the contrary, I observed with surprise that the artist had clearly intended to render a mischievousness bordering on the vicious.[20]

In another scene that prepares the reader for the statue's animation, Monsieur de Peyrehorade's son places his wedding ring on the finger of the statue during a game of *pelota* against a visiting team from Aragon, Spain, but later forgets his ring on the statue's finger. At the climax of the narrative of "The

Venus of Ille," Monsieur de Peyrehorade and his wife discover that their son has been murdered in bed on the night of his wedding. Various details from the story support the idea that he was killed in a deadly embrace by the statue of Venus, including the sound of heavy footsteps on the stairs heard the night before, the ring found discarded in the room, the broken frame of the bed, and the unusual condition of the body of the groom, which appeared to have been crushed, as well as by the testimony of the man's spouse, who gives an improbable account of feeling a cold, metal figure sneak into her wedding bed. When the reader aligns these details, it is difficult to arrive at a conclusion that attributes the man's murder to anything other than the living statue, although the inspector and the prosecutor discount such absurd possibilities. The result is a story that hovers with abundant hesitation at the borders of reality and fantasy, and is thereby justifiably acknowledged as one of Mérimée's best works of supernatural fiction.

Other stories of the fantastic by Mérimée follow similar patterns of narrative development. In "The Vision of Charles XI," Mérimée adapts the popular account of a ghostly vision seen by King Charles XI of Sweden portending the downfall of the Swedish monarchy within a few generations, as supposedly recorded in a historical document. A document of this sort circulated in Europe in the mid-eighteenth century and was published in Germany in 1810, although it was later discovered to be a forgery.[21] In Mérimée's adaptation of the account, King Charles XI witnesses lights coming from the closed and vacant meeting hall of his palace at night. He proceeds toward the hall with three of his subjects and finds that the oak paneling has been replaced by black drapery and German, Danish, and Muscovite flags. He then sees the room fill with apparitions, including a bloody corpse on the throne and crowds of witnesses and judges. An executioner's block is placed before the throne, where a young man is beheaded, spraying blood on the king's feet. The apparitions then fade away, implying that the vision was either an illusion or a hallucination, but the reality of the vision is suggested by a spot of blood remaining on the king's slippers. In the key scene reinforcing a supernatural interpretation of the narrative, Mérimée writes, "The black hangings, the severed head and the blood which had been flooding the floor had disappeared together with the other ghosts. But the red bloodstain on Charles's slipper could still be seen, and that would have been enough to remind him of what he had witnessed that night; in any case, these scenes had been too dramatic to easily be forgotten."[22] Mixing a forged historical narrative with vivid descriptions of the supernatural, Mérimée draws fantasy and reality together in a skillfully constructed tale of horror.

In addition to its scholarly content and puzzle-like narratives, another major element of Mérimée's fiction was the depiction of local traditions of folklore, magic, and the occult, including invented traditions and hoaxes. Mérimée's literary debut, *The Plays of Clara Gazul* (*Théâtre de Clara Gazul*, 1825), was a hoax that purported to present translations of six plays written by a Spanish actress of Moorish descent from Andalucía—in a demonstration of his commitment to the hoax, Mérimée even posed in drag for the portrait of "Clara Gazul" that appeared in the book.[23] This work was followed by *La Guzla* (1827), Mérimée's most explicitly supernatural collection of stories, as well as another literary hoax. *La Guzla,* whose title refers to a Serbian string instrument (usually rendered as *gusle*), was presented as a collection of ballads supposedly "translated" from a South Slavic dialect of the Balkans referred to as Illyrian (most likely Serbian or Croatian), but was actually written by Mérimée in French.[24] The collection includes stories set in countries corresponding to modern-day Serbia, Croatia, Bosnia and Herzegovina, Montenegro, and Turkey. Mérimée, who never visited the Slavic countries of the Balkan peninsula, gleaned most of what he learned about their cultures from literary sources of varying reliability, and the rest he made up.[25]

La Guzla features many elements that would come to define Mérimée's wider oeuvre, such as depictions of monsters and supernatural phenomena, grisly accounts of war and revenge, and the exoticization of cultures and literary traditions at the periphery of Europe. The supernatural stories featured in the collection center on themes of vampires, phantoms, and the evil eye, all situated within the exoticized landscapes of Illyria. The collection also reveals Mérimée's ongoing obsession with magic and the occult, particularly through references to classical texts on these subjects. As scholars have noted, in 1819, a young Mérimée spent six months studying texts on magic and supernatural creatures, including works such as *Treatise on Apparitions, Spirits, and Vampires, or the Ghosts of Hungary, Moravia, etc.* (*Traité sur les apparitions des esprits, et sur les vampires, ou les revenans de Hongrie, de Moravie, &c*, 1751) by Antoine Augustin Calmet (1672–1757); *The Enchanted World* (*De Betoverde Weereld*, 1691) by Balthasar Bekker (1634–1698); and *Natural Magic* (*Magia naturalis*, 1558) by Giambattista della Porta (1535–1615).[26] In addition to these classical texts, Mérimée was inspired in his approach to the fantastic by the work of Nodier, including Nodier's depiction of a vampiric monster in "Smarra or the Demons of the Night" ("Smarra, ou les Démons de la nuit," 1821), and by the frequent setting of Nodier's fiction in Illyria, or the Balkan peninsula.[27]

One more, lesser-known story of the fantastic by Mérimée, "Il Viccolo de Madame Lucrezia," again treats themes of ghosts and animated images, in ways that recall the themes of Kyōka's fiction. Like other works by Mérimée, the story mixes historical details with an invented narrative of modern fantasy. In "Madame Lucrezia," a narrator from France visiting Rome learns from a local woman that the ghost of the infamous Lucrezia Borgia is inhabiting an abandoned apartment in a backstreet, where she supposedly orchestrated the murders of her unsuspecting lovers after sleeping with them, in order to hide her promiscuous lifestyle. After accidentally sleeping with and killing her brother, Madame Lucrezia took her own life. Lucrezia makes her presence known to the narrator by throwing him a flower from the second-story window of the apartment, shaking the shutters, and laughing from behind the window. At the conclusion of the story, the ghostly figure is revealed to be a living woman named Lucrezia who has been hiding an affair with a young man studying for the priesthood, although details throughout the narrative suggest the presence of a separate Lucrezia, or a ghost of the historical figure hidden in the apartment. Other supernatural themes are introduced throughout the narrative, such as details of paintings and photographs with moving eyes, as well as an embedded tale of a murderous living statue. Similar images can be found throughout Kyōka's stories of the fantastic, particularly those of ghosts and living images, dolls, or statues, thereby suggesting a natural affinity between authors.

3. The Reception of Mérimée in Japan

Compared to Maupassant, the translation of Mérimée came relatively late in Japan, despite Mérimée being the earlier author chronologically. Translation of Mérimée largely began in the Taishō period, although the first work by Mérimée translated into Japanese appeared at the very end of the Meiji period, a translation of "Mateo Falcone" by Fujinami Suisho in 1911.[78] A collection of short stories titled *The Masterpieces of Mérimée* (*Merime kessakushū*) was translated by Kuriyagawa Hakuson and Ichinomiya Sakae in 1915 and included "The Etruscan Vase" ("La vase étrusque," 1830), "The Game of Backgammon" ("La partie de trictrac," 1830), "Mateo Falcone," and "Carmen." Notably, none of these are stories of the fantastic, suggesting the value that translators of European literature continued to place on realistic fiction, although most of these stories include at least some reference to superstition or the supernatural. Translation of Mérimée's work quickly accelerated in the 1920s, and soon many of his stories of the fantastic became widely available in Japanese. As is the case elsewhere in the world, "Carmen" quickly became Mérimée's most widely represented work in Japan, with eight different translations appearing during Kyōka's lifetime, followed by "Mateo Falcone," "Tamango," "The Etruscan Vase," and "The Venus of Ille," with four translations each.[29]

In terms of influence on major writers, three authors figure most prominently in the reception of Mérimée in Japan: Kyōka, Sōseki, and Akutagawa. Kyōka appears to have become familiar with Mérimée's work circa the early 1920s, shortly after translation of Mérimée's fiction began in Japan. He also appears to have sought out Mérimée's fiction in multiple translations and collections, some of which he probably owned at one point. Altogether, Kyōka references "The Etruscan Vase" in "Shepherd's Purse," *A Chronicle of the Reign of Charles IX* in "Signs of the Chinese Calendar," and "Carmen" in "The Cypress Vine." He was also described by Muramatsu as reading aloud from a collection of short stories translated by Ishikawa Takeshi that included "The Vision of Charles XI." In his reference to "The Etruscan Vase," Kyōka uses a translated title, "Etoruria no hanagame," that suggests that he encountered the story in *The Masterpieces of Mérimée*, which also featured a translation of "Carmen."[30] Muramatsu's anecdote suggests that Kyōka probably read "The Vision of Charles XI" in the collection *The Venus of Ille* (*Iru no megamizō*, 1924), translated by Ishikawa Takeshi and Okada Jitsumaro and named after the title story.[31] The collection features translations of three stories of the fantastic, "The Venus of Ille," "The Vision of Charles XI," and "Il Viccolo de Madame Lucrezia," in addition to a vendetta story, "Mateo Falcone." Finally, Kyōka refers to a version of *A Chronicle of the Reign of Charles IX* translated by Ishikawa Takeshi in 1923.[32]

Kyōka was preceded in his encounter with Mérimée by Sōseki, who owned copies of the author's fiction in English-language versions, prior to the translation of Mérimée's work into Japanese.[33] Sōseki referenced Mérimée twice in his fiction, first in *I am a Cat* (*Wagahai wa neko de aru*, 1905–1906), in a reference to a scene of women bathing in a river in Córdoba from "Carmen," and later in *Nowaki* (1907), in a summary of the plot of "The Venus of Ille" presented by a character in the novel.[34] Sōseki also annotated his personal copies of "Carmen," "The Venus of Ille," and *Colomba* with various critical observations. In these notes, Sōseki demonstrates his deep familiarity with the themes and structures of Mérimée's fiction.

In his notes for "Carmen," Sōseki writes that the novella is divided into four parts, each featuring different content and narrative techniques. As a work exemplifying Mérimée's scholarly style, the novella opens with the narrative frame of a researcher traveling to southern Spain to ascertain the precise location of the Battle of Munda, a battle fought by the forces of Julius Caesar in the ancient world, and also to use the libraries of the region to help him write his dissertation. While traveling through the arid mountains of Andalucía, the narrator meets José Navarro, a bandit from the Basque region whom he later encounters in a prison in Córdoba. In part two of the story, the geographer-narrator meets Carmen, who offers to read him his fortune, before stealing his watch. In part three of the narrative, which contains the main part of the story, José relates to the narrator that he fell in love with Carmen in Seville, after she brutally attacked a fellow worker with a knife at a cigar factory in revenge for an insult. Thereafter, José quickly fell into a life of banditry, smuggling, and violent rivalry with Carmen's other suitors. After months of a tumultuous relationship and life on the run, José murders Carmen, due to his jealousy over attention that she receives from other men, ending with a bullfighter in Córdoba. At the conclusion of the narrative, José accepts execution under the law. Part four of "Carmen," written later and included in later editions of the text, differs entirely from the first three parts, offering a scholarly examination of the language and culture of the Romani people.

In Sōseki's copy of "Carmen," the author describes the third part of the novella as being its most interesting and essential act, while describing part four as being entirely unnecessary for the narrative (part four of "Carmen" is often included as an index or addendum in later versions of the text). In a note conveying Sōseki's perception of literary history in a comparative global context, Sōseki compares Mérimée's work to *kusazōshi*, referring to "Carmen" as "Japanese *kusazōshi* enveloped in the atmosphere of the nineteenth century" and comparing its femme-fatale protagonist, Carmen, to Kijin no Omatsu, a female bandit and murderer who occupied a similar role in the illustrated fiction and theater of the Edo period.[35] Sōseki's identification of Mérimée's stories with *kusazōshi* suggests that he perceived commonalities in their themes, while also considering both forms of literature to be passé or outmoded in modern times. This might be compared to Sōseki's evaluation of Kyōka, cited in chapter 1, which similarly equated the author's work with *kusazōshi*, with an emphasis on the negative aspects of such influence.

Sōseki connects Kyōka directly to Mérimée in his notes for another story, "The Venus of Ille," particularly in terms of the content and style their fiction, but also their seemingly backward attachment to fantasy. Sōseki writes, in a private observation, that "The Venus of Ille" may be art, but that it is too "mystical" for the modern age, and that, in this respect, Mérimée's fiction resembles that of Kyōka. He furthermore adds, with acerbic wording, that Mérimée is "more than ten times better" than Kyōka.[36] Sōseki appears to have had at least a partially positive impression of Kyōka's work, however, because he personally met with Kyōka and mediated the publication of one of his most famous ghost stories, *White Heron* (*Shirasagi*, 1909), in the *Asahi shinbun*, a newspaper of high standing in which Sōseki regularly published his fiction.[37] This is the only work that Kyōka published in this newspaper. Sōseki's biting comments about Kyōka seem to indicate an undue sense of rivalry on Sōseki's part, perhaps because he recognized the unparalleled aesthetic qualities of Kyōka's fiction, or because he was truly averse to the writing of more fantastic literature in modern Japan.

An author more obviously influenced by Mérimée than Sōseki was Akutagawa, who references the French writer at least twelve times in his work.[38] Like Mérimée, Akutagawa wrote primarily short stories, many featuring fantastic themes, and often based on the author's research into historical literature, from Chinese mythology to Japanese literature of the Edo period to medieval Christian hagiographies from Europe. Akutagawa's familiarity with Mérimée was such that he even references the author's correspondence in two of his final works, "Literary, All Too Literary" ("Bungeiteki, amari ni bungeiteki na," 1927), a debate that took place between Akutagawa and Tanizaki, and "Cogwheels" (1927).[39] Scholars have interpreted many of Akutagawa's short stories as adaptations of fiction by Mérimée: for example, "Thieves" ("Chūtō," 1917) adapts elements of "Carmen"; "The Black-Robed Holy Mother" ("Kokui Seibo," 1920) borrows from "The Venus of Ille"; and "The Folding Fan of Hunan" ("Konan no ōgi") draws on both "Carmen" and *Colomba*.[40] As an example of such adaptations, "The Black-Robed Holy Mother" links Akutagawa's vision of the fantastic directly to "The Venus of Ille." Akutagawa's story presents the image of an eerie grimacing statue that brings about the death of a petitioner, along with her grandson, for whom she had been praying. In a parallel to Mérimée's Roman statue of Venus, Akutagawa's story features a historical artifact, that of a Kannon Maria, or a mixed image of the bodhisattva Kannon and the Virgin Mary. Such images were historically made by Japanese converts to the Roman Catholic religion during the Edo period, although Akutagawa's vision of the statue transforms religious imagery to suit the needs of a supernatural narrative. Deviating from the details of Mérimée's work, the petitioner's death in Akutagawa's story is caused by a curse, rather than by the physical embrace of the statue.[41]

Like Sōseki, Akutagawa drew a link between the literature of Kyōka and Mérimée, but he interpreted this link in a positive manner, particularly in his evaluation of Kyōka. Kyōka became acquainted with Akutagawa circa 1921, and the two remained friends until Akutagawa's passing in 1927. In 1925, Akutagawa met with Kyōka at a hot spring resort in Shūzenji, where

Kyōka and his wife, Izumi Suzu, were staying. In a letter written to a friend from the resort, Akutagawa described Kyōka as an author who maintained his youthful enthusiasm, including for one of his favorite writers in his later years, Mérimée. Akutagawa wrote, "Kyōka has been here with his wife since yesterday. That old man seems like he's even younger than me. He keeps saying that Mérimée is so great."[42] That same year, Akutagawa wrote a message advertising the publication of an early version of *The Complete Works of Izumi Kyōka* (*Kyōka zenshū*, 1925), published by Shun'yōdō. In the advertisement, Akutagawa asserts that Kyōka's fiction is even better than Mérimée's, an evaluation that reversed Sōseki's private opinion of Kyōka. Akutagawa wrote:

> As an experiment, Sensei's stories might be compared to the work of the great romantic writers from France on equal ground. The quality of his fiction is like a pillar of seven treasures reaching into the heavens, his skill even surpasses that of Mérimée. In terms of its quantity, his work is like an Ashoka tree that reaches beyond the earth, standing shoulder to shoulder with the great work of Balzac. Sensei's literature is truly impressive![43]

One might note that Akutagawa refers to Kyōka as "sensei," in common with Tanizaki, thereby signaling the respect he felt for the senior author. Akutagawa also praises Kyōka's fiction by drawing on the language and imagery of Buddhist sutras, thereby emphasizing the Japanese qualities of Kyōka's approach to fantasy.

Kyōka was so pleased with Akutagawa's recommendation of his work that he later reprinted Akutagawa's essay in the opening pages of one of his final collections of fiction, *To Hear Auspicious News* (1934). Because the advertisement includes the comparison to Mérimée, this might even be included as a fourth reference by Kyōka to the French author, although it was made vicariously. The publication of Akutagawa's message also serves as further evidence of the camaraderie that existed between these two authors, as well as the respect that Kyōka felt and returned to his departed friend. Furthermore, this late publication foregrounds the enthusiasm both authors felt for Mérimée as an aspect of their connection.

4. Kyōka and Mérimée

In his late work, Kyōka appears to have been influenced by Mérimée's modern experimentations with narrative framing and the depiction of supernatural themes. Scholar Jinzai Kiyoshi writes of the connection between the authors, "The most obvious point that Kyōka and Mérimée have in common would seem to be their interest in the supernatural [*yōi*]. . . . They were both people who never grew tired of endlessly expressing their thoughts about the supernatural."[44] Both authors also shared interests in themes such as popular religion, living images, the occult, and the character type of the femme fatale. Mérimée's most famous character, Carmen, falls into this category, as does Kyōka's most famous character, the witch of Mt. Kōya, both of whom are depicted as threatening, dangerous, and seductive, but also, at times, as maternal and caring. In their relation to the fantastic, however, these characters differ. The woman of Mt. Kōya is suggested to have supernatural powers, in the manner of fairytales, whereas Carmen's practice of fortune-telling is linked to local superstition and folkloric tradition, in a scholarly fashion.

Kyōka's first reference to Mérimée is to one of the author's more realistic works of fiction, "The Etruscan Vase," a work that appears to have been particularly popular in Japan, based on how frequently it was translated into Japanese.[45] "The Etruscan Vase" presents the story of Auguste Saint-Clair, a Parisian aristocrat who fears that his mistress, Countess Mathilde de Coursy, may have another lover, a handsome though famously boring man named Massigny, whose connection to her is indicated by an Etruscan vase that she received as a gift and that she keeps on her mantlepiece. To prove her innocence, the countess smashes the priceless vase, but Saint-Clair is soon killed in a duel with another man whom he offended while sulking over his suspicions of infidelity. The countess spends three years in mourning, then dies of illness, seemingly brought on by a broken heart.

Kyōka references "The Etruscan Vase" in "Shepherd's Purse" (1921), a story that represents one of Kyōka's clearest forays into naturalist fiction. It is part of a group of works, often short, that began to appear with greater frequency in Kyōka's later career. Although little discussed in scholarship, stories such as "Shepherd's Purse," "Maple and Dove" ("Kaede to shirahato," 1922), and "Two, Three Birds, Twelve, Thirteen Birds" ("Ni, san wa, jū ni, san wa," 1924) are among Kyōka's most subtle works of modern literature, featuring mostly autobiographical content related in a realistic manner. At the same time, they demonstrate the author's tendency to provide at least a hint of the supernatural in the majority of his work, in ways that infuse even his most ordinary tales of the modern world with a sense of enchantment or otherworldliness. Due to these traits, the style of these works might be compared to the genre of magical realism, a global genre of fiction that scholar Maggie Ann Bowers describes as featuring a "matter-of-fact, realist tone . . . when presenting supernatural happenings."[46]

"Shepherd's Purse" is one of Kyōka's most unusual stories, and also one of the most intimate portrayals of his family life and environment. Kyōka was known to spend much of his time with his wife, Suzu, primarily in a comfortable two-story home with a spacious garden in the central Rokubanchō neighborhood of the Kōjimachi district of Tokyo, where he lived for the final three decades of his life.[47] As suggested in Kyōka's fiction, often with a hint of disappointment, Kyōka's wife never bore children of her own, although following Kyōka's death she adopted a daughter, Izumi Natsuki (1933–2008), Kyōka's niece and the daughter of his brother, Izumi Shatei.[48] In "Shepherd's Purse," Kyōka describes interactions between a childless couple and the young daughter of a family in the narrator's neighborhood who practically becomes the couple's adopted daughter. According to Izumi Natsuki, the character from the story was based on a real girl from the neighborhood, who shares her name with the fictionalized character in the text.

Kyōka opens "Shepherd's Purse" by remarking that he loathes children, but then goes on to spend the rest of the story describing the happiness brought to a childless couple by a young girl, Mieko, the daughter of a neighborhood friend who works as an employee of a government tobacco agency. The couple help raise the child from the time that she is an infant through her early years, when she begins to crawl, babble, and eventually tell stories and sing songs. Despite the narrator's supposed dislike of children, he is deeply moved by the girl's presence in his life, writing of her, "Truly, it is only when one looks into the eyes of a child that one realizes that humans are all pure and beautiful, the transformed bodies of stars," and elsewhere remarking that her singing and her bunched-up nose make him want to cry.[49] The couple is also proud of the girl's mature taste in food (she eats pickled radish and dried squid) and her ability to tell humorous stories.

While sketching realistic scenes of life in modern Tokyo, Kyōka introduces details that gradually create a fairytale-like atmosphere for his narrative, in part by referencing Western folktales. This begins when the narrator relates a list of nicknames devised by the couple for Mieko, including Mīchan, Mībō, Mīkō, Minoji, and even Mimizuku, a word meaning "horned owl." The couple eventually settles on the nickname of Minmī, an unusual name for a Japanese child. The narrator even surmises that the name might best be spelled using the Western alphabet as "Mimmy," although he worries that this would lead to teasing from other children. Minmī begins to appear like a character from a fairytale when the narrator imagines that she was once a long-eared rabbit in her mother's womb, whose "gramophone" ears recorded the songs that she later sang.

In descriptions of his conversation with the child, Kyōka mixes references to Western and Japanese folklore and religion, thereby demonstrating his abiding interest in such topics. Kyōka writes:

> Recalling the song of the baby rabbit, it's not the Western story that I mean to speak of, but it seemed that she couldn't have arrived in this world in any other way than in the beak of a white bird. There are many other stories that I wish to relate, but let me tell you a little bit about the story of the baby bird . . .
>
> "Whose child are you, Minmi?" I asked.
> "Auntie's child."
> "Is that so? Where were you born?"
> "In the ginkgo tree."
> There was a giant ginkgo tree by the child's house directly across the way. Her parents were Christians, so they had skillfully adapted the fable of the stork and taught her this.
> "Who brought you to the ginkgo tree?"
> "A horned owl."
> "That's no good, a horned owl," auntie said, although I thought it made sense. It would be strange for a crane, like an origami crane, to land in a ginkgo tree. There are crows, kites, owls, starlings. . . . There are sparrows, but those are too small. So I guess that's why her parents went with a horned owl.[50]

The narrator follows his reference to the stork with a reference to a *kappa*, a popular *yōkai*. In the scene, the girl imagines that she is wearing a dish of water on her head, in the manner of *kappa*, who are said to preserve their life force in such dishes.

Kyōka's reference to Mérimée finally appears in the closing section of "Shepherd's Purse," in what might be considered an addendum or author's note. Having rambled on about Minmī for an entire short story, the narrator apologizes for presenting such boring content to the reader. He then links his discussion of boredom to a scene from "The Etruscan Vase." The relationship of the reference to the narrative appears to be entirely tangential, yet it is meaningful because it demonstrates the depth of Kyōka's familiarity with Mérimée's work. In reference to a slight anecdote from "The Etruscan Vase," Kyōka describes the darkly humorous scene of a character who is literally bored to death. In the scene being referenced, a traveler named Richard Thornton traveling through the vicinity of Naples decides to take a dangerous path through the countryside, notorious for its roaming thieves, to avoid the painfully boring banter of his travel companion, Massigny. On this alternative path, he is murdered by bandits. As Kyōka notes in "Shepherd's Purse," echoing Mérimée's dark humor, sometimes "boredom kills."[51] Kyōka ends the story with an anecdote about a woman who lost her mind from boredom because she was forced to play *hanagaruta*, a traditional Japanese card game, with her mother-in-law every evening. Kyōka then closes the literary sketch by reinforcing the disappointment of the childless couple, as the narrator remarks, "As one without children, I cried."

Kyōka's subsequent reference to Mérimée is more important for establishing a link between the two authors in terms of their mutual interest in the fantastic. The reference is to *A Chronicle of the Reign of Charles IX*, an ostensibly historical novel by Mérimée that includes references to magic spells, fortune-telling, and miraculous relics. The reference appears in Kyōka's short story "Signs of the Chinese Calendar" (1925), a tale of ghostly fantasy and horrific apparitions. The reference constitutes one of the most revealing descriptions of Kyōka's global literary influences and of his admiration for modern European literature, particularly the work of Mérimée. "Signs of the Chinese Calendar" opens within a naturalistic framework, in a hot springs resort, where the narrator's wife picks green onions with a maid in the fields and enjoys a local show of *manzai*, while the narrator enjoys miso soup and curry with rice in his room. At the beginning of the narrative, Kyōka describes the narrator as reading a novel by Mérimée in translation, in a scene that strongly suggests that Kyōka is describing his own recent reading habits. In the scene, the narrator lays in bed at the inn and reads a copy of *A Chronicle of the Reign of Charles IX*, translated into Japanese as *Churujisu fujin* (*Madame de Turgis*) by Ishikawa Takeshi in 1923.[52] The narrator apologizes for his poor posture, conceding that Merimée's novel should rightfully be read in an attentive position at one's desk. He then remarks that, on his bookshelf at home, he keeps a copy of *A Chronicle of the Reign of Charles IX* next to a Bunka-era (1804–1818) edition of *Bathhouse of the Floating World* (*Ukiyoburo*, 1809–1813) by Shikitei Sanba, a famous work of comic literature from the Edo period. Noting the incongruity of placing these books side by side, Kyōka suggests that this arrangement encapsulates his own approach to writing fiction as an author of the modern world. He remarks, "Without such daring measures, it is no longer possible to make one's career as a writer."[53] As one who was often scrupulous in preserving his image as an antiquarian writer influenced mainly by the art and literature of East Asia, the passage appears as something of a confession of the impossibility of avoiding European influences in the modern age.

Kyōka's suggestion that Mérimée's novel should be read at a desk indicates his understanding of *A Chronicle of the Reign of Charles IX* as a serious book dealing with historical subject matter—the conflict between Roman Catholic and Huguenot Protestant citizens of France during the French wars of religion (1562–1598), with a focus on the St. Bartholomew's Day massacre of Huguenots by French Catholic mobs in 1572. The scholarly nature of the book is reinforced in Ishikawa's translation, which retains quotations from writings by Molière, Shakespeare, Lord Byron, and other authors in their original English- and French-language versions, included as epigraphs at the beginning of each chapter. Ishikawa's translation is furthermore enhanced by the inclusion of a short biography and bibliography of Mérimée, which would have helped to expand Kyōka's familiarity with the author. Kyōka's interest in Mérimée's novel suggests that he continued to value historical, geographic, and cultural education later in life, a tendency that can be traced to his international education during his school days. However, *A Chronicle of the Reign of Charles IX* is not just a straightforward historical novel, but also a novel of romance, adventure, and even magic set in a historical time period. Although details of the French Wars of Religion and the St. Bartholomew's Day massacre are related at length in the novel, particularly in the last part of the narrative, much of the story focuses on the interactions of its main characters, who include Bernard de Mergy, a Protestant soldier, George de Mergy, Bernard's Catholic brother, and Madame de Turgis, Bernard's Catholic lover. The centrality of the romantic narrative is emphasized by the title chosen by Ishikawa for the Japanese translation: *Madame de Turgis*. As this choice suggests, much of the story revolves around a romantic relationship, particularly between people of different religious backgrounds, which encapsulates wider social and religious tensions. The narrative of the lovers is also colored by elements of the supernatural and by irreverent and even sacrilegious humor, of a kind that occasionally caused trouble for Mérimée.[54]

Although the narrative of *A Chronicle of the Reign of Charles IX* is largely realistic, it includes improbable and even fantastic details, such as a prediction made by a Romani fortune teller named Mila at the outset of the story that Bernard will eventually take the life of a relative, who turns out to be his brother, and a plotline about a relic given by Madame de Turgis to Bernard that saves his life when, miraculously, it is struck by a bullet during a duel. The novel also draws on Mérimée's lifelong interests in the occult and other supernatural themes in prominent scenes of magic. Mila, who is from Germany, is said to come from a country where conjurers are as common as monks are in France. Before reading Bernard's fortune, she tells him a fairytale, "The Pied Piper of Hamelin," in a version found in the writings of the Brothers Grimm (thereby suggesting a second possible intersection between Kyōka and the famous collectors of fairytales). As in other versions of the fairytale, the main part of the story describes a wandering piper who rids the town of Hamelin of rats by mesmerizing packs of rodents with his music and drawing them to a river, where they drown. In the version related by the Brothers Grimm, the piper proceeds to draw the children of Hamelin away to a cave when the town's citizens refuse to pay him for his services, and the children magically reappear in Transylvania.[55] Following Mila's recounting of the fairytale, she accurately predicts Bernard's fate, and he exclaims that she must truly be a witch.

The most involved scene of magic in *A Chronicle of the Reign of Charles IX* appears in a chapter whose subject is indicated by its title: "White Magic." In the chapter, Bernard spies on magic rituals, including a love spell and a healing spell performed by a witch, Camilla, at the request of Madame de Turgis. During the ritual, Camilla reveals that the pair had sacrificed a black ram, buried a black hen with a sword blessed by a priest, and stabbed an effigy of Bernard's enemy prior to his duel, thereby ensuring his success. In a new ritual, the witch anoints with scorpion oil a sword that was used to wound Bernard and burns a wax image over a fire, thereby aiming to secure Bernard's love and health. The ritual ends when the witch directs Madame de Turgis to burn a green candle before an image of the Virgin Mary. The magic ritual seems to work, but only for a time, because Bernard eventually loses his life, after taking the life of his brother, as predicted by Mila earlier in the narrative.

Kyōka's "Signs of the Chinese Calendar" delves more clearly into the realm of the fantastic than Mérimée's novel, although it perhaps took hints from the novel for its own mixture of vivid realism with dark and fantastic imagery. After the narrator describes his bookshelf at home, where *A Chronicle of the Reign of Charles IX* sits next to *Bathhouse of the Floating World*, he then presents a frame narrative that is related by another character at the inn, Akiba Toshiyuki, as the main narrative of the text. Akiba's story conveys a convincingly lifelike vision of modern Tokyo, but also includes supernatural details that blur the lines between reality and fantasy so thoroughly that the narrative is occasionally difficult to follow. One of the main elements of fantasy is found in a recurring motif, that of two geisha who have periodically reappeared to Akiba throughout his life, including in the buildings of his hometown, in his dreams, and as new geisha who resemble the earlier pair.

In the frame narrative, Akiba recalls that, during the Meiji period, there was a famous pair of geisha from Shinbashi in central Tokyo who decided to set out on a pilgrimage to expiate their sins. The pair, dressed as pilgrims with sedge hats and wooden boxes on their backs, deliberately chose deep mountain routes to ensure the authenticity of their pilgrimage. Their journeys proved to be a national sensation and were reported in newspapers around the country. According to Akiba, the pair ended up in his hometown of Kanazawa, where he spotted them in a neighboring building while studying for an upcoming geography exam with a friend. He describes their voices as reaching out to him as though from "another world" (*betsu no sekai*) and their shadowy figures as being framed by a "strange mountain like the kind from fairytales" in the background.[56] The two women are contrasted in ways that accentuate their differences, while also suggesting the caricatures of fairytales. One geisha is tall, slim, wears her hair in the *marumage* style, and is referred to as the "older sister"; the other is short, round, wears her hair in the *ichōgaeshi* style, and is referred to as the "younger sister." The identities of these geisha begin to blur with those of other women, however, beginning when Akiba spots them out at sea, while accompanying his father on a trip to negotiate for a potential future wife, following the death of Akiba's mother. Akiba believes one of the women to be his recently departed mother, and then nearly drowns at sea when trying to reach her.

The two geisha reappear, or are in some sense reincarnated or reflected in new characters, nearly thirty years later in Tokyo. In the later timeline of the story, they have become the hired companions of Akiba as an adult, who remarks, "From illusion to reality, the boy of fairytales became an annoying old man bringing geisha along with him on a trip."[57] Akiba arranges a rendezvous with the two geisha at a train station in Tokyo after a night of drinking, during which the group came up with the plan of visiting an inn on the Shōnan coast. After a moment of fantasy (the women appear to him like birds with human faces), Kyōka provides an image of modern transit in Tokyo that is so realistic that it still corresponds, in certain details, to travel in Tokyo today. The train is packed and stuffy; its passengers alternately scramble for seats, struggle to save seats for friends, or leave them open for other passengers. New crowds pour in at Shinagawa station in south-central Tokyo (a central hub of transport and transit exchange even today), and many are wearing Western clothes and white shirts. In a nod to his abiding interest in European classical antiquity, Kyōka describes one of the passengers as being as brave as a soldier from Sparta in his attempt to save a seat for his female traveling companion. When the woman arrives, Kyōka presents an erotic portrait of her that is rooted in the language of realism. Kyōka writes:

> The woman who came buoyantly floating onto the train wore a pleated blue hat with the bill tilted upward, a Western-style knee-length skirt, and an opera bag decorated with glittering glass beads that hung down to her knees. She held back breasts that seemed ready to pop out of her shirt, while, with her other hand—she wasn't quite waving it, but rather seemed to be letting it follow the momentum of tossing her umbrella aside. As expected, because her butt was so big that there was simply nothing that could be done about it, she landed onto the seat with a thud. . . . Resting her round chin on her hand, she just barely managed to cover her dangerously protruding nipples, while exposing the rest of the surface of her breasts and letting them bounce and sway with the movement of the train . . .[58]

One might note that Kyōka describes the full-bodied woman sensually, as he does in similar fashion throughout his fiction, including in his description of the woman of Mt. Kōya. This attention to the fleshliness of woman's bodies has been noted by scholars, who describe such depictions as deepening the eroticism of Japanese literature.[59] Kyōka's consistent emphasis on the thickness of women's bodies as a source of attraction might be further emphasized as a defining aspect of the eroticism of his fiction.

In a passage that conveys Kyōka's acute awareness of the effects of literary experimentation, the author suggests that such realistic description risks taking him far away from the worlds of fairytales and fantasy that he usually depicts in his fiction. He writes, "When the degree of realism becomes this dense, the images of *marumage* and *ichōageshi* [the two geisha] become too thin, like dreams. They disappear and even turn into ghosts."[60] The two geisha of the story oscillate between ghostly transparency and corporeal reality throughout the narrative, which continues to mix dense realism with ephemeral fantasy. An example of this mixed style follows almost immediately, when a man manages to wake up from a nap just before his stop (a scene frequently witnessed in Tokyo today) and grabs a Panama hat and a walking stick, but then is described as flying out of the train like a bird.

In the second part of the story, the trio arrives at an inn in a backwater bay on the Shōnan coast, somewhere in between Akiya and Tateishi. The landscape is muddy and less picturesque than they had hoped for and the inn appears to be in a state of disrepair. In a reference to contemporary events, the damage is attributed to the lingering effects of the Great Kantō Earthquake of 1923.[61] In his description of the inn, Kyōka presents one of the central images of the story, as well as a source of its horror, in the detail of a massive mosquito net that is covered with loosely patched holes that look like human faces. The destructive effects of the earthquake in the area are later related by an eerie old woman, who seems to share a spiritual connection with a black dog that unnerves Akiba. The old woman relates to the narrator that three people died in a fire that broke out at the inn during the earthquake, including an old woman and two children, and that a beautiful young maid who works at the inn, Oyuki, was partially blamed for their deaths, because she was busy trying to extinguish the fire rather than making sure that all of her customers were safe. Akiba sympathizes with Oyuki's self-preservation, considering that any attempt to save other people in such a dangerous situation might have led to her own death as well. Following this revelation, the mosquito net again becomes a haunting image, this time when all of its patched holes appear like human eyes, which are described as "staring, blinking, and moving their pupils around."[62] The eyes then gather into one spot and turn into the blank, featureless face of a *nopperabō*, a *yōkai* that appears frequently in Kyōka's fiction. The *nopperabō* then transforms into Oyuki, who has covered her face with a white cloth, and who deliberately walks around with her eyes covered in this way in atonement for her sin of letting the customers die in the fire. As a sign of Oyuki's guilty conscience, Akiba relates that when she prays before the Buddhist or Shinto altars in the inn, her own face appears clearly right in front of her, despite the absence of any mirrors to reflect her image. At the conclusion of the story, Akiba relates that he never saw the two geisha together again, but rather saw only one at a time, or otherwise saw them in new groups of three. Akiba then returns to the inn on the coast, where Oyuki has been expecting him. In a hint that her self-imposed punishment has been completed, Oyuki has gone blind, and the story ends as the pair embrace and shed tears together.

Kyōka's last reference to Mérimée appears in his final published work of fiction, "The Cypress Vine" (1939), in a reference to the character of Carmen.[63] "The Cypress Vine" is one of Kyōka's most profoundly haunting stories, because it suggests the author's awareness of his own impending death, while also conveying his fear of dying, as suggested by central imagery of gravestones. The handwritten manuscript for the story has become famous as material evidence of Kyōka's pained and anxious state, because so much of the manuscript is blacked out and rewritten.[64] The work belongs to a significant group of stories centering on graveyards, the so-called "graveyard-visit novels" (*bosan shōsetsu*), while implying more vividly than in earlier stories that Kyōka had been ruminating increasingly on death. Other works that fall into the category of *bosan shōsetsu* include "Marriage Ties" ("Enmusubi,"

1907), *Women of Fate* (1919–1921), "Blessings of the Holy Mother" (1924), "The Cemetery Angel" ("Rantōba no tennyo," 1927), "The Votive Light Volume" (1933), and "The Sacred Heron Volume" (1933).[65]

"The Cypress Vine" is a subtle work of fiction that mixes ghostly imagery with fleeting glimpses of scenes and ideas drawn from throughout Kyōka's oeuvre. It is difficult to fully appreciate without a thorough understanding of Kyōka's literature, because of its diffuse narrative, but for those familiar with the author's work, it presents a powerful summary of the themes that continued to guide his imagination late in life. In "The Cypress Vine," an elderly man, Tsujimachi Itoshichi, climbs a hill in Kanazawa to visit the grave of his elder sister, Okyō, along with his niece, Oyone, the woman's daughter. Amid hints of fiercely resisted erotic tension, Tsujimachi discusses the past with his niece. He tells her of the suicide of a woman named Hatsuji who died some thirty years earlier, and whose gravestone is also located on the hill. As Tsujimachi explains to Oyone, he had planned to commit suicide on the same night as the young woman by jumping into the moat of the castle of Kanazawa, and stopped only because she beat him to it. According to Tsujimachi, the woman committed suicide because she was relentlessly teased by the workers of a sewing factory where she worked. The reason for the harassment was that she sewed a handkerchief with a design of two dragonflies touching tails, a veiled reference to sexual union. Tsujimachi then relates to Oyone that he once saw thousands of dragonflies crowding the skies of Tokyo, thereby gesturing toward the irresistible sex drive and relentless cycles of procreation found throughout nature, which is also the subject of another late story, "Two, Three Birds, Twelve, Thirteen Birds."

As the narrative of "The Cypress Vine" continues, Kyōka begins to mix eroticism with inhuman horror. When Tsujimachi and his niece discover Hatsuji's grave, the narrator repeatedly compares the cold, moss-covered gravestone to the warm, white body of a naked woman. The gravestone is found turned over on its side and bound in ropes, which strikes the narrator as an image similar to that of a woman being bound and tortured. Oyone quickly removes her outer coat to cover the naked stone, whose surface is warm to the touch, like human skin. In a perverse modification of the bathing scene from *The Holy Man of Mt. Kōya*, Tsujimachi imagines that his older sister would have stripped completely naked to cover the gravestone with her kimono, and that she would insist that he do the same. At the conclusion of the narrative, Oyone boldly decorates a votive lantern with images of red dragonflies, before two "ghost dragonflies" (*yūrei tonbo*) fly out from behind Hatsuji's grave, in the closing image of Kyōka's fiction.

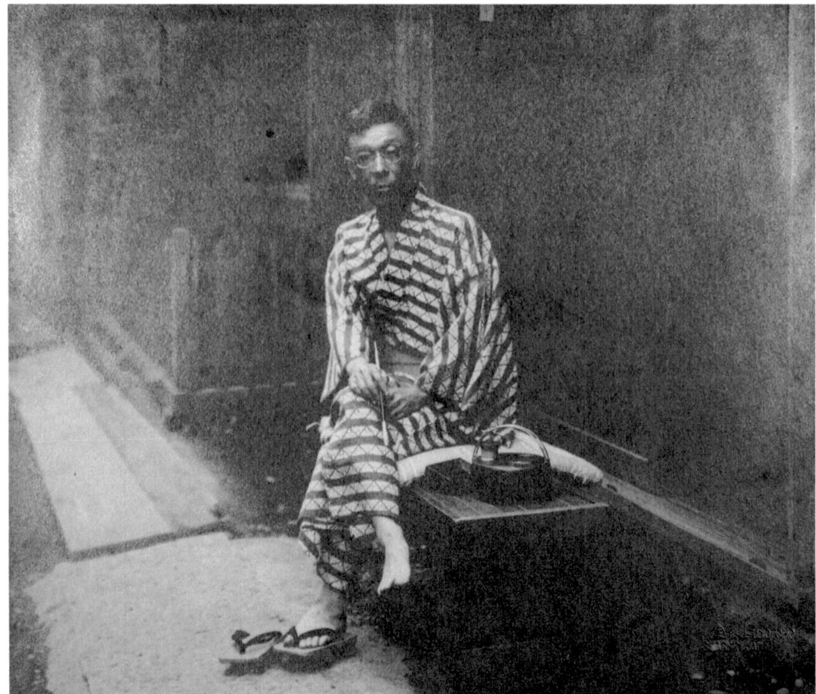

Fig. 24. Izumi Kyōka in 1933. (Photograph courtesy of Izumi Kyōka Kinenkan Museum.)

The reference to the character of Carmen in "The Cypress Vine" occurs toward the middle of the narrative, when Tsujimachi recalls the embarrassment that drove Hatsuji to suicide. Tsujimachi expresses the opinion that aristocratic women would rather be tortured with whips, water, and fire than be stripped naked, the most shameful punishment of all. The narrator then adds, "Tsujimachi, thinking of such weak-willed women, envied the tomboy of the tobacco factory in Seville, Spain."[66] The image is a clear reference to Carmen, a character who reacts to a woman taunting her at her workplace, a cigar factory in Seville, by slashing the woman's face with a knife, leaving her bloodied and scarred on the factory floor. Although Carmen is murdered by the conclusion of the novella, she resists all attempts to restrain her passions and her career as an outlaw until her violent demise. As evidenced by the frequent translation of "Carmen" throughout the 1920s and 1930s in Japan, she had become a familiar and favorite character from European literature for many Japanese readers. The reference to "Carmen" in Kyōka's final story suggests the lasting impact of the character Carmen on his literary imagination.

An additional reference to Mérimée in scholarship on Kyōka reinforces the idea that Kyōka had only become fonder of the author during his final years, nearly two decades after his first encounter with Mérimée's fiction. The reference, by Muramatsu, describes Kyōka as enthusiastically reciting passages from a translation of Mérimée's story "The Vision of Charles XI" while discussing foreign literature (*gaikoku bungaku*). Muramatsu writes:

> The venerable aged author constantly brought up the supernatural aspects of the work of Prosper Mérimée. He was particularly impressed with "The Vision of Charles XI." He would take the book (the one translated by Ishikawa [Takeshi]) out of his drawer and recite the climactic scene of the narrative aloud with great admiration, saying, "You see this part right here, where the ghosts disappear and only a fleck of blood remains on Charles's slipper, it's so good. There was no other way . . ."[67]

Kyōka's focus on this scene suggests that he recognized the key technique of Mérimée's fiction, the presentation of counterevidence that suggests an intrusion of the supernatural into the real world, and that he continued to search for new ways to present ghostly illusions in ways that would excite, surprise, and frighten his readers. The detail of Kyōka repeatedly reciting Mérimée's text aloud echoes the author's own description of his earlier obsession with *The Improvisatore* by Andersen, related two decades earlier, while also providing some of the most convincing evidence of the clear influence of European and other global literature on his work.

5. Kyōka and the Scholarly Fantastic

The influence of Mérimée is suggested in two late works by Kyōka, *The River Goddess* (1927) and *Commentaries on the Mountains and the Sea* (1929), specifically in Kyōka's framing of his ghost stories using scholarly research and documentation, both genuine and invented. Mérimée's influence is also suggested by Kyōka's deepening interest in depicting localized traditions of folkloric religion and magic, as well as literary history. In *Commentaries on the Mountains and the Sea*, Kyōka draws on the research of pioneering Japanese ethnographer Yanagita Kunio, a friend of his, to describe popular religious practices in northern and northeastern Japan.[68] In *The River Goddess*, he relates the story of a murderous living statue, thereby suggesting the influence of Mérimée's "The Venus of Ille," and he frames his account of the statue's origin with scholarly research on the history of *haikai* poetry in the remote Noto peninsula of northern Japan.

Kyōka's scholarly approach to the fantastic differs from Mérimée's in terms of its localization, dealing exclusively with Japanese folklore, history, and religion, whereas Mérimée's fiction describes folkloric beliefs and practices across European regions, including Spain, Corsica, French Catalonia, and the Baltic region, by drawing on the author's extensive knowledge of over half a dozen European languages. However, Kyōka's "scholarly fantastic" echoes Mérimée's in its focus on the remote provincial corners of the region of the world where he lived, Honshū island in Japan, with a focus on the Noto peninsula and the Hakusan mountain range in Ishikawa prefecture. Kyōka provides detailed descriptions of these locations by drawing on a combination of scholarly research and firsthand experience of places that most of his readers would probably never visit due to their remote locations. Kyōka again differs from Mérimée, however, in his status as a provincial informer, rather than a metropolitan observer, whose knowledge of the province that he writes about is linked to his personal identification with his native region.

Commentaries on the Mountains and the Sea is one of Kyōka's longest novels, at nearly 400 pages, and one of the most significant of his late career. It is also one of his most notoriously difficult works, due to its diffuse narrative style, multiple interweaving plotlines, and complex layering of loosely related scenes and images. Shinoda Hajime famously wrote of *Commentaries on the Mountains and the Sea*, "I don't read this novel as a novel per se, but rather I listen to it, enraptured, as though it were a piece of music. . . . The plot, however, is so unclear that it lies beyond description."[69] It is difficult to relate the narrative of Kyōka's novel without going into excessive detail, but one way to summarize the story would be to describe it as an episodic series of gradual revelations of a hidden inner image, that of a goddess, and particularly the locally venerated goddess of Mt. Hakusan, a towering, snow-capped mountain and associated mountain range that forms a backdrop to Kanazawa, to the southeast of the city.

Commentaries on the Mountains and the Sea is one of numerous Hakusan novels that Kyōka wrote throughout his career. Such novels include "The Female Mountain Immortal: Prelude" ("Josen zenki," 1902), "Kinuginu River" ("Kinuginugawa," 1902), *The Elegant Railway* (*Fūryūsen*, 1903–1904), "The Count's Hairpin" (1920), and *The River Goddess* (1927). Kyōka's Hakusan stories often focus on the goddess of the mountain, popularly known as Shirayama Hime (Princess of the White Mountain), as well as the wider veneration of Shirayama Hime and related female deities throughout the surrounding region. As Kyōka was well aware, Shirayama Hime was the central figure of popular religious and occult practices throughout northern and northeastern Japan that were propagated by female mediums known as *itako*, most of whom were elderly and blind.[70] As scholars have found, Shirayama Hime is associated with numerous other deities who are venerated on Hakusan, including a nine-headed dragon god known as Kuzuryū-Ō, an eleven-headed version of the bodhisattva Kannon, a syncretic Shinto-Buddhist deity known as Myōri Dai Gongen or Myōri Dai Bosatsu, the Shinto goddess Izanami no Mikoto from the *Kojiki*, and an obscure Shinto goddess named Kukurihime from the *Nihon shoki*.[71] Scholar Kawamura Jirō pictures Hakusan as the center of Kyōka's literary universe, and also as a major source of the female deities that he depicts throughout his fiction, in a book-length study of the connection between Kyōka, Mt. Hakusan, and the Hakusan faith.[72] In *Commentaries on the Mountains and the Sea*, Kyōka pays close attention to occult elements associated with popular veneration of Shirayama Hime, such as divination and rituals for promoting fortune and desired outcomes.

Commentaries on the Mountains and the Sea begins in rather loose fashion at an inn on the Noto peninsula, a location that also serves as the main setting of *The River Goddess*. The novel starts off in the mode of travel fiction, with the protagonist, a novelist named Yano Chikau, describing his lodging, the view from his window, and the routes and geographic features of the peninsula. The work soon takes a turn toward fantasy, however, by incorporating elements of folklore and fairytales. At the inn, Yano recalls the legend of a hunter who was haunted by a talking *tanuki*; in another eerie episode, Yano witnesses a ghostly female apparition wander through the dark hallways of the inn before disappearing into the women's bath. Later in the novel, after many episodes of diverse content, Yano discusses appearances of the goddess Oshirakami, one of various alternate names of Shirayama Hime, with a local driver, who claims to have seen the head of the goddess hovering in a grove of silk flower trees. Yano proceeds to describe Oshirakami as a goddess of secrets and hidden phenomena. According to Yano, images of the goddess are often shrouded in layers of thick, concealing kimono and hoods that cover their faces. She has no major places of worship and is venerated in shrines hidden in forests and among thick grasses far away from main roads. As a goddess of hidden phenomena, she is petitioned in connection with things that are normally concealed, such as silkworms in their cocoons, family fortunes, and conjugal relations.

At another point in the novel, Kyōka describes a children's game that originates in practices of divination associated with Shirayama Hime, or

Oshirakami. Drawing on research by Yanagita, Kyōka describes the game and iconography of *berobero no kami*.[73] He writes:

> The figure is wrapped in seven layers, eight layers, ten layers, twelve layers, and on top of that cloth or silk. As for the body of the goddess, I can only relate what scholars have told me of their research. Simply speaking, one takes a piece of wood, shaves it down, draws simple eyes and a nose and, on top of that, just as I was saying before, wraps numerous layers of cloth around the wooden figure. When you look at her, all you see is a hood draped deep over her head, down to her sleeves. A cord of cotton is tied neatly around her neckband so that her face is just slightly visible while still being kept hidden. . . . From the beginning the goddess had a hidden form, so whatever exquisite design might lie beneath, whether drawn by brush or carved by knife, however majestic or elegant, her mysterious visage remains unknown.[74]

In the narrative, Kyōka connects images of Shirayama Hime and *berobero no kami* to a female character named Himenuma Ayaha, who Yano recalls from his youth. As an example of one of Kyōka's female scholar characters, Ayaha is described as having been a prodigious artist skilled in *kanbun*, European languages, math, calligraphy, literature, and philosophy. She is also said to have been so beautiful that Yano's classmates in Kanazawa imagined her to be Cleopatra, whose beauty they had read of in their world history class, in a scene that once again suggests the lifelong impact of Kyōka's education on his literary imagination. Like the hidden goddess Oshirakami, however, Ayaha eventually goes into hiding, after marrying a jealous husband who attempts to keep his wife hidden from public view. At the conclusion of the novel, Yano drives up into the mountains on a trip with his friend, a young dance instructor named Rie, who features as a main character in the novel in lengthy episodes set in Tokyo. In a scene of shocking violence, Rie is attacked by a group of loggers in the mountains who attempt to sexually assault her, but she is rescued by a representative of the goddess of the mountain, who whips her attackers into submission. The narrative ends with the lyrics of a *temari uta* and a challenge posed by the narrator for modern authors to attempt to write novels that are as brilliant as *temari* songs.

A novel that suggests the influence of Mérimée even more strongly is *The River Goddess*, another of Kyōka's Hakusan novels, due to both the scholarly framing of the supernatural story and its central account of a statue that comes to life and causes death, just like "The Venus of Ille." Like many of Kyōka's late works, *The River Goddess* is one of the author's more confusing and surreal narratives. *The River Goddess* opens with an unusual historical frame, one that is so uncharacteristic of the writer that it might even take familiar readers of Kyōka by surprise. Specifically, the narrative opens by aiming to establish the importance of Kanazawa and the Noto peninsula in the history of *haikai* poetry, including in the history of the most famous practitioner of the art form, Bashō, and his disciples. Mixing real and imagined references, Kyōka writes:

> Kanazawa in the North Country, with Hokushi, Bokudō, and others in the Genroku era, its history of haikai is not shallow. Recently I came across something from spring in the third year of the Bunsei era. Though I say spring, that region still hibernates in the depths of winter snow. Kashin, as a certain haikai poet was once known, had pasted a poem from the *Utatsu Collection*, compiled by Hokushi, on an old folding screen to mend a tear, and the pasted poem had remained there. Thinking nostalgically of a past over one hundred years old, as a preface, I respectfully present this manuscript that Kashin transcribed by hand.
>
> Utatsu is still the name of the part of Kanazawa beyond the hills. It seems that Hokushi once lived there.
>
> According to Kashin's manuscript, Hokushi once wrote the following poem (although it cannot be found in *The Narrow Road to the Deep North*):
>
> Old man! A suspended mosquito net. A lesson learned from the grasses.
> —Hokushi
>
> There's a preface explaining that Hokushi had guided Bashō on a walk through the suburbs of Kanazawa and accompanied him to the foothills of Nodayama. Again:
>
> Upon taking leave from him in Maruoka, I wrote this on a fan:
>
> Scribbled on a fan and then discarded, a farewell poem. —Bashō[75]

A similar style of framework, providing a mix of historical and pseudohistorical content, might be seen in the work of Mérimée, as in the author's discussions of the local history of Andalucía in "Carmen" or of Perpignan, France, in "The Venus of Ille."

As Kyōka notes in the opening section of the novella, Bashō once visited

Kanazawa and wrote a haiku poem in Natadera Temple in nearby Komatsu. Furthermore, one of Bashō's closest followers, one of the so-called "ten wise disciples of Bashō" (*Shōmon jittetsu*), Tachibana Hokushi (ca. 1665–1718), was a native of Kanazawa. As Kyōka notes, Hokushi edited a collection of *haikai* poetry named after the northeastern Utatsu hills on the outskirts of the city, near the neighborhood where Kyōka was raised, known as the *Utatsu Collection* (*Utatsu shū*, 1691).[76] Kyōka proudly relates these details of Kanazawa's literary history, providing examples of Bashō's poetry, before introducing a fabricated text, *Records of Travel on the Noto Road* (*Notoji no ki*) by the fictitious *haikai* poet and founder of a local temple, Kashin.[77] Following the introduction of the historical framework, *The River Goddess* is related in a two-part structure, first as a summary of a chapter from *Records of Travel on the Noto Road* titled "Account of the Founding of Kawasuso Myōjin Shrine," complete with fabricated quotations, and then as a frame narrative related by traveler Koyama Natsukichi to the narrator at an inn in Noto. The fictional chapter from *Records of Travel on the Noto Road* relates the travels of Kashin in the Noto peninsula, the origin story of the fictional Kawasuso Myōjin shrine in the same area, and an account of the origin of the image of a goddess hidden in the inner sanctum of the shrine (the name Kawasuso looks suspiciously like *kawauso*, or river otter, a creature often depicted as a trickster *yōkai* in Japanese folklore). In the second part of the narrative, Natsukichi relates his own experience of the image's murderous power, and gives an account of a visit to the shrine and various grotesque and bizarre apparitions associated with the experience.

In the invented historical narrative from *The River Goddess*, Kashin describes taking a boat along the coast of the inner sea of the Noto peninsula, where he encounters a monk selling amulets from Mt. Sekidō, another sacred mountain in the area associated with the faith of Mt. Hakusan and Shirayama Hime. The account of the monk's travels across the Noto peninsula recalls Bashō's *haikai* travel narrative, *Narrow Road to the Deep North*, particularly in its vivid descriptions of the privations of travel, the difficulty of the road, and meaningful encounters with local people along the way. Kashin's encounter with a beautiful woman washing laundry sets the stage for the description of the origins of the Kawasuso Myōjin shrine, and for Kyōka's imagined depictions of folkloric religious practices and local lore. Kashin is surprised when the woman refuses to offer him a cup of tea, but her reticence is then explained as a result of local superstitions. As Kashin relates:

> In Noto, when 75 days have yet to pass after childbirth, the local people are accustomed to saying, "Older sister is still in the hut." The red

> god of Kuroshima, known as Akagami, is a wrathful deity and despises pollution. Birthing huts are set up near the shrines and the women confine themselves within. Such was the extent to which residents of the inner sea of the Noto peninsula feared the wrathful deity.[78]

Kyōka's description of belief in pollution associated with childbirth and the use of birthing huts echoes research into the Hakusan faith by Yanagita.[79] Kyōka then relates that the identity of the Kawasuso Myōjin deity is an apotheosis of the woman who was washing laundry, who later saves Kashin's life by rescuing him from the quicksand-like banks of the flooded Yonemachigawa river, only to lose her life in the rescue. Following her death, Kashin commissions a statue of the woman to be made by a master artisan, and then dedicates the rest of his life to guarding the shrine of Kawasuso Myōjin.

In the second part of the story, the narrator relates Natsukichi's personal account of his interactions with the image of the Kawasuso Myōjin shrine. Having opened the story in a historical setting with references to traditional Japanese literature, Kyōka then asserts the global character of his work with the description of a local engraver of ornamental objects whose goods are popular as far away as Europe. The gold engraver, who once again recalls the figure of Kyōka's own father, achieved international recognition, in an odd narrative detail, particularly for his ornamental melons, whose carved details of stems, leaves, seeds, and even insects turned them into lifelike objects. As Natsukichi relates, his father's golden ornamental melons were popular in France and Italy, and even in Belgium and Spain. In an additional reference to Europe, Kyōka quotes an anonymous French writer, to whom he attributes the phrase, "A woman who listens gladly to your conversation for a second time obviously loves you."[80] At another point in the story, the narrator demonstrates his global perspective by suggesting that a visit to the Noto peninsula was considered as essential for *haikai* poets of Bashō's era as a visit to the temple in Jerusalem was for modern pilgrims in the West, or a visit to Europe for modern academics from Japan.

After the change in narrative perspective, Natsukichi's description of the origin of the Kawasuso Myōjin deity takes a sudden turn into dark territory, with some of the more bizarre and grotesque content to be found in Kyōka's fiction. In his narrative, Natsukichi remarks that the statue is "said to be a witch" (*majo da to iu*) who caused the deaths of six local men who assaulted Natsukichi and his lover when they were both seventeen years old.[81] The local people set up six statues of the bodhisattva Jizō by the side of the road near a melon field as an attempt to expiate the sins of the men and create merit, but Natsukichi is still so angered by their actions that he asserts that he would gladly chisel off the faces of the statues to posthumously expose their shame. As Natsukichi relates, he once wandered around the vicinity of the melon field in a state of terrible poverty and hunger, thereby recalling Kyōka's early life as a writer. As Natuskichi wandered near the field, a loosely dressed prostitute with "large breasts as white as snow" appeared to him. In an eerie mixture of eroticism and grotesque horror, the woman tells Natsukichi, "You know, when you die, they strip you naked for the autopsy."[82] The prostitute, named Oyū, then invites Natsukichi to commit suicide with her by hanging themselves from a nearby tree using Oyū's red sash. Just as Oyū is about to hang herself, however, she spots a carp in the melon field, a miracle that convinces her to suddenly change her mind and climb down from the tree. As the narrator relates, the carp apparently landed in the field after being shot into the sky by a waterspout at sea. The couple then decide to steal a melon from the field to alleviate their hunger, but as soon as Oyū takes a bite into the melon, six local men appear and attack them. In a scene that is very unusual for Kyōka, the men threaten to tie the couple up and urinate on them, a punishment that Natsukichi considers to be too shameful to bear. In self-defense, Natsukichi escapes and burns down a local tea hut in an act of arson. Years later, when Natsukichi returns to Kanazawa, he learns that Oyū eventually went through with her decision to commit suicide, but by self-immolation in a hut in the melon fields rather than by hanging.

Having returned to Kaga province, Natsukichi decides to visit the main shrine of Kawasuso Myōjin in the Noto peninsula. At a hotel, he dreams of faceless naked women, described as *nopperabō*, who multiply and crawl out of a flooded field. After awaking from his nightmare, he learns from the proprietor of the hotel that the statue of Kawasuso Myōjin is alive and that a faint metallic sound can be heard from within the shrine when she combs her hair. Natsukichi then visits the shrine, hidden in a bamboo grove, where he observes a room with offerings of women's hair and a pond full of frogs who swim around with black hair trailing behind them. He then runs into a ghostly apparition of Oyū, who offers him a melon. Natsukichi splits the melon open and a fish falls out. When Natsukichi is finally offered access to the inner image of the shrine, he discovers a statue of a woman in a raincoat riding on a fish with a vaguely human or animal face. When the shrine closes, Natsukichi hears the metallic ringing described by the hotel proprietor, but the doors shut before he is able to see the statue move. The local people surmise that the statue might come to life via the working of some internal mechanism or spring that is only activated once the doors to the shrine have been closed. At the conclusion of the narrative, Kyōka describes the artist who created the image of Kawasuso Myōjin as some kind of scientist who practiced the arts of medicine, shamanism, fire magic, and photography, in addition to creating living dolls whose operative mechanisms were unknown to the people of the Kaga province. The scientist is rumored to have learned his techniques from Westerners, and possibly even from Christians. The story then ends with a description of living images attributed to the scientist-sculptor. The narrator relates: "He made a figure of a black kite (not a crane) and rode upon it, flying out of the second floor of a building, and proceeded to an unknown location. Kashin, who enjoyed mixing with odd types, enjoyed this. Drawing on supernatural methods such as these, the image of the goddess was formed."[83]

Considered as a whole, *The River Goddess* represents Kyōka at his most experimental and surreal. It is also, however, a story that benefits from the variety of scholarly narrative framework and fantastic content often found in the work of Mérimée. With its combination of local history, an invented travelogue, an imagined account of the origins of a shrine, and its tale of a living statue, the work is a strong candidate for a story that might have been directly influenced by Mérimée's fiction. It is also a story that proves, like so many others, that Kyōka was one of the most avant-garde writers of his era.

Conclusion

In common with previous scholarship on Kyōka and the fantastic in Japan, this study raises almost as many questions as it answers. Due to its focus on global elements of the fantastic, connections between Kyōka, Andersen, Maupassant, Mérimée, Hauptmann, and the *Arabian Nights* have been emphasized, but certainly more could be written on Kyōka's integration of the themes and narrative techniques of classical Japanese literature and theater into his modern fiction of the fantastic, not to mention the influence of premodern Chinese literature. On the author's death in 1939, the books that remained on Kyōka's desk included collections of poetry by Bashō and Li He, as well as *The Arabian Nights*, reflecting his eclectic influences late in life.[1] As described in this study, elements that Kyōka borrowed from traditional Japanese literature include the typical three-part *jō-ha-kyū* rhythmic structure of Nō plays, narratives of pacifying restless spirits from Nō, depictions of magic and monsters from *kusazōshi*, and scenes of *michiyuki* and double suicide from *bunraku* puppet theater. Nevertheless, as argued throughout this study, Kyōka's literature should not be interpreted as deriving entirely from classical sources, from which his stories differ greatly in so many respects, but should rather be treated as modern fiction that draws on a combination of literary tradition and modern literary techniques and influences to bring ghosts, monsters, and the supernatural into a recognizably modern world.

Kyōka's seamless integration of fantasy and realism and his treatment of the tensions between modernity and tradition in Japan suggest affinities with a recent global genre of literature of the fantastic, magical realism, which raises questions about the political and cultural relevance of Kyōka's work. As scholars have frequently argued, magical realism is an inherently political genre of global fiction that originated in politically marginalized and formerly colonized spaces in the modern world, beginning with Latin America and spreading to South Asia, North America, and beyond, where writers sought to integrate narrative traditions, literary techniques, worldviews, and cultural values that often seemed to exist in opposition.[2] As Susan J. Napier points out, the situation in Japan differs from that of almost any other regional producer of magical realism, because Japan was never colonized in the same way as other postcolonial states. However, as Napier adds, the Japanese government imposed foreign ideals and cultural values on its own people from within.[3]

Kyōka might be considered as a writer whose social marginalization and formative experiences placed him closer to global writers of magical realism than most in Japan, in part because he was educated at a Christian missionary school run by Americans in the outlying districts of a provincial Japanese city. As a migrant in Tokyo, Kyōka initially experienced hunger and homelessness, and later in life, as a literary outsider, he was met by critical rejection from the literary establishment. Throughout his career, he fought to preserve the legacy of traditional forms of Japanese art and literature within the frameworks of the modern novel, short story, and play. Like writers from Latin America who endeavored to integrate European, African, and indigenous traditions of storytelling, Kyōka brought the narrative traditions and worldviews of old Japan into the modern novel, allowing the past and the present to exist alongside each other in varying patterns of tension and harmony.

By drawing on traditional forms of Japanese storytelling and art, but also on global literature in translation, as well as the modern literary styles of contemporary Japanese authors, Kyōka created a unique brand of Japanese fantasy that is characterized by its hybrid nature. Kyōka's style is also distinguished, however, by its idiosyncrasy—a subject that is difficult to avoid when writing about an author who has been described as "unique" or "genius" more often than almost any other modern writer in Japan. As scholars have frequently argued, although Kyōka's prose recalls elements of classical Japanese literature, it is also deeply personal and creative. Many of the markers of Japanese tradition in Kyōka's work are also particular to his provincial background, suggesting an attachment to the local that is more precisely defined than national tradition. These markers include local cultural products from Kanazawa, such as handwoven *temari* and ornamental golden objects; local varieties of popular performance, such as amateur *kyōgen* and itinerant storytelling; and local forms of religious practice focusing on the veneration of sacred female figures, including Maya Bunin, Kishimojin, and Shirayama

Hime. Thus, Kyōka's literature pays homage not just to traditional Japan, but to Kanazawa, the Kaga province, and the north coast region of Japan, whose stories and religious practices transmit a local cultural history that diverges, in certain aspects, from the mainstream Japanese culture of Tokyo. The result of Kyōka's mixing and rearranging themes and literary techniques is a literature that feels rooted in tradition, while diverging considerably from premodern literature in terms of its modern language, avant-garde themes, and surreal narrative structures. By constantly pushing the boundaries of grammar and narrative sequencing, Kyōka produced stories that are diffuse, surreal, and kaleidoscopic. As Japanese scholars have frequently noted, such narratives are occasionally so complex and unusual that they take practice and experience to unravel.

If Kyōka has appeared to critics to be a writer entirely dedicated to tradition, this is in part because he cultivated this image himself. Virtually every photograph of Kyōka that exists depicts the author wearing kimono (the wide variety of kimono patterns that he wears suggests his close attention to matters of fashion), and usually tabi (traditional socks with a single split) and geta (wooden clogs). However, as author Satomi Ton (1888–1983) once noted, Kyōka's appearance could be deceiving. Satomi writes that when he first met Kyōka, he was surprised to find that the author was not quite the staunch traditionalist that his reputation had led many to believe, as indicated in part by his fondness for foreign products. As Satomi writes, Kyōka wore a hat from Christys' (a British hatmaker), used medicine and hygiene products from America, and was a fan of imported cigars, cigarettes, wine, brandy, whiskey, and vermouth.[4] According to Komura Settai, Kyōka frequently went to movie theaters, although his attendance apparently became less frequent after they banned smoking.[5] It is thanks to writers such as Akutagawa and Muramatsu Sadataka that we know that Kyōka was a major fan of French author Mérimée;[6] without their firsthand reports, we would never even know that Kyōka had a favorite European author. Kyōka's reticence to comment on global literature or culture can be interpreted as a protectionist outlook, a position of prioritizing the native, so that Japanese tradition could survive and eventually flourish once again. However, one has only to compare Kyōka to the modern Japanese writers who inspired him, such as Kōyō, Shōyō, and Rohan, all of whom maintained more clearly traditional literary styles than Kyōka, to recognize the novelty and experimental quality of Kyōka's writing. While remaining a traditionalist in certain aspects of his work, Kyōka also prioritized the aesthetic impact and creativity of his artistic vision, leading him to create a form of literature that has no immediate equal in either premodern or modern Japanese literature. Kyōka's vision of traditional Japan is not simply an inherited image, but rather a reimagining of both the past and the present through fantasy.

This study has emphasized many less frequently noted aspects of Kyōka's work and life, particularly those suggesting that the author was fully a citizen of the modern world. Most importantly, Kyōka was educated at an international school, where he studied world history and geography in English, while reading Western literature in Japanese translation in the *Yūbin hōchi shinbun*. Following this early education, he maintained a lifelong interest in classical antiquity, including the ancient Mediterranean and Middle Eastern regions, with references to Sparta and Cleopatra appearing in his late fiction. Kyōka mentions various countries and regions of the modern world in his writing, including Germany, France, Italy, Belgium, Spain, the United States, South America, and Ethiopia. He also read literature in translation throughout his life, including fiction from France, Germany, Denmark, and the Middle East. Although the list of Kyōka's posthumous library contains only three works of non–East Asian literature, including two volumes of writings by Lermontov and the *Arabian Nights*, Kyōka appears to have owned copies of two volumes of fiction by Mérimée late in life, including *A Chronicle of the Reign of Charles IX*, as late as 1925, and *The Venus of Ille*, as late as 1938. The disappearance of such works is a mystery that one might attribute to the chaos of World War II and the destruction of most of Kyōka's library. So many decades having passed since then, the details can never be ascertained.

Areas of research suggested by this study that could benefit from future scholarship include the broader development of *gensō bungaku* in modern Japan and Kyōka's influence on later writers. As emphasized in this study, no other author wrote nearly as much fiction with fantastic and supernatural themes as Kyōka during his lifetime, but the combined stories of the fantastic by contemporary writers are still a significant body of work. Such writers include Rohan, Sōseki, Akutagawa, Tanizaki, Kawabata, Okamoto Kanoko, Satō Haruo, Uchida Hyakken (1889–1971), Edogawa Ranpo (1894–1965), and Miyazawa Kenji (1896–1933), whose connections and divergences in terms of style, structure, and influences could be productively researched in future studies of *gensō bungaku*. Even more complicated is the matter of Kyōka's influence on later writers. When it comes to this question, one is tempted to concede to the opinions of writers such as Tanizaki and Kawabata, that simply put, no other Japanese author has ever written in a style quite like

Kyōka's, and probably nobody ever will. The writers who are the most likely candidates as successors to Kyōka, such as Tanizaki, Kawabata, and Mishima, wrote fiction that is far more accessible, in work that is far less dedicated to creating sprawling worlds of fantasy, ghosts, and monsters. The fiction of later writers who praised Kyōka's work, such as Yoshiya Nobuko, Tsushima Yūko, Kōno Taeko, and Kanai Mieko, is even more distantly removed from Kyōka's in terms of its literary style and themes. Perhaps the true successors to Kyōka are most clearly identifiable as other writers who similarly created inimitable worlds of literature of the fantastic, such as Takahashi Takako, an author of eerie stories of nightmares, madness, haunting images, and religious devotion; Abe Kōbō, one of Japan's most accomplished writers of dystopian dark fantasies and experimental sci-fi novels; or even Takahashi Rumiko, the author of such popular series of manga and anime as *Urusei Yatsura* and *Ranma 1/2*, whose richly detailed worlds of fantasy, combining traditional Japanese culture with modern global elements, recall the imaginative scope of Kyōka's fiction. Another likely successor to Kyōka is Mizuki Shigeru, one of the most influential creators of manga, and also one who was directly influenced by Kyōka's work.

Perhaps the greatest assurance of Kyōka's legacy is the Izumi Kyōka Prize for Literature, in part for the simple reason that it reminds today's readers and authors of the writer's name. Beyond this simple fact, however, is the unusual nature of the prize. It is Japan's top prize for literature with themes that are supernatural, ghostly, or dreamlike, and it has consistently been awarded to many of Japan's most critically acclaimed writers, including many who represent literature of the fantastic and related genres in Japan. As noted in the introduction to this book, winners of the award have also included many of the most successful women writers in Japan, such as Yoshimoto Banana, Yū Miri, Tawada Yōko, Kirino Natsuo, Ogawa Yōko, and Kawakami Hiromi, among many others. It seems reasonable that winners of the award would be familiar with at least part of Kyōka's oeuvre, while also indirectly conveying the author's name to fans of their own work. Certain winners of the prize have also been notable fans or scholars of Kyōka's fiction, including Kanai, Tsushima, Ogawa, Mori Mari, Tanemura Suehiro, and Shinoda Masahiro. Women writers continue to be strongly represented by the award, with nine of the twelve winners of the prize from 2013 to 2022 (the 40th through 50th editions of the prize) being women writers. Although a study of the prizewinners' fiction might not reveal direct influence, it probably would show the wider impact that Kyōka's work has had on Japanese literature by encouraging the continued production of serious and critically acclaimed works of *gensō bungaku*. All of these projects, on the wider formation of *gensō bungaku* in modern Japan, the influence of Kyōka on later writers, and the role of the Kyōka Prize in the field of fantasy literature and related genres, would make for worthwhile research, while helping to further ground and expand Kyōka's reputation for future readers.

Notes

Introduction

1. Tanizaki Jun'ichirō, "Junsui ni 'Nihonteki' na 'Kyōka sekai,'" *Izumi Kyōka [bungei dokuhon]* (Tokyo: Kawade Shobō, 1981), 67–68, originally published in *Tosho* (March 1940); Nakagawa Yoichi, "Kyōka to romanchishizumu," *Kyōka ron shūsei*, eds. Tanizawa Eiichi and Watanabe Ikkō (Tokyo: Rippū Shobō, 1983), 302, originally published in *Kokubungaku kaishaku to kanshō* (May 1949); Kasahara Nobuo, "Izumi Kyōka: hankindai-teki bi no yōshiki," *Henbō suru dentō* (Tokyo: Ōfūsha, 1971), 278–316; Mita Hideaki, *Izumi Kyōka no bungaku* (Tokyo: Ōfūsha, 1976), 6.

2. Ikushima Ryōichi, *Kyōka mangekyō* (Tokyo: Chikuma Shobō, 1992), 100–119.

3. Muramatsu Sadataka, *Izumi Kyōka* (Tokyo: Bunsendō, 1966), 240–62.

4. Yoshimura Hirotō, *Izumi Kyōka: geijutsu to byōri* (Tokyo: Kongō Shuppan Shinsha, 1970), 260–68.

5. Kasahara Nobuo, "Suikoden no keifu: *Fūryūsen* made," *Ronshū Izumi Kyōka* (Tokyo: Yūseidō, 1987), 95–110.

6. Mita Hideaki, *Izumi Kyōka no bungaku*, 6–10.

7. Saitō Nonohito, "Izumi Kyōka to romanchiku," *Kyōka ron shūsei*, 153, 164. Originally published in *Taiyō* (September–October 1907).

8. Ikuta Chōkō, "Izumi Kyōka-shi no shōsetsu o ronzu," *Kyōka ron shūsei*, 174–76. Originally published in *Shinshōsetsu* (June 1911).

9. Katsumoto Seiichirō, "Kyōka no ishinzō," *Kyōka ron shūsei*, 279. Originally published in *Kokubungaku kaishaku to kanshō* (May 1949).

10. Waki Akiko, *Gensō no ronri: Izumi Kyōka no sekai* (Tokyo: Kōdansha, 1974), 13–15.

11. Kanazawa Daigaku Furansu Bungakkai, Hirakawa Sukehiro, Watanabe Kaneo, et al., eds., *Gensō kūkan no tōzai: Furansu bungaku o tōshite mita Izumi Kyōka* (Kanazawa: Jūgatsusha, 1990).

12. Mishima Yukio and Shibusawa Tatsuhiko, "Kyōka no miryoku," *Kyōka ron shūsei*, 356. The text is a transcription of a combined interview with Mishima and Shibusawa that took place in Akasaka on November 4, 1968. Originally published

in *Nihon bungaku furoku 60* (Tokyo: Chūō Kōronsha, 1969). This interview, involving one of Japan's most popular authors, along with one of the most prominent early critics of *gensō bungaku*, has been characterized as launching the Kyōka revival. It was followed by Mishima's essay, "Izumi Kyōka," *Izumi Kyōka [bungei dokuhon]*, 10–14, originally published in *Ozaki Kōyō, Izumi Kyōka [Nihon no bungaku 4]* (Tokyo: Chūō Kōron, 1969).

13. Tsushima Yūko, "Pari no Izumi Kyōka," *Izumi Kyōka [Gunzō Nihon no sakka 5]*, eds. Ōoka Makoto, Takahashi Hideo, Miyoshi Yukio, et al., with an essay by Tsushima Yūko (Tokyo: Shōgakukan, 1992), 10–11.

14. As shown in later chapters, Kyōka first read the *Arabian Nights* as a middle-school student and later kept a copy of the book on his desk during the final days of his life.

15. Kyōka's frequent use of this type of narrative structure, referred to in Japanese as *ireko kōzō*, or "nesting doll structure," has been interpreted by scholars as having been influenced by the *Arabian Nights*. Yoshimura Hirotō, *Makai e no enkinhō: Izumi Kyōka ron* (Tokyo: Kindai Bungeisha, 1991), 10.

16. Muramatsu Sadataka, *Kotoba no renkinjutsushi: Izumi Kyōka* (Tokyo: Shakai Shisōsha, 1973), 13.

17. Kobayashi Hideo, "Kyōka no shi, sono ta," *Kyōka ron shūsei*, 217–19, originally published in *Bungei shunjū* 17, no. 19 (October 1939); Muramatsu, *Izumi Kyōka*, 189; Ikushima, *Kyōka mangekyō*, 212.

18. Kawamura Jirō translated literature from German by writers such as Friedrich Hölderlin (1770–1843), Hugo von Hofmannsthal (1874–1929), Rainer Maria Rilke (1875–1926), and Franz Kafka (1883–1924). He is the author of one of the most important texts on literature of the fantastic in Japan, *Ginga to jigoku: gensō bungaku ron* (Tokyo: Kōdansha, 1973). One of his most important essays on Kyōka is "Dōshi sareta kūkan: Izumi Kyōka," *Izumi Kyōka [bungei dokuhon]*, 54–65. Originally published in *Ginga to jigoku.*

19. Tanemura Suehiro translated authors such as E. T. A. Hoffmann, Heinrich von Kleist, and Ludwig Achim von Arnim (1781–1831), in addition to many stories about vampires. On Kyōka, he wrote "Suichūka henge," *Izumi Kyōka [Gunzō Nihon no sakka 5]*, 30–43. Originally published in *Bessatsu gendaishi techō 1: Izumi Kyōka: yōbi to gensō no majutsushi* (Tokyo: Shichōsha, 1972).

20. Shibusawa Tatsuhiko translated authors including Joris-Karl Huysmans (1848–1907), Georges Bataille (1897–1962), Charles Perrault (1628–1703), and, infamously, the Marquis de Sade (1740–1814). He also edited various publications in the 1970s that made early use of the term "*gensō*" as a translation for "fantasy" or "the fantastic." See Sunaga Asahiko, *Nihon gensō bungakushi* (Tokyo: Heibonsha, 2007), 11–12. On Kyōka, he wrote "Ranpu no kaiten," *Izumi Kyōka [bungei dokuhon]*, 115–23. Originally published in *Bungei* 14, no. 10 (October 1975): 128–37.

21. Waki Akiko has translated authors including Lewis Carroll (1832–1898), Ursula K. Le Guin (1929–2018), and Patricia McKillip (1948–2022). She wrote one of the first major studies of Kyōka and literature of the fantastic, *Gensō no ronri: Izumi Kyōka no sekai.*

22. Sunaga, *Nihon gensō bungakushi*, 10–12.

23. Sunaga, *Nihon gensō bungakushi*, 15.

24. Higashi Masao, ed., *Nihon gensō bungaku jiten* (Tokyo: Chikuma Shobō, 2013), 577–608.

25. Higashi, *Nihon gensō bungaku jiten*, 577.

26. Susan J. Napier, *The Fantastic in Modern Japanese Literature: The Subversion of Modernity* (London: Routledge, 1996), 26. Napier's book includes discussion of work by major writers of literature of the fantastic from Kyōka to Abe Kōbō (1924–1993) to Murakami Haruki, along with the work of many prominent women writers, including Enchi Fumiko (1905–1986), Kurahashi Yumiko (1935–2005), Ōba Minako (1930–2007), and Kanai Mieko. *The Fantastic in Modern Japanese Literature*, 80–92. A recent edited volume of essays on *gensō bungaku*, *Into the Fantastical Spaces of Contemporary Japanese Literature*, similarly highlights the fiction of women writers, including Ogawa Yōko, Tawada Yōko, Kawakami Hiromi, and Murata Sayaka, in addition to other popular authors such as Murakami Haruki and Murakami Ryū. Mina Qiao, ed., *Into the Fantastical Spaces of Contemporary Japanese Literature* (Lanham, MD: Lexington Books, 2022).

27. Susan J. Napier, "The Magic of Identity: Magic Realism in Modern Japanese Fiction," *Magical Realism: Theory, History, Community*, eds. Lois Parkinson Zamora and Wendy B. Faris (Durham: Duke University Press, 1995), 457–60.

28. Mark Cody Poulton, "Metamorphosis: Fantasy and Animism in Izumi Kyōka," *Japan Review* 6 (January 1995): 81. Scholar Taketomo Sōfū notes similarities between *The Holy Man of Mt. Kōya* and Homer's *Odyssey*. "Izumi Kyōka to kindai kaii shōsetsu," *Kyōka ron shūsei*, 238, originally published in *Kokubungaku kaishaku to kanshō* (March 1943). Others have compared Kyōka's novel *The Grass Labyrinth* to the myth of Ariadne and the Labyrinth. See Shibusawa, "Ranpu no kaiten," 119; Tanemura, "Suichūka henge," 34.

29. Poulton, *Spirits of Another Sort: The Plays of Izumi Kyōka* (Ann Arbor: Center for Japanese Studies, University of Michigan, 2001), 7–8.

30. Roger Caillois, *Images, images: essais sur le rôle et les pouvoirs de l'imagination* (Paris: José Corti, 1966), 15–16.

31. Tzvetan Todorov, *The Fantastic: A Structural Approach to a Literary Genre*, trans. Richard Howard, foreword by Robert Scholes (Ithaca: Cornell University Press, 1975), 25. Because this translation is widely referenced in English-language scholarship, I refer to the English-language edition, although I have consulted the original French version for technical terminology.

32. Rosemary Jackson, *Fantasy: The Literature of Subversion* (London: Methuen, 1981), 7–8.

33. Claire Whitehead, "On the Fantastic," *The Fantastic*, ed. Claire Whitehead (Ipswich, MA: Salem Press, 2013), 8–9.

34. Farah Mendlesohn, *Rhetorics of Fantasy* (Middletown, CT: Wesleyan University Press, 2008), xiv–xv.

35. Brian Attebery, *Strategies of Fantasy* (Bloomington: Indiana University Press, 1992), 1–2.

36. Todorov, *The Fantastic*, 25.

37. Todorov, *The Fantastic*, 45; Todorov, *Introduction à la littérature fantastique* (Paris: Éditions du Seuil, 1970), 49.

38. Todorov, *The Fantastic*, 24–27, 166.

39. Pierre-Georges Castex, *Le conte fantastique en France: de Nodier à Maupassant* (Paris: José Corti, 1951), 42–56; Marcel Schneider, *Histoire de la littérature fantastique en France* (Paris: Fayard, 1985), 9.

40. David Sandner, *Critical Discourses of the Fantastic, 1712–1831* (London: Routledge, 2011), 7–8.

41. Sandner, *Critical Discourses of the Fantastic*, 14.

42. Charles Nodier, "Du Fantastique en Littérature," *Contes Fantastiques par Charles Nodier* (Paris: Bibliothèque-Charpentier, 1904), 5–30. Originally published in *Revue de Paris* (November 1830): 205–26.

43. Nodier, "Du Fantastique en Littérature," 8; Todorov, *The Fantastic*, 54–56, 107–10, 164–65.

44. Todorov, *The Fantastic*, 43–44, 166; Castex, *Le conte fantastique en France*, 248–83, 365–94.

45. Louis Vax, *L'art et la littérature fantastiques* (Paris: Presses Universitaires de France, 1974), 5–6. Originally published in 1960. Translations from French are my own, except where otherwise noted.

46. Vax, *L'art et la littérature fantastiques*, 9.

47. Schneider, *Histoire de la littérature fantastique*, 8.

48. Schneider, *Histoire de la littérature fantastique*, 9.

49. In recognition of Izumi Seiji's influence on Kyōka's aesthetic values, Kyōka has often been referred to as a "sculptor" or "engraver" of literary texts by scholars. For example, see Mita, *Izumi Kyōka no bungaku*, 70; Kasahara Nobuo, *Izumi Kyōka: bi to erosu no kōzō* (Tokyo: Shibundō, 1976), 5; Ichihara Toyota, "Nihongo no majutsushi," *Kyōka ron shūsei*, 358, originally published in *Nihon kindai bungaku zenshū geppō* 52 (October 1969).

50. Gold engravers appear as characters in stories such as the *Volume One* series ("Ichi no maki" through "Chikai no maki," 1896–1897), *The Ashoka Tree* (*Muyūju*, 1906), and *The River Goddess* (*Kahaku reijō*, 1927). Common protagonists with artistic backgrounds in Kyōka's fiction include writers, poets, painters, sculptors, and actors.

51. Muramatsu, *Izumi Kyōka*, 18, 33.

52. For an in-depth description of Kyōka's phobias, obsessions, and superstitious behaviors, see Yoshimura, *Izumi Kyōka: geijutsu to byōri*, 50–111.

53. Waki Akiko, "Izumi Kyōka: bosei tsuibo," *Izumi Kyōka [Gunzō Nihon no sakka 5]*, 96–102.

54. Kyōka is referred to as a genius (*tensai*) in the following essays and reviews: Natsume Sōseki, "'Gin tanzaku'—*Kinsaku tanpyō* yori," *Kyōka ron shūsei*, 134, originally published in *Shinchō* (May 1905); Kawabata Yasunari, "Kiku awase," *Izumi Kyōka [Gunzō Nihon no sakka 5]*, 62, originally published in *Shinchō* (February 1932); Mishima Yukio, "Izumi Kyōka," 10.

55. Tanizaki, "Junsui ni 'Nihonteki' na 'Kyōka sekai,'" 68. All translations from Japanese are my own.

56. Ikushima, *Kyōka mangekyō*, 11, 212; Shinoda Hajime, "Izumi Kyōka no ichi," *Izumi Kyōka [bungei dokuhon]*, 39–45, originally published in *Subaru* (May 1971); Kobayashi Hideo, "Kyōka no shi, sono ta," 219. In my experience, professors and graduate students in Japan almost universally agree on the difficulty of Kyōka's writing.

57. Shinoda, "Izumi Kyōka no ichi," 39.

58. Yanagita Kunio, "Shako Kyōka kan," *Kyōka ron shūsei*, 201–3, originally published in *Tensai Izumi Kyōka [Shin shōsetsu rinji zōkangō]* (Tokyo: Shun'yōdō, 1925); Bandō Tamasaburō and Gunji Masakatsu, "Taidan: Kyōka geki o megutte," *Izumi Kyōka [Gunzō Nihon no sakka 5]*, 231–53, originally published in *Kokubungaku kaishaku to kyōzai no kenkyū* 36, no. 9 (August 1991): 6–25. Bandō, a traditional *onnagata* actor, has frequently portrayed the heroines and female characters of Kyōka's fiction on stage, as well as in the film *The Demon Pond* (1979), directed by Shinoda Masahiro.

59. Mori Mari was the daughter of famous author Mori Ōgai. In her essay, Mori relates her pleasure on receiving the third annual Izumi Kyōka Prize for Literature (Izumi Kyōka Bungakushō) for her novel *The Room of Sweet Honey* (*Amai mitsu no heya*, 1975). Mori, "Kioku no naka no Izumi Kyōka," *Kyōka ron shūsei*, 368–69. Originally published in *Nami* (December 1975).

60. Yoshiya Nobuko was a dedicated fan of Kyōka. She describes first encountering his fiction during her middle-school years, beginning with "A Song by Lantern Light" (1910) in *Shinshōsetsu* magazine, and followed by *Shining Leaf Theater* (1896), *Worship at Yushima* (1899), and *The Holy Man of Mt. Kōya* (1900) in book form soon afterward. She owned the fifteen-volume Shun'yōdō edition of his complete works, in addition to books of scholarship on Kyōka. In an anecdote, she describes encountering the complete works of Kyōka in Rome, Italy, on the bookshelf of Shimoi Harukichi (1883–1954), a poet and translator of Italian literature whom she visited. "Watashi no Izumi Kyōka," *Nihon kindai bungaku taikei 7: Izumi Kyōka shū*, eds. Muramatsu Sadataka, Asada Shōjirō, and Mita Hideaki, *geppō* 13 (Tokyo: Kadokawa Shoten, 1970), 1–2; Yoshiya Nobuko, *Yoshiya Nobuko zenshū 11: soku no nuketa hishaku, aru nyoninzō* (Tokyo: Asahi Shinbunsha, 1975), 490–91.

61. Kōno Taeko, "Kyōka to watashi," *Izumi Kyōka [Gunzō Nihon no sakka 5]*, 210–12, originally published in *Remon* (May 1969); Kōno Taeko, "Kyōka no seimei," *Izumi Kyōka [bungei dokuhon]*, 110–12, originally published in *Kyōka zenshū geppō 6* (Tokyo: Iwanami Shoten, 1974).

62. Tsushima Yūko was another major fan of Kyōka and describes reading works such as *The Holy Man of Mt. Kōya*, *The Grass Labyrinth*, and *The Castle Tower* more times than she could count. "Pari no Kyōka," 5–12.

63. Kanai Mieko, "Shisen ni hibiku kotoba," *Nihon kindai bungaku taikei 7: Izumi Kyōka shū*, *geppō 13*, 2–3.

64. Ogawa Yōko, *Ogawa Yōko no tōsui tanpenbako* (Tokyo: Kawade Shobō Shinsha, 2014), 35–54.

65. Matsuda Aoko adapts Kyōka's fantasy play, *The Castle Tower*, in her short story "On High" ("Orinai," 2016). Matsuda, *Obachan-tachi no iru tokoro: Where the Wild Ladies Are* (Tokyo: Chūō Kōron Shinsha, 2019), 241–52.

66. Mizuki Shigeru, *Mizuki Shigeru no Izumi Kyōka den*, ed. Akiyama Minoru (Tokyo: Shōgakukan, 2015).

67. Izumi Kyōka, *Tenshu monogatari/Tale of a Castle Keep*, trans. Don Kenny, illustrated by Uno Akira [Aquirax] and Yamamoto Takato, notes by Anakura Tamaki (Tokyo: Edishon Toreviru, 2016).

68. Kyōka, *Kusameikyū*, illustrated by Yamamoto Takato (Tokyo: Edishon Toreviru, 2014).

69. Kyōka, *Ehon ryūtandan*, illustrated by Nakagawa Gaku (Tokyo: Kokusho Kankōkai, 2023); Kyōka, *Shunikki*, illustrated by Nakagawa Gaku (Tokyo: Kokusho Kankōkai, 2015); Kyōka, *Kechō*, illustrated by Nakagawa Gaku (Tokyo: Kokusho Kankōkai, 2012).

70. Kyōka, *Gekashitsu*, illustrated by Honojiro Towoji (Tokyo: Rittōsha, 2018).

71. Kyōka, *Ehon no haru*, illustrated by Kanaida Etsuko (Tokyo: Asahi Shuppansha, 2020).

72. Asagiri Kafka and Harukawa Sango, *Bungō sutorei doggusu* (Tokyo: Kadokawa, 2012–present).

73. Araki Hirohiko, *Kishibe Rohan wa ugokanai* (Tokyo: Shūeisha, 2013).

74. Kyōka, *Sobre el dragón del abismo*, trans. Alejandro Morales Rama (Gijón: Satori, 2022).

75. Kyōka, *Labirinto d'erba*, trans. Alessandro Passarella (Milan: Luni Editrice, 2022).

76. Kyōka, *Tang dao zhi lian/Yūshima mōde*, trans. Zhou Qian (Beijing: Xiandai Chubanshe, 2019).

77. Attebery, *Strategies of Fantasy*, x.

78. Charles Shirō Inouye, *The Similitude of Blossoms: A Critical Biography of Izumi Kyōka (1873–1939), Japanese Novelist and Playwright* (Cambridge, MA: Harvard University Asia Center, 1998).

79. Izumi Kyōka, *Japanese Gothic Tales*, trans. Charles Shirō Inouye (Honolulu: University of Hawai'i Press, 1996).

80. Izumi Kyōka, *In Light of Shadows: More Gothic Tales*, trans. Charles Shirō Inouye (Honolulu: University of Hawai'i Press, 2005).

81. M. Cody Poulton, *Spirits of Another Sort*.

82. Nina Cornyetz, *Dangerous Women, Deadly Words: Phallic Fantasy and Modernity in Three Japanese Writers* (Stanford: Stanford University Press, 1999).

83. Tanaka Takako, *Kyōka to kaii* (Tokyo: Heibonsha, 2006).

84. Tominaga Maki, *Kyōka bungaku no shinkō to zuzō: monogataru koto e no ishi* (Tokyo: Kachōsha, 2023).

85. Suzuki Aya, *Izumi Kyōka no engeki: shōsetsu to gikyō ga kōsa suru tokoro* (Tokyo: Kachōsha, 2023).

86. Matsumura Tomomi, *Kyōka bungaku no ryūiki* (Tokyo: Insukuriputo, 2023).

87. Izumi Kyōka Kinenkan, Izumi Kyōka Kenkyūkai, eds., *Kyōka no ie: Izumi Kyōka seitan 150-nen kinen* (Tokyo: Heibonsha, 2023).

Chapter 1

1. Tanemura Suehiro, "Suichūka henge," 43.

2. Mendlesohn, *Rhetorics of Fantasy*, 35–36.

3. Caillois, *Images, images*, 40–41.

4. Todorov, *The Fantastic*, 100–1.

5. Schneider, *Histoire de la littérature fantastique en France*, 10.

6. Caillois, *Images, images*, 14. Caillois was one of the first scholars to study literature of the fantastic from Europe, Asia, and the Americas in a comparative context. His foundational essay on the fantastic, "From Fairytales to Science-Fiction: The Fantastic Image" ("De la féerie à la science-fiction: l'image fantastique," 1958) first appeared in a collection of global literature, *Fantastique: soixante récits de terreur* (Paris: Club Français du Livre, 1958).

7. I hope to address the illustration of Kyōka's literature in future research.

8. Numerous articles discuss the subject of Kyōka and illustration. See, for example, Tominaga Maki, "Monogatari ga tou mono: Izumi Kyōka *Sankai hyōbanki* to Komura Settai no sashie kara," *Mita kokubun* no. 60 (2015): 52–85; Deguchi Tomoyuki, "*Bungei kurabu* no mokuhan tashokuzuri kuchi-e: shōsetsu to no kankei kara," *Nihon kindai bungaku* 93 (2015): 152–59; Hinode Yumi, "Sashie no kinō: shinbun shōsetsu toshite no *Sankai hyōbanki*," *Ronshū Shōwaki no Izumi Kyōka*, ed. Izumi Kyōka Kenkyūkai (Tokyo: Ōfū, 2002), 78–101; Yoshida Masashi, "Izumi Kyōka to sashie gaka: Kaburaki Kiyokata," *Ronshū Izumi Kyōka 2*, ed. Izumi Kyōka Kenkyūkai (Osaka: Izumi Shoin, 1999), 190–223; Yoshida Masashi, "Izumi Kyōka to sashie gaka: Ikeda Shōen, Terukata," *Ronshū Izumi Kyōka 3*, ed. Izumi Kyōka Kenkyūkai (Osaka: Izumi Shoin, 1999), 133–57.

9. Inouye, *The Similitude of Blossoms*, 19–20; Inouye, "Pictocentrism," *Yearbook of Comparative and General Literature* 40 (1992), 37.

10. Inouye, *Similitude of Blossoms*, 141–43.

11. Cornyetz, *Dangerous Women, Deadly Words*, 91.

12. Poulton, *Spirits of Another Sort*, 2.

13. Tokuda Shūsei, "Izumi Kyōka to iu otoko," *Izumi Kyōka [Gunzō Nihon no sakka 5]*, 188. Originally published in *Bungei shunjū* (December 1935). Quoted in Muramatsu, *Izumi Kyōka*, 38

14. Nagai Kafū, "*Sato no konjaku* yori," *Kyōka ron shūsei*, 180–81. Originally published in *Chūō Kōron* (March 1935).

15. Muramatsu, *Izumi Kyōka*, 38; Kasahara Nobuo, *Izumi Kyōka: bi to erosu no kōzō*, 285.

16. Katsumoto, "Kyōka no ishinzō," 280.

17. Ikuta, "Izumi Kyōka-shi no shōsetsu o ronzu," 178.

18. Mita, *Izumi Kyōka no bungaku*, 69.

19. Kawabata Yasunari, "Kiku awase," 62.

20. Mishima, "Izumi Kyōka," 12; Mishima, Shibusawa, "Kyōka no miryoku," 352, 354.

21. Terayama Shūji, "Kyōka bigaku no disukūru: eiga *Kusameikyū* no dekiru made," *Izumi Kyōka [Gunzō Nihon no sakka 5]*, 229. Originally published in *Kinema junpō* (November 1979).

22. Tanemura, "Suichūka henge," 38.

23. Ikushima, *Kyōka mangekyō*, 13.

24. Katsumoto, "Kyōka no ishinzō," 279.

25. Tanemura, "Suichūka henge," 38.

26. Yoshimura, *Makai e no enkinhō*, 13.

27. Kawamura Jirō, "Dōshi sareta kūkan," 61.

28. Inouye discusses images of water, such as rivers and waterfalls, as being among the central visual motifs of Kyōka's fiction in "Water Imagery in the Work of Izumi Kyōka," *Monumenta Nipponica* 46, no. 1 (Spring 1991): 43–68.

29. For research on *yōkai*, see Michael Dylan Foster, *Pandemonium and Parade: Japanese Monsters and the Culture of Yōkai* (Berkeley: University of California Press, 2009); Gerald A. Figal, *Civilization and Monsters: Spirits of Modernity in Meiji Japan* (Durham: Duke University Press, 1999).

30. Izumi Kyōka, *Kyōka zenshū* (Tokyo: Iwanami Shoten, 1973–1976), vol. 28, 697–98.

31. Katsumoto, "Kyōka no ishinzō," 278.

32. Kasahara, *Izumi Kyōka: bi to erosu no kōzō*, 14.

33. Murakami Kenji, *Yōkai jiten* (Tokyo: Mainichi Shinbunsha, 2000), 16.

34. An *onibaba* figure, who tortures a bound woman suspended from the ceiling, appears in Kyōka's debut work of literature, *Kanmuri Yazaemon*. Kyōka, *Kyōka zenshū*, vol. 1, 128–29. Other references to the *onibaba* in Kyōka's literature are highlighted throughout this book.

35. Kyōka, *Kyōka zenshū*, vol. 23, 462.

36. An example of Kyōka's reference to the *hitotsuya* as an allusion to the lair of the *onibaba* can be found in his most famous story, *The Holy Man of Mt. Kōya*. Kyōka, *Kyōka zenshū*, vol. 5, 640–41.

37. J. Thomas Rimer, *Mori Ōgai* (Boston: Twayne, 1975), 17.

38. Damian Flanagan, "Sōseki in London," Natsume Sōseki, *The Tower of London: Tales of Victorian London*, trans. Damian Flanagan (Chester Springs, PA: Peter Owen, 2005), 47–48.

39. Mitsuko Iriye, "Translator's Introduction," Nagai Kafū, *American Stories*, trans. Mitsuko Iriye (New York: Columbia University Press, 2000), vii, xiii.

40. Muramatsu, *Izumi Kyōka*, 50–52.

41. For Pamphile, see Apuleius, *The Golden Ass*, trans. P. G. Walsh (Oxford: Oxford University Press, 1994), 21. For scholarship on Kyōka, *The Holy Man of Mt. Kōya*, and the influence of *The Golden Ass*, see Tezuka Masayuki, "*Kōya hijiri* seiritsukō," *Izumi Kyōka "Kōya hijiri" sakuhin ronshū* (Tokyo: Kuresu Shuppan, 2003), 38–61, originally published in *Kaishaku* (December 1959–August 1960); Suda Chisato, "Kyōka ni okeru 'ma' teki bijo no keisei to tenkai: *Kōya hijiri* o chūshin ni," *Izumi Kyōka "Kōya hijiri" sakuhin ronshū*, 267–91, originally published in *Kokugo kokubun* 59, no. 2 (November 1990).

42. Kawato Michiaki, Nakabayashi Yoshio, and Sakakibara Takanori, eds., "Meiji-ki hon'yaku bungaku nenpyō: Morita Shiken hen," *Morita Shiken shū I [Zoku Meiji hon'yaku bungaku zenshū hon'yakuka hen 5]* (Tokyo: Ōzorasha, 2002), 1.

43. Kyōka, *Kyōka zenshū*, vol. 28, 656.

44. Jules Verne, *Michael Strogoff: A Courier of the Czar*, anonymous translation (New York: Scribner, 1927).

45. Kyōka, *Kyōka zenshū*, vol. 28, 656.

46. Minakami Takitarō and Hamano Eiji, eds., "Shun'yōdō han *Kyōka zenshū* kan'ichi shoshū: Izumi Kyōka nenpu," *Kyōka zenshū*, suppl. vol., 718. Originally published in "Izumi Kyōka nenpu," *Kyōka zenshū* (Tokyo: Shun'yōdō, 1925–1927), vol. 1, 4.

47. Kyōka, *Kyōka zenshū*, vol. 28, 655–56.

48. Kyōka's knowledge of intimate details of Ichiyō's childhood suggests reasonably close familiarity between two of Japan's most famous authors. The idea of a friendship between these writers is further supported by two extant letters from Kyōka addressed to Ichiyō that show that the authors personally corresponded, as well as by allusions to Ichiyō's life and work throughout Kyōka's writings. Following Ichiyō's tragic death at an early age, Kyōka wrote two illustrated novels that featured a protagonist modeled on Ichiyō, who is given the author's birth name of Natsuko: *Triptych Print* (*Sanmai tsuzuki*, 1900) and *Shikibu Alleyway* (*Shikibu kōji*, 1906). Kyōka also describes a visit that he made to Ichiyō in one of his final novels, *Pale Plum Blossoms* (1937), in an anecdote that relates an event from many years earlier. For details of their correspondence, see Kyōka, *Kyōka zenshū*, suppl. vol., 300–303; Muramatsu, *Izumi Kyōka*, 362–70. For more on Kyōka and Ichiyō see Muramatsu, *Izumi Kyōka*, 117–20; Suda Chisato, "Ichiyō kara Kyōka e: 'Wakaremichi' to *Sanmai tsuzuki, Shikibu kōji*," *Kōka Joshi Daigaku kenkyū kiyō* 28 (1990): 51–69.

49. Kyōka, *Kyōka zenshū*, vol. 28, 657.

50. Koike Masatane, "Izumi Kyōka: *Kanmuri Yazaemon* to *Shinkyoku gyokuseki dōjikun*," *Kokubungaku: kaishaku to kanshō* 44, no. 13 (December 1979): 173–74.

51. Kyōka, *Kyōka zenshū*, vol. 28, 657–58.

52. Tsubouchi Shōyō, *Shōyō senshū* (Tokyo: Shun'yōdō, 1926–1927), suppl. vol. 1, 337–38.

53. Kyōka, *Kyōka zenshū*, vol. 28, 658.

54. Kyōka, *Kyōka zenshū*, vol. 28, 658–59; Muramatsu, *Izumi Kyōka*, 52.

55. Kyōka, *Kyōka zenshū*, vol. 28, 658–59.

56. Muramatsu, *Izumi Kyōka*, 46–49; *Izumi Kyōka [Gunzō Nihon no sakka 5]*, photograph 13.

57. Kyōka, *Kyōka zenshū*, vol. 2, 331.

58. Kyōka, *Kyōka zenshū*, vol. 2, 340.

59. Kyōka, *Kyōka zenshū*, vol. 2, 363–64.

60. Kyōka, *Kyōka zenshū*, vol. 2, 458.

61. Kyōka, *Kyōka zenshū*, vol. 2, 482.

62. Robert Irwin, "Introduction," *The Arabian Nights: Tales of 1001 Nights*, trans. Malcolm C. Lyons with Ursula Lyons (London: Penguin Books, 2008), vol. 1, ix–xviii.

63. Kyōka, *Kyōka zenshū*, vol. 5, 410.

64. Kyōka, *Kyōka zenshū*, vol. 5, 421.
65. Kyōka, *Kyōka zenshū*, vol. 5, 411.
66. Kyōka, *Kyōka zenshū*, vol. 5, 417.
67. Kyōka, *Kyōka zenshū*, vol. 5, 418–19.
68. Kyōka, *Kyōka zenshū*, vol. 5, 419–20
69. Kyōka, *Kyōka zenshū*, vol. 2, 30.
70. Kyōka, *Kyōka zenshū*, vol. 2, 486.
71. Kyōka, *Kyōka zenshū*, vol. 2, 486–87.
72. Kyōka, *Kyōka zenshū*, vol. 2, 488.
73. Hinatsu Kōnosuke, "Meijin Kyōka gei," *Kyōka ron shūsei*, 260, 265. Originally published in *Meiji bungaku sakkaron* (Tokyo: Shōgakukan, 1943).
74. Cornyetz, *Dangerous Women, Deadly Words*, 37.
75. See, for example, Tezuka, "*Kōya hijiri* seiritsu kō"; Suda, "Kyōka ni okeru 'ma' teki bijo no keisei to tenkai"; Higashi Masao, "Izumi Kyōka to *Arabian naito*," *Izumi Kyōka "Kōya hijiri" sakuhin ronshū*, 149–62, originally published in *Kin'yōmō* (March 1981).
76. See, for example, Takada Mamoru, "Yume to yamahime gensō no keifu: Kyōka e no shichū," *Izumi Kyōka "Kōya hijiri" sakuhin ronshū*, 179–201, originally published in *Bungaku* (June 1983); Kawamura Jirō, "Dōshi sareta kūkan," 54.
77. Miri Nakamura, *Monstrous Bodies: The Rise of the Uncanny in Modern Japan* (Cambridge, MA: Harvard University Asia Center, 2015), 23–29.
78. Kyōka, *Kyōka zenshū*, vol. 5, 574.
79. Kyōka, *Kyōka zenshū*, vol. 5, 583.
80. Kyōka, *Kyōka zenshū*, vol. 5, 610–12.
81. Katsumoto, "Kyōka no ishinzō," 278.

Chapter 2

1. Caillois, *Images, images*, 13–16; Todorov, *The Fantastic*, 54, 64–65; Vax, *L'art et la littérature fantastiques*, 5–6.
2. Kyōka, *Kyōka zenshū*, vol. 28, 658.
3. Okitsu Kaname, "Izumi Kyōka to Edo gesaku," *Meiji Taishō bungaku kenkyū* 21 (1957): 17.
4. Asada Shōjirō, "Kyōka no shōsetsu to Edo bungaku: ushinawareta toki no tansakusha-tachi," *Kokubungaku kaishaku to kanshō* 41, no. 14 (1976): 130.
5. Koike Masatane, "Kyōka bungaku no kosō: koten no sekai," *Kokubungaku kaishaku to kanshō* 46, no. 7 (1981): 115.
6. Later volumes were illustrated by Kunisada's apprentice and son-in-law, Utagawa Kunisada II, while part of a single volume (volume 53, part 2) was illustrated by Kawanabe Kyōsai (1831–1889).
7. Later volumes were written by Ryūtei Senka (1804–1868), then Ryūsuitei Tanekiyo (1823–1907), and were illustrated by Kunisada II, followed by Utagawa Yoshiiku (1833–1904), Toyohara Chikanobu (1838–1912), and numerous other illustrators. Because the archive of *kusazōshi* has yet to be thoroughly documented, variant names, titles, dates, and other details can be found in scholarship and archi-

val records. I have prioritized details included in the latest research on the subject, found in Laura Moretti and Satō Yukiko, eds., *Graphic Narratives from Early Modern Japan: The World of Kusazōshi* (Leiden: Brill, 2024). Details are also drawn from the Waseda University Library Kotenseki Sōgō Database, a vital source on this subject.

8. *Fake Murasaki, Rustic Genji* is unusual among long-running series for featuring the same writer and illustrator throughout its serialization.

9. Later volumes were written by Ryūkatei Tanekazu and then Ryūsuitei Tanekiyo. Illustrators who contributed to the series include Kuniyoshi, Kunisada II, Keisai Eisen (1790–1848), Utagawa Kuniteru (active ca. 1840s–1870s), Utagawa Yoshifusa (1837–1860), and Utagawa Yoshiiku (1833–1904), among others.

10. The majority of the long-running series was created by Shunsui II (also known as Somezaki Nobufusa) and Kunisada II, although the last few volumes were written by Ryūsuitei Tanekiyo and illustrated by Utagawa Kuniaki (active ca. 1840s–1860s), followed by Adachi Ginkō (1853–1902).

11. Natsume Sōseki, "'Gin tanzaku'—*Kinsaku tanpyō* yori," 134.

12. Quoted in Yoshida Masashi, "Izumi Kyōka to kusazōshi: *Shaka hassō Yamato bunko* o chūshin to shite," *Izumi Kyōka: bi to gensō*, ed. Tōgō Katsumi (Tokyo: Yūseidō, 1991), 172. The article by Yoshida was originally published in *Bungaku* 55, no. 3 (March 1987), 37–52. The comments by Osanai Kaoru were originally published in "Geki to naritaru Kyōka-shi no shōsetsu," *Yomiuri shinbun* (June 21, 1908).

13. Okitsu, "Izumi Kyōka to Edo gesaku," 16–17.

14. Asada, "Kyōka no shōsetsu to Edo bungaku," 130.

15. Jean Akemi Funatsu, *Through the Colored Looking Glass of Izumi Kyōka: Reflections of the Kusazōshi* (dissertation, Harvard University, 1972), 82–83; 112–13; 151–52.

16. The anecdote by Izumi Shatei is quoted by Muramatsu Sadataka in *Izumi Kyōka*, 37–38.

17. Inouye, *Similitude of Blossoms*, 13. In his dissertation, Inouye describes additional aspects of the influence of *kusazōshi* on Kyōka's fiction, including the influence of *The Life of Shakyamuni in Eight Phases*, Kyōka's hobby of collecting picture books, and literary criticism comparing Kyōka's work to *kusazōshi*. Charles Shirō Inouye, *Izumi Kyōka and the Visual Tradition* (dissertation, Harvard University, 1988).

18. Yoshida Masashi, "Izumi Kyōka to kusazōshi," 175.

19. Yoshida relates such imagery to that of the *kechō*, who appears as an angelic protector of the protagonist in one of Kyōka's early stories, "The Bird Changeling" ("Kechō," 1897), "Izumi Kyōka to kusazōshi," 179–84.

20. Kyōka, *Kyōka zenshū*, vol. 19, 383–99.

21. Ikushima, *Kyōka mangekyō*, 42; Noguchi Takehiko, ed., *Izumi Kyōka [Shinchō Nihon bungaku arubamu 22]*, with an essay by Tsushima Yūko (Tokyo: Shinchōsha, 1985), 16, 51, 63.

22. For a description of Kyōka's veneration of the image of Maya Bunin, as well a note on the rarity of such images in Japan, see the essay "Bunindō" ("Hall of the Sacred Mother," 1911), Kyōka, *Kyōka zenshū* vol. 28, 474–76.

23. Kyōka, *Kyōka zenshū*, vol. 16, 291.

24. Kyōka, *Kyōka zenshū*, vol. 28, 792.

25. Caillois, *Images, images*, 15.

26. Andrew Lawrence Markus, *The Willow in Autumn: Ryūtei Tanehiko, 1783–1842* (Cambridge, MA: Council on East Asian Studies, Harvard University, 1992), 67.

27. Markus, *The Willow in Autumn*, 86.

28. Markus, *The Willow in Autumn*, 62.

29. Adam Kern, *Manga from the Floating World: Comicbook Culture and the Kibyōshi of Edo Japan* (Cambridge, MA: Harvard University Asia Center, 2006), 184.

30. Suzuki Jūzō, *Ehon to ukiyoe: Edo shuppan bunka no kōsatsu* (Tokyo: Bijutsu Shuppansha, 1979), 16–17.

31. Suzuki, *Ehon to ukiyoe*, 17–18.

32. Kern, *Manga from the Floating World*, 181–82.

33. Suzuki, *Ehon to ukiyoe*, 13.

34. Michael Emmerich, *The Tale of Genji: Translation, Canonization, and World Literature* (New York: Columbia University Press, 2013), 114.

35. Many artists share the name "Utagawa" because it was derived from the Utagawa school of woodblock-printing, the most prominent artistic school in the illustration of *kusazōshi* during the nineteenth century.

36. Markus, *The Willow in Autumn*, 145–46.

37. Satō Yukiko, *Edo no eiri shōsetsu: gōkan no sekai* (Tokyo: Perikansha, 2001), 1.

38. Markus, *The Willow in Autumn*, 61.

39. Satō, *Edo no eiri shōsetsu*, 150; Nozaki Sabun, "Kusazōshi to Meiji shoki no shinbun shōsetsu," *Waseda bungaku* 261 (October 1927): 148.

40. Markus, *The Willow in Autumn*, 146–48.

41. Markus, *The Willow in Autumn*, 146.

42. Maeda Ai, *Kindai dokusha no seiritsu* (Tokyo: Chikuma Shobō, 1989), 118–19.

43. Maeda, *Kindai dokusha no seiritsu*, 118–19.

44. Maeda, *Kindai dokusha no seiritsu*, 117.

45. Kyōka, *Kyōka zenshū*, vol. 28, 654.

46. Ryūkatei Tanekazu, Ryūtei Senka, Ryūsuitei Tanekiyo, Utagawa Kunisada, Utagawa Kunisada II, Utagawa Yoshiiku, et al., *Shiranui monogatari*, eds. Takada Mamoru and Satō Yukiko (Tokyo: Kokusho Kankōkai, 2006).

47. Kyōka, *Kyōka zenshū*, vol. 28, 774.

48. Kyōka, *Kyōka zenshū*, vol. 28, 773.

49. Some of Kyōka's more interesting female characters include the following: a magician, traveling performer, and murderer in *Noble Blood, Heroic Blood* (*Giketsu kyōketsu*, 1894); a gang leader who takes revenge on the wealthy elite of Tokyo in *Poverty Club* (*Hinmin kurabu*, 1895); an American teacher and missionary in *Volume One* (1896–1897) and "Story of a Famous Princess" (1900); a troupe of *kyōgen* actresses in *Shining Leaf Theater* (*Teriha kyōgen*, 1896); a mother who becomes a

realtor after a career of prostitution and her daughter who becomes a nurse in "The Glittering Sands of Katsushika" ("Katsushika sunago," 1900); a maid who evades the police and encounters a goddess in the mountains in "The Female Mountain Immortal: Prelude" ("Josen zenki," 1902) and "Kinuginu River" ("Kinuginugawa," 1902); a scholar of Russian literature who once lived in Siberia in *The Phantom Votive Image* (*Maboroshi no ema*, 1917); an agile thief and assassin in *A Peony Song* (*Shakuyaku no uta*, 1918); a film actress in "The Count's Hairpin" ("Hakushaku no kanzashi," 1920); and a fortune teller who practices Zen Buddhist meditation and studies Chinese philosophy and literature in "Picture Books in the Springtime" ("Ehon no haru," 1926). These are in addition to characters modeled on modern authors Higuchi Ichiyō and Kitada Usurai (1876–1900), both featured in *Pale Plum Blossoms* (*Usukōbai*, 1937), and stories that memorialized modern painter Ikeda Shōen (1886–1917), a friend of Kyōka, including "The Silver Three-Pronged Vessel" ("Gin kanae" / "Zoku gin kanae," 1921) and "Maple and Dove" ("Kaede to shirohato," 1922).

50. Kyōka, *Kyōka zenshū*, vol. 28, 653–54.

51. Kyōka, *Kyōka zenshū*, vol. 28, 654.

52. Kyōka, *Kyōka zenshū*, vol. 28, 654–55.

53. Kyōka, *Kyōka zenshū*, vol. 28, 659–60.

54. Kyōka, *Kyōka zenshū*, vol. 28, 693.

55. Later volumes were written by Ryūtei Senka and illustrated by Utagawa Sadahide (1807–1873).

56. Later volumes were written by Kakutei Shūga (active ca. 1860s–1880s) and illustrated by Kunisada II.

57. The earlier list can be found in Hasegawa Satoru, "Kyōka Sensei no kusazōshi mokuroku," *Izumi Kyōka: bi to gensō*, 224–25. Originally published in *Kyōka zenshū*, vol. 16, *geppō* 19 (April 1942). The later list can be found in Hinotani Teruhiko, Suzuki Isamu, and Matsumura Tomomi, eds., "Izumi Kyōka zōsho mokuroku," *Kyōka zenshū*, suppl. vol., *geppō* 29 (March 1976): 15–19. Further details of the extant collection housed at Keiō University appear in Keiō Gijuku Toshokan, Matsumura Tomomi, Suzuki Aya, and Tominaga Maki, eds., *Kyōka no shosai: "gensō" no umareru basho* (Tokyo: Keiō Gijuku Toshokan, 2016), 96–102.

58. Hinotani, Suzuki, and Matsumura, "Izumi Kyōka zōsho mokuroku," 15.

59. *Izumi Kyōka [Shinchō Nihon bungaku arubamu 22]*, 62–63.

60. Takada, Satō, *Shiranui monogatari*, vol. 3, 300.

61. Later volumes were illustrated by Utagawa Kuniyasu (1794–1832).

62. Writers involved in the series include Santō Kyōzan, Ryūtei Tanehiko, Ryūtei Senka, and Shōtei Kinsui (1797–1862). All volumes were illustrated by Utagawa Kuniyoshi. See Satō Satoru, "*Kanagaki Suikoden* o megutte," *Kokugo to kokubungaku* 58, no. 9 (September 1981): 50–51. Kyōka discusses the publication history and shifting literary style of the series in his essay "*The Water Margin in Japanese*" ("*Kanagaki Suikoden*," 1905). The essay includes an aside that he "knows nothing of Tolstoy" in a discussion of Edo period fiction. Kyōka, *Kyōka zenshū*, vol. 28, 350.

63. Later volumes were illustrated by Kuniyoshi and Utagawa Yoshiiku.

64. Later volumes were written by Ryūhasha Odoriko (an otherwise unknown writer) and illustrated by Utagawa Yoshitora (active ca. 1850s–1870s) and Utagawa Kunimasa (1773–1810).

65. Later volumes were written by Ryūtei Senka and Santei Shunba (active ca. 1830s–1860s).

66. For more on the work of Kunisada, one of the most talented and prolific artists of the Edo period, see Hinohara Kenji, *Utagawa Kunisada: kore zo Edo no iki*, ed. Ōta Kinen Bijutsukan (Tokyo: Tōkyō Bijutsu, 2016).

67. Illustrators are also listed on covers and in opening pages of *kusazōshi*.

68. Kyōka, *Kyōka zenshū*, vol. 12, 688.

69. Kyōka, *Kyōka zenshū*, vol. 12, 702–3.

70. Kyōka, *Kyōka zenshū*, vol. 12, 702.

71. Kyōka, *Kyōka zenshū*, vol. 22, 525.

72. Mantei Ōga's story is based on an earlier popular rendition of the life of the Buddha, the similarly titled *Tale of Shakyamuni in Eight Phases* (*Shaka hassō monogatari*, 1666), an anonymous text that scholar Micah L. Auerback describes as "the single most influential Japanese biography of the Buddha from that time until the late nineteenth century." *A Storied Sage: Canon and Creation in the Making of a Japanese Buddha* (Chicago: University of Chicago Press, 2016), 75. Auerback lists many unorthodox details of the life of the Buddha from the earlier narrative that are adopted by Ōga in the *kusazōshi* series, *A Storied Sage*, 75–87. See also, Bernard Faure, *The Thousand and One Lives of the Buddha* (Honolulu: University of Hawai'i Press, 2022), 189–99.

73. Kyōka, *Kyōka zenshū*, vol. 22, 498–99.

74. Akiyama Minoru, "Izumi Kyōka 'Bunin rishōki' ron: seiritsu haikei o chūshin ni," *Ronshū Shōwaki no Izumi Kyōka*, 12.

75. Kyōka, *Kyōka zenshū*, vol. 22, 510–12. The images described in this story correspond with varying levels of accuracy to illustrations from *The Life of Shakyamuni in Eight Phases*. According to scholar Akiyama Minoru, *oshi-e* based on different illustrations by Kunisada can actually be found at Shinjōji temple in Kanazawa, thereby demonstrating a real-life meeting between religious devotion, entertainment, and the print culture of nineteenth-century Japan. Akiyama, "Izumi Kyōka 'Bunin rishōki' ron," 13–20.

76. Kyōka, *Kyōka zenshū*, vol. 23, 12.

77. Kyōka, *Kyōka zenshū*, vol. 23, 14.

78. Kyōka, *Kyōka zenshū*, vol. 23, 671.

79. Kyōka also references Bashō's famous text in "Blessings of the Holy Mother" and *The River Goddess*, thereby demonstrating his deep interest in Bashō during the 1920s.

80. Kyōka, *Kyōka zenshū*, vol. 23, 671, 771–72.

81. Kyōka, *Kyōka zenshū*, vol. 23, 708–9.

82. Rebecca Salter, *Japanese Popular Prints: From Votive Slips to Playing Cards* (Honolulu: University of Hawai'i Press, 2006), 73–74.

83. Kyōka, *Kyōka zenshū*, vol. 23, 767.

84. Resources on Settai's work in illustration and graphic design, including his work for Kyōka, are extensive. Such sources include Harada Osamu, Hirata Masaki, Yamashita Yūji, eds., *Ishō no tensai Komura Settai* (Tokyo: Shinchōsha, 2016); Ōkoshi Hisako and Saitama Kenritsu Kindai Bijutsukan, eds., *Komura Settai: monogataru ishō* (Tokyo: Tōkyō Bijutsu, 2014); and Saitama Kenritsu Kindai Bijutsukan, eds., *Komura Settai to sono jidai: iki de modan de sensai de* (Saitama: Saitama Kenritsu Kindai Bijutsukan, 2009); among others.

85. Kyōka, *Kyōka zenshū*, vol. 28, 595.

Chapter 3

1. It is not clear why Kyōka would pair Leo Tolstoy, a Russian writer, with Auguste Rodin (1840–1917), a French sculptor, as his two examples of European artists, although he is perhaps gesturing toward his understanding of the relation between literary and visual arts. Noguchi, *Izumi Kyōka [Shinchō Nihon bungaku arubamu 22]*, 60.

2. Hasegawa Satoru, "Izumi Kyōka zōsho mokuroku," *Izumi Kyōka: bi to gensō*, 221–23. Originally published in *Kyōka zenshū*, vol. 3, *geppō* 14 (December 1941). Hasegawa characterizes the list as being an initial accounting of the gift of Kyōka's personal library from his wife, Suzu, to the library at Keiō University. He suggests that the list may be less than complete and possibly includes oversights. Most of Kyōka's library was destroyed during World War II, with the exception of part of his *kusazōshi* collection, and so its original contents are no longer possible to ascertain. The work by Lermontov is listed only as *Lermontov Collection* (*Rērumontofu shū*) in two volumes. It is unclear what publication the entry corresponds to. The collection probably included Lermontov's only major novel, *A Hero of Our Time* (1840), a romantic tragedy set in the Caucasus region. Kyōka may have been interested in the detailed descriptions of local cultures and landscapes featured in the novel.

3. Sugita Hideaki, *Arabian naito to Nihonjin* (Tokyo: Iwanami Shoten, 2012), 70; Tayama Katai, *Tōkyō no sanjūnen* (Tokyo: Nihon Tosho Sentā, 1983), 70, originally published in 1917.

4. Poulton, *Spirits of Another Sort*, 100–13; Muramatsu, *Izumi Kyōka*, 304–19.

5. Robert Irwin, "Introduction," *The Arabian Nights: Tales of 1001 Nights*, vol. 2, ix.

6. Irwin, "Introduction," *Arabian Nights*, vol. 2, x.

7. Castex, *Le conte fantastique en France*, 25; Todorov, *The Fantastic*, 24–27; Schneider, *Histoire de la littérature fantastique en France*, 99–119.

8. Castex, *Le conte fantastique en France*, 26–27, 90–92.

9. Tezuka, "*Kōya hijiri* seiritsukō," 38–61; Higashi Masao, "Kyōka to *Arabian naito*," 149–62.

10. Sugita, *Arabian naito to Nihonjin*, 63–70, 173–80.

11. In addition to being one of the first works of global literature translated into Japanese during the modern period, Nagamine's the *Arabian Nights* was one of

the first modern books in Japan to feature lithographic illustrations. Sugita, *Arabian naito to Nihonjin*, 19; Higashi, "Kyōka to *Arabian naito*," 149.

12. Alternate collected editions printed between 1886 and 1888, in eleven volumes, reach 700 pages. Sugita, *Arabian naito to Nihonjin*, 27; Higashi, "Kyōka to *Arabian naito*," 152.

13. Sugita, *Arabian naito to Nihonjin*, 28.

14. Sugita, *Arabian naito to Nihonjin*, 70. Originally published in Yamagishi Kayō, "Ko Kōyō daijin no koe," *Uzue* 2, no. 1 (January 1904).

15. *The Arabian Nights: Tales of 1001 Nights*, vol. 2, 549–50.

16. Sugita, *Arabian naito to Nihonjin*, 63.

17. The lecture was given and transcribed in December 1899, then serialized in the *Yomiuri shinbun* from January 23 to February 5, 1900. Sugita, *Arabian naito to Nihonjin*, 66; Sakai Miki, *Ozaki Kōyō to hon'an: sono hōhō kara yomitoku "kindai" no gugen to genkai* (Fukuoka: Kashoin, 2010), 195.

18. Sugita, *Arabian naito to Nihonjin*, 70; Sakai Miki, *Ozaki Kōyō to hon'an*, 196.

19. Kyōka, *Kyōka zenshū*, vol. 28, 392.

20. Sugita, *Arabian naito to Nihonjin*, 82–83.

21. Kyōka, *Kyōka zenshū*, vol. 28, 398–99.

22. Sugita, *Arabian naito to Nihonjin*, 81–82.

23. Kyōka, *Kyōka zenshū*, vol. 28, 392.

24. Sugita, *Arabian naito to Nihonjin*, 173–76.

25. Sugita, *Arabian naito to Nihonjin*, 177.

26. Sugita, *Arabian naito to Nihonjin*, 176–77.

27. Muramatsu, *Izumi Kyōka*, 72–90.

28. Sakai, *Kōyō to hon'an*, 32.

29. Kyōka, *Kyōka zenshū*, vol. 28, 741.

30. Sakai, *Ozaki Kōyō to hon'an*, 30–34.

31. Seki Hajime, *Shinbun shōsetsu no jidai: media, dokusha, merodorama* (Tokyo: Shin'yōsha, 2007), 53–54.

32. For scholarship on Kōyō and his career, see Baba Mika, *"Shōsetsuka" tōjō: Ozaki Kōyō no Meiji nijūnendai* (Tokyo: Kasama Shoin, 2011). For scholarship on Kōyō's most famous novel, *The Gold Demon*, see Jonathan E. Zwicker, *Practices of the Sentimental Imagination: Melodrama, the Novel, and the Social Imaginary in Nineteenth-Century Japan* (Cambridge, MA: Harvard University Asia Center, 2006), 169–91.

33. Sakai, *Ozaki Kōyō to hon'an*, 101, 146–48.

34. Sakai, *Ozaki Kōyō to hon'an*, 36–37.

35. Matsumura Tomomi, "Kaidai," *Kōyō zenshū* (Tokyo: Iwanami Shoten, 1995), suppl. vol., 533; Kawato Michiaki, Nakabayashi Yoshio, and Sakakibara Takanori, eds., "Meiji-ki hon'yaku bungaku nenpyō: Ozaki Kōyō-hen," Ozaki Kōyō, Oguri Fūyō, *Ozaki Kōyō, Oguri Fūyō shū [Meiji hon'yaku bungaku zenshū hon'yakuka hen 12]* (Tokyo: Ōzorasha, 2002), 3–4.

36. Matsumura, *Kōyō zenshū*, suppl. vol., 531–32.

37. Sakai, *Ozaki Kōyō to hon'an*, 39.

38. Uchida Roan, *Omoidasu hitobito* (Tokyo: Shunjūsha, 1925), 91. Quoted in Sakai, *Ozaki Kōyō to hon'an*, 39.

39. Kashiwagi Takao, "Kyōka, Merime, Yugō: juyō no mondai," *Bungaku* 57, no. 9 (September 1989): 28–34.

40. Hans Christian Andersen, *Hans Andersen's Fairytales: A Selection*, trans. L. W. Kingsland (Oxford: Oxford University Press, 1998), 11–27.

41. Jacob Grimm and Wilhelm Grimm, *The Original Folk and Fairy Tales of the Brothers Grimm*, trans. Jack Zipes, illustrated by Andrea Dezsö (Princeton: Princeton University Press, 2014), 92–97.

42. Muramatsu, *Izumi Kyōka*, 313.

43. Poulton, *Spirits of Another Sort*, 110.

44. Kyōka, *Kyōka zenshū*, vol. 26, 452–53, 474.

45. Muramatsu, *Izumi Kyōka*, 334–38.

46. Muramatsu, *Izumi Kyōka*, 338–39.

47. Shibusawa Tatsuhiko, "Gosō no tenshukaku," *Kyōka ron shūsei*, 374. Originally published in *Shingeki* 24, no. 12 (December 1977).

48. Ōgai's translation was based on the German translation by Heinrich Denhardt from 1876. Nagashima Yōichi, "Hans Christian Andersen Remade in Japan: Mori Ōgai's Translation of *Improvisatoren*," *Hans Christian Andersen: A Poet in Time*, eds. Johan de Mylius, Aage Jørgensen, and Viggo Hjørnager Pedersen (Odense, Denmark: Odense University Press, 1999), 398.

49. John Timothy Wixted, "Mori Ōgai: Translation Transforming the Word/World," *Japonica Humboldtiana* 13 (October 2009): 104–5.

50. Muramatsu, *Izumi Kyōka*, 287–91.

51. Yoshida Seiichi, "Kaisetsu," Mori Ōgai, *Mori Ōgai zenshū* (Tokyo: Chikuma Shobō, 1971), vol. 8, 377.

52. Nagashima Yōichi, *Mori Ōgai no hon'yaku bungaku: "Sokkyō shijin" kara "Perikan" made* (Tokyo: Shibundō, 1993).

53. Muramatsu Sadataka, "Mori Ōgai no hon'yaku bungaku," *Kokubungaku kaishaku to kyōzai no kenkyū* 4, no. 5 (March 1959): 64–65.

54. Muramatsu, "Mori Ōgai no hon'yaku bungaku," 64.

55. Yoshida, "Kaisetsu," *Mori Ōgai zenshū*, vol. 8, 380–81. Original in Satō Haruo, *Kindai Nihon bungaku no tenbō* (Tokyo: Kōdansha, 1950), 73.

56. Yoshida, "Kaisetsu," *Mori Ōgai zenshū*, vol. 8, 381; Muramatsu, "Mori Ōgai no hon'yaku bungaku," 65.

57. Itō Sei, *Kindai Nihon no bungō 2* (Tokyo: Yomiuri Shinbunsha, 1967), 126.

58. Kyōka, *Kyōka zenshū*, vol. 28, 509–10.

59. Kinoshita Mokutarō, Kojima Masajirō, et al., eds., "Kōki," Mori Ōgai, *Ōgai zenshū* (Tokyo: Iwanami Shoten, 1971), vol. 1, 640. Editions of stories in translation referenced in this section are listed in the bibliography.

60. Yoshida Seiichi, "Kaisetsu," *Mori Ōgai zenshū*, 382.

61. Mori Ōgai, "Kaitei *Minawashū* jo," *Minawashū* (Tokyo: Shun'yōdō, 1892), 3. Despite Ōgai's personal lack of interest, he recommends the story by Hoffmann to fans of Poe.

62. E. T. A. Hoffmann, *Tales of Hoffmann*, trans. R. J. Hollingdale (London: Penguin Books, 1982), 28–29; Ōgai, *Ōgai zenshū*, vol. 1, 108.

63. Wixted, "Mori Ōgai: Translation Transforming the Word/World," 63.

64. Nagashima, "Hans Christian Andersen Remade in Japan," 399.

65. Nagashima, "Hans Christian Andersen Remade in Japan," 397.

66. Nagashima, "Hans Christian Andersen Remade in Japan," 400–4.

67. Nagashima, "Hans Christian Andersen Remade in Japan," 401.

68. Quoted in Yoshida, "Kaisetsu," *Mori Ōgai zenshū*, vol. 8, 382–83. Originally published in *Shiragami zōshi* (May 1893).

69. Hans Christian Andersen, *The Improvisatore: A Novel of Italy*, trans. Frank Hugus (Minneapolis: University of Minnesota Press, 2018), 254; the corresponding passage in *Sokkyō shijin* can be found in Ōgai, *Ōgai zenshū*, vol. 2, 484.

70. Andersen, *The Improvisatore*, 256; Ōgai, *Ōgai zenshū*, vol. 2, 487–88.

71. Andersen, *The Improvisatore*, 213. Ōgai translates "fata morgana" simply as "mirage" (*shinkirō*). He also includes what might be considered as an early translation of "fantasy" into Japanese, translated as *fāntajia* (phantasia) in *katakana*, with "daydream" (*kūsō*) appearing in parentheses. Ōgai, *Ōgai zenshū*, vol. 2, 435.

72. Andersen, *The Improvisatore*, 197; Ōgai, *Ōgai zenshū*, vol. 2, 420.

73. Kyōka, *Kyōka zenshū*, vol. 28, 507–8.

74. Kyōka, *Kyōka zenshū*, vol. 28, 511.

75. Kyōka, *Kyōka zenshū*, vol. 28, 511–12.

76. Andersen, *The Improvisatore*, 49–50; Ōgai, *Ōgai zenshū*, vol. 2, 263–64.

77. Ōgai literally writes, "Italy is heaven [*tengoku*], it is the Pure Land [*jōdo*]," thereby equating Italy with the pure world of the afterlife in Buddhism. Andersen, *The Improvisatore*, 177; Ōgai, *Ōgai zenshū*, vol. 2, 398.

78. Muramatsu, *Izumi Kyōka*, 289.

79. Noguchi Tetsuya, "'Teriha kyōgen' o kataru koe: Mori Ōgai hon'yaku *Sokkyō shijin* to no kanren kara," *Kokubungaku kaishaku to kanshō* 74, no. 9 (September 2009): 105.

80. Muramatsu, *Izumi Kyōka*, 291; Noguchi, "'Teriha kyōgen' o kataru koe," 105–6.

81. Author Tsushima Yūko, a fan of Kyōka's literature, once wrote that she read these three texts too many times to count. "Pari no Kyōka," 5.

82. Todorov, *The Fantastic*, 44–45.

83. Tanemura Suehiro describes the influence of the ghost stories of Hirata Atsutane (1776–1843) on *The Grass Labyrinth* in "Meikyū no kai," *Izumi Kyōka shūsei* (Tokyo: Chikuma Shobō, 1995–1997), vol. 5, 468.

84. Kyōka, *Kyōka zenshū*, vol. 2, 544.

85. Kyōka, *Kyōka zenshū*, vol. 28, 697–98.

86. Kyōka, *Kyōka zenshū*, vol. 2, 549.

87. Kyōka, *Kyōka zenshū*, vol. 2, 621.

88. Japanese scholars have often noted the extreme difficulty of the narrative. Ikushima, *Kyōka mangekyō*, 11.

89. This last quote is by Tanemura. "Suichūka henge," 43.

90. Kyōka, *Kyōka zenshū*, vol. 11, 170.

91. This succession of images has been widely noted by scholars as the structuring sequence of the story and is clearly visualized in the cinematic adaptation by Terayama, as well as in the illustrations by Takato. See Shibusawa, "Ranpu no kaiten," 118.

92. Kyōka, *Kyōka zenshū*, vol. 11, 258.

93. Kyōka, *Kyōka zenshū*, vol. 11, 313.

94. Kyōka, *Kyōka zenshū*, vol. 11, 316.

95. Kyōka, *Kyōka zenshū*, vol. 11, 327.

96. Kyōka, *Kyōka zenshū*, vol. 11, 332.

97. A variation of this *temari uta* also appears in *The Castle Tower*. Kyōka, *Kyōka zenshū*, vol. 26, 451–52.

98. Kyōka, *Kyōka zenshū*, vol. 11, 333–34.

Chapter 4

1. Kyōka, *Kyōka zenshū*, vol. 28, 695.

2. Ōnishi Tadao, "Mōpassan to sono Nihon e no eikyō," *Shizen shugi bungaku*, ed. Kawachi Kiyoshi (Tokyo: Keisō Shobō, 1962), 305; Matsuda Minoru, "Nihon bungaku to Furansu bungaku," *Hikaku bungaku: Nihon bungaku o chūshin to shite*, eds. Nakajima Kenzō, Yoshida Seiichi, et al. (Tokyo: Yajima Shobō, 1953), 193–98; Nobori Shomu, "Nihon bungaku to Roshia bungaku," *Hikaku bungaku: Nihon bungaku o chūshin to shite*, 237–49, 272–77.

3. Ōnishi Tadao, "Mōpassan to Nihon kindai bungaku," *Nihon kindai bungaku no hikaku bungaku teki kenkyū*, ed. Yoshida Seiichi (Tokyo: Shimizu Kōbundō Shobō, 1971), 187–88.

4. Ōnishi, "Mōpassan to Nihon kindai bungaku," 179–96.

5. Kawato Michiaki and Sakakibara Takanori, eds., "Meiji hon'yaku bungaku nenpyō: Mōpassan-hen," *Mōpassan shū I [Meiji hon'yaku bungaku zenshū shinbun zasshi hen 31]* (Tokyo: Ōzorasha, 1997), 1–12.

6. Christopher Lloyd, *Guy de Maupassant* (London: Reaktion Books, 2020), 7–8, 88–89.

7. Didier Philippot, *Guy de Maupassant et l'affolant mystère de la vie: essai sur l'œuvre fantastique* (Paris: Classiques Garnier, 2019), 55–57; Lloyd, *Guy de Maupassant*, 109–10.

8. Yoshimura, *Izumi Kyōka: geijutsu to byōri*, 101; Komura Settai, "Izumi Kyōka-sensei no koto," *Nihonbashi Himonochō* (Tokyo: Chūō Kōronsha, 1990), 80–81, originally published in *Hōmuraifu* (November 1939).

9. Komura Settai, "Izumi Kyōka-sensei no koto," 81; Yoshimura, *Izumi Kyōka: geijutsu to byōri*, 107.

10. Yoshimura, *Izumi Kyōka: geijutsu to byōri*, 102, 144. Kyōka's *fudezuka* can be found at Yushima Shrine in Tokyo.

11. Teraki Teihō, *Hito Izumi Kyōka* (Tokyo: Nihon Tosho Sentā, 1983), 212–13, originally published in 1943. Quoted in Inouye, *Similitude of Blossoms*, 78–79. Settai, "Izumi Kyōka-sensei no koto," 80.

12. Kawamura, "Dōshi sareta kūkan," 62–63; Kobayashi Hideo, "Kyōka no shi sono ta," 219; Poulton, *Spirits of Another Sort*, 69; Tsushima, "Mashō no sekai," *Izumi Kyōka [Shinchō Nihon bungaku arubamu 22]*, 102.

13. Philippot, *Guy de Maupassant et l'affolant mystère de la vie*, 57.

14. Miri Nakamura points out the centrality of themes of hygiene (*eisei*) and modern medical discourse in *The Holy Man of Mt. Kōya*. *Monstrous Bodies*, 15–16. Themes of contamination, disease, and concerns over hygiene can be found throughout Kyōka's literature, reinforcing the idea of the author's unusual concern with cleanliness. Entire chapters of anecdotes have been written about Kyōka's efforts to avoid contamination, particularly through food. For example, he was known to drink liquids at extremely hot temperatures, excessively boil food, abstain from foods such as shellfish, octopus, and shrimp, and even to avoid fish and meat more generally. He was also known to have a strong fear of bacteria and flies. Yoshimura, *Izumi Kyōka: geijutsu to byōri*, 55–96.

15. Clive Barker, cover endorsement, Guy de Maupassant, *The Dark Side: Tales of Terror and the Supernatural*, trans. Arnold Kellett, foreword by Ramsey Campbell (New York: Carroll and Graf, 1989).

16. Siân Miles, "Introduction," Guy de Maupassant, *A Parisian Affair and Other Stories*, trans. Siân Miles (London: Penguin Books, 2004), xxiv.

17. Arnold Kellett, "Introduction," *The Dark Side*, xi.

18. Caillois, *Images, images*, 37; Castex, *Le conte fantastique en France*, 382–84; Vax, *L'art et la littérature fantastiques*, 21; Jackson, *Fantasy: The Literature of Subversion*, 24.

19. Kawato, Sakakibara, eds., "Meiji hon'yaku bungaku nenpyō: Mōpassan-hen," 4.

20. Ikari Akira, "Tayama Katai to Mōpassan," *Shizen shugi bungaku [Nihon bungaku kenkyū shiryō sōsho]* (Tokyo: Yūseidō, 1975), 137.

21. Schneider, *Histoire de la littérature fantastique en France*, 281.

22. Because multiple accurate translations into English of Maupassant's work have been made, passages from Maupassant's fiction are quoted from widely available English-language translations. References to corresponding pages in French are also provided. Maupassant, *The Complete Short Stories of Guy de Maupassant* (Garden City, NY: Hanover House, 1955), 732. Translation originally from Maupassant, *The Works of Guy de Maupassant*, anonymous translator, compiled by M. Walter Dunne (New York: M. Walter Dunne, 1903); original French-language version in *Le Horla et autres contes cruels et fantastiques*, ed. Marie-Claire Bancquart (Paris: Garnier, 1989), 9.

23. Castex, *Le conte fantastique en France*, 382.

24. Arthur Schopenhauer (1788–1860) was a famous philosopher from Germany whose pessimistic philosophy influenced Maupassant's worldview, whereas Gustave Flaubert, the renowned author of *Madame Bovary* (1857), a pinnacle of French naturalist fiction, was Maupassant's mentor early in his career. Castex, *Le conte fantastique en France*, 367.

25. Philippot, *Guy de Maupassant et l'affolant mystère de la vie*, 57.

26. Philippot, *Guy de Maupassant et l'affolant mystère de la vie*, 102–3.

27. Guy de Maupassant, *Guy de Maupassant's Selected Works*, trans. Sandra Smith, ed. Robert Lethbridge (New York: W. W. Norton & Company, 2017), 214; Maupassant, *Onze histoires fantastiques*, ed. Henri Parisot, illustrated by Aristide Caillaud (Paris: Robert Marin, 1949), 173.

28. Maupassant, *Guy de Maupassant's Selected Works*, 216; Maupassant, *Onze histoires fantastiques*, 175.

29. Maupassant, *Guy de Maupassant's Selected Works*, 200, 202; Maupassant, *Le Horla et autres contes cruels et fantastiques*, 1, 3. The original is "land of mirages and phantasmagoria" (*le pays des mirages et des fantasmagories*).

30. Maupassant, *Guy de Maupassant's Selected Works*, 203; Maupassant, *Le Horla et autres contes cruels et fantastiques*, 4–5. The original describes his "fantastic imagination" (*imaginations fantastiques*).

31. Ōnishi, "Mōpassan to sono Nihon e no eikyō," 306–7.

32. Kawato, Sakakibara, eds., "Meiji hon'yaku bungaku nenpyō: Mōpassan-hen," 1–12.

33. Ōnishi, "Mōpassan to Nihon kindai bungaku," 179; Katai, *Tōkyō no sanjūnen*, 281.

34. Matsumura, *Kōyō zenshū*, suppl. vol., 531–32.

35. Kawato, Nakabayashi, and Sakakibara, "Meiji-ki hon'yaku bungaku nenpyō: Ozaki Kōyō-hen," 3.

36. Ōnishi, "Mōpassan to Nihon kindai bungaku," 190–91.

37. Ōnishi, "Mōpassan to Nihon kindai bungaku," 181–85.

38. Ōnishi, "Mōpassan to Nihon kindai bungaku," 193–96.

39. Ōnishi, "Mōpassan to sono Nihon e no eikyō," 311.

40. Ōnishi, "Mōpassan to sono Nihon e no eikyō," 313.

41. Ōnishi, "Mōpassan to sono Nihon e no eikyō," 317.

42. Ōnishi, "Mōpassan to sono Nihon e no eikyō," 316–17.

43. Ikari, "Tayama Katai to Mōpassan," 129–30.

44. Artinian, "Introduction," *The Complete Short Stories of Guy de Maupassant*, xii.

45. Ikari, "Tayama Katai to Mōpassan," 136–37.

46. Ikari, "Tayama Katai to Mōpassan," 136.

47. Ikari, "Tayama Katai to Mōpassan," 137–38.

48. Kyōka, *Kyōka zenshū*, vol. 28, 685–86.

49. Kyōka, *Kyōka zenshū*, vol. 28, 689; Miya Elise Mizuta Lippit, *Aesthetic Life: Beauty and Art in Modern Japan* (Cambridge, MA: Harvard University Asia Center, 2019), 208–11.

50. According to Francis Steegmuller, at least sixty-five stories published in English that were attributed to Maupassant were in fact forgeries, thereby proving the tremendous popularity and marketability of the author. These can all be found in early sets of English-language translations of Maupassant's work that were anonymously translated and issued by bookseller M. Walter Dunne beginning in 1903. These works continued to circulate widely in English for decades. *Maupas-*

sant: A Lion in the Path (New York: Random House, 1949), 353–60. Such forgeries were also frequently translated into Japanese.

51. Kyōka, *Kyōka zenshū*, vol. 28, 690.

52. Maupassant, "Kane no oto," trans. Baba Kochō, *Taisei meichoshū* (Tokyo: Josandō, 1907), 106.

53. Kyōka, *Kyōka zenshū*, vol. 28, 695.

54. Napier, *The Fantastic in Modern Japanese Literature*, p. 223.

55. Kyōka, *Kyōka zenshū*, vol. 10, 234–35.

56. Kyōka, *Kyōka zenshū*, vol. 10, 237.

57. Kyōka, *Kyōka zenshū*, vol. 28, 677.

58. Kyōka, *Kyōka zenshū*, vol. 28, 679–80.

59. Kyōka, *Kyōka zenshū*, vol. 10, 282–83.

60. Kyōka, *Kyōka zenshū*, vol. 6, 594. The meaning of this passage is clarified in notes by Asada Shōjirō and Mita Hideaki in one of the very few annotated collections of Kyōka's stories, *Nihon kindai bungaku taikei 7: Izumi Kyōka shū*, 459. The production of annotated versions of Kyōka's fiction would greatly facilitate understanding of his work, although such a project seems unlikely at this point in time. The most extensively annotated edition of a novel by Kyōka nearly doubles the length of the text, which reflects the density, allusiveness, and difficulty of Kyōka's writing. Izumi Kyōka, *Chūkai kōsetsu Izumi Kyōka Nihonbashi*, annotated by Asada Shōjirō (Tokyo: Meiji Shoin, 1974).

61. Kyōka, *Kyōka zenshū*, vol. 6, 595.

62. Kyōka, *Kyōka zenshū*, vol. 6, 611.

63. Kyōka, *Kyōka zenshū*, vol. 6, 628.

64. Kyōka, *Kyōka zenshū*, vol. 15, 711.

65. Kyōka, *Kyōka zenshū*, vol. 15, 712–13.

66. Kyōka, *Kyōka zenshū*, vol. 15, 713.

67. Chiyoko Kawakami, "The Metropolitan Uncanny in the Works of Izumi Kyōka: A Counter-Discourse on Japan's Modernization," *Harvard Journal of Asiatic Studies* 59, no. 2 (December 1999): 560.

68. Kyōka, *Kyōka zenshū*, vol. 15, 681 (ellipses in original).

69. Kyōka, *Kyōka zenshū*, vol. 15, 703.

70. Kyōka, *Kyōka zenshū*, vol. 11, 458.

71. Tanemura, "Meikyū no kai," 465.

72. Kyōka, *Kyōka zenshū*, vol. 11, 486.

73. C. Andrew Gerstle, *Circles of Fantasy: Convention in the Plays of Chikamatsu* (Cambridge, MA: Council on East Asian Studies, Harvard University, 1986), 121–23.

74. Kyōka, *Kyōka zenshū*, vol. 11, 529.

75. Kyōka, *Kyōka zenshū*, vol. 11, 539.

Chapter 5

1. Kashiwagi Takao, "Futari no kaii sakka: Izumi Kyōka ni miru Purosuperu Merime," *Gallia* 12 (March 1973): 43; Muramatsu, *Kotoba no renkinjutsushi*, 13.

2. Phil Powrie, Bruce Babington, Ann Davies, and Chris Perriam, *Carmen on Film: A Cultural History* (Bloomington: Indiana University Press, 2007), 243–59.

3. Marcel Schneider, *Histoire de la littérature fantastique*, 241.

4. Castex, *Le conte fantastique en France*, 251; Schneider, *Histoire de la littérature fantastique*, 130, 145–50.

5. Maxwell A. Smith, *Prosper Mérimée* (New York: Twayne, 1972), 17, 47; A. W. Raitt, *Prosper Mérimée* (London: Eyre & Spottiswoode, 1970), 69–71.

6. Tomita Hitoshi, *Furansu shōsetsu i'nyūkō* (Tokyo: Tokyo Shoseki, 1981), 214–15.

7. Castex, *Le conte fantastique en France*, 268–69; Todorov, *The Fantastic*, 87–88.

8. Smith, *Prosper Mérimée*, 180.

9. Mérimée began studying Russian in his fifties and did not attain fluency in the language, although he studied it seriously and received assistance in his translations from the Russian language, including by Turgenev himself. Raitt, *Prosper Mérimée*, 279–85.

10. Raitt, *Prosper Mérimée*, 158–59, 214–15, 228–46, 279–92.

11. Raitt, *Prosper Mérimée*, 198–200; Jean Balsamo, "Introduction," Prosper Mérimée, *Carmen* (Paris: Librairie Générale Française, 1996), 6–13.

12. For details on Mérimée's visits to England, see Raitt, *Prosper Mérimée*, 64–65, 250–51, 299–300, 311, 338–40.

13. Sasaki Akio, "Ōgai to Merime," *Hikaku bungaku kenkyū* 10 (February 1966). Quoted in Tomita, *Furansu shōsetsu i'nyūkō*, 206.

14. Castex, *Le conte fantastique en France*, 248.

15. Castex, *Le conte fantastique en France*, 249.

16. Peter Cogman, "Prosper Mérimée's Playful Fantastic," *The Fantastic*, ed. Claire Whitehead, 144–45.

17. "The Venus of Ille" was translated into Japanese at least four times during Kyōka's lifetime, in 1924, 1930, 1934, and 1939, and was used as the title for two separate collections of translations. Prosper Mérimée, *Iru no megamizō*, trans. Okada Jitsumaro and Ishikawa Takeshi (Tokyo: Kaibunsha, 1924); Mérimée, *Vīnasu no satsujin*, trans. Yano Tsuneari (Tokyo: Shun'yōdō, 1934). Eguchi Kiyoshi and Tomita Hitoshi, "Nihon ni okeru Purosuperu Merime shoshi," *Hikaku bungaku* 21 (1978): 61–70.

18. Caillois, *Images, images*, 37–38.

19. Todorov, *The Fantastic*, 80, 87–88.

20. Mérimeé, *Carmen and Other Stories*, trans. Nicholas Jotcham (Oxford: Oxford University Press, 1989), 141; Mérimée, *Colomba, La Vénus d'Ille, Les Ames du Purgatoire* (Paris: Calmann Lévy, 1883), 259.

21. Cogman, "Prosper Mérimée's Playful Fantastic," 138.

22. Mérimée, *The Etruscan Vase and Other Stories*, trans. Douglas Parmée (London: Alma Classics, 2012), 21; Mérimée, *Oeuvres complètes de Prosper Mérimée: Mosaïque*, ed. Maurice Levaillant (Paris: Librairie Ancienne Honoré Champion, 1933), 33–34.

23. Smith, *Prosper Mérimée*, 20–21.

24. Prosper Mérimée, *Songs for the Gusle*, trans. Laura Nagle (Philadelphia:

Frayed Edge Press, 2023); Eguchi, Tomita, "Nihon ni okeru Purosuperu Merime shoshi," 64.

25. According to scholars, Mérimée's early works were recognized as hoaxes by leading European writers, but they were positively reviewed nonetheless, such as in reviews for *La Guzla* by Goethe, Hugo, and Mary Shelley. Shelley translated excerpts of *La Guzla* in an issue of the *Westminster Review* in January 1829, but these translations were almost entirely lost until 1970. Shelley was also a friend of Mérimée. Raitt, *Prosper Mérimée*, 43, 69–71; Smith, *Prosper Mérimée*, 63–64; Nagle, "Translator's Note," *Songs for the Gusle*, 137.

26. Castex, *Le conte fantastique en France*, 250.

27. Castex, *Le conte fantastique en France*, 251; Smith, *Prosper Mérimée*, 22.

28. Tomita, *Furansu shōsetsu i'nyūkō*, 202.

29. Eguchi, Tomita, "Nihon ni okeru Purosuperu Merime shoshi," 61–71.

30. Kyōka, *Kyōka zenshū*, vol. 20, 466.

31. Muramatsu, *Kotoba no renkinjutsushi*, 13. The *kanji* character for Ishikawa's first name appears to be misprinted in Muramatsu's account, as does the word used to translate "vision," with *gensō* appearing instead of *gen'ei*. However, Ishikawa Takeshi is the only figure with a corresponding last name who translated "The Vision of Charles XI" in a collected volume of Mérimée's fiction, and thus this seems to be the collection that Muramatsu was referring to.

32. Kyōka, *Kyōka zenshū*, vol. 22, 580–81.

33. The collection was *Little French Masterpieces, vol. 1, Prosper Mérimée*, trans. George Burnham Ives, ed. Alexander Jessup (New York: Putnam, 1903); Kashiwagi Takao, "Sōseki to Merime: Mineko no shōzō o megutte," *Eigo seinen* 122 (January 1977): 34.

34. Kashiwagi, "Sōseki to Merime," 34.

35. Quoted in Tomita, *Furansu shōsetsu i'nyūkō*, 203.

36. Tomita, *Furansu shōsetsu i'nyūkō*, 211.

37. Muramatsu, *Izumi Kyōka*, 171–72.

38. Tomita, *Furansu shōsetsu i'nyūkō*, 216.

39. Tomita, *Furansu shōsetsu i'nyūkō*, 218.

40. Tomita, *Furansu shōsetsu i'nyūkō*, 219.

41. Akutagawa Ryūnosuke, *Akutagawa Ryūnosuke zenshū* (Tokyo: Iwanami Shoten, 1977), vol. 3, 478–85.

42. Kashiwagi, "Futari no kaii sakka," 43; Tomita, *Furansu shōsetsu i'nyūkō*, 212–13.

43. Akutagawa Ryūnosuke, "Kyōka zenshū mokuroku kaikō," *Izumi Kyōka [bungei dokuhon]*, 66. Originally published in *Shinshōshetsu* (May 1925).

44. Jinzai Kiyoshi, "Kyōka to Merime," *Gendai Nihon bungaku zenshū: Kyōka, Roka hen geppō* (Tokyo: Chikuma Shobō, 1955). Quoted in Tomita, *Furansu bungaku i'nyūkō*, 210.

45. Eguchi, Tomita, "Nihon ni okeru Purosuperu Merime shoshi," 62–63.

46. Maggie Ann Bowers, *Magic(al) Realism* (London: Routledge, 2004), 3.

47. Izumi Natsuki, "Kyōka to sumai," *Kyōka ron shūsei*, 114–17. Originally pub-

lished in *Izumi Kyōka zenshū geppō 15* (Tokyo: Iwanami Shoten, 1975). For details of Kyōka's house in Rokubanchō, see Izumi Kyōka Kinenkan, *Kyōka no ie*, 17–85.

48. Izumi Natsuki, "Kyōka to sumai," 114.

49. Kyōka, *Kyōka zenshū*, vol. 20, 447, 459–60.

50. Kyōka, *Kyōka zenshū*, vol. 20, 462–63.

51. Kyōka, *Kyōka zenshū*, vol. 20, 466.

52. Prosper Mérimée, *Churujisu fujin: Sharuru kyūsei nendaiki*, trans. Ishikawa Takeshi (Tokyo: Shun'yōdō, 1923).

53. Kyōka, *Kyōka zenshū*, vol. 22, 581.

54. Smith, *Prosper Mérimée*, 147.

55. Jacob Grimm and Wilhelm Grimm, *The German Legends of the Brothers Grimm*, trans. Donald Ward (Philadelphia: Institute for the Study of Human Issues, 1981), vol. 1, 208.

56. Kyōka, *Kyōka zenshū*, vol. 22, 587.

57. Kyōka, *Kyōka zenshū*, vol. 22, 591.

58. Kyōka, *Kyōka zenshū*, vol. 22, 593–94.

59. Katsumoto, "Kyōka no ishinzō," 278; Kasahara, *Izumi Kyōka: bi to erosu no kōzō*, 14.

60. Kyōka, *Kyōka zenshū*, vol. 22, 595.

61. Scholars have often discussed the Great Kantō Earthquake as a major turning point in the fiction of Izumi Kyōka, as it was in the work of many other authors. Following this disaster, Kyōka's fiction became grimmer and more abstract and gradually moved away from the space of Tokyo and back to Kyōka's home region and other prefectures of central Japan. See Kaneko Ayumi, "Yume no tenki: 'Kinoe kinoto' ni okeru Kantō daishinsai no eikyō," *Bungei to hihyō* 11, no. 4 (November 2011): 11–20; Maari Sumika, "Izumi Kyōka to Kantō daishinsai: 'Kinoe kinoto' o shiza to shite," *Geijutsu shijō shugi bungei* 24 (November 1998): 118–26.

62. Kyōka, *Kyōka zenshū*, vol. 22, 611.

63. This reference to "Carmen" in Kyōka's final published work of fiction has received surprisingly little attention in scholarship on Kyōka. It appears to be noted most prominently by Kashiwagi Takao in "Yōi no katarikata: Izumi Kyōka to Furansu bungaku," *Gensō kūkan no tōzai*, 218–19.

64. Noguchi, *Izumi Kyōka [Shinchō Nihon bungaku arubamu 22]*, 92.

65. Muramatsu, *Izumi Kyōka*, 208.

66. Kyōka, *Kyōka zenshū*, vol. 24, 694.

67. Muramatsu, *Kotoba no renkinjutsushi*, 13.

68. For discussions of Yanagita's folkloric research and its adaptation by Kyōka in *Commentaries on the Mountains and the Sea*, see Abe Ayumi, "*Sankai hyōbanki*: minzokugaku to no kakawari," *Kokubungaku kaishaku to kanshō* 74, no. 9 (September 2009): 168–74; Nakanishi Yukiko, "*Sankai hyōbanki* o yomu tame ni: fōkuroa no kaitei saikō," *Kindai bungaku ronshū* 29 (2003): 55–64.

69. Shinoda, "Izumi Kyōka no ichi," 39–40.

70. Maeda Hayao, *Shiro no minzokugaku e: Hakusan shinkō no nazo o otte* (Tokyo: Kawade Shobō Shinsha, 2006), 93.

71. Takase Shigeo, *Hakusan Tateyama to Hokuriku shugendō* (Tokyo: Meicho Shuppan, 2000), 31, 38–39; Hongō Masatsugu, *Hakusan shinkō no genryū: Taichō no shōgai to kodai Bukkyō* (Kyōto: Hōzōkan, 2001), 97–110.

72. Kawamura Jirō, *Hakusan no mizu: Kyōka o meguru* (Tokyo: Kōdansha, 2008), 358–59.

73. See Tanemura Suehiro, "Sannin no onna," *Izumi Kyōka shūsei*, vol. 10, 473.

74. Kyōka, *Kyōka zenshū*, vol. 24, 143–44.

75. Kyōka, *Kyōka zenshū*, vol. 23, 191–92.

76. Yi Hyŏn-yŏng (I Hyon'yon), *Kaga haidan to Shōfū no kenkyū* (Toyama: Katsura Shobō, 2002), 121–42.

77. While the *Utatsu Collection* was a real collection of poetry, *Records of Travel on the Noto Road* is a fictionalized account that appears to draw on multiple historical sources, while also presenting Kyōka's own literary inventions. Suzuki Keiko, "Shōwa ninen no Izumi Kyōka: *Kahaku reijō* to *Rantōba no tennyo* no shōsetsu kikō," *Kokugo to kokubungaku* 95, no. 12 (December 2018): 3–20; Abe Ayumi, "Izumi Kyōka *Kahaku reijō* ron," *Kokugo kokubun* 72, no. 8 (August 2003): 21–39.

78. Kyōka, *Kyōka zenshū*, vol. 23, 209.

79. Maeda Hayao, *Hakusan shinkō no nazo to hisabetsu buraku* (Tokyo: Kawade Shobō Shinsha, 2013), 83–84.

80. Kyōka, *Kyōka zenshū*, vol. 23, 227.

81. Kyōka, *Kyōka zenshū*, vol. 23, 219.

82. Kyōka, *Kyōka zenshū*, vol. 23, 229.

83. Kyōka, *Kyōka zenshū*, vol. 23, 258.

Conclusion

1. Noguchi, *Izumi Kyōka [Shinchō Nihon bungaku arubamu 22]*, 94.

2. See, for example, Lois Parkinson Zamora and Wendy B. Faris, "Introduction: Daiquiri Birds and Flaubertian Parrot(ie)s," *Magical Realism: Theory, History, Community*, 1–11; Stephen M. Hart and Wen-chin Ouyang, "Globalization of Magical Realism: New Politics of Aesthetics," *A Companion to Magical Realism*, eds. Stephen M. Hart and Wen-chin Ouyang (Woodbridge, Suffolk: Tamesis, 2005), 1–22; Bowers, *Magic(al) Realism*, 1–7.

3. Napier, "The Magic of Identity," 452. Japanese literature has not often been discussed in terms of magical realism, with the exception of a few authors, most prominently Nakagami Kenji and Murakami Haruki. See, for example, Mark Morris, "Magical Realism as Ideology: Narrative Evasions in the Work of Nakagami Kenji," *A Companion to Magical Realism*, 199–209; Matthew Strecher, *Dances with Sheep: The Quest for Identity in the Fiction of Murakami Haruki* (Ann Arbor: Center for Japanese Studies, University of Michigan, 2002).

4. Satomi Ton, "Kyōka no kōokan," *Izumi Kyōka [bungei dokuhon]*, 72–73. Originally published in *Satomi Ton zenshū* (Tokyo: Chikuma Shobō, 1941).

5. Settai, "Izumi Kyōka-sensei no koto," 82.

6. Kashiwagi, "Futari no kaii sakka," 43; Muramatsu, *Kotoba no renkinjutsushi*, 13.

Bibliography

Abe Ayumi. "Izumi Kyōka *Kahaku reijō* ron." *Kokugo kokubun* 72, no. 8 (August 2003): 21–39.

Abe Ayumi. "*Sankai hyōbanki*: minzokugaku to no kakawari." *Kokubungaku kaishaku to kanshō* 74, no. 9 (September 2009): 168–74.

Akiyama Minoru. "Izumi Kyōka 'Bunin rishōki' ron: seiritsu haikei o chūshin ni." In *Ronshū Shōwaki no Izumi Kyōka*, eds. Izumi Kyōka Kenkyūkai, 7–26. Tokyo: Ōfū, 2002.

Akutagawa Ryūnosuke. *Akutagawa Ryūnosuke zenshū*. Tokyo: Iwanami Shoten, 1977–1978.

Akutagawa Ryūnosuke. "*Kyōka zenshū* mokuroku kaikō." In *Izumi Kyōka [bungei dokuhon]*, 66–67. Tokyo: Kawade Shobō, 1981.

Andersen, Hans Christian. *Hans Andersen's Fairytales: A Selection*. Translated by L. W. Kingsland. Oxford: Oxford University Press, 1998.

Andersen, Hans Christian. *The Improvisatore: A Novel of Italy*. Translated by Frank Hugus. Minneapolis: University of Minnesota Press, 2018.

Andersen, Hans Christian. *Ninin mukusuke*. Translated by Ozaki Kōyō. Tokyo: Hakubunkan, 1891.

Andersen, Hans Christian. *Sokkyō shijin*. Translated by Mori Ōgai. Tokyo: Shun'yōdō, 1902.

Anonymous. *The Arabian Nights' Entertainments*. Translated by George Fyler Townsend. London: Frederick Warne, 1865.

Anonymous. *The Arabian Nights: Tales of 1001 Nights*. Translated by Malcolm C. Lyons with Ursula Lyons. London: Penguin Books, 2008.

Anonymous. *A Plain and Literal Translation of the Arabian Nights' Entertainments Now Entitled the Book of the Thousand Nights and a Night*. Translated by Richard Francis Burton. Burton Club: 1885–1888.

Anonymous. *Zen sekai ichidai kisho: genmei Arabiyan naito*. Translated by Inoue Tsutomu. Tokyo: Hōkokusha, 1883–1885.

Apuleius. *The Golden Ass*. Translated by P. G. Walsh. Oxford: Oxford University Press, 1994.

Araki Hirohiko. *Kishibe Rohan wa ugokanai.* Tokyo: Shūeisha, 2013.
Artinian, Artine. "Introduction." In *The Complete Short Stories of Guy de Maupassant*, ix–xvii. Garden City, NY: Hanover House, 1955.
Asada Shōjirō. "Kyōka no shōsetsu to Edo bungaku: ushinawareta toki no tansakusha-tachi." *Kokubungaku kaishaku to kanshō* 41, no. 14 (1976): 130–33.
Asagiri Kafka and Hurakawa Sango. *Bungō sutorei doggusu.* Tokyo: Kadokawa, 2012–present.
Attebery, Brian. *Strategies of Fantasy.* Bloomington: Indiana University Press, 1992.
Auerback, Micah L. *A Storied Sage: Canon and Creation in the Making of a Japanese Buddha.* Chicago: University of Chicago Press, 2016.
Baba Kochō, trans. *Taisei meichoshū.* Tokyo: Josandō, 1907.
Baba Mika. *"Shōsetsuka" tōjō: Ozaki Kōyō no Meiji nijūnendai.* Tokyo: Kasama Shoin, 2011.
Balsamo, Jean. "Introduction." In Prosper Mérimée, *Carmen*, 6–13. Paris: Librairie Générale Française, 1996.
Bandō Tamasaburō and Gunji Masakatsu. "Taidan: Kyōka geki o megutte." *Izumi Kyōka [Gunzō Nihon no sakka 5]*, 231–53. Tokyo: Shōgakukan, 1992.
Barker, Clive. Cover endorsement for Guy de Maupassant, *The Dark Side: Tales of Terror and the Supernatural.* New York: Carroll and Graf, 1989.
Bowers, Maggie Ann. *Magic(al) Realism.* London: Routledge, 2004.
Caillois, Roger. *Fantastique: soixante récits de terreur.* Paris: Club Français du Livre, 1958.
Caillois, Roger. *Images, images: essais sur le rôle et les pouvoirs de l'imagination.* Paris: José Corti, 1966.
Calderón de la Barca, Pedro. *Six Dramas of Calderón.* Translated by Edward FitzGerald. London: De la More Press, 1903.
Castex, Pierre-Georges. *Le conte fantastique en France: de Nodier à Maupassant.* Paris: José Corti, 1951.
Cogman, Peter. "Prosper Mérimée's Playful Fantastic." In *The Fantastic*, ed. Claire Whitehead, 136–54. Ipswich, MA: Salem Press, 2013.
Cornyetz, Nina. *Dangerous Women, Deadly Words: Phallic Fantasy and Modernity in Three Japanese Writers.* Stanford: Stanford University Press, 1999.
Deguchi Tomoyuki. "*Bungei kurabu* no mokuhan tashokuzuri kuchi-e: shōsetsu to no kankei kara." *Nihon kindai bungaku* 93 (2015): 152–59.
Eguchi Kiyoshi, Tomita Hitoshi. "Nihon ni okeru Purosuperu Merime shoshi." *Hikaku bungaku* 21 (1978): 61–77.
Eiichi Tanizawa and Watanabe Ikkō, eds. *Kyōka ron shūsei.* Tokyo: Rippū Shobō, 1983.
Emmerich, Michael. *The Tale of Genji: Translation, Canonization, and World Literature.* New York: Columbia University Press, 2013.
Faure, Bernard. *The Thousand and One Lives of the Buddha.* Honolulu: University of Hawai'i Press, 2022.
Figal, Gerald A. *Civilization and Monsters: Spirits of Modernity in Meiji Japan.* Durham: Duke University Press, 1999.

Flanagan, Damian. "Sōseki in London." In Natsume Sōseki, *The Tower of London: Tales of Victorian London*, 47–48. Translated by Damian Flanagan. Chester Springs, PA: Peter Owen, 2005.

Foster, Michael Dylan. *Pandemonium and Parade: Japanese Monsters and the Culture of Yōkai*. Berkeley: University of California Press, 2009.

Funatsu, Jean Akemi. *Through the Colored Looking Glass of Izumi Kyōka: Reflections of the Kusazōshi*. Dissertation, Harvard University, 1972.

Gerstle, Andrew C. *Circles of Fantasy: Convention in the Plays of Chikamatsu*. Cambridge, MA: Council on East Asian Studies, Harvard University, 1986.

Grimm, Jacob, and Wilhelm Grimm. *The German Legends of the Brothers Grimm*. Translated by Donald Ward. Philadelphia: Institute for the Study of Human Issues, 1981.

Grimm, Jacob, and Wilhelm Grimm. *The Original Folk and Fairy Tales of the Brothers Grimm*. Translated by Jack Zipes, illustrated by Andrea Dezsö. Princeton: Princeton University Press, 2014.

Grimm, Jacob, and Wilhelm Grimm. *Ukigimaru*. Translated by Ozaki Kōyō. Tokyo: Shun'yōdō, 1896.

Harada Osamu, Hirata Masaki, and Yamashita Yūji, eds. *Ishō no tensai Komura Settai*. Tokyo: Shinchōsha, 2016.

Hart, Stephen M., and Wen-chin Ouyang. "Globalization of Magical Realism: New Politics of Aesthetics." In *A Companion to Magical Realism*, eds. Stephen M. Hart and Wen-chin Ouyang, 1–22. Woodbridge, Suffolk: Tamesis, 2005.

Hasegawa Satoru. "Izumi Kyōka zōsho mokuroku." In *Izumi Kyōka: bi to gensō*, 221–23. Tokyo: Yūseidō, 1991.

Hasegawa Satoru. "Kyōka Sensei no kusazōshi mokuroku." In *Izumi Kyōka: bi to gensō*, 224–25. Tokyo: Yūseidō, 1991.

Hauptmann, Gerhart. *The Sunken Bell: A Fairy Play in Five Acts*. Translated by Charles Henry Meltzer. Garden City, NY: Doubleday, Page & Company, 1914.

Higashi Masao. "Izumi Kyōka to *Arabian naito*." In *Izumi Kyōka 'Kōya hijiri' sakuhin ronshū*, 149–62. Tokyo: Kuresu Shuppan, 2003.

Higashi Masao, ed. *Nihon gensō bungaku jiten*. Tokyo: Chikuma Shobō, 2013.

Hinatsu Kōnosuke. "Meijin Kyōka gei." In *Kyōka ron shūsei*, 248–75. Tokyo: Rippū Shobo, 1983.

Hinode Yumi. "Sashie no kinō: shinbun shōsetsu toshite no *Sankai hyōbanki*." In *Ronshū Shōwaki no Izumi Kyōka*, eds. Izumi Kyōka Kenkyūkai, 78–101. Tokyo: Ōfū, 2002.

Hinohara Kenji. *Utagawa Kunisada: kore zo Edo no iki*, eds. Ōta Kinen Bijutsukan. Tokyo: Tōkyō Bijutsu, 2016.

Hinotani Teruhiko, Suzuki Isamu, and Matsumura Tomomi, eds. "Izumi Kyōka zōsho mokuroku." In *Kyōka zenshū* supplementary volume [*bekkan*] *geppō* 29 (March 1976): 15–19. Tokyo: Iwanami Shoten, 1973–1976.

Hoffmann, E. T. A. *Tales of Hoffmann*. Translated by R. J. Hollingdale. London: Penguin Books, 1982.

Hongō Masatsugu. *Hakusan shinkō no genryū: Taichō no shōgai to kodai Bukkyō*. Kyōto: Hōzōkan, 2001.

Hugo, Victor. *Shōrōmori: Nōtorudamu do Pari*. Translated by Ozaki Kōyō [and Osada Shūtō]. Tokyo: Waseda Daigaku Shuppanbu, 1903.

Ichihara Toyota. "Nihongo no majutsushi." In *Kyōka ron shūsei*, 357–59. Tokyo: Rippū Shobō, 1983.

Ikari Akira. "Tayama Katai to Mōpassan." In *Shizen shugi bungaku [Nihon bungaku kenkyū shiryō sōsho]*, 129–40. Tokyo: Yūseidō, 1975.

Ikushima Ryōichi. *Kyōka mangekyō*. Tokyo: Chikuma Shobō, 1992.

Ikuta Chōkō. "Izumi Kyōka-shi no shōsetsu o ronzu." In *Kyōka ron shūsei*, 168–80. Tokyo: Rippū Shobō, 1983.

Inouye, Charles Shirō. *Izumi Kyōka and the Visual Tradition*. Dissertation. Harvard University, 1988.

Inouye, Charles Shirō. "Pictocentrism." *Yearbook of Comparative and General Literature* 40 (1992): 23–39.

Inouye, Charles Shirō. *The Similitude of Blossoms: A Critical Biography of Izumi Kyōka (1873–1939), Japanese Novelist and Playwright*. Cambridge, MA: Harvard University Asia Center, 1998.

Inouye, Charles Shirō. "Water Imagery in the Work of Izumi Kyōka." *Monumenta Nipponica* 46, no. 1 (Spring 1991): 43–68.

Iriye, Mitsuko. "Translator's Introduction." In Nagai Kafū, *American Stories*. Translated by Mitsuko Iriye. New York: Columbia University Press, 2000.

Irving, Washington. *The Legend of Sleepy Hollow and Other Stories*. London: Penguin Books, 2014.

Irwin, Robert. "Introduction." In *The Arabian Nights: Tales of 1001 Nights*. Translated by Malcolm C. Lyons with Ursula Lyons. London: Penguin Books, 2008.

Itō Sei. *Kindai Nihon no bungō 2*. Tokyo: Yomiuri Shinbunsha, 1967.

Izumi Kyōka. *Chūkai kōsetsu Izumi Kyōka Nihonbashi*. Annotated by Asada Shōjirō. Tokyo: Meiji Shoin, 1974.

Izumi Kyōka. *Ehon no haru*. Illustrated by Kanaida Etsuko. Tokyo: Asahi Shuppansha, 2020.

Izumi Kyōka. *Ehon ryūtandan*. Illustrated by Nakagawa Gaku. Tokyo: Kokusho Kankōkai, 2023.

Izumi Kyōka. *Gekashitsu*. Illustrated by Honojiro Towoji. Tokyo: Rittōsha, 2018.

Izumi Kyōka. *In Light of Shadows: More Gothic Tales*. Translated by Charles Shirō Inouye. Honolulu: University of Hawai'i Press, 2005.

Izumi Kyōka. *Japanese Gothic Tales*. Translated by Charles Shirō Inouye. Honolulu: University of Hawai'i Press, 1996.

Izumi Kyōka. *Kechō*. Illustrated by Nakagawa Gaku. Tokyo: Kokusho Kankōkai, 2012.

Izumi Kyōka. *Kusameikyū*. Illustrated by Yamamoto Takato. Tokyo: Edishon Toreviru, 2014.

Izumi Kyōka. *Kyōka zenshū*. Tokyo: Iwanami Shoten, 1973–1976.

Izumi Kyōka. *Kyōka zenshū*. Tokyo: Shun'yōdō, 1925–1927.

Izumi Kyōka. *Labirinto d'erba*. Translated by Alessandro Passarella. Milan: Luni Editrice, 2022.

Izumi Kyōka. *Nihon kindai bungaku taikei 7: Izumi Kyōka shū*, annotated by Muramatsu Sadataka, Asada Shōjirō, and Mita Hideaki. Tokyo: Kadokawa Shoten, 1970.

Izumi Kyōka. *Shunikki*. Illustrated by Nakagawa Gaku. Tokyo: Kokusho Kankōkai, 2015.

Izumi Kyōka. *Sobre el dragón del abismo*. Translated by Alejandro Morales Rama. Gijón: Satori, 2022.

Izumi Kyōka. *Tang dao zhi lian/Yūshima mōde*. Translated by Zhou Qian. Beijing: Xiandai Chubanshe, 2019.

Izumi Kyōka. *Tenshu monogatari/Tale of a Castle Keep*. Translated by Don Kenny, illustrated by Uno Akira [Aquirax] and Yamamoto Takato, notes by Anakura Tamaki. Tokyo: Edishon Toreviru, 2016.

Izumi Kyōka. *Yoki koto kiku*. Tokyo: Shōwa Shobō, 1934.

Izumi Kyōka Kenkyūkai, eds. *Ronshū Shōwaki no Izumi Kyōka*. Tokyo: Ōfū, 2002.

Izumi Kyōka Kinenkan and Izumi Kyōka Kenkyūkai, eds. *Kyōka no ie: Izumi Kyōka seitan 150-nen kinen*. Tokyo: Heibonsha, 2023.

Izumi Natsuki. "Kyōka to sumai." In *Kyōka ron shūsei*, 113–17. Tokyo: Rippū Shobō, 1983.

Jackson, Rosemary. *Fantasy: The Literature of Subversion*. London: Methuen, 1981.

Jinzai Kiyoshi. "Kyōka to Merime." In *Gendai Nihon bungaku zenshū: Kyōka, Roka hen geppō*. Tokyo: Chikuma Shobō, 1955.

Kanai Mieko. "Shisen ni hibiku kotoba." In *Nihon kindai bungaku taikei 7: Izumi Kyōka shū*, eds. Muramatsu Sadataka, Asada Shōjirō, and Mita Hideaki, vol. 7, *geppō* 13, 2–3. Tokyo: Kadokawa Shoten, 1970.

Kanazawa Daigaku Furansu Bungakkai, Hirakawa Sukehiro, Watanabe Kaneo, et al., eds. *Gensō kūkan no tōzai: Furansu bungaku o tōshite mita Izumi Kyōka*. Kanazawa: Jūgatsusha, 1990.

Kaneko Ayumi. "Yume no tenki: 'Kinoe kinoto' ni okeru Kantō daishinsai no eikyō." *Bungei to hihyō* 11, no. 4 (November 2011): 11–20.

Kasahara Nobuo. *Henbō suru dentō*. Tokyo: Ōfūsha, 1971.

Kasahara Nobuo. *Izumi Kyōka: bi to erosu no kōzō*. Tokyo: Shibundō, 1976.

Kasahara Nobuo. "Suikoden no keifu: *Fūryūsen* made." In *Ronshū Izumi Kyōka*, 95–110. Tokyo: Yūseido, 1987.

Kashiwagi Takao. "Futari no kaii sakka: Izumi Kyōka ni miru Purosuperu Merime." *Gallia* 12 (March 1973): 41–61.

Kashiwagi Takao. "Kyōka, Merime, Yugō: juyō no mondai." *Bungaku* 57, no. 9 (September 1989): 28–34.

Kashiwagi Takao. "Sōseki to Merime: Mineko no shōzō o megutte." *Eigo seinen* 122 (January 1977): 34–36.

Kashiwagi Takao. "Yōi no katarikata: Izumi Kyōka to Furansu bungaku." In *Gensō kūkan no tōzai: Furansu bungaku o tōshite mita Izumi Kyōka*, 191–258. Kanazawa: Jūgatsusha, 1990.

Katsumoto Seiichirō. "Kyōka no ishinzō." In *Kyōka ron shūsei*, 275–84. Tokyo: Rippū Shobō, 1983.

Kawabata Yasunari. "Kiku awase." In *Izumi Kyōka [Gunzō Nihon no sakka 5]*, 62. Tokyo: Shōgakukan, 1992.

Kawakami, Chiyoko. "The Metropolitan Uncanny in the Works of Izumi Kyōka: A Counter-Discourse on Japan's Modernization." *Harvard Journal of Asiatic Studies* 59, no. 2 (December 1999): 559–83.

Kawamura Jirō. "Dōshi sareta kūkan: Izumi Kyōka." In *Izumi Kyōka [bungei dokuhon]*, 54–65. Tokyo: Kawade Shobō, 1981.

Kawamura Jirō. *Ginga to jigoku: gensō bungaku ron*. Tokyo: Kōdansha, 1973.

Kawamura Jirō. *Hakusan no mizu: Kyōka o meguru*. Tokyo: Kōdansha, 2008.

Kawato Michiaki, Nakabayashi Yoshio, and Sakakibara Takanori, eds. "Meiji-ki hon'yaku bungaku nenpyō: Morita Shiken hen." In Morita Shiken, *Morita Shiken shū I [Zoku Meiji hon'yaku bungaku zenshū hon'yakuka hen 5]*, 1–7. Tokyo: Ōzorasha, 2002.

Kawato Michiaki, Nakabayashi Yoshio, and Sakakibara Takanori, eds. "Meiji-ki hon'yaku bungaku nenpyō: Ozaki Kōyō-hen." In Ozaki Kōyō and Oguri Fūyō, *Ozaki Kōyō, Oguri Fūyō shū [Meiji hon'yaku bungaku zenshū hon'yakuka hen 12]*, 1–6. Tokyo: Ōzorasha, 2002.

Kawato Michiaki and Sakakibara Takanori, eds. "Meiji hon'yaku bungaku nenpyō: Mōpassan-hen." In *Mōpassan shū I [Meiji hon'yaku bungaku zenshū shinbun zasshi hen 31]*, 1–12. Tokyo: Ōzorasha, 1997.

Keiō Gijuku Toshokan, Matsumura Tomomi, Suzuki Aya, and Tominaga Maki, eds. *Kyōka no shosai: "gensō" no umareru basho*. Tokyo: Keiō Gijuku Toshokan, 2016.

Kellett, Arnold. "Introduction." In Guy de Maupassant, *The Dark Side: Tales of Terror and the Supernatural*, xi–xvi. New York: Carroll and Graf, 1989.

Kern, Adam. *Manga from the Floating World: Comicbook Culture and the Kibyōshi of Edo Japan*. Cambridge, MA: Harvard University Asia Center, 2006.

Kirschner, Aloisia [Ossip Schubin]. *The Story of a Genius*. Translated by E. H. Lockwood. New York: R. F. Fenno & Company, 1898.

Kleist, Heinrich von. *The Marquise of O—and Other Stories*. Translated by David Luke and Nigel Reeves. London: Penguin Classics, 1978.

Kobayashi Hideo. "Kyōka no shi, sono ta." *Kyōka ron shūsei*, 217–23. Tokyo: Rippū Shobō, 1983.

Koike Masatane. "Izumi Kyōka: *Kanmuri yazaemon* to *Shinkyoku gyokuseki dōjikun*." *Kokubungaku kaishaku to kanshō* 44, no. 13 (December 1979): 167–75.

Koike Masatane. "Kyōka bungaku no kosō: koten no sekai." *Kokubungaku kaishaku to kanshō* 46, no. 7 (1981): 114–17.

Komura Settai. "Izumi Kyōka-sensei no koto." In Komura Settai, *Nihonbashi Himonochō*, 75–83. Tokyo: Chūō Kōronsha, 1990.

Kōno Taeko. "Kyōka no seimei." In *Izumi Kyōka [bungei dokuhon]*, 110–12. Tokyo: Kawade Shobō, 1981.

Kōno Taeko. "Kyōka to watashi." In *Izumi Kyōka [Gunzō Nihon no sakka 5]*, 210–12. Tokyo: Shōgakukan, 1992.

Lermontov, Mikhail. *A Hero of Our Time*. Translated by Paul Foote. London: Penguin Books, 2001.

Lessing, Gotthold Ephraim. *Emilia Galotti.* Translated by Anna Johanna Gode von Aesch. In *Nathan the Wise, Minna von Barnhelm, and Other Plays and Writings*, ed. Peter Demetz, 75–135. New York: Continuum, 1991.

Lippit, Miya Elise Mizuta. *Aesthetic Life: Beauty and Art in Modern Japan*. Cambridge, MA: Harvard University Asia Center, 2019.

Lloyd, Christopher. *Guy de Maupassant*. London: Reaktion Books, 2020.

Maari Sumika. "Izumi Kyōka to Kantō daishinsai: 'Kinoe kinoto' o shiza to shite." *Geijutsu shijō shugi bungei* 24 (November 1988): 118–26.

Maeda Ai. *Kindai dokusha no seiritsu.* Tokyo: Chikuma Shobō, 1989.

Maeda Hayao. *Hakusan shinkō no nazo to hisabetsu buraku*. Tokyo: Kawade Shobō Shinsha, 2013.

Maeda Hayao. *Shiro no minzokugaku e: Hakusan shinkō no nazo o otte*. Tokyo: Kawade Shobō Shinsha, 2006.

Markus, Andrew Lawrence. *The Willow in Autumn: Ryūtei Tanehiko, 1783–1842*. Cambridge, MA: Council on East Asian Studies, Harvard University, 1992.

Matsuda Aoko. *Obachan-tachi no iru tokoro: Where the Wild Ladies Are*. Tokyo: Chūō Kōron Shinsha, 2019.

Matsuda Minoru. "Nihon bungaku to Furansu bungaku." In *Hikaku bungaku: Nihon bungaku o chūshin to shite*, eds. Nakajima Kenzō, Yoshida Seiichi, et al., 177–216. Tokyo: Yajima Shobō, 1953.

Matsumura Tomomi. "Kaidai." In Ozaki Kōyō, *Kōyō zenshū*, supplementary volume, 521–34. Tokyo: Iwanami Shoten, 1995.

Matsumura Tomomi. *Kyōka bungaku no ryūiki*. Tokyo: Insukuriputo, 2023.

Maupassant, Guy de. *Bel-Ami*. Translated by Douglas Parmée. London: Penguin Books, 1975.

Maupassant, Guy de. *The Complete Short Stories of Guy de Maupassant*. Garden City, NY: Hanover House, 1955.

Maupassant, Guy de. *The Dark Side: Tales of Terror and the Supernatural*. Translated by Arnold Kellett, foreword by Ramsey Campbell. New York: Carroll and Graf, 1989.

Maupassant, Guy de. *Guy de Maupassant's Selected Works*. Translated by Sandra Smith, ed. Robert Lethbridge. New York: W. W. Norton & Company, 2017.

Maupassant, Guy de. *Le Horla et autres contes cruels et fantastiques*, ed. Marie-Claire Bancquart. Paris: Garnier, 1989.

Maupassant, Guy de. *The Odd Number: Thirteen Tales by Guy de Maupassant*. Translated by Jonathan Sturges. New York: Harper & Bros, 1888.

Maupassant, Guy de. *Onze histoires fantastiques*, ed. Henri Parisot, illustrated by Aristide Caillaud. Paris: Robert Marin, 1949.

Maupassant, Guy de. *Pierre and Jean*. Translated by Leonard Tancock. London: Penguin Books, 1979.

Maupassant, Guy de. *Short Stories, by Guy de Maupassant [The After-Dinner Series]*. Translated by R. Whitling. London: Mathieson & Co., 1896.

Maupassant, Guy de. *The Works of Guy de Maupassant*, anonymous translator, compiled by M. Walter Dunne. New York: M. Walter Dunne, 1903.

Mendlesohn, Farah. *Rhetorics of Fantasy*. Middletown, CT: Wesleyan University Press, 2008.

Mérimée, Prosper. *Carmen and Other Stories*. Translated by Nicholas Jotcham. Oxford: Oxford University Press, 1989.

Mérimée, Prosper. *Churujisu fujin: Sharuru kyūsei nendaiki*, translated by Ishikawa Takeshi. Tokyo: Shun'yōdō, 1923.

Mérimée, Prosper. *Colomba, La Vénus d'Ille, Les Ames du Purgatoire*. Paris: Calmann Lévy, 1883.

Mérimée, Prosper. *The Etruscan Vase and Other Stories*. Translated by Douglas Parmée. London: Alma Classics, 2012.

Mérimée, Prosper. *Iru no megamizō*. Translated by Okada Jitsumaro and Ishikawa Takeshi. Tokyo: Kaibunsha, 1924.

Mérimée, Prosper. *Oeuvres complètes de Prosper Mérimée: dernières nouvelles*, ed. Léon Lemonnier. Paris: Librairie Ancienne Honoré Champion, 1929.

Mérimée, Prosper. *Oeuvres complètes de Prosper Mérimée: Mosaïque*, ed. Maurice Levaillant. Paris: Librairie Ancienne Honoré Champion, 1933.

Mérimée, Prosper. *Songs for the Gusle*. Translated by Laura Nagle. Philadelphia: Frayed Edge Press, 2023.

Mérimée, Prosper. *Vīnasu no satsujin*. Translated by Yano Tsuneari. Tokyo: Shun'yōdō, 1934.

Miles, Siân. "Introduction." In Guy de Maupassant, *A Parisian Affair and Other Stories*, translated by Siân Miles, xiii–xxvi. London: Penguin Books, 2004.

Minakami Takitarō and Hamano Eiji, eds. "Shun'yōdō han *Kyōka zenshū* kan'ichi shoshū: Izumi Kyōka nenpu." In *Kyōka zenshū*, supplementary volume [*bekkan*], 717–21. Tokyo: Iwanami Shoten, 1973–1976.

Mishima Yukio. "Izumi Kyōka." In *Izumi Kyōka [bungei dokuhon]*, 10–14. Tokyo: Kawade Shobō, 1981.

Mishima Yukio and Shibusawa Tatsuhiko. "Kyōka no miryoku." In *Kyōka ron shūsei*, 349–57. Tokyo: Rippū Shobō, 1983.

Mita Hideaki. *Izumi Kyōka no bungaku*. Tokyo: Ōfūsha, 1976.

Mizuki Shigeru. *Mizuki Shigeru no Izumi Kyōka den*, ed. Akiyama Minoru. Tokyo: Shōgakukan, 2015.

Molière. *The Misanthrope and Other Plays*. Translated by John Wood and David Coward. London: Penguin Books, 2000.

Molière. *The Miser and Other Plays*. Translated by John Wood and David Coward. London: Penguin Books, 2000.

Molière. *Natsu kosode*. Translated by Ozaki Kōyō. Tokyo: Shun'yōdō, 1892.

Moretti, Laura, and Satō Yukiko, eds. *Graphic Narratives from Early Modern Japan: The World of Kusazōshi*. Leiden: Brill, 2024.

Mori Mari. "Kioku no naka no Izumi Kyōka." In *Kyōka ron shūsei*, 368–69. Tokyo: Rippū Shobō, 1983.

Mori Ōgai. *Minawashū*. Tokyo: Shun'yōdō, 1892.

Mori Ōgai. *Mori Ōgai zenshū*. Tokyo: Chikuma Shobō, 1971.

Mori Ōgai. *Ōgai zenshū*. Tokyo: Iwanami Shoten, 1971–1975.

Mori Ōgai. *Shokoku monogatari.* Tokyo: Kokumin Bunko Kankōkai, 1915.

Morris, Mark. "Magical Realism as Ideology: Narrative Evasions in the Work of Nakagami Kenji." In *A Companion to Magical Realism*, eds. Stephen M. Hart and Wen-chin Ouyang, 199–209. Woodbridge, Suffolk: Tamesis, 2005.

Murakami Kenji. *Yōkai jiten.* Tokyo: Mainichi Shinbunsha, 2000.

Muramatsu Sadataka. *Izumi Kyōka.* Tokyo: Bunsendō, 1966.

Muramatsu Sadataka. *Kotoba no renkinjutsushi: Izumi Kyōka.* Tokyo: Shakai Shisōsha, 1973.

Muramatsu Sadataka. "Mori Ōgai no hon'yaku bungaku." *Kokubungaku kaishaku to kyōzai no kenkyū* 4, no. 5 (April 1959): 60–65.

Nagai Kafū. "*Sato no konjaku* yori." In *Kyōka ron shūsei*, 180–81. Tokyo: Rippū Shobō, 1983.

Nagashima Yōichi. "Hans Christian Andersen Remade in Japan: Mori Ōgai's Translation of *Improvisatoren*." In *Hans Christian Andersen: A Poet in Time*, eds. Johan de Mylius, Aage Jørgensen, and Viggo Hjørnager Pedersen, 397–406. Odense, Denmark: Odense University Press, 1999.

Nagashima Yōichi. *Mori Ōgai no hon'yaku bungaku: "Sokkyō shijin" kara "Perikan" made.* Tokyo: Shibundō, 1993.

Nakagawa Yoichi. "Kyōka to romanchishizumu." In *Kyōka ron shūsei*, 301–5. Tokyo: Rippū Shobō, 1983.

Nakamura, Miri. *Monstrous Bodies: The Rise of the Uncanny in Modern Japan.* Cambridge, MA: Harvard University Asia Center, 2015.

Nakanishi Yukiko. "*Sankai hyōbanki* o yomu tame ni: fōkuroa no kaitei saikō." *Kindai bungaku ronshū* 29 (2003): 55–64.

Napier, Susan J. *The Fantastic in Modern Japanese Literature: The Subversion of Modernity.* London: Routledge, 1996.

Napier, Susan J. "The Magic of Identity: Magic Realism in Modern Japanese Fiction." In *Magical Realism: Theory, History, Community*, eds. Lois Parkinson Zamora and Wendy B. Faris, 451–75. Durham: Duke University Press, 1995.

Natsume Sōseki. "'Gin tanzaku'—*Kinsaku tanpyō* yori." In *Kyōka ron shūsei*, 134. Tokyo: Rippū Shobō, 1983.

Nobori Shomu. "Nihon bungaku to Roshia bungaku," In *Hikaku bungaku: Nihon bungaku o chūshin to shite*, eds. Nakajima Kenzō, Yoshida Seiichi, et al., 237–86. Tokyo: Yajima Shobō, 1953.

Nodier, Charles. "Du Fantastique en Littérature." In *Contes Fantastiques par Charles Nodier*, 5–30. Paris: Bibliothèque-Charpentier, 1904.

Noguchi Takehiko, ed. *Izumi Kyōka [Shinchō Nihon bungaku arubamu 22]*, with an essay by Tsushima Yūko. Tokyo: Shinchōsha, 1985.

Noguchi Tetsuya. "'Teriha kyōgen' o kataru koe: Mori Ōgai hon'yaku *Sokkyō shijin* to no kanren kara." *Kokubungaku kaishaku to kanshō* 74, no. 9 (September 2009): 105–11.

Nozaki Sabun. "Kusazōshi to Meiji shoki no shinbun shōsetsu." *Waseda bungaku* 261 (October 1927): 144–50.

Ogawa Yōko. *Ogawa Yōko no tōsui tanpenbako.* Tokyo: Kawade Shobō Shinsha, 2014.

Okitsu Kaname. "Izumi Kyōka to Edo gesaku." *Meiji Taishō bungaku kenkyū* 21 (1957): 12–17.

Ōkoshi Hisako and Saitama Kenritsu Kindai Bijutsukan, eds. *Komura Settai: monogataru ishō.* Tokyo: Tōkyō Bijutsu, 2014.

Ōnishi Tadao. "Mōpassan to Nihon kindai bungaku." *Nihon kindai bungaku no hikaku bungaku teki kenkyū*, ed. Yoshida Seiichi, 173–97. Tokyo: Shimizu Kōbundō Shobō, 1971.

Ōnishi Tadao. "Mōpassan to sono Nihon e no eikyō." In *Shizen shugi bungaku*, ed. Kawachi Kiyoshi, 305–33. Tokyo: Keisō Shobō, 1962.

Ōoka Makoto, Takahashi Hideo, Miyoshi Yukio, et al., eds. *Izumi Kyōka [Gunzō Nihon no sakka 5].* With an essay by Tsushima Yūko. Tokyo: Shōgakukan, 1992.

Ozaki Kōyō. *Kōyō zenshū.* Tokyo: Iwanami Shoten, 1993–1995.

Ozaki Kōyō. *Tōzai tanryo no yaiba: Musashi no meikō Arabia no yaiba.* Tokyo: Shun'yōdō, 1902.

Ozaki Kōyō. *Yamato Shōkun.* Tokyo: Yoshioka Shosekiten, 1895.

Philippot, Didier. *Guy de Maupassant et l'affolant mystère de la vie: essai sur l'œuvre fantastique.* Paris: Classiques Garnier, 2019.

Poulton, Mark Cody. "Metamorphosis: Fantasy and Animism in Izumi Kyōka." *Japan Review* 6 (January 1995): 71–92.

Poulton, M. Cody. *Spirits of Another Sort: The Plays of Izumi Kyōka.* Ann Arbor: Center for Japanese Studies, University of Michigan, 2001.

Powrie, Phil, Bruce Babington, Ann Davies, and Chris Perriam. *Carmen on Film: A Cultural History.* Bloomington: Indiana University Press, 2007.

Qiao, Mina, ed. *Into the Fantastical Spaces of Contemporary Japanese Literature.* Lanham, MD: Lexington Books, 2022.

Raitt, A. W. *Prosper Mérimée.* London: Eyre & Spottiswoode, 1970.

Rimer, J. Thomas. *Mori Ōgai.* Boston: Twayne, 1975.

Ryūkatei Tanekazu, Ryūtei Senka, Ryūsuitei Tanekiyo, et al., illustrated by Utagawa Kunisada, Utagawa Kunisada II, Utagawa Yoshiiku, et al. *Shiranui monogatari*, eds. Takada Mamoru and Satō Yukiko. Tokyo: Kokusho Kankōkai, 2006.

Saitama Kenritsu Kindai Bijutsukan, eds. *Komura Settai to sono jidai: iki de modan de sensai de.* Saitama: Saitama Kenritsu Kindai Bijutsukan, 2009.

Saitō Nonohito. "Izumi Kyōka to romanchiku." In *Kyōka ron shūsei*, 143–68. Tokyo: Rippū Shobō, 1983.

Sakai Miki. *Ozaki Kōyō to hon'an: sono hōhō kara yomitoku "kindai" no gugen to genkai.* Fukuoka: Kashoin, 2010.

Salter, Rebecca. *Japanese Popular Prints: From Votive Slips to Playing Cards.* Honolulu: University of Hawai'i Press, 2006.

Sandner, David. *Critical Discourses of the Fantastic, 1712–1831.* London: Routledge, 2011.

Sasaki Akio. "Ōgai to Merime." *Hikaku bungaku kenkyū* 9 (March 1965): 1–54.

Satō Haruo. *Kindai Nihon bungaku no tenbō.* Tokyo: Kōdansha, 1950.

Satō Satoru. "*Kanagaki Suikoden* o megutte." *Kokugo to kokubungaku* 58, no. 9 (September 1981): 50–64.

Satō Yukiko. *Edo no eiri shōsetsu: gōkan no sekai.* Tokyo: Perikansha, 2001.

Satomi Ton. "Kyōka no kōokan." *Izumi Kyōka [bungei dokuhon]*, 72–73. Tokyo: Kawade Shobō, 1981.

Schneider, Marcel. *Histoire de la littérature fantastique en France*. Paris: Fayard, 1985.

Seki Hajime. *Shinbun shōsetsu no jidai: media, dokusha, merodorama*. Tokyo: Shin'yōsha, 2007.

Shibusawa Tatsuhiko. "Gosō no tenshukaku." In *Kyōka ron shūsei*, 370–74. Tokyo: Rippū Shobō, 1983.

Shibusawa Tatsuhiko. "Ranpu no kaiten." In *Izumi Kyōka [bungei dokuhon]*, 115–23. Tokyo: Kawade Shobō, 1981.

Shinoda Hajime. "Izumi Kyōka no ichi." In *Izumi Kyōka [bungei dokuhon]*, 36–53. Tokyo: Kawade Shobō, 1981.

Smith, Maxwell A. *Prosper Mérimée*. New York: Twayne, 1972.

Steegmuller, Francis. *Maupassant: A Lion in the Path*. New York: Random House, 1949.

Strecher, Matthew. *Dances with Sheep: The Quest for Identity in the Fiction of Murakami Haruki*. Ann Arbor: Center for Japanese Studies, University of Michigan, 2002.

Suda Chisato. "Ichiyō kara Kyōka e: 'Wakaremichi' to *Sanmai tsuzuki, Shikibu kōji*." *Kōka Joshi Daigaku kenkyū kiyō* 28 (1990): 51–69.

Suda Chisato. "Kyōka ni okeru 'ma' teki bijo no keisei to tenkai: *Kōya hijiri* o chūshin ni." In *Izumi Kyōka "Kōya hijiri" sakuhin ronshū*, 267–91. Tokyo: Kuresu Shuppan, 2003.

Sugita Hideaki. *Arabian naito to Nihonjin*. Tokyo: Iwanami Shoten, 2012.

Sunaga Asahiko. *Nihon gensō bungakushi*. Tokyo: Heibonsha, 2007.

Suzuki Aya. *Izumi Kyōka no engeki: shōsetsu to gikyō ga kōsa suru tokoro*. Tokyo: Kachōsha, 2023.

Suzuki Jūzō. *Ehon to ukiyoe: Edo shuppan bunka no kōsatsu*. Tokyo: Bijutsu Shuppansha, 1979.

Suzuki Keiko. "Shōwa ninen no Izumi Kyōka: *Kahaku reijō* to *Rantōba no tennyo* no shōsetsu kikō." *Kokugo to kokubungaku* 95, no. 12 (December 2018), 3–20.

Takada Mamoru. "Yume to yamahime gensō no keifu: Kyōka e no shichū." In *Izumi Kyōka "Kōya hijiri" sakuhin ronshū*, 179–201. Tokyo: Kuresu Shuppan, 2003.

Takase Shigeo. *Hakusan Tateyama to Hokuriku shugendō*. Tokyo: Meicho Shuppan, 2000.

Taketomo Sōfū. "Izumi Kyōka to kindai kaii shōsetsu." In *Kyōka ron shūsei*, 234–47. Tokyo: Rippū Shobō, 1983.

Tanaka Reigi, ed. *Izumi Kyōka "Kōya hijiri" sakuhin ronshū*. Tokyo: Kuresu Shuppan, 2003.

Tanaka Takako. *Kyōka to kaii*. Tokyo: Heibonsha, 2006.

Tanemura Suehiro. "Meikyū no kai." In *Izumi Kyōka shūsei*, vol. 5, 465–71. Tokyo: Chikuma Shobō, 1995–1997.

Tanemura Suehiro. "Sannin no onna." *Izumi Kyōka shūsei*, vol. 10, 469–75. Tokyo: Chikuma Shobō, 1995–1997.

Tanemura Suehiro. "Suichūka henge." In *Izumi Kyōka [Gunzō Nihon no sakka 5]*, 30–43. Tokyo: Shōgakukan, 1992.

Tanizaki Jun'ichirō. "Junsui ni 'Nihonteki' na 'Kyōka sekai.'" In *Izumi Kyōka [bungei dokuhon]*, 67–68. Tokyo: Kawade Shobō, 1981.

Tayama Katai. *Tōkyō no sanjūnen*. Tokyo: Nihon Tosho Sentā, 1983.

Teraki Teihō. *Hito Izumi Kyōka*. Tokyo: Nihon Tosho Sentā, 1983.

Terayama Shūji. "Kyōka bigaku no disukūru: eiga *Kusameikyū* no dekiru made." In *Izumi Kyōka* [*Gunzō Nihon no sakka 5*], 222–30. Tokyo: Shōgakukan, 1992.

Tezuka Masayuki. "*Kōya hijiri* seiritsukō." In *Izumi Kyōka "Kōya hijiri" sakuhin ronshū*, 38–61. Tokyo: Kuresu Shuppan, 2003.

Todorov, Tzvetan. *The Fantastic: A Structural Approach to a Literary Genre*, translated by Richard Howard, foreword by Robert Scholes. Ithaca: Cornell University Press, 1975.

Todorov, Tzvetan. *Introduction à la littérature fantastique*. Paris: Éditions du Seuil, 1970.

Tōgō Katsumi, ed. *Izumi Kyōka: bi to gensō*. Tokyo: Yūseidō, 1991.

Tokuda Shūsei. "Izumi Kyōka to iu otoko." In *Izumi Kyōka [Gunzō Nihon no sakka 5]*, 180–91. Tokyo: Shōgakukan, 1992.

Tolstoy, Leo. "Lucerne." In *Collected Shorter Fiction*, translated by Louise Maude, Aylmer Maude, and Nigel J. Cooper. New York: Knopf, 2001.

Tominaga Maki. *Kyōka bungaku no shinkō to zuzō: monogataru koto e no ishi*. Tokyo: Kachōsha, 2023.

Tominaga Maki. "Monogatari ga tou mono: Izumi Kyōka *Sankai hyōbanki* to Komura Settai no sashie kara." *Mita kokubun* no. 60 (2015): 52–85.

Tomita Hitoshi. *Furansu shōsetsu i'nyūkō*. Tokyo: Tokyo Shoseki, 1981.

Tsubouchi Shōyō. *Shōyō senshū*. Tokyo: Shun'yōdō, 1926–1927.

Tsushima Yūko. "Mashō no sekai." In *Izumi Kyōka [Shinchō Nihon bungaku arubamu 22]*, 97–103. Tokyo: Shinchōsha, 1985.

Tsushima Yūko. "Pari no Kyōka." In *Izumi Kyōka [Gunzō Nihon no sakka 5]*, 5–12. Tokyo: Shōgakukan, 1992.

Uchida Roan. *Omoidasu hitobito*. Tokyo: Shunjūsha, 1925.

Vax, Louis. *L'art et la littérature fantastiques*. Paris: Presses Universitaires de France, 1974.

Verne, Jules. *Michael Strogoff: A Courier of the Czar*. Anonymous translation. New York: Scribner, 1927.

Waki Akiko. *Gensō no ronri: Izumi Kyōka no sekai*. Tokyo: Kōdansha, 1974.

Waki Akiko. "Izumi Kyōka: bosei tsuibo." In *Izumi Kyōka [Gunzō Nihon no sakka 5]*, 96–102. Tokyo: Shōgakukan, 1992.

Whitehead, Claire. "On the Fantastic." *The Fantastic*, ed. Claire Whitehead, 1–17. Ipswich, MA: Salem Press, 2013.

Wixted, John Timothy. "Mori Ōgai: Translation Transforming the Word/World." *Japonica Humboldtiana* 13 (October 2009): 61–109.

Yanagita Kunio. "Shako Kyōka kan." In *Kyōka ron shūsei*, 201–3. Tokyo: Rippū Shobō, 1983.

Yi Hyŏn-yŏng (I Hyon'yon). *Kaga haidan to Shōfū no kenkyū*. Toyama: Katsura Shobō, 2002.

Yoshida Masashi. "Izumi Kyōka to kusazōshi: *Shaka hassō Yamato bunko* o chūshin to shite." In *Izumi Kyōka: bi to gensō*, 172–86. Tokyo: Yūseidō, 1991.

Yoshida Masashi. "Izumi Kyōka to sashie gaka: Ikeda Shōen, Terukata." In *Ronshū Izumi Kyōka 3*, eds. Izumi Kyōka Kenkyūkai, 133–57. Osaka: Izumi Shoin, 1999.

Yoshida Masashi. "Izumi Kyōka to sashie gaka: Kaburaki Kiyokata." In *Ronshū Izumi Kyōka 2*, eds. Izumi Kyōka Kenkyūkai, 190–223. Osaka: Izumi Shoin, 1999.

Yoshida Seiichi. "Kaisetsu." In Mori Ōgai, *Mori Ōgai zenshū*, vol. 8: 377–84. Tokyo: Chikuma Shobō, 1971.

Yoshimura Hirotō. *Izumi Kyōka: geijutsu to byōri*. Tokyo: Kongō Shuppan Shinsha, 1970.

Yoshimura Hirotō. *Makai e no enkinhō: Izumi Kyōka ron*. Tokyo: Kindai Bungeisha, 1991.

Yoshiya Nobuko. "Watashi no Izumi Kyōka." In *Nihon kindai bungaku taikei 7: Izumi Kyōka shū, geppō* 13, 1–2. Tokyo: Kadokawa Shoten, 1970.

Yoshiya Nobuko. *Yoshiya Nobuko zenshū 11: soko no nuketa hishaku, aru nyoninzō*. Tokyo: Asahi Shinbunsha, 1975.

Zamora, Lois Parkinson, and Wendy B. Faris. "Introduction: Daiquiri Birds and Flaubertian Parrot(ie)s." In *Magical Realism: Theory, History, Community*, eds. Lois Parkinson Zamora and Wendy B. Faris, 1–11. Durham: Duke University Press, 1995.

Zwicker, Jonathan E. *Practices of the Sentimental Imagination: Melodrama, the Novel, and the Social Imaginary in Nineteenth-Century Japan*. Cambridge, MA: Harvard University Asia Center, 2006.

Index